VLADIMIR'S CARROT

John Peter

VLADIMIR'S CARROT

Modern drama and the modern imagination

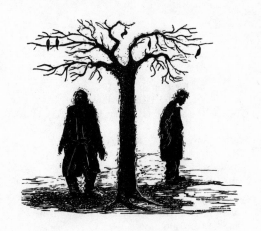

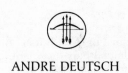

ANDRE DEUTSCH

First published 1987 by
André Deutsch Limited
105–106 Great Russell Street London WC1B 3LJ

Copyright © 1987 by John Peter

British Library Cataloguing in Publication Data

Peter, John
  Vladimir's carrot: modern drama and the
  modern imagination.
  1. Drama – 19th century – History and
  criticism 2. Drama – 20th century – History
  and criticism
  I. Title
  809.2′034   PN1851

ISBN 0–233–98014–8

Printed in Great Britain by
St Edmundsbury Press Limited
Bury St Edmunds, Suffolk

For my wife, Linette

'Where the heart lies, let the brain lie also.'
Robert Browning

TABLE OF CONTENTS

ACKNOWLEDGEMENTS

Acknowledgements is an inadequate word to describe my sense of indebtedness to those I mention here. Their interest in my work and their unstinted generosity not only saved me from errors of fact and judgement: they also helped my morale during the years it took, working entirely in my spare time, to complete this book. Whatever it is worth I share with them; its faults are mine alone.

Most of all I want to thank Professor John Carey, who read the entire book chapter by chapter and gave me a great deal of time, pertinent criticism and warm encouragement.

David Cairns, Professor John Golding, Dr Michael Patterson, Dr Anthony Storr and Marina Vaizey read substantial parts of the book and helped me greatly with corrections and advice.

R.J. Hollingdale replied to my inquiries on Nietzsche; T.J. Reed and Dr K.H. Segar gave generously of their time and knowledge to talk to me about Kafka; Patrick Gardiner replied to queries about Schopenhauer; Dr Jane Grayson wrote to me in the most helpful detail on a point about Dostoyevsky; Jeremy Brooks, Dusty Hughes and Michael Meyer generously put at my disposal unpublished material; Mrs Bertram Smith allowed me to see her private collection of paintings in New York and was most hospitable to me.

I also want to thank those who helped me by lending, or suggesting to me, books and articles to read; by supplying references; or by patiently listening to me talking about my ideas. They are: Dannie Abse, Stephen Aris, Patrick Carnegy, Michael Gearin-Tosh, Ronald Harwood, Ronald Hayman, Dr Elisabeth Jakab, Dorothy Koenigsberger, Professor H.G. Koenigsberger, Caroline Lee, Boris Kidel, Rosalind Newcomen, John Russell, George Schöpflin, Desmond Shawe-Taylor, Professor George Steiner, Janet Suzman, Mrs Magda Vámos, Irving Wardle, Angelica Zander-Rudenstein.

T.G. Rosenthal first suggested that I might 'have a book in me' when he was Managing Director of Secker and Warburg. Patient, imaginative and generous publisher, he is this volume's onlie begetter.

I am grateful to Frank Giles, former Editor of the *Sunday Times*, and to the present Editor, Andrew Neil, for allowing me to take seven months' leave to complete the book. I also want to express my gratitude to Godfrey Smith who, during his short period as Arts Editor, helped me to make sensible use of my free time.

I am indebted for financial assistance to the Arts Council of Great Britain.

I also want to thank the Phoenix Trust for financial help.

I want to thank the Librarians and Staffs of the following: the London Library; the British Library, the Bodleian Library, Oxford; the Radcliffe Science Library, Oxford; the Taylorian Institute, Oxford; the British Theatre Association; the Tate Gallery; the Courtauld Institute; the Royal Shakespeare Company; Centre Pompidou, Musée d'Art Moderne, Paris; the Phillips Collection, Washington; the Museum of Art, Baltimore.

My greatest debt of all is acknowledged after the title page.

INTRODUCTION

What is modern in modern drama? What is it that defines it, unmistakably, as being of our time?

The answer usually depends on when modern drama is thought to have begun. Did it begin with the impudent iconoclasm of Jarry's *Ubu Roi* (1896), or with the extravagant Symbolism of Villiers's *Axël*, first performed in 1894? Did it begin with the moral earthquake of Ibsen's great prose dramas, or with the portrayal of sexual and psychological warfare in the plays of Strindberg? Or did it only really begin with Samuel Beckett's *Waiting for Godot*?

Each of these examples has led to a different kind of drama and implies entirely different notions of what 'modern' means. Have they anything in common?

Again, is Brecht modern? Most of us would say yes; yet at the same time we would withold the title from his contemporary J.B. Priestley, despite the fact that some of Priestley's plays deal with ideas about time which are distinctly modern. Clearly, being modern is not simply a question of dates. Nor does it depend on the quality of the dramatist's imagination: when we say that, compared with Priestley, Brecht or Beckett are modern, this is not only because we judge their work to be better. There is something else.

This book explores a quality which cuts across schools, styles and accepted categories. It also assumes that drama does not live and grow on its own. A glance at the table of contents will indicate that the argument which follows aims at setting drama in a wider context. There is something in the modern imagination which links together plays, novels and paintings; and the way all these depict the world echoes, and is echoed by, the work of some modern thinkers. In some ways modern drama is closer to us than we think.

I

VLADIMIR'S CARROT

This book is an investigation into modern literature, and modern drama in particular, as pictures of the world.

This may not sound a very original enterprise, but the words are chosen with care. Usually, when we talk about, say, Chekhov's world, we mean the people and the milieu he writes about: stagnant provincial society blanketed by disillusionment, cushioned by self-deception, populated by people with small imaginations and large grievances. If we were asked to define a typical example of 'Chekhov's world', we would describe a drawing-room or a garden in which indolent, deeply egotistical middle-class people, middle-aged in body, or in mind, or both, consume endless refreshments, make desultory conversation laden with malice, mostly unintended, and fret about things they might once have done but did not, or would like to do but cannot. In other words, when we talk about 'Chekhov's world', we mean both his characters and the physical and social settings in which they move.

This 'world' is partly made by the characters in it. One of the reasons why the Prozorov sisters cannot go to Moscow is that they do not really want to. They do not want to because they are the sort of people whose lives are nourished by undernourished hopes. But also, they were born into a society which, stagnant and unconcerned by nature, frames their lives with a sense of futility. These people may have made this world, but this world has also made them. 'Chekhov's world' includes this sense of mutual dependence. It also includes the personalities of these people, their feelings and their actions, their past, present and future. And all this, the setting and the people, are rooted in a particular place and time: they are defined geographically and historically. All this, too, is 'Chekhov's world'.

But when we speak, as we sometimes do, about 'Chekhov's picture of the world', what we really mean is a sense of identity between Chekhov and 'his world'. We sense, or we think we sense, that Chekhov felt in a certain way about his characters and their settings, and wrote his plays in order to tell us what this feeling was. So when we talk about Chekhov's picture of the world we are implying, not so much that we are observing this world but that we are listening to Chekhov. This means something both more and less than considering 'the world' of one of his plays. For we are not talking about one specific picture in our minds, a memory that we can 'see': we might be talking about a scene in a drawing-room as well as one in a garden or at a crossroads; we might be thinking of several characters or groups of characters, and of several things they said or did. All these things combine loosely and unpredictably to define memories and feelings in ourselves which we choose to call 'Chekhov's picture of the world' — a vague metaphor which means neither *picture* nor *world* but our complex emotional memory of what it was like to see one of his plays. We contemplate, not so much the contents of the play, but what it made us feel like.

It may seem pedantic to stalk these words and then put them under a net to examine them. But it is, after all, one of the commonplaces of criticism to talk about a writer's picture of the world, and we might as well realise that the phrase does not always mean what it says. Nor does it quite fit Chekhov, because he did not write his plays with the intention of depicting 'a world', let alone 'the world'; and he did not write them as if he were creating a 'picture'. No, Chekhov wrote about people, and these people make up their own world. At which point we, the audience, join in: we witness events, we experience feelings, we draw conclusions, and we try to understand the playwright's intentions, so that we can square what is happening inside us with what has been happening on the stage. We are 'involved'. The life of the play awakens an answering life in us, and we turn to the play for confirmation. It talks to us and we question it. We question it and it talks to us again. To experience the theatre is to take part in a dialogue.

Now when we turn to a play like Samuel Beckett's *Waiting for Godot*, the relationship between us and the play seems to be entirely different. It is almost as if the dialogue had broken down. Most people describe the experience of such a breakdown by saying that they do not understand the play. That phrase is our first clue to the difference between *Waiting for Godot* and the plays that Chekhov and others wrote. Because, to paraphrase E.M. Forster, oh, dear, yes, a play also tells a story[1]; and insofar as it tells a story we can understand it. All narratives can be understood. We may protest that they are illogical, improbable, ridiculous or confusing — but we can understand them. Let us take Lautréamont's famous definition of beauty[2], much loved by the surrealists, and turn it into a story by saying that 'a sewing machine met an umbrella, by chance, on an operating table'. We can understand this miniature narrative perfectly; only we regard the story it tells us as preposterous. But of course Lautréamont was not thinking of a story. And when we say that we do not understand a play we imply, whether we realise it or not, that the play does not tell a story either: that it is not concerned, at least not primarily, with relating events. We imply that such a play is 'about' something, something other than a story, and something which we cannot grasp.

Is this true? Can the dialogue ever really break down? If so, why? What is the nature of plays with which, at least at first, we cannot conduct the kind of dialogue prompted by Chekhov's plays; or by *Hamlet*, Ibsen's *Ghosts* or Aeschylus's *Agamemnon*? Beckett's *Waiting for Godot* has something both more and less than these plays. What is it? That is the subject of this book.

Let us begin with simple matters. We shall find their simplicity deceptive. When, for example, the curtain rises on *Ghosts*, we see a drawing-room furnished in a way consistent with the way of life of an upper-middle-class northern European family in the 1880s. The furniture includes a table, and on it there are, among other things, some books. Ibsen's stage directions specifically mention books, because they are there for a purpose. They are Mrs Alving's lifeline to her lost freedom. Some twenty-eight years earlier, after a year of marriage, she had run away from the dissolute Captain Alving, but then allowed herself to be led back to him by Pastor Manders. She has been paying the price for this ever since. The most terrible price is yet to be paid, but she is not to know that until the end of the play. Meanwhile she is determined to break free of the Alving bondage. On the one hand, she is devoting all her dead husband's money to the building of an orphanage; on the other hand, she is reading books that would outrage conventional public opinion and religious feeling to the core. Ibsen does not mention any of the books by title

or author, but they might have included Renan's *Life of Jesus*, the
writings of Kierkegaard; or Darwin's *The Descent of Man* and *The
Origin of Species*, which appeared in Scandinavia in translation six
and nine years, respectively, before *Ghosts* was written. She might
have been reading some novels by Zola, or indeed plays by Ibsen.
The sight of these books certainly upsets Pastor Manders, who
disapproves of them thoroughly and gives Mrs Alving a sharp rebuke
for reading them, even though he has not read any of them himself.
'There are many occasions in life,' he informs her, 'when one must
rely on the judgement of others.'[3]

The full irony of this remark will dawn on us later, when we
realise that Mrs Alving herself may have made the greatest mistake
of her life precisely when she relied on the judgement of another –
namely Pastor Manders, who had told her to go back to Alving. But
now the books represent for Mrs Alving the freedom she did not
have the courage to hold on to all those years ago. To read them now
is a gesture, safe because private: it commits her to no action. And
when the time for action finally comes, we can see that she has
benefited very little from her reading. Of course we should not be
too hard on Mrs Alving. For a middle-class provincial lady in the
1880s to find out that her son, conceived after she had gone back to
her dissolute husband, has hereditary syphilis, is the equivalent of
damnation, and no amount of freethinking books will tell her what
to do. But this is precisely the point. Mrs Alving has been living
with her books in an entirely private freedom of the mind. She is no
more fitted now to deal with the consequences of her marriage than
she was when she tried to break out of it. When her bid for freedom
failed she condemned herself to moral imprisonment for life. All of
which means that Mrs Alving's books are more than just stage
props. Both she and Pastor Manders reveal a great deal about
themselves when they discuss these books: they are defined, both
psychologically and morally, through their attitudes to them.

Such objects sometimes come to be called symbolic: for as the play
goes on, they acquire an increasing significance in relation to what
the characters say and do, so much so that, finally, the people in the
play can sometimes be judged by some moral standard which is both
established and measured by these objects. Thus Mrs Alving's books
lead us to regard Manders as a hypocrite and Mrs Alving herself as a
coward: she has no more courage than to read about her convictions.
Once we see the two of them in this way, the books become symbolic,
both of her cowardice and of his hypocrisy.

It is worth making another commonplace observation: namely, that what we see on stage are real books. People pick them up and examine them. A conscientious director could find out, just as we did, what sort of books they would have had to be to shock a clergyman of that time and place. We, the spectators, could ask ourselves, too, without being obtuse, how Mrs Alving could have come by them. Libraries? Bookshops? Unlikely. Friends? Possibly. Pastor Manders clearly asks himself the same question, and comes to the conclusion that she orders them by post, judging from the way he reacts when, at the end of Act One, a parcel arrives for Mrs Alving. (It turns out to contain songs for the dedication service at the orphanage.) The thing to remember about Mrs Alving's books is that, to her and to others in the play, they are real. They, and we, can ask questions about them which can be answered; and both the questions and the answers have a plausible place in the life of the play. If the books have any moral or symbolic significance, it rests on their solid physical reality and dramatic function.

Now let us take a very different play: Aeschylus' *Agamemnon*[4]. When King Agamemnon returns to Argos victorious from the Trojan War, his wife Clytemnestra welcomes him in a language of hyperboles, as if he were a demigod. The crucial moment comes when Clytemnestra asks her husband to step down from his chariot onto some crimson cloths which her servants are about to spread before him on the ground. Agamemnon protests that only a god deserves such courtesies — and well he might. For these cloths are not carpets, as some translations have it. Indeed, carpets were rare in Greece until the time of Alexander the Great. Even Xenophon, who was born a century after Aeschylus, still regarded them as examples of oriental effeminacy[5]. We gather from him that to have any kind of cloth on the ground was regarded by Greeks as an oriental and therefore by definition barbaric custom. To take one's shoes off, too, was thought to be an oriental way of showing respect. In Aeschylus' own time, which was that of the Persian wars (he himself fought at Marathon and Salamis), anything with oriental associations was frowned upon. What Clytemnestra wanted Agamemnon to step on were precious tapestries, specially woven and dyed: they were probably used as hangings or curtains in palaces and temples. One way or another, and this is the most important thing of all, they were associated with religious worship.

From all this, several things follow. Agamemnon is being made to behave like an oriental despot: he is, against his own better judgement, committing a public outrage against traditional Greek standards of behaviour. It is as if a British Prime Minister accepted a welcoming ceremony organised like a Nazi rally. Moreover, since these cloths were woven for religious purposes, for a man to tread on them was sacrilege. Yet Clytemnestra prevails upon Aga- memnon to do precisely that, thus demonstrating her superior will and cunning. He in turn shows that he is weak-willed and short- sighted. Once he steps on the crimson tapestries, they lead him to, and become symbolic of, his bloody end.

Note, once again, that Clytemnestra's tapestries, like Mrs Alving's books, are real objects. Their precise function is a matter of some academic controversy; but the text is quite clear about their colour, their method of weaving and dyeing; and the original audiences would have understood their significance without having to do any homework. And so, when Agamemnon stepped on these costly, delicately-woven cloths, dyed the colour of blood, they would have known that they were in the presence of sacrilege and death. Like Mrs Alving's books, these tapestries tell us important things about the world of the play and about its people: what Clytemnestra and Agamemnon say and do in relation to them is closely bound up with their characters, their situation and their fate.

Now let us turn to *Waiting for Godot*. In Act One Estragon asks Vladimir for a carrot. Vladimir rummages in his pockets which are full of turnips. At last he finds a carrot and hands it to Estragon: 'Make it last; that's the end of them.'[6]

Where did Vladimir get that carrot? Where did he get all those turnips? There is nothing in the play to tell us. Moreover, the question seems utterly fatuous. Our response is: What does it matter where he got them? What, quite simply, does it have to do with anything?

In Act Two the eating ceremony, like all Beckett's ceremonies, is repeated. Vladimir offers a radish; his pockets turn out to be full of turnips. Finally, a black radish emerges, but Estragon gives it back because he only likes pink ones.

ESTRAGON: I'll go and get a carrot. (*He does not move.*)[7]

where, indeed, would he go?

The point about Vladimir's carrot is how little it tells us. It comes out of his pocket and Estragon eats it; but it tells us nothing about the two men or their world. One commentator has noted that 'Carrots and turnips ... were staples of the actual diet of the occupied under the occupier'[8] — an allusion to the fact that Beckett, who was involved in the French Resistance during the Second World War, lived for a while as a refugee from the Nazis, and worked in Southern France as an agricultural labourer. This is an important fact for Beckett's biographers, but it has nothing to do with the play. It is irrelevant, not because biography is not relevant to criticism, but because these facts about carrots and turnips in France in the 1940s tell us nothing about Vladimir's carrot in the play. Like all objects in the play — hats, boots, belts, basket, rope — the carrot is there for no other purpose than to fulfil (or fail to fulfil) its most basic function. It reveals nothing about anyone, unless we are to call it a revelation that Estragon is hungry and prefers a carrot to a turnip; and it symbolises nothing whatever, unless the act of eating it is symbolic of anything.

If there were no carrot and no turnip, and if Estragon ate nothing, it would not make *Godot* a significantly different play; but think how different *Ghosts* would be without Mrs Alving's books, or *Agamemnon* without Clytemnestra's tapestries. They have a significance which is both specific and symbolic. It is a matter both of what they simply are, and what they stand for. In this sense, they are irreplaceable. But if the pernickety spectator should want to know where Vladimir had got his provisions, he would find nothing in the play to suggest an answer; and no such answer would add anything to his experience of the play. This is one of many things in *Waiting for Godot* which are not open to questioning, because there are no answers available, either actual or implied. There are, also, many other things, which are more essential to what happens in the play, and which, in most other plays, would need an explanation, but which seem irrelevant to what we sense the play to be 'about'.

What, for example, do Vladimir and Estragon do, what do they live on? What kind of families do they come from? How long and how often have they been here? What is the nature of their appointment with Godot? What does Pozzo live on? Did he and Lucky ever get to the fair? If not, where had they been between Act One and Act Two? Questions like these are the very lifeblood of a play like *Ghosts*, and they all have an answer in Ibsen's world. A sense of time, of past, present and future, are part of the texture of such a world: we sense that the characters and the objects in it had existed before the curtain rose, and may exist after the curtain has fallen, in a way which is relevant, sometimes even vital, to the way we experience the play.

Of course, this is the metaphorical language of criticism. We must once again risk the commonplace by admitting that the characters of *Ghosts* do not exist in the way you or I exist, and that to talk about their past and future is an act of the imagination. Indeed, the whole of *Ghosts* is an act of the imagination: a fictional creation, of which an implied past and an implied future are organic parts. In the fictional creation called *Waiting for Godot* such parts do not exist at all. Vladimir and Estragon do not have a fictional past: the play is written in such a way as to function in an endless present. It conveys an experience of time to which actual length of time is irrelevant.

Now one of the reasons why this play is thought by some people to be incomprehensible is that we approach plays, as we do everything else in life, in a logical frame of mind. If we see a man we assume, consciously or not, that he comes from somewhere, and that he is probably going somewhere. This simple assumption implies a past and a future. In this sense life, like a play, is a story. To be faced with a play which seems entirely unconcerned with such matters, and which provides no answers if we should want to ask, can be disconcerting because it lacks the comforting props of explanation and context. It is like meeting someone entirely articulate but suffering from amnesia.

Of course an amnesiac is not only unable to tell us where he has come from: he cannot tell us why. Let us look again at *Ghosts*. Why has Oswald come home? Why had he left home in the first place? Why does Pastor Manders not want to insure the orphanage? Why has he not been to Mrs Alving's house for so very long? Ibsen has provided answers to these questions, even if some of them are only implied, or even equivocal. The reader may then object that Ibsen is hardly a fair example because his plays are exceptionally tightly constructed, and *Ghosts* almost ostentatiously so; and that there are many plays by other playwrights that leave behind unanswered questions. Is this true?

Take *Hamlet*. Does Hamlet spare Claudius at prayer because he thinks that by killing him at that moment he might send his repentant soul to heaven? Or is he merely procrastinating? The controversy on this point is very old. The point for us is not that Shakespeare gives or implies no explicit answer; nor that Hamlet's character is in some respects vague and elusive; nor even that the answers to both questions could be yes. No, the point is that such questions *make sense*. They are provoked by the events of the play, and they can lead to a coherent interpretation of Hamlet's character.

Depending on which reading of the episode we accept, we will end up with a different view, both of Hamlet the man and of *Hamlet* the play. We may finally decide that our chosen interpretation is wrong and follow another; and even come to the conclusion that both man and play are hopelessly enigmatic. But all this is possible only because it *makes sense* to ask questions in the first place. Hamlet changes his mind and gives a reason for it; we, the spectators, test the sense and the logic of his decision against our own ideas of what thought and action are. If then, we still arrive at an enigma, it will be after we have conducted a dialogue with the play. And in this sense *Waiting for Godot* is not an enigma at all, just as an amnesiac is not an enigmatic person: it is simply that the past is not part of his mind.

If, once again, we turn to *Ghosts*, a whole network of causes and effects opens up before us. If Mrs Alving had not returned to her husband she might not now have a syphilitic son. Why did she go back? Why did Pastor Manders take her back? Was he aware of his own reasons? Was Mrs Alving aware both of his reasons and of her own? It is in the very nature of someone with a past that such questions can be asked about them: indeed, this is what having a past means. And when we ask why Mrs Alving went home, we are in fact asking two questions. One is: could she have done otherwise? And the possibility that she could is what gives her a psychological density, a sense of personal identity. She once did certain things; she might also have done other things; she might yet do other things still. She carries within her a sense of possible alternatives, past, present and to come. This is the meaning of character in drama.

The other question we imply when we ask why Mrs Alving went home is this: *should* she have done otherwise? In other words, was she right? And did she herself think at the time that she was right? Does she think so now? And what, finally, do *we* think? The point about questions like these is not only that they make sense: it is the very essence of Ibsen's play that it makes us ask them. If he has a purpose beyond relating events, beyond telling a story, it is this: that we should ask such questions, and by doing so pit our imaginative and moral natures against that of his characters.

Minutes before the play ends Oswald turns on his mother and says, with terrible lucidity: 'I didn't ask you for life. And what kind of life have you given me? I don't want it. Take it back.'[9]

This is one of those rare moments in the theatre when the earth seems to move under our feet. Oswald Alving, whose existence has been blighted by his own parents in his very conception, tears up the most sacred bonds of human life as they were known to men and women in Ibsen's time. He repudiates the ties of the family, the natural right, urge and duty to have children, and the divinely ordained obligation of a human being to preserve his own life. The moral impact of all this has diminished in the hundred years since it was written, but that is partly because Ibsen's own plays have taught the intervening generations to think more responsibly about such things. Still, in a good production, Oswald's words can have, even now, a shattering effect; in the 1880s they were breathtaking and monstrous. They challenged the very foundations of moral life. The questions that *Ghosts* asks are moral questions; the characters stand before us to receive moral judgement from us and to deliver it, in turn, back to us. The dialogue with such a play is a moral dialogue.

Aeschylus' *Oresteia*, of which the *Agamemnon* is the first part, is a drama whose actual subject is the nature of moral judgement[10]. Its ending, the conclusion of *The Eumenides*, is the dramatic demonstration of Aeschylus' faith in civic justice as opposed to tribal revenge; of his belief that crimes can be purged by atonement as well as by punishment; and of his conviction that the forces of punishment can and should be transformed into forces of strong and benevolent protection.

When Agamemnon steps on the tapestries, his own imminent doom assumes a physical form before us. Commentators[11] have pointed out how this central moment of the play envisions Agamemnon's murder later in the play, as well as the murder of Clytemnestra in *The Libation Bearers*; and how it also takes us back to the past, before the play began, when Agamemnon had sacrificed his daughter Iphigenia so that his fleet could sail to Troy. The crimson of the tapestries is like Agamemnon's own blood which is about to be shed, as well as Iphigenia's blood which he had shed himself. Thus the outrage Agamemnon commits when he steps down from his chariot enmeshes us in moral questions. Clearly, walking on these tapestries is not merely a capital offence in itself: it also stands for larger matters. Agamemnon is about to lose his own life as a recompense for that of his daughter. Is this just? Was Agamemnon right when he sacrificed Iphigenia? Is Clytemnestra right in exacting revenge?

Modern scholarship has taught us that it is wrong to see these people as mere tools of divine confrontations, just as it was wrong to see them steeped in personal motivations and struggling with the forces of fate and personal will, like characters in nineteenth-century novels or in an Ibsen play[12]. What interests Aeschylus is precisely that difficult area where human will and divine ordinance meet and clash. Agamemnon, Clytemnestra and Orestes were commanded by gods to do certain things; but they also acted as men and women, and they share in the responsibility for their deeds. Indeed, it is precisely because they have to make a choice, because they cannot *not do* anything, that we can, through the nature of their choice, question not only them but also the world they live in, and the nature of the justice they bring upon themselves and others. And when, in *The Eumenides*, the Furies are transformed from vengeful monsters into the kindly guardians of justice, we reach a plateau of dramatic action and argument. We have been led here by a chain of events which followed one another with remorseless logic throughout the course of the trilogy, and which also stretch back into the past, beyond the beginning of the *Agamemnon*, to Agamemnon's ancestors, to Zeus himself, and the curse on the House of Atreus. Aeschylus' drama spans the time from divine dictatorship and the primitive law of revenge to the establishment of civic law in the Athenian democracy. It is a drama of two conflicting social organisations, two conflicting moral codes; and its resolution represents the victory of what Aeschylus and many of his contemporaries clearly held to be higher moral and civic values.

In other words, the whole work is held together by the logic of its events, its past and present; and its purpose is to confront life in the spirit of moral questioning. What do we do with criminals? Can crime be justified? What is punishment? Who has the right to judge? It has been suggested[13] that Aeschylus may not have been entirely in favour of the Athenian legal reforms which resulted in the establishment of the Areopagus, the court of citizens which sits in judgement at the end of *The Eumenides*. For me, such a view is negated by the moral and dramatic drive of the whole trilogy, and by the overwhelming nobility of its ending. *The Oresteia* is not civic or legal propaganda; but the grandeur of its ending is clearly backed by a moral will, a consent of the creative mind. Yet to question Aeschylus' attitude in this way seems to me both possible and necessary, because he himself subjects the new justice to rigorous questioning. He also lets us see that this new justice arose out of profound needs, and that it must at all times be safeguarded against offenders. The menace of the Furies is not expelled from the world:

it is held in check by judges who are kindly yet rigorous. Aeschylus does not wish to 'make a scarecrow of the law'.[14] His Furies represent the ideals of justice implied by Shakespeare's *Measure for Measure*: they are both fair and fearful. They represent a justice which a citizen can both question and understand, because it operates in the context of a society: it is based on both nature and reason. Thus logic and morality are intimately and essentially intertwined in *The Oresteia*. This is why it is open to our questions. Our dialogue with *The Oresteia* is moral or it is nothing.

Now let us look again at *Waiting for Godot*. It has been described as a play in which 'nothing happens, twice.'[15] Strictly speaking, of course, that is not true. Things do happen. Conversations take place. Pozzo and Lucky come and go, twice. Estragon eats a carrot and refuses a radish. Lucky delivers a virtually incomprehensible speech. The point is not that some of these events are minor, uninteresting or inconsequential: Chekhov's plays, for example, are full of events that are minor, uninteresting and inconsequential. No, the point about these events is that they appear not to have causes. Events and people in *Godot* do not seem to be shaped by intentions or decisions. That may seem a simple matter in a play, but this simplicity, too, is deceptive. Why, we ask, did Mrs Alving take what we think was the wrong decision? The answer is: because of the sort of person she was and still is, and also because of the influence of Manders, who was a moral coward, and still is. Equally, we could say that the 'cause' of what happens in Molière's *Tartuffe* is Orgon's gullibility, or Tartuffe's hypocrisy or ambition, or both; that the 'cause' of what happens in *Macbeth* is the intervention of the Weird Sisters, or Macbeth's dormant hunger for power, or the impact of the one on the other. Such causes can be elusive, debatable, even contradictory. We might say, for example, that Othello's susceptibility to Iago's intrigues is due to a certain lack of sophistication, but that this same susceptibility is somewhat at odds with his high standing as a successful leader of men. Or could Shakespeare have been portraying just such a self-contradictory character? The matter is debatable. What is not debatable is that some 'cause', something in Othello's nature, combined with something that happens to him, sets in train a sequence of specific events. We 'understand' the play because it is a sequence of events we can follow, and because behind the events we see, or dimly sense, some cause. And such an understanding of a play implies that we have already, even if subconsciously, questioned it. We could not identify, let alone understand, any cause, however vaguely and imprecisely, without first questioning their effects — and the 'effects' are the things that happen in the play.

Plays like the *Agamemnon* or *Ghosts* are open to our questions, and our simplest and most fundamental question is always 'Why?' And to ask why? about people is, more often than not, a moral question. Certainly, if we ask this about almost anything or anyone in *Ghosts*, we will find an answer which, whether we agree with it or not, has a moral value. Now the point about *Waiting for Godot* is that it is not open to such questioning. It has events, such as they are, but they have no obvious cause. It is not for nothing that Beckett's theatre has been described as the drama of the non-specific. Why exactly are Vladimir and Estragon here? Since we have no idea what the appointment with Godot is all about, we do not really know. And if we do not know, we can neither approve nor disapprove of what they are doing. That, indeed, would be a moral reaction; and it is simply not part of our experience of the play. So perhaps this play is outside the realm of moral judgement: perhaps it has nothing to do with right or wrong, because in drama such concepts have explanations, just as events have causes. Vladimir and Estragon wait for Godot without any precise cause, because Beckett was not interested in events with precise causes.

Yet he seems to have sensed that this lack of dramatic reasoning was intimately involved with a lack of moral content. In *Texts for Nothing*, which he was writing at about the same time as *Waiting for Godot*, he left behind a clue, in the form of a nagging question.

> Why did Pozzo leave home, he had a castle and retainers, insidious question, to remind me I'm in the dock.[16]

So Pozzo existed in Beckett's imagination as someone with a castle and retainers. That means a past, a context. But, apart from a solitary reference to his 'manor'[17] (*château* in the original French version[18]), the Pozzo we meet in the play carries virtually none of this context with him. Beckett excluded it because he was interested only in a figure who embodied a sense of garrulous command. But the playwright, in the privacy of his *Texts*, feels oddly guilty, 'in the dock', as if his omission of Pozzo's past and possessions, with all the sense of dramatic causation it would have brought with it, had been a moral omission. And indeed it is: Beckett, with his haunting sense of being in the dock, has put his finger on the deep-lying and essential connexion between the logical and the moral. And it is because his characters lack this sense of cause and morality that they seem to exist almost independently of the world we find them in. Aeschylus', Shakespeare's and Ibsen's characters make their world as much as it makes them; but there is no sense, in *Waiting for Godot*, that the place Beckett's characters inhabit is in any way different because they have inhabited it.

It has been said that the two tramps have different personalities, and it is true that Vladimir is on the whole more aggressive, Estragon more introverted and dreamy. But these differences are slight when you compare them with what you can find in any of the other plays I have mentioned. *Godot* has long passages where the two men's dialogue, if that is the word, is almost homogeneous: their antiphonal lines sound like answering echoes within the same poem. But plays are not poems; and dramatic writing like this can, in a fundamental sense, frustrate our experience of the play as drama. It replaces a sense of action with feeling. It is, of course, easy to tell Pozzo and Lucky apart; but when, in Act Two, they come back from wherever they may have been, their relationship and condition have changed, for no reason that we or they can comprehend. And so, all in all, the way in which human character exists, unfolds or changes in this play is no easier to 'understand' than anything else. Here, as in his 'plot', Beckett is not interested in precise causes. Events and people are subordinated to something else.

I spoke, at the beginning, about plays as pictures of the world. *Waiting for Godot* is a picture of the world in two senses. In the first, and much the simpler, sense, it works *as a picture*: it leaves in our minds a single visual memory which is that of two tramps doing nothing in particular under a bare tree. That may indeed be how the play was born: in the same section of *Texts for Nothing*, which is really all about writing, Beckett meditates:

> It's an image, in my helpless head, where all sleeps, all is dead, not yet born, I don't know, or before my eyes, they see the scene, the lids flicker and it's in.[19]

Other plays, of course, have memorable scenes: the entry of the blinded Oedipus, for example, or Hamlet with Yorick's skull, or the shooting of Kattrin in Brecht's *Mother Courage*. Such scenes can represent what the play is about: they are like a compact reminder of the story it tells. They can sum up and express its central relation-ship, or the essence of its plot, or its principal characters, with a concentrated intensity. They encapsulate the world of the play with a lyrical power that burns it into the memory.

But that does not make them pictures of the world. Such scenes do not 'stand for' the play; we do not feel that the play's meaning is fully expressed in them. We question such scenes in the simple but essential way we question representational paintings: why are these people in this place? Why do they behave in this way? Is this what they really feel? A sense of such questioning defines, at the same time, both the play's nature as a narrative, and its meaning. By contrast, our visual memory of *Waiting for Godot* virtually sums up the essence of the whole play: it is about that waiting which we see. It strikes us as static, not because 'nothing happens, twice,' but because things that are not clearly caused or explained take place, with only minor variations, in the same place, between the same people, twice; and because the same things may already have happened, we do not know how often, and may all happen again. This waiting, and the repetition of this waiting, is what the play is 'about'. And if the single picture it leaves in our minds corresponds so closely, almost literally, to what the play is about, it is because the play is a statement.

Agamemnon and *Ghosts* are arguments. Arguments are dynamic: they move from point to point and from fact to fact. In drama, this means not only that the play's events progress, but also that its intellectual life is on the move. At the end of *The Oresteia* and *Ghosts* both the play's world and ours have changed: both Argos and the Alving household have become different places, and we know more about them and their inhabitants. This is the real meaning of dramatic action. An argument also implies questions: the nature of Aeschylus' and Ibsen's plays implies that between us and its events there is a dialogue of comprehension. There is no such dialogue between us and *Waiting for Godot*, because it does not relate events we can challenge or explain. It makes, instead, a statement about the world, about the human condition. This is the second, metaphorical, sense in which such a play is a 'picture of the world': it offers a distilled statement about human experience, and encloses it in a small, still, visual frame. Such a dramatic statement does not provoke questioning in any detail: it asks only to be accepted or rejected. We either feel that it is an accurate summing up of life, or that it is not. Is life an endless waiting, without cause or fulfilment? Yes, or no? There is no half-way reply, because that would mean that we accept certain things in the play but not others.

The difficulty is that there is no ground within the play from which we could challenge it in this way. If someone said that Shakespeare's *King Lear* depicted an utterly evil world, we might object by pointing out that the play's world not only contains Edmund, Cornwall, Goneril and Regan, but also Edgar, Albany, Kent and Cordelia, and the servant who comes to Gloucester's defence. But how do you *partly* disagree with *Waiting for Godot*? To repeat: we know virtually nothing about the characters. Their past, their education (if any), their motivations, their friends or families, are never revealed. It is an essential part of our experience of the play that such questions do not arise in our minds: the play contains or implies no answers to them, and to ask them at all seems both pedantic and fatuous.

Now what we call conventional plays are full of precisely such things. To understand them is part of our dialogue with the play. We cannot conduct such a dialogue with *Waiting for Godot*, because it has no such hidden implications. There is nothing in it, in this sense, to search for. It is a total statement of what it says. It is not open to questions. I shall call it *a closed play*. By contrast, *Agamemnon* and *Ghosts* are *open plays*. These terms are not derived from Karl Popper's *The Open Society and Its Enemies*: a book which, at the time of planning and writing this, I had not read — indeed, I was not then acquainted with Popper's work at all. I mention this, not in order to insinuate that my work is somehow on a level with Popper's, which would be impertinent, but to suggest that the preoccupations which made me write this book may have led me into an important area of imaginative and critical thought, one which is central to our experience of the modern world. Popper's terminology derives from a personal engagement with the life of politics and the life of the mind. I, too, had been trying to understand and to define something about plays like *Waiting for Godot*: something that made it, for me, fundamentally different from *Agamemnon* or *Ghosts*. I came to realise that Aeschylus and Ibsen offered me experiences which had to be challenged in order to be verified and understood: indeed, that such a challenge was an essential part of understanding what they had to say. I was like a questioner, and they were open to my questions. But with *Waiting for Godot* things were different: here I sensed that I was permitted to share someone else's unique vision of the world, but that asking questions about either this unique vision or that world was not meant to be part of the experience. Beckett's world was closed to my inquiries. I had to accept, and share, what he felt. Here, it seems to me, lies an essential difference between two kinds of drama, and also between two profoundly different types of aesthetic experience.

When I finally came to read Popper, it was both exhilarating and sobering. He sets out the central perception on the very first page of his text, contrasting the primitive tribe, the oldest form of 'closed' society, with later, 'open' societies[20]. The first, Popper tells us, is characterised by a *'submission* to magical forces'; while the latter 'sets free the *critical powers* of man' (my italics). Man's relationships to such social structures, it seemed to me, were not unlike a spectator's reaction to two different types of play. It is part of the purpose of *Agamemnon* and *Ghosts* to awaken and free our critical powers, while *Waiting for Godot* thwarts our questioning impulses at their very roots. *Submission* seems to me an accurate description of our experience of this play. The moral probing, the social inquisitiveness, the psychological questioning which *Agamemnon* and *Ghosts* call forth from us are not an important part of our response here. We submit to Beckett's vision; we accept his picture of the world. Or, alternately, we reject it entirely: this vision, we say, is not ours.

We are left with an extraordinary paradox. Here is a play which defies most of the rules of what we understand by drama. It has structure, but virtually no plot. Its characters have little in the way of personality, and practically no social background. There they are, in no particular place and no particular time; much of what they do seems to be purposeless; how long they have been here is obscure and irrelevant. This play may turn out to be the single most important event in the theatre since Aeschylus. It represents a change in the very subject matter of drama — which is a specific action, unfolding and concluding through the actions of characters who, in their turn, have both a social and a psychological density. The social and psychological density of Beckett's characters is almost nil. This is partly why his play also lacks plot: for plot rests on the comprehensible and 'question-able' actions of comprehensible and 'question-able' people. If we want to grasp the meaning of an action, we must first make sense of the characters who act. Furthermore, all drama is to some extent moral: even a boulevard farce makes us say, Serve him right. And insofar as morality has to do with conduct, with the way people live, act and behave, *Waiting for Godot* seems to have nothing moral about it whatever. And yet this play, which appears to have almost nothing of what we call conventionally dramatic about it, has been both a critical and, to a lesser extent, a popular success: it can hold audiences and say something to them.

But say what? In *The Theatre of the Absurd* Martin Esslin quotes a famous passage from the *San Quentin News*, the prisoners' journal in the San Quentin gaol in the United States. Here, in 1957, 1400 convicts sat spellbound by a performance of *Waiting for Godot*. The leading article said that the play

> was an expression, symbolic in order to avoid all personal error, by an author who expected each member of his audience to draw his own conclusions, make his own errors. It asked nothing in point, it forced no dramatized moral on the viewer, it held out no specific hope . . . We're still waiting for Godot, and shall continue to wait[21].

It is worth quoting this classic piece of theatre history again, because it shows Beckett's picture of the world being received by people who are already perfectly at home in it. The anonymous author may not have been a master of sophisticated critical prose, but he gives an unforgettable picture of one state of mind responding to another because it happens to be identical. The prisoners, he tells us, 'all shook'[22] as they left the performance. These words make us sense that shock of recognition which needs no explanation and provokes no questions. This is your life.

The rest of this book will try to answer two questions. The first is straightforward: is *Waiting for Godot* the single most important event in the theatre since Aeschylus? Or is it the fulfilment of forces that have been at work long before Beckett wrote it? If there is such a thing as a 'closed' play, what is its history?

The second question is much more difficult. It has to do with the existence of 'closed' art in general.

The prisoners of San Quentin responded to *Waiting for Godot* with deep emotion because, in Beckett's picture of the world, they recognised their own. In other words, the play did not tell them anything new. It is, we can see, a play which confirms. The full and proper response to it consists in the recognition of spiritual and emotional identity through a shared experience. If the experience is alien to us, we reject the play without questioning; and when we say that we do not understand it we mean, not only that we do not grasp its 'story', but also that it confirms nothing within us and that we do not share its vision. By contrast, a playwright like Ibsen provokes us to look and to think in a new way. The purpose of his mature plays is to alter our mental and moral habits: perhaps even to make us do things we might not have done before. All this makes up our response to his plays: it is part of the way in which we talk back to them. But we do not talk back to *Waiting for Godot* like this, because it does not tell us anything new. It speaks to us of our condition as it is, or as we feel it is. Its appeal is to our expectations, conscious or unconscious. It sets the seal on what we think and what we feel; or it fails and we turn away in incomprehension, dislike, or both.

To all this, there is an unexpected and most unpleasant analogy. In a book called *Hitler: The Führer and the People*, J.P. Stern analyses the psychology of German totalitarianism and looks, among other things, at the impact of the Nazi rallies. These events, Professor Stern observes, were 'perlocutionary' acts: they involved no *interlocution*, or proper communication in both directions. In Hitler's speeches the 'informational element' was slight: he usually said nothing that was new to his audience. Indeed, the effect of these speeches actually depended 'on an all but complete foreknowledge of their informational content.'[23]

It is impossible to read this without discomfort. Could there conceivably be something in common between the reception of Hitler's speeches by his audiences and the reception we accord to *Waiting for Godot*? No play could be more unlike a source of mindless and evil intoxication. No one could ever have left a performance of it wishing to intimidate or kill: indeed, one might expect that most people would leave the theatre wishing not to do anything at all. And yet the similarities remain: both this play, and the 'perlocutionary act' described by Professor Stern, expect, and depend on, complete and unreserved acceptance; they both ask for a suspension of what Popper calls 'the critical powers of man'. Such a reaction is contrary to everything we have come to understand by the experience of art. Art of any kind is, or we think it is, the creation of other worlds with which we can have a dialogue. And if we are engaged in a dialogue we can neither suspend judgement nor simply submit, not even in delighted recognition or a feeling of identity. Yet those are precisely the things that *Waiting for Godot* asks us to do.

And so we must ask: is the resemblance between the play and the totalitarian event merely superficial? Or is there such a thing as the totalitarianism of the creative mind? Is there an aesthetic which functions on the principle of recognition and assent, with recognition (or incomprehension) and dissent as the only alternatives? Pascal said that to think well was the basic principle of morality. Could it be that, in an art which demands submission and no inquisitive thought, there resides an essential amorality? If art is the creation of communicating worlds, can there be such a thing as totalitarian art? Or is the very phrase a contradiction in terms?

What follows is an attempt to understand what 'closed' art might mean, and what is its special appeal to the modern imagination. How, we must ask, could 'closed' art come to be created in what is an 'open' world? For information and understanding are essential properties of mental and physical life, and our ability to question our world purposefully and successfully is vital to our moral and physical survival. So, when we respond to 'closed' art, we might be denying, for a time at least, the fundamental human instinct to investigate. Instead of questioning, our imagination submits.

Is this a kind of abdication? The rest of this book will try to make sense of that question; and to find out how it happens and why.

Notes

1. E.M. Forster: *Aspects of the Novel*, ed. Oliver Stallybrass, Harmondsworth, repr. 1980, p. 40.
2. In *Maldoror*, tr. Paul Knight, Harmondsworth, 1978, p. 217.
3. *Ghosts*, tr. Michael Meyer, London, 1973, p. 38.
4. For commentaries on this passage, see *Agamemnon*, ed. Eduard Fraenkel, Oxford, 1950, pp. 412 ff.; *Agamemnon*, ed. J.D. Denniston and Denys Page, Oxford, 1957, pp. 148–54; Oliver Taplin: *The Stagecraft of Aeschylus*, Oxford, 1977, pp. 314–5; Oliver Taplin: *Greek Tragedy in Action*, London, 1978, esp. pp. 78–83. In an article in *The Proceedings of the Cambridge Philological Society*, 1963, pp. 21 ff., R.D. Dawe argues eloquently against the accepted view that Agamemnon's act in treading on the tapestries is a case of extreme *hybris*: he points out that the Chorus make no comment on Agamemnon's action, which would be unusual if the action carried great significance. On the other hand, we know that Aeschylus was an innovator and not averse to spectacle: might he not have made Agamemnon tread the tapestries in silence (as Taplin points out, he would have had a long way to walk), and allowed the silence to make its own, unexpected, and damning, comment?
5. Xenophon: *Cyropaedia*, tr. J.S. Watson and H. Dale, London, 1898, Book 8, Ch.8, p. 284.
6. *Waiting for Godot*, London, 1959, p. 20.
7. *ibid.*, p. 68.
8. 'All Mankind Is Us', by Kay Boyle, in *Samuel Beckett: A Collection of Critical Essays*, ed. Ruby Cohn, New York, 1975, p. 19.
9. *Ghosts*, Meyer, p. 96

10. See George Thomson: *Aeschylus and Athens*, 2nd edn., London, 1946, Ch. XV, esp. pp. 265 ff.; John Jones: *Aristotle and Greek Tragedy*, London, 1962, esp. Section II; Hugh Lloyd-Jones: *The Justice of Zeus*, California, 1971, esp. Ch. I and Ch. IV.

11. See Taplin, *Stagecraft*, p.356; Robert F. Goheen: 'Aspects of Dramatic Symbolism: Three Studies in the 'Oresteia',' *American Journal of Philology*, 76, 1955, pp. 113 ff.

12. See Lloyd-Jones, *The Justice of Zeus*, passim.

13. *ibid.*, p. 94.

14. Shakespeare: *Measure for Measure*, II.1., London, 1965, Arden Edition, ed. J.W. Lever, p. 27.

15. Vivian Mercier: 'The Mathematical Limit,' *The Nation*, February 14, 1959.

16. *Texts for Nothing* in *No's Knife: Collected Shorter Prose, 1947–66*, London, 1967, p. 92.

17. *Godot*, p. 46.

18. *En Attendant Godot*, ed. Colin Duckworth, London, 1966, p. 41.

19. *No's Knife*, p. 91.

20. K.R. Popper: *The Open Society and Its Enemies*, London, 5th edn., 1977, Vol.I., p. 1.

21. Martin Esslin: *The Theatre of the Absurd*, Harmondsworth, 1968, p. 20.

22. *ibid.*

23. J.P. Stern: *Hitler: The Führer and the People*, London, 1975, pp. 35–8.

II

SCHOPENHAUER
The Circular Hell

Closed art is not a movement, like Romanticism or Surrealism. It has no theoreticians or critical apologists; no one has written manifestos for it, or created for it a body of aesthetic doctrine. The importance of Schopenhauer in the argument of this book lies in the fact that his writings contain a body of aesthetic judgements and doctrines which, in retrospect, read as if they were heralding a new form of artistic expression. When his principal work, *The World as Will and Idea*, fell into the hands of Richard Wagner in 1854, Schopenhauer was virtually unknown even in Germany: indeed, it is not often realised that Wagner was a pioneering Schopenhauerian. His admiration for the philosopher, whose book he read on the casual recommendation of a friend, was not part of an intellectual fashion or movement but a matter of personal enthusiasm.

What attracted Wagner to Schopenhauer was not philosophy in the technical sense. He was overwhelmed by the book because he found in it a picture of the world very like his own. He responded, not with the fervour of an analytical mind, but with the mental and emotional excitement of someone who has been labouring in isolation and has unexpectedly found a fellow creature.

Schopenhauer held that the business of a philosopher was to make sense of the world. That is precisely what his work did for Wagner: after reading him, the composer knew that his deeply felt but incompletely formulated ideas about the world and the meaning of human life had been clarified for him by a kindred spirit. His reaction to Schopenhauer was, strictly speaking, an emotional and aesthetic one; and what interests us here is the nature of the emotion, the nature of the aesthetic perceptions that the two men might have had in common.

The English reader may have a reservation about all this: namely, that what Schopenhauer meant to Wagner was somehow an exclusively German affair. It is one of the purposes of this book to dispel that notion. I shall argue in the next chapter that if there is such a thing as closed drama, then Wagner was its first great practitioner. The dramas on which his mature operas rest are his pictures of the world; and Schopenhauer's picture of the world was for him, in turn, both a confirmation and an inspiration.

Erich Heller has written, in connection with Schopenhauer, about 'that mysterious elective attraction that coldly figures in literary histories as "influence"'[1]; and the way in which writers and other artists have responded, some more consciously than others, to Schopenhauer, is one of the threads which will run through all the following chapters. It is true that the philosopher's most famous appearance is in a German novel: Thomas Mann's *Buddenbrooks*, in the celebrated passage where Consul Thomas Buddenbrook, ageing and disillusioned, sits in his garden pavilion and reads, for four hours, 'a book which had, partly by chance, come into his hands'. It is, we are told, the second part of 'a famous philosophical system'[2]. Other than that, Mann does not tell us what the book is: in an act of intellectual complicity which is both arrogant and ironical, he assumes that we know. It is, in fact, *The World as Will and Idea*; and the pages of the novel that follow are both a concise summary of Schopenhauer's philosophy, and the portrait of a mind under the impact of its first encounter with it. The Consul's afternoon culminates in his reading of the chapter 'On Death and its Relation to our Personal Immortality'.

> Only a few lines remained when the servant came through the garden at four o'clock to call him to dinner. He nodded, read the remaining sentences, closed the book, and looked about him. He felt that his whole being had unaccountably expanded, and at the same time there clung about his senses a profound intoxication, a strange, sweet, vague allurement which somehow resembled the feelings of early love and longing. He put away the book in the drawer of the garden table. His hands were cold and unsteady, his head was burning, and he felt in it a strange pressure and strain, as though something were about to snap. He was not capable of consecutive thought.[3]

What has taken place is very like a perlocutionary act. Thomas
Buddenbrook is moved by Schopenhauer's book because it reveals to
him something that, however vaguely, already exists within his own
mind.

> He remained the rest of the day in this condition, this heavy
> lethargy and intoxication, overpowered by the heavy draught
> he had drunk, incapable of thought.

This is not the picture of a questing intellect but a mind subjugated
by a revelation: Consul Buddenbrook has seen Schopenhauer's
picture of the world and submitted to it. And we may note in passing
that Mann is a little perfunctory about the actual book. The Consul
had apparently bought it years ago, secondhand and in poor condition. Yet until now we have had no indication that he was interested
in books at all, let alone in a book of philosophy: unlike Mrs Alving,
he has no real reason for wanting to read them. And yet the battered
book by the unknown philosopher makes a perfectly natural appearance here, and any questions as to why it should have occurred to
the Consul to read it now, or why precisely he should have bought it
in the first place, would seem, at this point in the narrative, both
pedantic and fruitless. For by now Mann is less concerned with
telling a story, and more with how he wants us to interpret it. We
might say that, as *Buddenbrooks* progresses, it changes from being a
novel about 'Mann's world' into 'Mann's picture of the world'.

The case of *Buddenbrooks* is unusual, because Schopenhauer
makes almost a personal appearance in it. But he exercised a wide
and subtle influence, which went well beyond German literature and
culture, and which is intimately connected with the subject of this
book. August Strindberg, for example, was a passionate reader and
admirer of Schopenhauer. He called him a disciple of Christ (which
would hardly have pleased the philosopher), and declared in one of
his letters that he had been 'educated by three Buddhists,
Schopenhauer, von Hartmann, and lastly Nietzsche'[4]. Strindberg is
getting a little muddled here as to what a Buddhist is; but his
admiration for Schopenhauer might make us look again at his late
plays. Their abrupt, apparently arbitrary and nihilistic endings, in
which the world of the plays virtually dissolves without its conflicts
being in any way resolved, may be difficult or unsatisfactory
theatre; but they may turn out to have a profound kinship with
Schopenhauer's vision of the world.

The Swiss architect and stage designer, Adolphe Appia, who was
to have such an enormous influence on the modern theatre, was

another devotee of Schopenhauer. When Appia writes about music as 'an element springing from our inner selves'[5], he uses, as we shall see, deeply Schopenhauerian language. His stage designs are a visual expression of that impatience with the accidental and the episodic which is so characteristic of Schopenhauer's thought, and which has also proved to be a source of important insights into the meaning of Wagner's operas. (What Schopenhauer himself would have thought of such stage designs is another matter.)

Schopenhauer once summed up the relationship between the human will and the human intellect as being like 'the strong blind man who carries on his shoulders the lame man who can see'[6]. It may not be fanciful to see in W.B. Yeats's play *The Cat and the Moon* a dramatisation of this image; and again a variation on it, in the characters of the Blind Man and The Fool, in *On Baile's Strand* — especially when we find that Yeats, too, read and admired Schopenhauer. 'Schopenhauer can do no wrong in my eyes,' he wrote; 'I no more quarrel with him than I do with a mountain cataract.'[7] Readers of Yeats will know that he is not usually so unreserved in his praise of other writers. But Schopenhauer was clearly a special case: Yeats responds to him, as Consul Buddenbrook does, with passionate abandon. Again, it may not be fanciful to see in Samuel Beckett's *Endgame*, with its domineering, self-deluding and blind master, Hamm, and its sardonic, clear-sighted and lame servant, Clov, another dramatised version of Schopenhauer's image. And it turns out that Beckett, too, is a reader of Schopenhauer: he has said that Schopenhauer was the only philosopher whom he has continued to read into his old age[8].

Was the image, then, in Beckett's mind when he wrote the play? We cannot say; and what concerns us here is a profound kinship of the imagination: a tendency in both men to see the world and human relationships in a bleak but sardonically humorous way, and a way of summing them up in images which are both dramatic and concise.

'All original thinking,' Schopenhauer said, 'takes place in images'[9] — a remark which we might apply to the passage from Beckett's *Texts for Nothing*:

> It's an image, in my helpless head, where all sleeps, all is dead, not yet born, i don't know, or before my eyes, they see the scene, the lids flicker and it's in.[10]

Perhaps the plays that we want to call pictures of the world are created under the spell of such images, so compulsively perceived;

perhaps such images speak for these 'pictures'. Perhaps, when we respond to pictures of the world we respond to images which inspired them and enclose their meaning. And their impact on us, their statement-like dominance over our minds, may have to do with the way in which we respond to images. Nor is it all a question of dominance. 'A mental image,' P.N. Furbank has pointed out,

> is no less and no more than what you put there. You can never learn anything from mental images, since they are merely a way of presenting to yourself what you already know.[11]

Now on this reading, an image, too, might be a perlocutionary act: we would have to know its meaning in order to understand it. Of course, if we were to take such an argument to its logical end, we would finish up calling language itself a perlocutionary act too, and might indeed find ourselves trying to prove that no literary work communicates anything. But the fact is that we are dealing with plays (and novels) which have stories; and it is the unfolding of these stories which, for us, is their principal 'informational content': what we do not know at the beginning, but find out by the end, is how the story would be told and how it would end. And when a playwright is not telling a story so much as summing up feeling in an image, he is engaged in a perlocutionary act. And so, when the young Wagner wrote, in 1850, long before he ever heard of Schopenhauer, that artistic expression was 'the inner image' of the world[12], he was speaking the language of Schopenhauer without knowing it; and he was already a creator of pictures of the world in the making.

Wagner's enthusiasm for Schopenhauer was no mere youthful intellectual infatuation. He was forty-one; he had already written his most important theoretical works; *Tannhäuser* and *Lohengrin* had been composed, respectively, nine and six years earlier. When, in the autumn of 1854, his friend the writer Georg Herwegh brought Wagner a copy of *The World as Will and Idea*, the entire libretto of *The Ring* had been written and published; the music of *The Rhinegold* was complete; and Wagner was composing Act Two of *The Valkyrie*. He was at the height of his intellectual and creative powers. Before the year was out he completed the composition of *The Valkyrie*, read Schopenhauer's book, and sent the philosopher a copy of the libretto of *The Ring*, inscribed 'With reverence and gratitude'.

Wagner welcomed Schopenhauer as a liberator. He told Hans von Bülow: 'A great boon has come to me through acquaintance with the works of the great philosopher Schopenhauer.'[13] To Liszt, he described him as 'the greatest philosopher since Kant', and added that 'His chief idea, the final desire of the negation of life, is terribly serious, but [sic] it shows the only salvation possible.'[14] To his friend August Röckel Wagner wrote:

I have only arrived at last at an understanding of my own works of art ... by the aid of another ... it required the great re-volution of my rational concepts, ultimately effected through Schopenhauer ... to give my poem [*The Ring*] a fitting keystone.

Wagner explains how, as he was writing the text, he was conscious of creating

a conceptual universe upon the Hellenic-optimistic model, which I believed entirely possible of realisation, if mankind would only will it, and in it I attempted ingeniously to bridge for myself the problem as to why, in that case, they do not actually will it.

Siegfried, at this stage was going to be a character presenting 'life without sorrow'; and the audience were to be given

a lesson on how we should recognise ... evil, tear it out by the roots and establish a righteous world in its stead. And all the time I scarcely noticed that in the execution, indeed at bottom even in the planning of my design, I was unconsciously follow-ing a quite different and far deeper perception and instead of a phase of world evolution, had discerned the nature of the universe itself in all its conceivable phases and had recognised its nothingness; whence it naturally happened that, since I was faithful not to my concepts but to my intuitions, something emerged quite different from what I had actually proposed.[15]

Wagner is being both perceptive and honest. Only a few months earlier, before he had encountered Schopenhauer, he was describing to Röckel how Wotan, faced with

the necessity of recognising and submitting to the multiplicity, the ever-changing aspects, the eternal renewals of Reality and of Life ... rises to the tragic dignity of *willing* his own destruction.[16]

There was, indeed, a Schopenhauerian in Wagner who was liberated by the philosopher: it was revealed to Wagner that he was much more of Wotan's mind than he had realised.

Schopenhauer was now sixty-six. *The World as Will and Idea* had been published in 1818, when he was thirty; its second, greatly enlarged edition appeared in 1844. Both were virtually ignored. Two years after the first edition was published Schopenhauer decided on an academic career, and began delivering a course of lectures on philosophy at the University of Berlin. Hegel, whom Schopenhauer detested, was also lecturing at the University, and Schopenhauer chose to give his lectures at precisely the same hour. The result was that they were unattended; but rather than change the hour, he decided to discontinue the course, and, at the age of thirty-two, his academic career was over.

Earlier, in 1816, he had written a treatise on colour under the influence of, and with some encouragement from, Goethe: some eighty years later it was to be avidly read by Kandinsky when he was working on his essay *On the Spiritual in Art*. In 1839, Schopenhauer, now over fifty, won a prize, offered by a Norwegian scientific society, for an essay on whether 'free will could be proved from the evidence of consciousness'. Later in the same year he sent another prize essay, about the basis of morality, to the Royal Danish Academy of Sciences. It was the only entry; but it was rejected for, among other reasons, containing too many uncomplimentary references to other philosophers. Schopenhauer published the two essays together two years later under the title *The Two Fundamental Problems in Ethics*.

In 1831 there had been a cholera epidemic in Berlin. Schopenhauer fled and, two years later, he settled in Frankfurt-am-Main where he lived for the rest of his life, resentful of his obscurity, in rented rooms but on a comfortable private income which he handled with great competence. The philosopher of renunciation did not go in much for renunciation. Meanwhile his books still remained unsold. He was to write one more, *Parerga and Paralipomena*, a large, two-volume collection of essays, whose Greek title means, roughly, things that are ancillary to and omitted from a work (the work being, clearly, *The World as Will and Idea*). It was this book, published in 1851, that received a review, two years later, from the English writer, playwright and drama critic John Oxenford, on the pages of the *Westminster Review*. The article was soon translated into German for a Berlin periodical, and the cloud of obscurity under which the ageing philosopher lived began to lift.

His last years were spent in gradually increasing fame — something which he wished constantly to reassure himself of by getting his disciples to hunt through newspapers and other publications for references to his work. He never altered his habits, which included lunching at the same hotel, and reading *The Times* in a public library, every day. He did not care for Wagner, disliking the composer's prose almost as much as his music. He had seen *The Flying Dutchman* and *Tannhäuser* and disliked both; and he did not live to hear either *The Ring* or *Tristan*. What he made of *The Ring*'s libretto is one of the entertaining minor episodes of cultural history. The philosopher commented acidly on the expensive quality of the paper; but the drama, in which he might have seen his own picture of the world, irritated him, and he left us traces of his incomprehension and dislike in brief marginal notes. On the love scene between Siegmund and Sieglinde in Hunding's house he commented 'Monstrous ingratitude!' When, in Act Two of *The Valkyrie*, Wotan gives in to Fricka, Schopenhauer noted: 'Hen-pecked Wotan.' And, against the final curtain, he wrote 'Not a moment too soon!'[17] This is the first of many examples of a 'closed' mind feeling uneasy, uncomprehending or indifferent in the face of a world other than its own: the philosopher of renunciation did not recognise another's picture of renunciation either. For this matter, we find Wagner, too, writing solemnly to Liszt, how, when sitting in trains, his

> gaze always tried involuntarily to read in the eyes of fellow travellers whether they were capable of, or destined for salvation, that is, negation of the world.

Did it occur to him, one wonders, to question whether he himself was destined for such salvation? For later in the same letter he drily informs Liszt:

> The object of my journey has been the securing of the rights of property in my operas.[18]

Schopenhauer said that a philosopher's business was to make sense of the world: his philosophy springs from looking at the world and finding it inexplicable as to its origins and unreal as to its existence. The apprehension of death gives to such puzzled astonishment a special sense of urgency and intensity. 'Without death,' Schopenhauer said, 'men would scarcely philosophise.'[19] This may provide the easiest key, for the non-philosopher, to Schopenhauer's work. Thinkers like him (and Plato and Kant) look at the world and ask what enduring reality it and its creatures can possibly have, since sooner or later they all die. Is this present existence of theirs and ours, then, all there is to life? Is reality not permanent? Does the world as we see it consist of decaying things and dying creatures? And if it does, how does it survive? How can life consist of continuous death?

Seen like this, the world might indeed appear incomprehensible to the point of seeming to be unreal — and, as far as it may be real, an extremely depressing place. And yet all its objects and its living creatures are *there*: they exist, and some of them even show signs of enjoying it. At this point we either conclude that these meditations are futile, or that there must be some other explanation. And we can then see why some people, to whom such thinking is painfully real, come to believe that there must be some other reality that we cannot see; a hidden but essential principle which, once revealed and understood, would explain the nature of the world. It is as if, faced with the unending and insoluble complexity of the universe, one wanted to find something that held it all together and could not be further questioned. Such an explanation would make the world both comprehensible and endurable. Philosophy, in this sense, is both a rational inquiry and an exercise in consolation; and such a solution gives us a sense of order which is both reassuring and imperative.

Such thinking also implies that what we see as real is not really real; that there are things which are more real than the things our perceptions report to us about; that beyond the things we perceive in ordinary life there is another reality, and we can somehow apprehend what it is; that this hidden reality — and this is an important jump — may not be clearly and rationally expressible; but that — an even more important jump — it is more significant than the one we are used to. Seen in this light, the revolution in Western painting which began at the turn of the century with Cézanne, the ageing Monet, and Picasso, ought to be clearly comprehensible to a reader of Schopenhauer. We must not over-simplify here; but the painters I have mentioned have in common a rising impatience with what we might call 'the merely real'. They were not interested simply in reality as they saw it: they wanted to grasp what made reality *seem* real, and they wanted to show us this insight in their pictures. They came to the conclusion that what made things seem real served only to conceal their essential quality, their basic what-ness. Their problem was how to show us this insight, and that basic what-ness, in paintings which we would approach with eyes accustomed to 'mere' reality.

I must reserve these matters for a later chapter. Our focus of interest here is the fact that Schopenhauer, too, wanted to know what this basic what-ness, the essence of things, might be. He thought he had discovered it; and that is the subject of his book.

Schopenhauer regarded himself as the disciple of Immanuel Kant, and to understand his thinking we must recall that for Kant the world consisted of the *phenomenal* and the *noumenal*. Put very simply, the phenomenal world is the world of things: we perceive it, and our mind makes sense of these perceptions. But, for Kant, there is something inherent in all things and objects: something that constitutes their very essence. This is what Kant calls the thing-in-itself, or the *noumenon*. If we could understand the real nature of the *noumenon*, then everything that is merely *phenomenon* would make sense, and seem less important. Schopenhauer called this hidden thing the Will. It was, for him, 'the inner content, the essence of the world'[20]. The essence of Schopenhauer's philosophy, which we must grasp if we are to understand him, is the relationship between this Will and the rest of the phenomenal world.

This is far from easy: indeed, it has been suggested that Schopenhauer has not clearly shown what this relationship is. That would amount to saying that his philosophy does not make sense. Therefore when we read him we must bear in mind that perhaps those who came under his sway did so, not because his ideas made coherent sense, but because he presented them with a picture of the world: that is to say, an account of the world which included Schopenhauer's feelings about the world.

The greatest difficulty in this picture is the Will itself. Schopenhauer has been criticised for using the word *will*, because it implies a sense of intention, of purpose; yet the Will, as Schopenhauer presents it, has neither. Essentially, it is like energy: 'blind striving, obscure inarticulate impulse'[21]. It is the principle of all existence: something that both *makes* it and *is* it. It is a 'motion, a striving forward, in boundless space, without rest and without end'[22]. It is 'outside time and space and therefore knows no multiplicity and is consequently *one*'[23] (my italics). It 'lies outside the ... law of motivation'[24], and is not subject to causes or changes. Change and causality, Schopenhauer tells us, 'have only to do with states and conditions' but not with the thing that caused them. And, he goes on, increasing our perplexity, 'the law of causality applies to all things in the world but not to the world itself'[25]. In other words, we are being told that things in the world can change but the world itself cannot, because the world is Will.

The Will is also entirely free; you cannot apply any laws to it at all; and the meaning of good and evil can only be understood as either conforming to it or opposing it. Indeed, for Schopenhauer 'every good is essentially relative, for its being consists in its relation to a desiring Will. *Absolute good* is, therefore, a contradiction of terms; the highest good, *summum bonum*, really signifies the same thing — a final satisfaction of the Will.'[26]

So much for the nature of the Will. As for any purpose it might have, Schopenhauer notes that 'since what the Will wills is always life', it is simply identical with the will to live [27]. We must observe that this is not 'purpose' as we understand it in ordinary life: what Schopenhauer means is that the will *issues in* life, indeed virtually *is* life. It is easy to understand, reading this, how Schopenhauer's philosophy could be distorted. When Nietzsche re-interpreted the Will as being essentially a Will to Power, the way was clear for the hijacking of both philosophers by Nazi ideologists. The gospel of naked power that knows no legality is of course a gross distortion of what Schopenhauer meant; but we must grasp how his choice of the word *will*, which can say one thing and mean another, lends itself to such subversion. He meant general, almost aimless willing; whereas the word suggests purposeful intent. Philosophical imprecision helped to create a creed of murder.

One guesses that Schopenhauer would have rejected Nazi ideology, not only for moral reasons, but also on philosophical grounds. He could have pointed out that what he meant by Will was something far more fundamental than political, military or racial visions. The Will, for him, is something that permeates the world, indeed takes shape as the world. Look at your body, Schopenhauer says, and you will see yourself as a thing and, like other things, an object of perception. But you have, too, another kind of awareness of yourself: an awareness *from within*. When you are conscious of yourself in this way, then you know yourself as an example of the Will in action. Schopenhauer's expression to describe this is that the Will *objectifies itself* in your body: you are, as it were, a living specimen of it. And if you have a sense of individuality, if you say, this is me, I walk, act or behave in such and such a way, then you must not think that those movements, those actions and that behaviour are related to each other or to 'you' in the way of cause and effect. They do not produce one another; nor do you cause them. They are, in reality, the same thing, manifested in different ways. 'The notion of free will,' we are told, 'is nothing but the act of Will objectified, i.e. passed into perception.' Observe yourself, that is, and you see a mechanism operated by the Will [28].

This is not a very elevated view of humanity; but Schopenhauer sees the whole world as such objectifications of the Will. When he called his book *The World as Will and Idea* (or *Representation*, as it is also translated), he meant that everything we saw or perceived was an Idea, a Representation, of something in the Will. Idea, or Representation, he said, was simply the way in which the Will 'objectified' itself for us. 'Matter,' he summed up, 'is the visibility of the *Will*.'[29] So, if we could ever apprehend what sort of thing the Will was, we should understand the world. And *The World* is also a crucial part of Schopenhauer's title. His book sets out to account for existence as a whole. The entire world is his subject, from the silent growth of crystals and the murderous struggles of animal survival, to human life and its vilest and most refined spiritual products. His vision is both total and final. He shows us how everything can be understood through the dependence of all things on the Will; but also that the Will itself, and therefore ultimately the world, too, are beyond questioning.

Now the ordinary inquiring mind may already find it hard to understand how 'the world' can exist as something separate from the things in it; and how those things can be subject to change and causality, while 'the world' is free of them. Moreover, Schopenhauer claims that the Will is subject to the law of necessity, which leaves us puzzled about how anything, even the Will, can be subject to any law, however abstract, unless a relationship resembling cause and effect exists between them.

Such contradictions are in the very nature of Schopenhauer's picture of the world. He is describing a causally structured universe, at the heart of which lives a non-causal principle: a force which is unknowable, unaccountable, self-contained and self-referential. This force is therefore also, by definition, amoral: that is, outside moral considerations. Propelled by this aimless, amoral thing, we live in 'eternal becoming, endless flux'. We always desire new things, trying to keep up 'the game . . . of constant transition from desire to satisfaction, and from satisfaction to desire'; and our only alternative is 'stagnation . . . fearful ennui that paralyses life . . . deadening languor'[30]. And the Will, as exemplified in you or me, also clashes with itself as exemplified in other men. Animals prey on animals; even clusters of crystals are images of this conflict. 'The will to live,' Schopenhauer concludes, 'everywhere preys on itself.'[31]

It is an utterly bleak picture. Like Samuel Beckett's characters, Schopenhauerian man finds himself in an unfriendly world. It is not in any sense his own creation, nor that of any being he could understand or look up to; nor is it a place he could improve upon. In this sense, Schopenhauer drew up one of the earliest coherent accounts of alienation. It is a world without any sense of progress, and thus one in which man has neither a real past nor a real future. His very extinction makes no difference to the survival of the Will which, as we have been shown, is both his own essence and the world's. (Hence Schopenhauer's view that suicide is futile.) It is a time-less universe, not unlike the end-less present of *Waiting for Godot*.

Schopenhauer's way of putting this is to say that time is only a form in which we comprehend matter: it has nothing to do with the essence of life. Time is like an unceasing stream; and when we talk about the 'present', we mean that we have found a way of isolating and understanding things which would otherwise merge into the flux of time. For us, if something or someone exists in time, then they have a past which could be subject to our questioning inquiry. But to the Schopenhauerian imagination time is both troublesome and essentially meaningless. This explains Schopenhauer's mistrust of history, and his preference for myths and epic poetry as ways of interpreting the world. For, again, if time is meaningless in itself, then history, a causal account of time, is not a reliable way of understanding anything. To the historian, things may look as though they were guided by some conception of an end; but in reality they are without any such guidance. (The young Wagner held very similar views, long before he encountered Schopenhauer.)

The fact is that, as Schopenhauer sees it, what we think of as means and ends are but manifestations of the unity of one and the same Will. In other words, things do not cause other things; events do not bring other events in their wake: it is the Will at work, assuming a kind of multiplicity in space and time, so that we might know it. That sounds almost like a version of the Incarnation; and it is not the only time that Schopenhauer writes like a religious mystic, with the Will as his inscrutable and probably malevolent God.

Within such a vision individual man does not have much significance. Consul Buddenbrook was consoled by Schopenhauer because he accepted the vision of his philosophy: he saw that he was but an objectification of the one great Will which would remain, forever striving, long after he himself had gone. For Schopenhauer the matter was majestically simple: 'We are at bottom something that ought not to be: therefore we cease to be.'[32] (Note how the visionary has taken over from the philosophical inquirer: the *fact* of death follows from the metaphysical statement that we *should not* exist at all.) Thomas Buddenbrook read those words and accepted them. 'Was not every human being,' he meditated afterwards in the night, 'a mistake and a blunder?' It was, he felt, merely a delusion that he was his own individual self; he was but a part of the world which was all Will.

> The deceptive perceptions of space, time, and history, the preoccupation with a glorious historical continuity of life in the person of his own descendants, the dread of some future final dissolution and decomposition — all this his spirit now put aside. He was no longer prevented from grasping eternity. Nothing began, nothing left off. There was only an endless present; and that power in him which loved life with a love so exquisitely sweet and yearning — the power of which his person was only the unsuccessful expression — that power would always know how to find access to this present.[33]

The consul lives only a few more months after this, and what is left of his life is once again consumed by the civic and commercial activities of a Hanseatic merchant. He never reads the book again, because he is 'too weak-willed to arrive at a reasonable and fruitful arrangement of his time'. But the experience of reading it was for him an ecstasy of submission and liberation. For those few hours he was freed from the shackles of identity; he experienced a temporary, blissful release from the responsibilities, the causes and effects of existence, the aches and pains of life. As a recognisable individual, he almost ceased to exist. We said that to live in an endless present, like Beckett's tramps, was bleak. To Consul Buddenbrook it meant the cessation of all 'becoming' and an assumption of a state of pure 'being'; and he found it intoxicating and blissful. The experience to which he so joyfully submitted was an encounter with a totalitarian spirit.

A sense of character in literature (and life) is inextricably bound up with time; and a denial of time obliterates our sense of an individual person. Consul Buddenbrook's experience of being freed from time and his own self brings us to consider Schopenhauer's ideas about character. He regarded himself as a moral philosopher: what did he think of people? What, for him, did *character* mean?

Schopenhauer was a moral philosopher, describing a world which he regarded as in its essence amoral; and it will not surprise us that human character is, for him, merely 'an immediate manifestation of the Will, and therefore *groundless*' (my italics)[34]. I take this to mean that for him character is morally unaccountable. Yet he also recognises that what he calls the inner meaning and content of a man's life proceed from his character: and to say that is to put character in a moral context. So where do we stand? Does human character have anything to do with morality? Schopenhauer distinguishes between *empirical* and *intelligible* character. A man's *empirical* character manifests itself in events and actions which Schopenhauer loftily calls 'unessential': they are determined only by outward circumstances and character reacts to them according to its nature. What, then, is its nature? We find that a man's empirical character is the image and manifestation of his other, *intelligible character*; and that this intelligible character, in turn, is a special Idea which corresponds to a special act of the objectification of the Will.

This is beginning to sound less and less like human character as you and I understand it. Still, it does seem clear that Schopenhauer leaves us little room for moral judgement. For if actions and events are 'unessential', and if the empirical character (for which they provide the material) is only an image, twice removed, of the Will itself, then a man's character is simply a man's character: it is merely something determined by its own cause and its other self, the inaccessible and amoral Will. On this reckoning, no one is to be condemned for any action, however evil, or praised for anything, however generous. We are being led irresistibly towards the dilemma of determinism or free will, which I am not qualified to deal with. But in literature the matter is simpler: to be a character means to have a will of your own. If Schopenhauer were to comment on Shakespeare's *Measure for Measure*, he would, one imagines, give short shrift to Angelo and his moral predicament. When Angelo tells Isabella, 'Look, what I will not that I cannot do,' Schopenhauer would note that Angelo's Will was manifesting itself through his intelligible character by making his empirical character react to the unessential circumstance of Isabella pleading for her brother's life. But what Shakespeare tells us is precisely that Angelo has a choice:

it is fully in his power to release Claudio, and our moral questioning of Angelo and the play turns on the fact that he decides one way rather than another. As the play goes on, we both apprehend and judge his character by watching him take decision after decision. Drama is character in moral action; and moral character in a play is meaningless without a sense of responsibility.

The problem of morality haunts Schopenhauer's work: it is something that the philosopher of the Will is on uneasy terms with. The world is, for him, clearly a moral place: it has not just a physical but an 'ethical significance'. Anyone who denies this is committing in Schopenhauer's view, 'the greatest and most pernicious of errors, the fundamental error,' for it is an 'intrinsically perverse view'. It is this denial of the ethical significance of the world which, he says, lies behind our idea of the Anti-Christ[35]. And within this moral world Schopenhauer is content to take a reassuringly straightforward view of human morality. In his essay *The Basis of Morality* the subject is much more what you or I would understand by the word, namely, everyday human conduct. Writing about malice and cruelty, for instance, Schopenhauer describes them as examples of 'a higher degree of moral turpitude'; and concludes this section with the words:

> Here I bring to an end my review of these terrible powers of evil; it is an array reminding one of the Prince of Darkness in Milton's *Pandemonium* . . .[36]

This is the sturdy language of conventional bourgeois moral indignation. But a little earlier[37] Schopenhauer said that 'the conception of *ought*, in other words the *imperative form* of Ethics', is entirely meaningless, since you cannot be good under duress. This is clearly a more radical voice; yet now it begins to ring a little hollow: for how can you so cavalierly dismiss moral imperatives when you yourself are capable of such vehement condemnation of evil actions? The problem of goodness is no easier. The good man, we are told, is someone who, inspired by a sense of identity with other people, respects the Will in them and overcomes it in himself. The bad man, by contrast, is bad because he prevents someone else's will from functioning.

Once again, we seem to be leaving the world of recognisable human behaviour behind and entering the land of theoretical speculation. For could not this 'bad man' have perfectly good reasons for getting in the way of another person's will? Suppose this other person was about to commit an act of cruelty or malice which Schopenhauer so deplores? And how, again, will the 'good man' overcome his own will, considering how powerful the Will is? Schopenhauer seems to have been aware of this. He is anxious that we should not think of his 'good man' as a feeble ninny: he makes a point of emphasising that goodness does not imply a weak Will.

The fact is that Schopenhauer always sounds more convincing and passionate when he describes the all-powerful, amoral Will than when he observes simple, uncomplicated goodness or generosity. For him, they are not uncomplicated at all: he admits, almost helplessly, that 'every purely beneficial act, all help entirely and genuinely unselfish . . . is in fact . . . a dark enigma, a piece of mysticism put into practice.'[38] Schopenhauer is torn between two worlds: on the one hand, that of ordinary human charity, which he views with all the incomprehension of a predator red in tooth and claw, and, on the other, that of the primal, unscrupulous, amoral Will, which he paints almost with hatred, but with a dark, vehement, lyrical conviction.

Now Schopenhauer may sometimes speak of the Will, and the world it creates, with hatred; but he is not condemning the world in the way one would criticise a faulty system. What is there to condemn in something which you know can never change, and which you yourself cannot hope to alter? How do you criticise an elemental, amoral force? How do you challenge a universe which is all one piece? This is why Schopenhauerian man is trapped in the world. The entire argument is circular because the world is circular. Its prime mover and its essence, the Will, is characterised by eternal becoming and endless striving: an idea which confers on Schopenhauer's universe a sense of both open-endedness and claustrophobia. The insatiable Will drives us on and causes all our suffering; and yet we and our world are but pieces of this same Will. This is a picture of the world which we cannot challenge by taking it on piece by piece: we can only accept it or reject it. It is entirely characteristic of Schopenhauer that he disapproves of suicide because it merely puts an end to our 'phenomenal' existence without making any impression on the everlasting Will; and that he does not believe in the moral reformation of people since character, too, is determined by the Will. This is why he held the now familiar view that punishment can only deter, but not improve. The morality implied in Schopenhauer's work is the morality, not of challenge, engagement and argument, but of unshrinking acceptance. Pain, for him, is inherent in all life because it is at the source of the Will: 'The basis of all willing is need, deficiency and thus pain.' Man's nature is like an unquenchable thirst and 'subject to pain originally through its very being'[39]. Happiness is thus, by definition, something negative: it is merely the alleviation of pain; and the pain of needing, and hence of willing, is ever ready to begin again. This is a circular hell.

Is there any escape? Schopenhauer tells us that there is: it is *to deny the Will*. But, the astonished reader might reply, that would amount to the denial of everything there is: the world and all there is in it, including ourselves! Here we reach the commanding height and the central paradox of Schopenhauer's thought. One of the reasons why it is hard to understand what he is about at this point is that he is struggling with an invisible gaoler. He is grimly eloquent about what the Will does, but baffled by the question of what the Will 'ultimately and absolutely is in itself'. Indeed, he admits that this question 'can never be answered'[40]. It is, after all, part of the Will's very nature that it cannot be known. Schopenhauer's answer is to close in with his adversary. Yes, he admits, 'we are ourselves the thing in itself,' and therefore 'a *way from within* stands open for us to that inner nature belonging to things themselves, to which we cannot penetrate *from without.*'[41]

What is this 'way from within'? Schopenhauer's answer is *knowledge*. One way, we are told, in which the Will asserts itself is to make us want to *know* the world; or, to use the appropriate language, the 'phenomena' of the world act as motives for our willing to know. To put it simply: the world is full of things which make us curious to know what they really are. Then, once we know, once 'that knowledge is attained, volition ends, because the particular known phenomena no longer act as *motives* for willing'. In other words, the Will has attained its aim; and once you know a thing you need strive no further. And so, we seem somehow to have acquired a 'knowledge of the nature of the world'; and 'through the comprehension of *Ideas*' this knowledge of ours 'becomes a *quieter* of the Will; and thus free, the Will suppresses itself.'[42]

What does all this mean? These passages are at the very heart of what Schopenhauer has to say, and what made him so important to Wagner; yet to an ordinary inquiring mind they sound almost incomprehensible. How did we get here? How is it possible for the Will which, we have been told, has no aim, to attain any aim at all? How is this restless, aimless force going to be appeased by simply satisfying a cosmic curiosity? How do Ideas help? If we recall that

Ideas, or Representations, are objectifications of the Will then it
might seem incomprehensible that the Will itself can cause us so
much suffering and yet its own objectifications can hold our salvation. And finally, can we suppress the Will? For we can only
suppress something by an act of willing; and if what we have read is
true, then we are supposed to exercise precisely that power which we
are meant to suppress.

An ultimate obscurity is an essential part of Schopenhauer's
picture of the world. Why, he might ask us, should we be able to
know how the Will is to be overcome, when we cannot ever know
what the Will is in itself? A circular universe is by nature obscure:
if we knew its origin or its destination, it would, by definition, be
neither obscure nor circular. (Jorge Luis Borges's prose poem, 'The
Library of Babel', is a meditation on this subject.)

Schopenhauer's way out of his circular hell is to put an end to the
striving which is its essence. It is a turning away, an obliteration, a
denial: and it is all-inclusive. He admits that to abolish the Will
means to abolish the world which is its objectification and mirror. It
is thus inevitably the end of all effort; of all forms, of time and
space. There are no more subjects who perceive, or objects that are
perceived. We are in a no man's land of the mind, where cause and
effect, by means of which we understand the world, no longer exist.
A peace is attained which is 'above all reason'; a 'perfect calm of the
spirit'; a 'deep rest'; an 'inviolable confidence and serenity'. 'Only
knowledge remains, the Will has vanished.'[43]

The alert reader may well wonder what kind of knowledge we
might be talking about, since we have just obliterated both subject
and object, the knower and the known. What is there left to know
and who is there to know it? Schopenhauer replies that this knowledge is a state which 'cannot properly be called knowledge, because it
has not the form of subject and object.' And if we should object that
this is no answer, Schopenhauer puts an end to the matter by declaring magisterially that this state is 'only attainable in one's own
experience and cannot be further communicated'. The totalitarian
aesthetic defines itself partly by declaring itself to be inaccessible.

And yet this note of lordly finality contains a note of failure. All
this time, Schopenhauer has been trying to make sense of the world.
Appearances, the world of phenomena, have been by definition
misleading. We could never, he complained,

   arrive at the real nature of things from without. However much
   we investigate, we can never reach anything but images and

names. We are like a man who goes round a castle seeking in vain for an entrance, and sometimes sketching the façades. And yet this is the method that has been followed by all philosophers before me.[44]

Readers of Kafka will respond to that passage with sombre familiarity. But these words also define Schopenhauer's own dilemma. The world he is trying to make sense of is entirely determined by the Will which is ultimately unknowable. We only know it in its objectifications; and it now seems that to achieve salvation we need to deny them both, the Will and its objectifications, at the same time. And if we do that, we are left in a strange condition, which both is and is not a state of knowledge. Essentially, it is a condition that no one can understand except the person who has experienced it. In practice, this means the person whose account of it we have been reading. Schopenhauer's book is an account of the world; and yet it is also, in a very personal sense, his own book. What sort of knowledge is it which cannot be communicated at all? How do we know what it is that we are supposed to understand? For all his immense eloquence and conviction, Schopenhauer himself has ended up with a world of his own, which is essentially an image and a name.

To Schopenhauerian man, imprisoned in the world of the Will, one possible escape route is art. To understand what Schopenhauer means by this, we should return to that other escape route, which is knowledge. To know something properly, he tells us, we have to lose ourselves in it. This is what happens:

> If, raised by the power of the mind, a man relinquishes the common way of looking at things, gives up tracing ... their relations to each other ... ceases to consider the where, the when, the why, and the whither of things, and looks simply and solely at the *what*; ... [if he] gives the whole power of his mind to perception, sinks himself entirely in this, and lets his whole consciousness be filled with the quiet contemplation of the natural object actually present, whether a landscape, a tree, a mountain, a building, or whatever it may be; inasmuch as he *loses* himself in this object, ... *i.e.*, forgets even his individuality, his Will and only continues to exist as the pure subject, the clear mirror of the object, so that it is as if the object alone were there, without any one to perceive it ... if thus the object has to such an extent passed out of all relation to something outside

it, and the subject out of all relation to the Will, then that which
is so known is no longer the particular thing as such; but it is
the *Idea*, the eternal form, the immediate objectivity of the Will
at this grade; and, therefore, he who is sunk in this perception
is no longer individual, for in such perception the individual has
lost himself; but he is *pure*, will-less, painless, timeless *subject
of knowledge*.[45]

It is worth quoting this at such length, because it shows the
rhetorical skill at Schopenhauer's command, and the emotional
conviction with which he could invest an abstract argument. It is
worth quoting, too, because for Schopenhauer art is a special kind of
knowledge. This is one of the purest examples of the perlocutionary
act: the beholder virtually obliterates himself in front of the thing he
contemplates. It tells him nothing: it takes him over. Erich Heller
has analysed brilliantly the intellectual duplicity and the sheer
emotional power of such writing. He wrote, with reference to
Thomas Mann, though it applies to Wagner too, that Schopenhauer
supplied him 'with the comforting metaphysical sanction of the
artist's nonentity', and confirmed for him 'the ethical superiority of
"being" over the moral intentions of "doing" '[46].
 And an uneasy relationship with the real world, with its relations
and pressures and its 'moral intentions of "doing"', is characteristic
of Schopenhauer's attitude to art. Art, for him, is by definition
something *achieved*. Science is always on the move; art 'is everywhere at its goal'. The practice of art, which is an act of genius, is the
condition of the purest objectivity in which the mind is turned away
from the world and the self and towards the contemplated object.
Both of them are taken out of the stream of time and of all other
relations. The reader may object that an art which is independent of
all relations sounds extremely vague; and Schopenhauer duly miti-
gates the elusiveness of all this by cautiously allowing that genius,
too, is only human. He, too, can only know the Ideas of those objects
which have come within his perception, and he will therefore be
'dependent upon the chain of circumstances that brought these
objects to him'. In simple words, you cannot know Ideas of things
you have never seen. This is a crucial reservation because, by saying
this, Schopenhauer asserts that art springs from what actually exists
in the first place[47]. One might presume that he would have had little
time for the fantasy interiors of Piranesi.
 Schopenhauer's mind is a battleground between representation

and what we might almost call mysticism. Take his views on the beautiful and the sublime[48]. We experience the beautiful, he says, when our pure will-less knowing, which is the condition of all aesthetic contemplation, is 'reached without opposition, by the *mere disappearance of the Will* from our consciousness' (my italics). The sublime is different: we experience it by consciously transcending the Will. Imagine, for example, that you are looking at something that bears what Schopenhauer calls 'a hostile relation to the human will in general'. He might have given the example of a picture showing a frightening event. You may, when you look at it, experience a sense of fear. But if you recognise what it is that frightens you in the picture, and then deliberately detach yourself from its effect on you, then you have raised yourself above this frightening thing. You have also raised yourself above your own Will. You contemplate, in spiritual peace, the 'Idea' of the frightening. Schopenhauer describes this state as having 'a constant remembrance of Will; yet not of a single particular volition'. But if you allowed yourself to be conscious of something frightening in that picture, through a sense of 'actual personal pressure and danger from the object', then your will, 'thus actually influenced, would at once gain the upper hand, the peace of contemplation would be impossible' and it would yield to anxiety.

So what is the role of the Will in art? Do we give ourselves up to art, or do we work towards it? If our will comes between us and a picture, do we not need some other kind of will to overcome it? And if so, does the frightening thing in the picture, indeed the picture itself, become more or less 'real'? Indeed, what, in such an experience, is 'real'? What is the 'real' doing *in* art and *to* art? What is it doing *in* the spectator and *for* the spectator?

One of the most extraordinary passages in Schopenhauer's analysis of art is his unexpected tribute to Dutch still-life and landscape painters[49]. These 'admirable' artists, he tells us, achieve that state of pure will-less knowledge, that losing of themselves in the object, in the act of perception, which for him is the essential condition of art. They do so, we are told, by their inward disposition, the predominance in them of knowing over willing. They direct their purely objective perception to the most insignificant objects, and they present them in a 'peaceful, still frame of mind ... free from Will'. As we participate in this state, we are moved to emotion by the contrast between it and our own unquiet minds, 'disturbed by vehement willing'.

Schopenhauer clearly senses the emotional intensity of the best Dutch painting; but there is no implication, in what he says, that the objects might be for human use, or that the landscape might be traversed by people of identifiable age, class, sex or nationality. Indeed, he has some strict exceptions to make. He objects to the 'charming' or the 'attractive', by which he means paintings that excite the Will by 'presenting to it directly its fulfilment, its satisfaction'. Some Dutch painters show us fruit, which is just permissible because fruit is 'the further development of the flower', and because we are not obliged to think of it as edible. But pictures of 'prepared and served dishes, oysters, herrings, crabs, bread and butter, wine, and so forth' excite our appetite for the things they represent. This excitement of the Will 'puts an end to all aesthetic contemplation', and such pictures are, in Schopenhauer's view, 'altogether to be condemned'. The same goes for naked figures in historical paintings, their 'position, drapery and general treatment'.

That is not the end of the problems for a contemplative mind saddled with an easily susceptible Will. For example, the best way of looking at a tree, for Schopenhauer, is 'aesthetically, i.e., with artistic eyes'[50], when the hypothetical spectator recognises 'not it but its Idea'. In such moments both the tree and the man who looks at it become 'at once of no consequence' compared with the Idea of the tree, and our old friend the pure will-less subject of knowing — in this case, the artist. The tree will get a better deal later on, when Schopenhauer admits that 'works of art themselves are always *representations of particular things*' (my italics). But the problem remains: if a painter is to represent a tree, even if only to go beyond the material tree and reveal the Idea of it, the tree itself can hardly become 'at once of no consequence'. How can the artist manage without the tree in its ordinary reality? Schopenhauer is wrestling with the same problem as Monet, Picasso and Kandinsky came to face less than a century later. He is torn in an aesthetic conflict. He is hungry for the apprehension of the essence of things; but he is also nagged by the need to represent, to portray. The point about Schopenhauer's vision of the tree is that neither it, nor the artist looking at it, are subject to our questioning. If his imaginary painter were to show us a coconut tree in a Norwegian landscape we could ask, on the grounds of simple incongruity, who ever painted such a picture and why. Looking at one of Constable's trees, we could ask about its age and type; its appearance could tell us what season it was.

Schopenhauer is not interested in any of these things: they are *phenomena*. His *noumenal* artist is contemplating a *noumenal* tree. Nor does his vision allow for the fact that for some people one tree can be more beautiful than another, or indeed that for some people the picture of one can be more beautiful than either the picture of another or another picture of the same. There is no room for comparisons in the absolute. And where, in all this, does the *Idea* of the tree come in? For if we admit such differences of appreciation, we will be dragging the Idea down from its godlike pedestal into the muddy world of the much-despised 'relations'. If we allow that someone might find, as Caspar David Friedrich frequently did, an old bare tree more beautiful than a flourishing one, we would have to allow for the existence of an Ideal Scraggy Tree. Alternatively, the Idea of a tree would have to include elements of scragginess. But if scragginess is a deficiency in beauty, as it is for some, how could it be part of any Idea of a tree when, according to Schopenhauer, the Idea is independent of all relations and subject to no change? (A scraggy tree must have changed, once, from being a perfectly healthy tree.)

At this point Schopenhauer's burgher-like honesty comes to his rescue, and to ours. He cannot help admitting that we can look at everything 'in a purely objective manner and apart from all relations', and that 'the will manifests itself in everything at some grade of its objectivity'. That, in Schopenhauerian terminology, amounts to saying that everything is something. And it leads him, as it must, to say that 'everything is also *beautiful*'[51]. Remember, he tells us, what he has said before about Dutch still lifes. We duly recall his tribute; but we recall, too, that he had excommunicated all pictures of edible matter and of touchable bodies. Schopenhauer himself reminds us of this, by stating that 'one thing is more beautiful than another, because it makes pure objective contemplation easier.' In other words it is more fitting to admire the painting of a pot than a painting of a dead pheasant because, with the latter, we would keep wishing that we could eat it. But might we not, we ask, if the pot was a nice pot, start wishing that we could possess it? We are never told. Food, for Schopenhauer, is simply more desirable than pots. And yet, he admits, even 'unorganised and formless' things have a beauty of their own, because they 'reveal the Ideas through which the will objectifies itself at its lowest grades'. In other words, they are what they are. At the end of it all, the dilemma is still with us: do we try to copy the appearance of things, or do we try to apprehend their hidden, inexpressible essence?

One thing emerges from all this: that only the true genius is equipped to comprehend and transmit the experience that is art. This true genius, the unconscious vessel of perception, will be familiar to readers of Romantic literature. Its Schopenhauerian version, the pure will-less subject, is a man who 'can give no justification for what he does'. He works 'unconsciously, indeed instinctively'. His starting point is the *Idea*, which is a self-contained, eternal form, and which assumes the forms of time and space so that the artist can grasp it, and pass the experience on to us. This sounds a little cloudy; but it may be clearer if we compare it with what, according to Schopenhauer, mere 'imitators' and 'mannerists' do. They start, we are told, from the *concept*, which is 'a unity reconstructed out of multiplicity by the abstraction of our reason'. In other words, they paint a tree, not because they have had a mystical apprehension of the essence of tree-ness, but because they have seen lots of trees and can paint a fairly typical one[52].

Translated into literature, this *concept* sounds very like an *argument*: for example, the 'argument' of a play. One way of describing what Ibsen does, for example, is to say that he applies his reason to a multiplicity of phenomena, or people and events, and then builds a coherent unity out of them. Those people and events, and that unity make up 'Ibsen's world', and that world is open to our questioning: a relationship between artist and audience which is precluded by Schopenhauer's vision of the genius suspended in will-less, isolated contemplation. Indeed, the Schopenhauerian audience shares the artist's remoteness from the mundane world of the Will. The artist *'understands the half-uttered speech of Nature'*; he has 'an anticipation of that which nature . . . strives to express . . . saying, as it were, to her, 'That is what you wanted to say!' And whoever is able to judge replies, "Yes, that is it."'' The artist anticipates beauty, and the critic (by which Schopenhauer clearly means the ideal audience) recognises it at once. This is because both 'are themselves the "in-itself" of nature, the Will which objectifies itself. For,' Schopenhauer concludes, 'like can only be known by like . . . only spirit can understand spirit.'[53]

This lofty view is entirely in keeping with Schopenhauer's picture of art as an act of pure, will-less contemplation. It has little to do with communication as we understand it. We are in the presence of art which so absorbs its creator that the idea of an audience becomes almost irrelevant. It is what Nietzsche, nearly seventy years later, came to call monological art, or art without witnesses[54]. It is of the essence of such an experience that it puts itself beyond questioning. Appia, too, was to describe the same thing when he wrote, in his hugely influential meditations about a theatre, of 'boundless space, with no witness but ourselves'; of a work which 'lives for itself — without the spectator. The author expresses it, and contemplates it at the same time.' In the theatre, Appia feels, 'we overhear bits of life never intended for us'[55]. Common humanity is excluded from such visions. The Schopenhauerian artist is like the Will; relentless and unknowable, remote from the pressures and relations of the ordinary world and concentrating entirely on a vision which cannot be properly communicated, he strains towards the Idea which already possesses him.

This is not a real artist in a real world, of course, but the Idea of the Artist. Still, to anyone who thought, or was willing to agree, that art and artists were not accountable and beyond questioning, it would have seemed a dangerously attractive picture. Schopenhauer made it even more so when he called genius an 'abnormity', and drew a contrast between this genius and 'merely moral beings'[56]. For Schopenhauer, both the Will, and its conqueror the visionary artist, have the same amoral existence, living only in and for what they are. In their world, both the thing that torments the spirit, and the only possible means of escape from this torment, have something essentially inhuman about them: they are, both, a malign god and an indifferent saviour.

It does not seem to occur to Schopenhauer that art might be created to fulfil a need; to provide something missing in a man's life; or to liberate a surplus of energy or feeling — views which will be familiar to readers of both Aristotle and Freud. Still less does it occur to him that art might start by wanting to question, to investigate; that it might want to alter someone's attitude to the world; and that in wanting to do this, art might open itself up to questions rather than demand mute acceptance. And it certainly did not occur to him that art might tell us something we did not already know.

Schopenhauer's treatment of art reaches its peak when he turns to music. Music is unique. Like architecture, it does not imitate anything; unlike architecture, it is not functional. We do not, in music, 'recognise the copy or repetition of any Idea of existence in the world'[57]. Accordingly, Schopenhauer has no time for what we have come to call 'programme music'. He accepts that music can be expressive of something: he explains somewhat uneasily that this is because both 'a composition and a perceptible representation [are] simply different expressions of the same inner being of the world'. Or, a little more specifically, 'The composer has been able to express in the universal language of music the emotions of Will which constitute the heart of an event.' And the composer can only do this because he has a 'direct knowledge of the nature of the world unknown to his reason'[58]. That is to say, the composer has apprehended intuitively, almost in a trance, something beyond definition, such as 'the inner being of the world' or 'the emotions of the Will'.

But if a composer should write such music deliberately, 'with conscious intention by means of conceptions', then his work is doomed. And so Haydn's *The Seasons*, as well as 'many passages' of *The Creation*, stand condemned (along with 'all battle-pieces'), because in them the 'phenomena of the external world are directly imitated'. Schopenhauer tells us that 'such music is entirely to be rejected.'[59] He does not pause to ask how precisely we go about identifying the contents of such music; nor does he offer any evidence that Haydn's imitative passages were composed with 'conscious intention' and not by 'direct knowledge'. How can we, the readers and listeners, tell the difference? We are not told.

Schopenhauer does not labour under the illusion that any of this is easy to understand: he freely admits that his interpretation of music is 'essentially impossible to prove'. But, he argues, so great is the effect that music can have on people that it must possess some profound and unique quality. Other arts, we have already learnt, are copies of Ideas: they are thus twice removed from the Will itself. But music is different. It is 'as *direct* an objectification and copy of the whole *Will* as the world itself, nay, as the Ideas.' It is, indeed, 'the *copy of the Will itself*, whose objectivity the Ideas are.' The other arts 'speak only of the shadows'; music 'speaks of the thing itself'[60]. It is something we fully understand but cannot explain. It is the metaphysical to everything physical in the world, the thing-in-itself to every phenomenon. The world itself is 'embodied music', just as it is embodied Will. Explain music and you explain the world. Music is thus very like philosophy.

Yet, in any precise terms, what Schopenhauer is saying here is impossible to grasp. Always impatient with the mere appearance of things, with the nagging need to represent them, he strives to initiate us into the reality of an art which does not have to bother with the relations between the thing and its image. And yet he ends up calling music the 'copy' of the Will. The expression is, strictly speaking, meaningless: for how do you copy that which is unknowable? The upshot of Schopenhauer's attempt to make sense of the world has been that, at its core, he found something that could not be made sense of. Now, at the heart of the artistic experience, he has found a copy of this same unknowable thing. He is, once again, dealing in nothing but images and names: philosophy as metaphor.

What he conveys is, essentially, feeling: the feeling of someone experiencing profound aesthetic pleasure. And he expresses its force and magnitude by translating it into cosmic terms. Music is like the world. The structure of harmony, the changing relations of melody to the key-note, changes of key and tempo are all, for him, ways in which music represents the entire world, from unorganised nature, through animal life, to man as the embodiment of the highest grade of Will. The composer 'reveals the inner nature of the world, and expresses the deepest wisdom in a language which his reason does not understand; as a person under the influence of mesmerism tells of things of which he has no conception when he awakes.' Music 'restores to us all the emotions of our inmost nature, *but entirely without reality and far removed from their pain.*'[61]

Thus, when we listen to music, we experience the world: both the outer world of nature and the inner world of the self. With such passages Schopenhauer gave a special dignity and importance to the experience of art: he recognised this experience as having an elemental importance to man. His pages on the way music both reflects and excites human feelings, and on the difficulties of putting this into words, are hard to read without emotion. But he also, at the peak of his utterance about art, lays down the doctrine of the artist, obsessed by the deepest wisdom to the point of trance, and of the listener, in profound mystical union with the whole of known creation. It is a majestic vision: passionate, persuasive, perceptive and vague. What is missing from it is a sense of confrontation: of engagement, questioning and challenge. There is no room here for rational or moral inquiry. If there is such a thing as closed art, passages like these are its cornerstones.

Note, now, the words I italicised at the end of the last paragraph but one. What does Schopenhauer mean?

When he says that music restores to us the emotions of our

inmost nature, he seems to be describing the opposite of what we
have come to know as *catharsis*: instead of purging our surplus
feelings, music appears to regain our lost feelings or to revive
numbed ones. We are enriched rather than purified. But if we want
to understand the phrase 'entirely without reality and far removed
from . . . pain', we should go back to Schopenhauer's analysis of the
artistic experience. There, the pure will-less subject was last seen
lost in contemplation of the object, attending, we may remember,
not to its *why* or its *how*, but to its *what*. The artistic experience, we
recollect, is not something we distil from comparing it with the
rough-and-tumble of actual life: it is a taking part in something 'up
there', which is shared with us, in a way that is beyond words, by
the will-less, clairvoyant artist. The Schopenhauerian spectator
attends, not to the accidental but to the essence.

On this reckoning, if Schopenhauer, watching *The Thieving Mag-
pie* by his favourite composer Rossini, ever felt any anxiety on
behalf of its poor little heroine under an unjust death-sentence, it
should have mattered little to him. Music, in opera, he tells us, is far
more important than words: it is like the soul in relation to the
body. It has

> a completely independent, separate, and . . . abstract existence
> for itself to which the incidents and persons in the piece are
> foreign . . . it becomes the expression of the inner significance
> of all those incidents and their ultimate and secret necessity.[62]

And so, for Schopenhauer, poor Ninetta's terror would have been a
mere incident, and the pain it implied would have had no significance. Schopenhauer is not interested in the story and its transient
realities: we must imagine him sitting there, waiting for Rossini's
music to reveal some 'ultimate and secret necessity'. Indeed, he
wrote that Rossini's music spoke '*its own language* so distinctly and
purely that it requires no words, and produces its full effect when
rendered by the instruments alone.'[63]

So, 'without reality and far removed from . . . pain' means
beyond 'relations', beyond cause and effect, time and change. The
world itself, its *what*, its essence and totality, is being conveyed by
one mind to another, both being free of willing and strife, unresist-
ing, and needing no help from reason. And music, which brings this
about, is also the direct copy of the Will. That, in turn, means that
music is the nearest we can ever get to that blind, ceaselessly striving
force, subject to no moral law, bound by no time or space, uncaused,

inexplicable, ultimately unknowable, aimless and end-less, which for Schopenhauer is the inmost kernel of the world. Music, in other words, is both the thing we are contemplating and the thing that brings about the state of contemplation. It is what we experience, the way we experience it, and the reason for experiencing it. The argument has a majestic circularity, both crushing and thrilling, with which we ought by now to be familiar. It implies the freedom of art from the shackles of cause and effect, and its nature as a total, all-engulfing experience. Such art is a 'perlocutionary act'.

Schopenhauer's description of the composer at work, like a 'person under the influence of mesmerism', saying things 'of which he has no conception when he awakes', and creating nothing less than a representation of the world, finds its perfect counterpart in the words of Cosima Wagner, writing in her diary after listening to Wagner playing from Act Two of *Tristan and Isolde*.

> I literally shudder at the power of genius which suddenly lays bare before us the unfathomable secrets of existence, even when there is nothing I cherish and esteem more than this divinely daemonic power. I find myself thinking of [Wagner's] words ... 'Art is perhaps a great crime'; and certainly those can be counted happy who, like animals, know nothing of it, though this sort of happiness seems to me like eternal darkness. I watch till I am blind, hear till I am deaf, feel to the point of oblivion all its splendour; I am drawn to the shining, star-filled abyss, look irresistibly down, and sink senseless into it.[64]

This is almost somnambulistic pleasure. The senses are paralysed by the very exercise of their functions; physical faculties and intellectual integrity both surrender in the face of something felt to be elemental, all-powerful and essentially incomprehensible. It is not what *happens* in *Tristan* that matters here: Cosima has seen Wagner's picture of the world and has submitted to it in grateful self-annihilation. She has written one of the earliest records of what it can be like to experience closed art.

Notes

1. 'The Glory of Pessimism', *Times Literary Supplement*, October 10, 1975, pp. 1167–68.
2. *Buddenbrooks*, tr. H.T. Lowe-Porter, Harmondsworth, 1957, p. 504.

3. *ibid.*, p. 505.

4. Quoted in *The Strange Life of August Strindberg*, by Elizabeth Sprigge, London, 1969, p.165. (Letter to Torsten Hedlund.)

5. Adolphe Appia: *The Work of Living Art: A Theory of the Theatre*, tr. H.D. Albright, Florida, 1960, p. 55.

6. *The World as Will and Idea* (*WWI*), tr. R.B. Haldane and J. Kemp, London, 1883, Vol. II p. 241.

7. Quoted in *W.B. Yeats 1865–1939*, by Joseph Hone, London, 1942, p. 392.

8. I owe this information to Mr John Montague.

9. *WWI* Vol II p. 245.

10. cf. p. 14 above. When André Breton wrote, 'Almost all images . . . strike me as spontaneous creations', he was meditating on the same subject. See *The Dada Painters and Poets*, ed. Robert Motherwell, *The Documents of Modern Art*, Vol.8, New York, 1951, p. 201.

11. *Reflections on the Word 'Image'*, by P.N. Furbank, London, 1970, p. 13.

12. In *Opera and Drama*, first publ. 1851. In *The Prose Works of Richard Wagner*, tr. W. Ashton Ellis, London, 1900, Vol. II p. 152.

13. *Letters of Richard Wagner*, ed. Wilhelm Altmann, tr. M.M. Bozman, London, 1927, Vol. I p. 225.

14. *Correspondence of Wagner and Liszt*, tr. Francis Hueffer, London, 1888, Vol. II pp. 53–4.

15. Altmann, *ed. cit.*, pp.310–1.

16. *ibid.*, pp. 260–62.

17. Schopenhauer's marginal notes are quoted in Ashton Ellis, *ed. cit.*, Vol. III.

18. *Wagner-Liszt*, Vol. II pp. 224–5.

19. *WWI* III. 249.

20. *ibid.*, I. 354.

21. *ibid.*, I. 195.

22. *ibid.*, I. 193–4.

23. *ibid.*, I. 166.

24. *ibid.*, I. 138.

25. *ibid.*, II. 215–6.

26. *ibid.*, I. 467.

27. *ibid.*, I. 354.

28. *ibid.*, I. 130. The mutual interdependence, indeed virtual identity, of the Will and its objectification is vividly expressed by Ronald Gray when he writes: 'The Will feels hunger which is nothing but hunger until it takes shape as teeth.' See *The Wagner Companion*, ed. Peter Burbidge and Richard Sutton, London, 1979. 'The German Intellectual Background', pp. 34–59, esp. p. 40.

29. *ibid.*, III. 51.

30. *ibid.*, I. 214–5.

31. *ibid.*, I. 192.

32. *ibid.*, III. 300.

33. *Buddenbrooks*, pp. 506–8.

34. *WWI*, I. 180.

35. 'On Ethics' in *Essays and Aphorisms*, ed. and tr. R.J. Hollingdale, Harmondsworth, 1970, p. 133.

36. *The Basis of Morality*, tr. A.B. Bullock, London, 1903, pp. 157–8.

37. *ibid.*, pp. 147–8.

38. *ibid.*, p. 278.

39. *WWI* I. 402.
40. *ibid.*, II. 408.
41. *ibid.*, II. 405.
42. *ibid.*, I. 367.
43. *ibid.*, I. 531.
44. *ibid.*, I. 128.
45. *ibid.*, I. 231.
46. Erich Heller: *The Ironic German: A Study of Thomas Mann*, London, 1958, p. 143.
47. *WWI* I. 239–41.
48. *ibid.*, I. 259–68.
49. *ibid.*, I. 255; 268–70.
50. *ibid.*, I. 271.
51. *ibid.*
52. *ibid.*, I. 304.
53. *ibid.*, I. 287–8.
54. *The Gay Science*, tr. Walter Kaufmann, New York, 1974, p. 324.
55. *The Work of Living Art*, pp. 53–4.
56. *WWI*, III. 139; 156.
57. *ibid.*, I. 330.
58. *ibid.*, I. 341.
59. *ibid.*
60. *ibid.*, I. 333.
61. *ibid.*, I. 336–41.
62. *ibid.*, III. 234.
63. *ibid.*, I. 338.
64. *Cosima Wagner's Diaries*, ed. Martin Gregor-Dellin and Dietrich Mack, tr. Geoffrey Skelton, London, 1978–80, Vol. I p. 47.

III

'I AM THE WORLD'
Wagner the Dramatist

When Cosima Wagner listened to Wagner playing *Tristan* on the piano she was experiencing the impact of closed art: reading her account we sense, not that Cosima is following a story, but that she is responding to a mood. But of course it is not quite so simple as that. For one thing, stories, too, can convey moods. Besides, Cosima had actually seen *Tristan*: her first husband, Hans von Bülow, conducted the première in Münich in 1865. Therefore Cosima knew what the music was *about*: she had witnessed the opera taking place on stage as action. She would have known that the passage Wagner was playing to her was the music of a passionate, illicit and ultimately disastrous love encounter, and it might have recalled to her the scene she had seen. In this sense, for Cosima, the music did tell, or re-tell, a story.

And yet this short diary entry is still a remarkable document. It is a spontaneous and personal record of an encounter with art, describing it as something beautiful but also demonic, even evil: it would have been perfectly comprehensible to the poet of 'La Belle Dame Sans Merci' and to the author of *Doctor Faustus*. And even if Cosima did know the story behind the music, her response of unreserved and uncritical submission has something to do with the fact that she does not write of *Tristan* as a drama involving people. It is as if, for her, this music were not telling a story; as if it were concerned with something other than relating events. In this respect, Cosima's diary entry is very like some of the most famous examples of Wagnerolatry. In *The Birth of Tragedy*, for example,

Nietzsche wondered whether anyone who really understood music

> would be able to perceive the third act of *Tristan and Isolde*,
> without any aid of word and image, purely as a tremendous
> symphonic movement, without expiring in a spasmodic unhar-
> nessing of all the wings of the soul?

Suppose, Nietzsche went on, that

> a human being has thus put his ear, as it were, to the heart
> chamber of the world will and felt the roaring desire for
> existence pouring from there into all the veins of the world, as a
> thundering current or as the gentlest brook, dissolving into a
> mist — how could he fail to break suddenly?[1]

What saves such a man, Nietzsche tells us, is the physical presence
of Tristan on stage: the myth and the tragic hero, he says, 'intervene
between our highest musical emotion and this music'. To anyone
who has seen *Tristan and Isolde* in a passably good production, this
may sound distinctly odd: it simply does not correspond to our sense
of what happens on stage. To us, Tristan comes across as a mixture
of indomitable will and utter helplessness; and the music heightens
and intensifies these qualities to a point where he becomes both
pitiable and almost inhuman.

Nietzsche writes as someone who is totally under the spell of the
opera as a spiritual event, without any real sense of it as a dramatic
event. And it turns out that when he wrote this passage he had never
actually seen *Tristan*. He knew the score and the libretto; he could
even play the piano transcript; but he had never experienced it as a
work of living drama. Six months after *The Birth of Tragedy* was
published, Nietzsche finally saw two performances of *Tristan*, in
Munich in June 1872; but in an important sense this made little
difference. Later on, he was to see *The Mastersingers* and the entire
Ring; but all his life the emotional and spiritual impact of Wagner's
operas remained more important to him than their contents. His
mind was haunted not by what happened in them but by what they
stood for.

Sixteen years later, a few months before he went insane, Nietzsche dashed off *The Case of Wagner*: a short, vitriolic book in which
brilliant perceptions fight a losing battle against uncivilised, almost
unhinged arrogance. Nietzsche looks at the events in the operas only
to lampoon them.

> Who if not Wagner would teach us that innocence prefers to

redeem interesting sinners? (The case in *Tannhäuser*.) Or that even the Wandering Jew is redeemed, settles down, when he marries? (The case of *The Flying Dutchman*.) Or that old corrupted females prefer to be redeemed by chaste youths? (The case of Kundry.)[2]

This is merely clever, in the way that a precocious and unpleasant schoolboy is clever. When Nietzsche turns to *The Ring*, his handling of it is both more dishonest and more obtuse. 'I shall relate the story of the *Ring*,'[3] he tells us; but what he does is to describe the story of the writing of *The Ring* and how, as he sees it, the whole enterprise was, for Wagner, an act of shallow self-redemption. He also asserts that Wagner's Siegfried declares war against contracts, tradition and morality; that 'he overthrows everything traditional, all reverence, all *fear*'; that 'without the least respect he tackles old deities.'[4] The misrepresentation here is subtle but crucial. Nietzsche's description suggests purposeful action; but the point about Siegfried is that he has not the remotest idea that he is doing any of these things. Nietzsche is crediting Siegfried with what he imagines were Wagner's motives in creating him. Siegfried himself knows no more about contracts, tradition or morality than he knows about fear; and when he 'tackles' Wotan in Act III of *Siegfried* he does not know who Wotan is. Perhaps it would make no difference if he did; but it is essential to the understanding of this scene, and of *The Ring* as a whole, that Siegfried is wholly unconscious of the real nature of his actions.

Now to argue with Nietzsche in this way implies that we regard *The Ring* as an open drama: a work which may be confronted in a spirit of engagement and questioning. But Nietzsche, at the end of his short creative life, confronts it as a closed work and rejects it without reservation, just as sixteen years earlier he responded to *Tristan* in astonished and submissive joy. And in his last book, *Ecce Homo*, we find him writing of 'the dangerous fascination and the gruesome and sweet infinity of *Tristan*'[5]. 'One pays heavily for being one of Wagner's disciples,' Nietzsche admits in *The Case of Wagner*, with an irony he could not have intended; and he concludes:

Does Wagner liberate the spirit? — He is distinguished by every ambiguity, every double sense, everything quite general-ly that persuades those who are uncertain without making them aware *of what* they have been persuaded. Thus Wagner is a seducer on a large scale. There is nothing weary, nothing decrepit, nothing fatal and hostile to life in matters of the spirit that his art does not secretly safeguard: it is the blackest obscurantism that he conceals in the ideal's shrouds of light ... Open your ears: everything that ever grew on the soil of *impoverished* life, all of the counterfeiting of transcendence and beyond, has found its most sublime advocate in Wagner's art — *not* by means of formulas: Wagner is too shrewd for formulas — but by means of a persuasion of sensuousness which in turn makes the spirit weary and worn-out. Music as Circe.[6]

As with Wagner and Schopenhauer, the reader might feel that what Wagner meant to Nietzsche was an exclusively German affair. Once again, I shall argue that this is not so. Nietzsche was the most profound and cultivated mind Wagner ever came into personal contact with; and he was the only great thinker and critic to have reflected on Wagner's works as they first confronted the world. He was also, as the next chapter will attempt to show, one of the foremost shapers as well as diagnosticians of that aspect of the modern imagination which finds its fulfilment in closed art. When Nietzsche wrote about 'the demonic *transmissibility* and self-relinquishment of [Wagner's] nature'[7], he defined the sense of despotism and submission which characterises artist and audience in the Wagnerian experience.

The quotation is taken from *Richard Wagner at Bayreuth*, an essay written just before the parting of the ways. Nietzsche is still under Wagner's spell. He describes his sense of Wagnerian opera as that of a powerful current which, with

convulsive restlessness has passed over into a broad, fearfully strong movement towards an as yet unknown goal; and suddenly the whole breadth of the stream ends by plunging down into the depths with a demonic joy in the abyss and in its seething waves.[8]

When Cosima Wagner read this she must have responded with joyful familiarity.

Nietzsche describes *Tristan* as

the actual *opus metaphysicum* of all art, a work upon which there lies the broken glance of a dying man with his insatiable sweet longing for the mysteries of night and death, far distant from life, which, as evil, deception and separation, shines with an uncanny ghostly morning brightness and distinctness.[9]

This is a famous passage, and it is worth pointing out how much of its effect depends on its ambiguous phrasing. Who is this dying man, whose glance lies upon this work? Is it Tristan, or is it Wagner? The sentence could be understood either way, but each sense would be incomplete and perhaps slightly absurd. Nietzsche's description is moving because he is moved by the essential identity he perceives, perhaps unconsciously, between Tristan and Wagner. It does not matter what *happens* in the opera: what it conveys to Nietzsche, and what he conveys to us, is its sense of redemptive suffering which embraces both composer and hero. The description carries no sense of action or event: Nietzsche might be describing a symphony by Mahler. If *Tristan* has a mood, Nietzsche has submitted to it.

By the time Nietzsche came to write *Daybreak* (1880), he was more wary and perturbed. He called Germany a 'nation of *unconditional* feelings', and wrote about how difficult it was, with Wagner, to admire some of his music and forget the rest. 'Where,' Nietzsche wonders, 'shall we satisfy our thirst for wholesale homage?' Perhaps, he goes on, it would be better to be different: perhaps the Germans should become 'a nation of conditional consent and benevolent opposition'[10]. This is one of those asides in Nietzsche which justify his reputation as a prophetic thinker. And, ironically, when we read his own writings on Wagner, we can see how that spirit of conditional consent is being replaced by unconditional feelings. What concerns us here is what it is in Wagner's operas that demands unconditional feelings: wholesale homage or wholesale rejection.

Part of the reason lies in the nature of music. Schopenhauer, we recall, placed music at the pinnacle of the arts because it imitated nothing. It was not the servant of accidental, *phenomenal* things: it was, quite simply, expression; or, as Schopenhauer put it, a copy of the Will. In this sense we may regard music as the closed art form *par excellence*. Schopenhauer disliked programme music because it was contaminated by *things*: it tried to represent mundane physical reality and thus lost its purity as a copy of the Will. From our point of view this means that music which imitates things is a form of open art. If we know that we are meant to hear the musical representation of a thunderstorm, we can say whether we find it convincing or not: we know what a thunderstorm is like, and we judge the composer's performance according to that knowledge. It is in this simple and fundamental sense that all imitative art is open to our questioning, and that all imitative art is, by definition, open art.

In the case of programme music we might say that, by imitating things, it tells a story: the musical representation of a bird singing, or waves crashing on the shore tells us of something that has *happened*. But it is not all that easy to divide music into two kinds: one in which 'things happen' and another where they do not. When we call a symphony 'The Bear' or 'The Hen' we acknowledge our need to read 'stories' into a structure and sequence of sounds that may have had no such imitative designs on us. Conversely, when works of 'pure' music were given descriptive titles by their composers (the 'Pathétique' Sonata, the 'Eroica' Symphony), those titles usually described not things or events, but moods, feelings, states of mind, which we may or may not have identified on our own.

Such music, too, tells a kind of 'story' ('that is how Beethoven felt, that was the mood in which he recollected his feelings'); but our relationship to it is different. It is not the kind of story where we can check the facts; and it would add nothing essential to our experience of the music if we could. In this sense it would be pointless to ask what Beethoven felt sad *about* when he composed his sonata, or to inquire into his views of Napoleon when he wrote the 'Eroica'. As it happens we know what those views were and they changed; but the biographical facts do not add to the work: they only confirm an emotional intensity which is inherent in the music.

Opera is different. It is, by definition, an open art form. Music and libretto work together in a relationship of mutual dependence: we can assess an opera by, among other things, asking how the music and the text serve one another. We can also approach opera by asking how the music and the words express and serve the dramatic action. In opera the music, by definition, has to tell a story. In view of all this, the reader may be puzzled to recollect a reference to Wagner in the previous chapter, describing him as one of the earliest practitioners of closed drama. It will also sound odd to anyone in the least familiar with Wagner's dramatic technique. It is essential to the nature of his mature operas that they invite questioning. For one thing, his *leitmotivs* hold these works together, both psychologically, in the sense of describing his characters, and structurally, in the sense of building up his narrative.

Take Act I of *The Valkyrie*. Siegmund and Sieglinde are strangers to one another, and ignorant of their own origins. But when Siegmund tells her the story of his life, and how one day he found that his father had gone, the orchestra plays a theme which we associate with Valhalla — and we sense that the absent father must be Wotan. We hear this same music again, when Sieglinde tells Siegmund that he reminds her of a mysterious old man who came to her wedding feast and drove a sword into the tree. Such music is both narrative and conspiratorial. It tells us as much of the past as we need to know at this point; and it hints at something about Siegmund and Sieglinde which neither of them know, but which is now gradually dawning upon them. It is as if the orchestra were speaking to us, and to the characters, about their subconscious thoughts.

And this turns out to be exactly what Wagner intended. His young disciple, Heinrich Porges, has left us an eyewitness account of Wagner's rehearsals for the first performance of *The Ring*. Describing the preparations for *The Valkyrie*, Porges adds a note about 'the connection between the instrumental music and the silent stage action. Both,' he explains, 'are the expressions of emotions slumbering . . . in the depths of the soul and now on the verge of becoming conscious.'[11] Porges confirms for us that, for Wagner, music was inseparable from dramatic action. There is a profound and constant psychological bond between the orchestra pit and the stage. We are even told that, in Act III of *Siegfried*, Brünnhilde's 'excitement is expressed by a slight trembling of her fingers that corresponds with the figure of the harps.'[12] One may wonder whether such delicate movements could have been seen from the Bayreuth stage; but Porges's devotion was such that we can safely take such directions and interpretations to be Wagner's own: we are listening to the Master's voice.

Or take the opening of Act II of *Siegfried*. Wotan comes to the mouth of the cave where Fafner guards the ring and the gold. Alberich, from whom Wotan had taken it all by force and cunning, is already there. Both know that Siegfried is on his way; both hope that he will kill Fafner; and both hope to lay their hands on the treasure to which neither of them has any right. Their confrontation is truly a meeting of equals. Both are tainted by corruption; and both have a certain grim dignity that comes from a sense of loss and a consciousness of past misdeeds. Alberich taunts Wotan with his, and reminds him how he paid off the giants, who had built Valhalla for him, with the stolen gold. The music we hear at this point has come to be known as the Treaty Motiv. We hear it again a moment later, when Wotan retorts:

> No symbols of contractual trust
> bound you,
> villain, to me.[13]

We first heard this music in *The Rhinegold*. There, too, Wotan was being reminded, by his wife Fricka, of his treaty with the giants; and there too, the music returned a moment later when he boasted to her:

> By contract I tamed
> their insolent race
> and made them build
> me this glorious hall.[14]

Now if dramatic character consists in having a past, a sense of past decisions, and a sense that those decisions could have been different, then Wagner has created characters who are as open to our questions as anyone in Aeschylus or Ibsen. The music acts here as a moral force. When the Treaty Motiv returns in *Siegfried*, we are being reminded of another time, in the past, when Wotan was first warned against acting unwisely and wrongly. At that time, he had already made a misguided treaty with the giants; but he had not yet damned himself by committing robbery to get out of it. The music is a moral force here because it reminds us that Wotan could have acted differently; and it is also challenging us to consider whether he *should* have acted differently. Indeed, the whole action of *The Ring* could be seen as a long drawn-out realisation by Wotan that he has committed a crime, and also as the slow unfolding of the consequences of this wrongdoing. In this sense, our confrontation with *The Ring* is as with the *Oresteia*: it is moral or it is nothing.

When we question people's actions, motivations and decisions, it is a moral questioning because actions are deeply bound up with causes and effects. Indeed, morality could be described as a system of ethical convictions and beliefs which is based on the principle of cause and effect, in the simple sense that there is, in ordinary life, always a reason for things, and that actions have consequences.

When we approach Wotan and *The Ring* in this way, we are treating it as open drama. In a world of causes and effects contracts,

such as Wotan's, are binding, and you break them at your peril.
Thus character here is not Schopenhauerian man, driven, through
his 'empirical' and 'intelligible' character, by the Will: it is someone
who exists in a causal world, and with the freedom to exercise a
personal will of his own. A sense of cause and effect worked hand in
hand with a sense of time, a sense of the past, in the very creation of
The Ring. Wagner first wrote Siegfried's Death, which became what
we know as The Twilight of the Gods; but he found that too much of
the past had to be implied or explained, so that The Young Siegfried
had to be written to precede it. Wagner then found that Siegfried's
parentage, and the origin of the conflict which brought him into the
world, had also to be made clear: and so, finally, the tetralogy we
know was born. In this sense, too, The Ring is an open drama: it
owes its very structure to an act of dramatic and moral reasoning.

We have seen how Wagner put the leitmotiv at the service of open
drama. It has also another role to play. Wagner uses it, essentially,
to recall the past; but by using it so often he subtly undermines the
very sense of the past he has created. The progression of a mature
Wagner opera is one of growing complexity of interweaving motives: themes referring to people, objects, thoughts and actions
answer each other in ever more intricate patterns. The effect is,
increasingly, of timelessness, almost of immobility. As each opera
goes on we sense, more and more, that the past is constantly
present; we are witnessing actions which are, in part at least,
repetitions of themselves. In this elusive but insistent sense Wagner's operas are time-less.

    And so it is not surprising that he could afford to leave certain
matters vague. How long, for example, have Siegmund and Sieglinde been on the run from Hunding? (Long enough, it would
seem, for Fricka to have heard all about them.) How old is Siegfried?
How much time passes between Siegfried's departure from Brünnhilde's rock and his arrival at the Gibichung's Hall? How much
time passes between the acts in Parsifal? The vast time span of the
operas, and the ever-present sense of the past in them, make such
questions seem pedantic, and the events of the action imply no
answers.

    The leitmotiv can also be something of an obstacle. Those who do
not know their Wagner well will know that sensation of general
familiarity one has when one hears a Wagnerian passage: we

recognise the familiar sounds, the motives of the sword and the treaty, of Freia and the giants, of Valhalla and Alberich's curse, but we do not always know precisely where in the action we are. For all Wagner's insistence on the interaction of music and drama, the teeming world of his *leitmotivs* constantly creates a sense of the unspecific. Of course, this is not true of all the operas all the time; but I believe that it is, for most people, an accurate description of what it is like to get to know Wagner's music. And the sort of experience we have when we get acquainted with a work has a vital bearing on what kind of work we will finally think it is. Baudelaire called Wagner's music 'ardent and despotic'[15] — a description which was based on very limited knowledge (at the time of writing Baudelaire had never seen a complete Wagner opera), but which expresses a central truth. Wagner's operas speak to us, among other things, of an ardent need to communicate; an urge to enmesh us, all along, in what both the characters and the composer think of the inevitable present and the ever-present past. There is something despotic in this urge; in the completeness with which we are required to experience it. By an irresistible paradox, the intensity of Wagner's questioning of the past is such that it demands from us a type of unquestioning submission.

The moral impact of Wagner's music is an aspect of its drama. When we say that his *leitmotivs* have a moral significance we mean, not that the music is in some way moral in itself, but that it shows us relations between people, events and things which have the causal, moral logic of open drama. The music at the end of *The Rhinegold*, for example, is grandiose, almost heady. The gods march to Valhalla while the dispossessed Rhinemaidens wail below, and the stage is disfigured by the corpse of Fasolt, the first of those who are to die for the gold which Wotan, defender of treaties, has just taken by force. The gods may feel relieved, even elated; but this is a doomladen moment, and Wagner makes sure that we know it. The words we hear are the sceptical aside of Loge, and his dismissal of the Rhinemaidens who lament the loss of their treasure almost to the end of the scene:

> They are hurrying to their end,
> though strong and enduring
> they think themselves.
>
> No longer gleams
> the gold on you girls,

> but in the gods' new radiance
> you can happily bask now.[16]

Against these lines, the music of the gods has a hollow ring. The moral clarity of Wagnerian music drama at its best depends on such masterful balance between music, words and action. In the scene in *Siegfried* between Wotan and Alberich, which we discussed earlier, this balance undergoes a subtle dislocation. When we think about it coolly, this meeting of equals is actually deeply sordid, Alberich's motive being greed and revenge, and Wotan's the somewhat less ignoble desire to save himself from the consequences of his own acts. Inside the cave lies a murderer whose entire existence consists in guarding his hoard; and the two men outside await the coming of a third who will kill him for them. We have seen how Wagner's use of the Treaty Motiv recalled for us the causes and origins of this murky meeting. But the music of this scene as a whole has a turbulent, barbaric magnificence: it has a monstrously intoxicating effect which proves stronger than the moral argument behind the encounter. We are thrilled and excited. In *The Rhinegold* music and action combine to speak the same moral and dramatic language; but here the moral meaning resides in the action, while the music speaks a language of almost amoral grandeur. Wagner the despotic musician undermines Wagner the dramatist of morality. We begin to perceive that the total action of Wagnerian music drama is not always all of a piece.

We can see this in *Tannhäuser*, where the music mostly communicates restless ecstasy, while the action speaks of failure. Tannhäuser's failure is, in a sense, a purely social one: he has ideas of love which are unacceptable to his courtly medieval world. And yet this world, for all Wagner's researches into the world of the medieval *Minnesinger*, has only a heraldic sort of reality: it never becomes more than a backdrop to what we realise is the essential drama — and that takes place within Tannhäuser himself. Carl Dahlhaus has written about the 'casualness of motivation' in *Tannhäuser*: 'How he got into Venusberg in the first place is as unclear and unexplained as the origins of his love for Elisabeth.'[17] Nor, we may add, does it become clear why, despite his love, Tannhäuser had left the Wartburg, or how long he has lived on Venusberg. These matters belong to the outward action of the opera, which, for all its authenticity, remains lifeless and detached from what, we sense, is its real subject.

Tannhäuser is the restless, unsatisfiable Will in action. In contrast

to Venus's languidly erotic music in the first scene, his is energetic
and decisive, fuelled by the urge to depart. It is not that he wants to
go anywhere in particular: he simply expresses an impulse to move
on, which seems to be the condition of his existence. For Tannhäuser, life exists only to puzzle the Will: Venus's love is too consuming,
while Elisabeth is made unattainable to him by what, in the chivalric
context of the opera, is his own sinful desire. If we tried to read
Tannhäuser as an open drama, we might say that Tannhäuser and
Elisabeth die of broken hearts; but in fact they never acquire enough
human reality for that. The death of Tannhäuser is simply the
expiry of a Will which cannot, by its nature, achieve fulfilment.
Only when he is dead can the Pope's barren staff bear leaves; and the
young pilgrims who bring it on bring a symbol of deliverance only
when there is no one there to receive it. If we did not know that
Wagner was not to read Schopenhauer for another ten years, we
might wonder whether *Tannhäuser* was not written to dramatise
Schopenhauer's notion that 'death is the great reprimand'; that 'we
are at bottom something that ought not to be: therefore we cease to
be'[18].

In this sense, even Tannhäuser himself is of little consequence:
the reprimand is not administered to him as a person. Indeed, in one
sense, this outward action, the plot, is relatively unimportant. The
real dramatic life of *Tannhäuser*, as of *The Flying Dutchman*,
consists in its great confrontations. What matters is Tannhäuser
wanting his freedom from Venus, and Tannhäuser defying the
world of the Wartburg; the machinery of the plot which gets him
from one place to the other merits only the most perfunctory
attention. In the same way, the core of *The Flying Dutchman* is
Senta's ballad and her sudden meeting with the Dutchman. It is a
meeting of two obsessions made flesh: obsessions of such inhuman
intensity that it would not occur to anyone to wonder what these
two people would do with each other if they were to survive the
encounter. Nietzsche's little joke about redemption by settling down
and getting married shows quite unusual obtuseness: to think of any
subsequent contact between Senta and the Dutchman is to read the
mutual relationships and elusive potentials of open drama into a
dramatic world closed by an obsession of the imagination.

In terms of this imagination, once Senta and the Dutchman have
laid eyes on each other the drama is over: its essence consists in their
mutual, unquestioning recognition. After this, there is nothing for
either of them to live for. Hence the clumsy disposal of their bodies.

No matter that Senta insists on her loyalty to the Dutchman: he must be on his way again, ostensibly because he saw her talking to Erik and is now convinced that she is faithless like all other women. The elements of coincidence and misunderstanding in this episode belong to the world of the clumsiest melodrama; the spirit of the work demands, with an air of lofty metaphysics, that the Will can only have fulfilment after it has expired. Thus the Dutchman must depart, and then be released into death by Senta's self-sacrifice.

Now the alert spectator might have wondered from the beginning why the Dutchman's original crime of defying the heavens could find redemption only in the love of a woman: what, morally speaking, has one thing got to do with the other? It is true that these things featured variously in Wagner's sources; but Wagner was capable, all his life, of altering his sources when they did not suit him. This tale appealed to him in this form; and it is, as we shall see, entirely characteristic of the nature of his moral imagination that the long held-out redemption bears no logical relationship to the original offence. The spectator might also wonder, somewhat more pedantically, why the Dutchman has to perish at the end at all: has not a woman, after all, shown her faith in him, albeit by killing herself? His death may be his punishment, or it may be his ultimate forgiveness: one way or another, it bears no relationship to his crime. And, indeed, the opera is designed so as to give us no time for such reflections: it is, once again, a portrayal of the Will in action, unappeasable, obsessional, and extinguishing itself by a form of spontaneous combustion.

As in *Tannhäuser*, this is the true inner action; and it tells us, with a finality worthy of Schopenhauer, that salvation depends on the cessation of existence. Who, then, we ask, is there left to be saved? That question would be more appropriate to open drama; here, we approach a world which is partly closed to our questioning. The people in this world elude us because of their very intensity. Tannhäuser and the Dutchman are both characteristic Wagnerian types, whose existence is entirely exhausted in being, and being compulsively. For them, the world consists of their condition, their state of mind: they are conceived entirely in terms of some urge which drives them on. 'Here I lie, and possess'[19], Fafner will observe laconically in *Siegfried*. And the innocence of Siegfried himself is merely an unawareness of the awareness in other people. His ignorance of fear is simply an ignorance of the way causes and effects operate in the human mind, including his own. When he realises that Mime is plotting his death he kills him as casually, instinctively and without anger as we would swat a fly; and the experience teaches him nothing, as we see later in his credulous dealings with Hagen. When Brünnhilde is punished by Wotan it is, among other things, for deviating from this same single-minded unawareness of the nature of others. Brünnhilde had spoken with Siegmund: she was moved because she saw that there was a form of unselfish existence other than being merely the bearer of someone else's heroic will. For this, her father sentences her to love and, ultimately, to death. Indeed, we may read the whole of *The Ring* as Wotan's gradual realisation that moral awareness and moral participation are fatal; that the world can only be saved, if at all, by someone who understands nothing but who simply *is*.

Tristan and Isolde, too, could be described as a tragedy of two people on whose self-obsessed consciousness the outside world insists on impinging, with all its conditions, obligations and fretful sense of mutual dependence. By the time Wagner composed *Tristan* he had come a long way from *The Flying Dutchman*, even from *Tannhäuser*: his mastery of his material was now complete. The world around the lovers is, in one sense, all too real. There is nothing metaphysical about their drinking what they think is a death-potion in Act I: it is an escape from an intolerable situation which is social as much as erotic. Tristan and Isolde both owe complex feudal and personal loyalties to King Marke, and their passion for each other is incompatible with every one of these obligations. The whole Act is tense with a sense of events taking place against the will of the characters. The very setting expresses this sense of unbearable inevitability: the ship is sailing eastwards, while its chief passenger looks back westwards with longing and resentment. Indeed, Isolde is desperate never to arrive, while Tristan, at his post by the rudder, can hardly wait to reach land. Physical and emotional forces pull us in opposite directions and give the action a sense of stillness and imminent disaster. But at this stage, according to the outward action, the disaster that looms for the lovers is identifiable and measurable. It is a disaster of precise personal and social significance: the impending betrayal of King Marke is implicit in everything Tristan and Isolde say to each other, and it is their deep-seated desire to avoid this that gives their feelings for each other a hideous intensity.

How much time passes between Act I and Act II? Is Isolde married to King Marke in Act II? Such sober factualities of open drama sound

hopelessly pedantic in this context. Looked at in such a way, the
events of Act II do not even, strictly speaking, make sense. What
takes place on stage is a passionate conversation: its language, dense,
terse and ornate, speaks of feelings of huge intensity. But this
language is by no means incoherent: it expresses the feelings of two
people with feverish turbulence, but this turbulence is under
control.

> If I died for her now,
> for whom I would so gladly die,
> how could love
> die with me,
> and eternal life
> end with my death?
> But if my love cannot die,
> how can Tristan die
> of love?[20]

The logic of these lines of Tristan's would make passionate and
perfect sense to a poet like Donne.

Meanwhile, the music describes the sexual act, twice, with
stupendous intensity[21]. Thus, once again, the music tells us one
thing, the action another. Jacques Barzun put this succinctly when
he said that the realism of this scene depended on 'whether one uses
one's eyes or one's ears'[22]. Questioning this scene with the mental
habits of open drama, we might ask whether anything is actually
meant to have happened between the two lovers. For if we are to
believe the visible action it may be that the music merely describes
what the lovers are thinking about – a device which Wagner uses
with consummate mastery in *The Ring*. And if so, then perhaps no
adultery has taken place? Indeed, when Marke arrives, he talks to
Tristan about how his heart is filled with suspicion: hardly the sort
of language a man uses when he has caught his wife in adultery.

The point about such questions is that, in their logical persistence,
they are utterly alien to one's experience of the opera in performance. There is a profound and crucial sense in which *Tristan and
Isolde* as a whole is not open to our questioning. Such questioning, if it is to make any sense at all, relates to the outer action of the
opera, which is about two people straining with all their might, first
to evade each other, and then to reach each other and achieve
fulfilment in love. This action takes place in a moral world, of which
King Marke and his court are the focal point: his great, sad outburst

at the end of Act II confirms the reality of this, and confirms, too, that here once again a moral dramatist is at work. But the inner action of *Tristan* is beyond questioning. This action consists in the incurable yearning and final annihilation of the Will which takes physical form ('objectifies itself') in the two lovers and is enacted by them. In this sense it is fatuous to ask what 'really' happens in Act II: we witness the Will taking shape as two people and enacting itself as love.

But the intensity of their presentation does not bring with it a greater sense of human reality. On the contrary: we have only to compare *Tristan* with Verdi's *La Traviata*. Both were composed in the same decade; both open with the reluctant beginning of what is to be a tragic love affair; and both end with one of the lovers on the point of death, waiting for a final reunion. Now the remarkable thing about *La Traviata* is how little we see of Alfredo and Violetta on the stage together. Their meeting in Act I is brief; and as they sing of their hopes at the end of the Act, he is already off stage. In Act II, Scene 1, we only see them together for a few moments. In Act II, Scene 2, after she has left him, they meet in public, in a state of uncontrollable anguish, barely able to communicate with each other. They meet only once more: at Violetta's deathbed. Indeed, in several of Verdi's major operas the hero and the heroine seldom meet. The greatest of Italian romantic composers wrote relatively few love duets. Passion flowers in these works with total dramatic conviction but off stage, almost *in absentia*. In *Aida*, *Il Trovatore*, *Un Ballo in Maschera* and *La Forza del Destino* the lovers see remarkably little of each other. Compare this with the massively long scenes between Tristan and Isolde; the relentless intensity with which they explore their feelings together. And yet how much less we know about them than about Alfredo and Violetta. For Verdi's lovers are social, as well as erotic and spiritual creatures: they partake of the lives of others around them, and the plot implies that they and the others have a life that goes on between the acts too. The question of money, for example, which would be meaningless in the world of *Tristan*, plays a vital part in *La Traviata*: we know who pays the bills. And so, each time Alfredo and Violetta reappear, however briefly, they possess a greater density of personality: as the drama goes on they acquire a character by acquiring, before our eyes, a past.

And so, when Wagner's first wife, Minna, described Tristan and Isolde as 'a much too odious and slippery couple'[23], she was speaking in the mundane ethical language of open drama, in which people can be known, understood and judged, about two beings who exist in a condition of pure amoral striving and who are, in a crucial sense, both unjudgeable and unknowable. Who indeed would think of considering Tristan and Isolde as inhabitants of a calculable and logical world? It is true that they have a past; but it would not occur to us to stop and contemplate their future. We might pause to think that the life of Alfredo and Violetta might, in other circumstances, have turned out differently; we might, perhaps naively, say that Alfredo's father could have taken a different attitude, given them a decent allowance, and let them go on living the life we have briefly witnessed.

It is all too easy to dismiss such surmises as naive: but it is precisely because *La Traviata* can provoke them in us that it affects us as sad, even tragic. For this story takes place in a life we can recognise; a life where everyday questions make sense; a life which holds, for its characters, other options, other possibilities. Our sense of the ending of *La Traviata* is defined by the fact that it might have had a different ending; that it might have implied an entirely different future. But in the inner action of *Tristan* there are no other options or possibilities. The Will, whom Tristan and Isolde both represent, is all one, and there is only one course it can take. At the height of the intensity of Act II the lovers sing together: 'I am the world'.

Note, too, that at the end of Marke's lament in Act II neither of the lovers offers an apology or an explanation to him, and that no one, not even Marke, comments on this. Isolde never speaks to him at all (just as she will entirely ignore him in the last Act); and Tristan only turns him aside with the lines:

> O King, that
> I cannot tell you.
> And what you ask
> that you can never find out.[24]

This is certainly no repentance: it is barely even an acknowledgement. Anything resembling either comes only in one line ('. . . the king whom I betrayed') before Tristan provokes Melot to attack him. This situation is beyond the dreary formalities of explanation or penitence: Tristan really only speaks to Isolde all the time, as if to emphasise that the others are mere props to their private drama. It is hardly an exaggeration to say that, towards the end of the opera the text, too, becomes little more than a prop: commentators have noted its almost cryptic conciseness, its frequent disregard of grammar, sometimes even sense. The things the lovers say to each other become less and less precise: more and more, they become mere signals of feeling. In the final scene Isolde's vocal line gradually breaks up: fragmented and almost discontinuous, it begins to sound like a musical instrument. Her last sentence contains an idea but does not have a verb. The famous conductor who told Thomas Mann after a performance that 'This is hardly even music any more'[25], could equally well have said that it was hardly even drama any more.

And it is because of its very intensity that *Tristan and Isolde* lacks moral value. This is not the accepted view. A critic as erudite and perceptive as Joseph Kerman writes about 'a new integrity' for Tristan at the end, and sums up by saying that 'Tristan finds in death no longer oblivion but triumph'.[26] This seems to me a total misunderstanding of the work. Professor Kerman has listened to the delirious Tristan in Act III, when he cries out:

> That fearful drink
> which acquainted me with torment
> I myself, myself
> I brewed it[27]

and he accepts this as the true reading of *Tristan*. But the entire emotional and psychological drive of the opera, as well as the carefully prepared catastrophe of Act I, prove that it is nothing of the kind. The world of *Tristan* is an amoral world where blame is meaningless, and where, for this same reason, there can be no atonement. Tristan did not brew the fatal drink, either literally or metaphorically. He is not responsible for anything that happens after he and Isolde drink what they believe is a death potion: Wagner has wrenched them away from the world of causes, reasons and responsibilities, and flung them into that Schopenhauerian world where the unknowable and relentless Will makes playthings of people. This is the true action of *Tristan and Isolde*. As a mere man, and an actor of the outer action, Tristan clings heroically to life in Act III until Isolde comes. This gives him a sense of moral worth, and makes us regard him with horrified pity. But as the actor of the inner action, Tristan achieves nothing. What 'triumph' does he find? According to the outer action he redeems his honour by allowing Melot to kill him for something he may or may not have done.

According to the inner action, the Will in him has come to an end, and with it his existence. While he is in its grip he has, as a dramatic character, no choices to make. To compare him to, say, Angelo in Shakespeare's *Measure for Measure* would be fatuous. Michael Tanner is much more to the point when he writes, in connection with *Tristan and Isolde*, that 'so enormous is Wagner's eloquence that one forgoes the mean luxury of raising logical or moral objections.'[28] This is an uncomfortably perceptive remark, diagnosing perfectly our sense of reluctant submission in the face of despotic artistic amorality. In this sense we cannot 'defend' or 'condemn' Tristan. Schopenhauer could have been thinking of *Tristan and Isolde* when he described tragedy as 'the strife of the Will with itself'. That is Wagner's picture of the world. Tristan is a useless passion.

When we call *Tristan and Isolde* a closed drama we mean that it eludes our questioning in a fundamental way. We had thought that it was telling us one kind of story, only to find that such a reading did not quite explain what was really going on; that besides and beyond this story, which we thought we had understood, Wagner was telling us another, more important one. This, we sense, is the real story; this is what carries the real meaning of what we have seen. It is in this sense that Tristan is a Schopenhauerian work.

Wagner, too, thought it a Schopenhauerian work, but for different reasons. If we compare *Tristan* to Shakespeare's *Troilus and Cressida*, for example, we find that in the play the world of hard facts and unscrupulous men destroys a love which is not strong enough to defend itself. The lovers are still alive at the end of the play, but their love is destroyed because the society in which they live is destructive. In other words, the outer and the inner story are one: Shakespeare is telling us that love can be killed by something destructive and cruel in the world. What Wagner is telling us in *Tristan* is that the world of men can destroy lovers and their loving, but not love itself: his drama is the affirmation that love survives its human victims. Love, we are told, is something greater and more essential than the mere phenomenal world: it is something that can even transcend the Will.

In a famous letter to Mathilde Wesendonck Wagner explained that in *Tristan* he was going to extend and even correct Schopenhauer's philosophy: a notion which Erich Heller has called, with charitable irony, 'one of the most revealing jokes in the history of ideas'[29]. The fact is that Wagner entirely missed the point: he was hoping to show, in a way which was deeply un-Schopenhauerian, that when all willing and striving had ceased, love would be there as a universal fulfilment and comfort. But a comfort to whom? A fulfilment to what? Schopenhauer's idea of how all our striving dissolves in nothingness is grim enough; Wagner's improvement on it is merely an abstraction. *Tristan* is a music drama with human characters; and Wagner is continuing it by musical means, even when the human drama is over, and the characters who are the vessels of his ideas are dead. But we, the spectators, are still there; what, we ask, can love mean in a drama where there is no one left to love or be loved?

All this means that the inner action of *Tristan* takes a different course from the outer action; and it is the inner action that commands our assent and belief. But, and this is where we sense that we are in the presence of closed drama, this assent is undermined by the events we witness. Tristan's and Isolde's love is something elemental, something 'unquestionable', but it is not in itself *good* or *evil*: indeed, it is not essentially *moral*. We only have to compare it with Romeo's love for Juliet or Othello's for Desdemona: such love, seen in a full human context, is good, just as Angelo's for Isabella, or Phèdre's for Hyppolite, can be seen as reprehensible, almost evil. These relationships are portrayed from a moral standpoint. The love of Tristan and Isolde is, after the drinking of the potion, something amoral; and, being amoral, it wreaks havoc on them, and on the world around them — a world which is moral and which can only understand them in a moral sense. The inner story of *Tristan*, which is beyond the grasp of our reason and our moral sense, tells us that the outer story is almost irrelevant. Closed drama intimates to us that there is something at the core of dramatic experience which is essentially beyond human grasp.

The Ring of the Niebelung is different: here the outer story is as important as the inner story. Indeed, the terms 'outer' and 'inner' do not sound entirely appropriate when applied to *The Ring*. But the fact is that there are two narrative forces working within the tetralogy, and they pull it in different directions. *The Ring* is simultaneously a drama of moral restitution and a drama of amoral disintegration. The opening of *The Rhinegold* is set under water, the primal element; and this, together with the long, low, brooding opening note of the music, suggests primeval nature, the beginning of all things: as if we were witnessing the first moments of creation. 'Consider well my poem,' Wagner wrote to Liszt, 'it contains the beginning and end of the world.'[30] It is vital, if we are to grasp the meaning of *The Ring*, to see that in one sense Wagner had set out to draw what we have been calling a picture of the world. We are meant to feel that before the curtain rose on *The Rhinegold*, only a primordial world had existed; and that when the curtain falls on *The Twilight of the Gods* the world we have known has perished. Neither of these things, as we shall see, is entirely true; but *The Ring* as a whole is imbued with an almost tyrannical sense of personal creation and destruction. There is a sense of identity between Wagner and 'his world', in the way we suggested at the beginning of this book: he set out, not merely to tell a story but also to tell us how, in a deeply personal way, he felt about its contents.

This sense of personal and apocalyptic inspiration is one of the reasons why *The Ring* is also, in part, a closed drama. Another is that if we were to approach the opening of *The Rhinegold* in an inquisitive frame of mind we would not get very far. Why, for example, are the Rhinemaidens guarding the gold? It is clear that no one had ever tried to steal it; and Alberich's arrival arouses no suspicion. In any case, he is not even looking for the gold: he wants to seduce one of the Rhinemaidens and knows nothing, either about the existence of the gold or its power, until the Rhinemaidens tell him about it. But such an analysis of what happens in *The Rhinegold* is useless, because Wagner has simply created a scene of primeval passivity in which nothing happens. Nothing, that is, until something does happen. Dramatically speaking, the arrival of Alberich is almost as inexplicable as the birth of the first living cell: it is not the result or culmination of past events or specific circumstances. And then, as we come to Scene 2, and as the tetralogy unfolds, we gather that, in any case, what we have seen may not have been the beginning of all things. Did Wotan and the gods exist before the gold? Is the World Ash Tree, ancient symbol and depository of all knowledge, guarded by the Norns who are themselves the daughters of the earth goddess Erda – is this tree older than the Rhine and the gold? To ask such questions is to lose oneself in irrelevant pedantries: we sense that we are not speaking Wagner's language.

If the world of the Rhine is one of blissful unawareness, the world of the gods above is one of pervasive but unspecific anxiety. Wotan's first words are:

> The sacred hall of delight
> has gates and doors to guard me.[31]

Guard from what? Why had Wotan built Valhalla? What is he afraid of? At this stage he knows nothing about Alberich's theft of the gold, nor that, in him and the Niebelungs, he now has rivals for power. There is a sense of foreboding and imminent dissolution about our first encounter with the gods which has no dramatic explanation.

The Beginning also implies The End. This is reflected in the nature of the action. Wagner's operas are often called static, meaning that, for long stretches of time, nothing happens, no events take place, except for a small number of characters, usually only two, discoursing at length, mostly about the past. Carl Dahlhaus has partly dispelled this facile generalisation by pointing out that such passages of narrative and reflection are not necessarily undramatic: they contribute to the psychological movement of the drama. But when Wagner's characters reflect on the past, they are not only uncovering the causes of events: they also make the past a part of these events. The sense of stasis in Wagnerian opera is due in part to this constant backward movement. And, while the narrative action moves steadily forward, there is another action which strives to return to the beginning. The central moral enterprise of *The Ring* is to return the gold to the Rhinemaidens and to re-establish the state of undisturbed innocence which we saw in the first scene of *The Rhinegold*. This action, which is essentially moral, strives to cancel and undo the inevitable events of the other action, which is not. We have a sense, as we watch a performance of *The Ring*, that the end is determined and unavoidable, and not in the facile sense in which we sometimes think of plays as having been 'bound to end this way'. As the drama of *The Ring* progresses we realise that its two actions are powerless against each other. The turbulence of the events is subtly undermined by this moral stalemate. This is the real source of the sense of stasis in Wagnerian opera.

The paradox of the moral action of *The Ring* is the amorality of its resolution. The moral nature of the conflict is clear. Wotan had committed himself to an inhuman bargain in order to have Valhalla built in a hurry: he offered the giants his own sister-in-law, Freia, in payment. When his wife Fricka drives home to him the monstrosity of what he has done, he casts around for a different method of settlement. The news, brought by Loge, that Alberich has stolen the powerful Rhinegold is, as it were, a godsend: Wotan is all too easily persuaded that it would be no crime to steal it from a thief. And when he can see how Freia's absence would affect the gods' very life (she grows the golden apples that keep them young and vigorous forever), his resolve becomes firm.

But note that throughout this scene Wotan's attitude to what should actually happen to the gold remains ambiguous. The Rhine-maidens have appealed to him to restore their treasure to them, and he, the lord of contracts, senses that he is in the wrong. In the meantime, he also needs the gold to pay the giants; and he is tempted, too, by the power over the whole world which the ring would give him. But once he robs Alberich it is too late: what he now possesses can also be demanded of him in payment. Wotan is trapped in the moral web of his own world. 'What you are,' Fasolt tells him, 'you only are through contracts.' Deryck Cooke has pointed out how important this was to Wagner's conception: Wotan's spear as an instrument of law was Wagner's own idea, not borrowed from any of his sources, and so was the notion that the possession of the gold could give one absolute dominion over the world. The idea of being bound by contracts holds the key to all that follows. Wotan might have argued that he was not bound to Alberich by anything: Alberich was merely a thief from whom things could be taken in a just cause. But once Wotan committed robbery, he himself became a wrongdoer like Alberich; and once he gave the gold and the ring in payment he could not take it back by force. As he explains to Brünnhilde in Act II of *The Valkyrie*:

> Fafner guards the treasure
> for which he slew his brother.
> From him I would have
> to seize the ring
> which I myself paid him as wages.
> But since I covenanted with him
> I may not attack him.
> Powerless before him
> my courage would fail me.[32]

Wotan is both a criminal and a prisoner of his own legality.

With all this, we are still in the world of open drama. Wotan has got to this point by a series of decisions: at several points in the action he could have decided differently. Indeed, we might ask whether it would be all that wrong of him to take the ring from Fafner: after all, Fafner got it by murdering his own brother, and we could argue that it is no greater a crime to rob a murderer than to rob a thief. Moreover, Wotan would then be able to return the gold and the ring to the Rhinemaidens, which, he knows all along, is what he ought to do.

Wotan's answer to the dilemma of legality is to create a hero without responsibility. This is how he explains the matter to Fricka:

> The crisis calls for a hero
> who, free from divine protection,
> will be released from divine law.
> So alone he will be fit
> to do the deed
> which, much as the gods need it,
> a god is nevertheless
> prevented from doing.

On the practical level, Fricka sees through Wotan's device at once.

> What marvels could
> heroes perform
> that their gods
> were unable to do,
> by whose favour
> alone men can act?[33]

And when Wotan claims that Siegmund is a free agent, with a bravery all his own, Fricka is quick to point out that Siegmund is entirely Wotan's creature: he is not only his son but is armed and protected by him. Wotan is defeated in this argument; and when he unburdens himself to Brünnhilde in the next scene he outlines a dilemma which is Wagner's as much as his:

> How can I create a free agent
> whom I have never protected,
> who by defying me
> will be most dear to me?
> How can I make that Other,
> no longer part of me,
> who of his own accord will do
> what I alone desire?

> With disgust I find
> only myself, every time
> in everything I have created.
> The Other man for whom I long,
> that Other I can never find:
> for the Free man has
> to create himself;
> I can only create subjects
> to myself.[34]

And when, in due course, we encounter Siegfried, we find that he too is no more the free man created by himself than his father Siegmund was. In Act I of *Siegfried* Wotan comes to Mime's smithy; he engages Mime in that long question-and-answer game which never quite pays its way as drama because it has one overriding aim: to lead Mime to the thought that Siegfried should re-forge Siegmund's broken sword. Without this sword Fafner cannot be killed and the ring cannot be recovered. And this, we must remember, is Wotan's own sword: the same sword that, long ago, he had driven into the tree in Hunding's hut so that Siegmund could find it. Now it is the turn of Siegmund's son, Wotan's grandson, to come into possession of this magic weapon and to use it as a 'free' agent.

But the fact is that Wotan stage-manages Siegfried as completely as he had stage-managed Siegmund: without his intervention Siegfried would be powerless. Nor does Wotan seem to realise that this 'free man' will have to commit an act which is as immoral in its way as Wotan's own had been: he is being set up to kill Fafner and seize the treasure to which he has no more right than Fafner, Wotan or Alberich. The moral balance of the world is about to be restored by an amoral agent committing an immoral act.

Wotan's plan implies, not the morality of reparation, restitution or atonement, but the morality of transcendence and self-release. To what extent can this be called morality at all? Wotan accepts his responsibilities, but this does not take the form of action. He explains this by implying that further action by him would mean robbing and killing someone to whom he is bound by contract; but it could also be read as merely a desire not to soil his hands any further. Now it is in the nature of moral restitution that it can endanger any moral integrity we may have left. When we make reparations we do not always emerge very well from the experience — indeed we sometimes emerge rather worse because making reparations involves us in having to deal with the unpleasant consequences of our own earlier deeds. The fact is that Wotan has done something that can only be put right by committing another act of injustice, and he simply cannot go on any longer. Wagner has drawn, in Wotan, a portrait of moral bankruptcy and impotence: a state of weariness in which the mind has no inner resources left and can only hope for outside help or destruction. In our own time he might have contemplated psychoanalysis or suicide. Indeed, Wotan does now long for the end; but in the meantime what he wants Siegmund and then Siegfried to do for him is, in some respects, not unlike what psychoanalysis would promise him: someone else would come to his aid, with an independent will and with motives of his own, and make peace between him and the world. But there is an important difference: the psychoanalyst restores the patient's moral equilibrium in full knowledge of the patient's past whereas Wotan wants a saviour who is innocent of knowledge and has no motives.

Here lies the core of the moral weakness of *The Ring*. There is no relationship of cause and effect between crime and redemption, which means that the act of redemption has no moral value. Siegfried is an amoral figure because he is neither intellectually nor morally touched by, or involved in, the sin he is supposed to redeem. And yet we have only to listen to his music to be convinced that he is Wagner's hero in every sense: with his death the chance of salvation is gone.

Of course, if we turn on all this the pedantic eye of open drama, we might wonder what precisely Wotan's plans had been. How exactly was he going to get the ring from Siegfried? We may surmise that the free warrior would have been little amenable to either persuasion or force. And yet, throughout the drama, Wotan is determined to get the ring back: even as late as Act I or *The Twilight of the Gods*, Waltraute, sent by Wotan, is begging Brünnhilde for the ring so that it can be returned to the Rhinemaidens. Such questioning leads us, once again, to a point where *The Ring* as open drama ends and *The Ring* as closed drama begins. For the fact is that the Rhinemaidens very nearly get their ring back from Siegfried himself; but when he is finally about to offer it to them they refuse with these words:

> Keep it, hero,
> and look after it well

till you know the peril
at which you keep the ring.
Then you'll be pleased
if we free you from its curse.[35]

This probably means as little to Siegfried as it would to us, if we did not by now surmise that we are dealing with events where questions of ordinary motivations do not apply. For, in terms of plain dramatic logic, the rest of this scene with the Rhinemaidens is quite super-fluous. They work Siegfried up to a fit of male pride, where he plainly tells them that they could have the ring if he could have his way with them, but he would think it cowardly to give it up merely to save his skin. Theodor Adorno writes solemnly that Siegfried rejects this last chance 'with an appeal to the ultimate shibboleth, the formula of private property'[36]. He does nothing of the kind. If anything, it is clear how little Siegfried considers the ring as his private property: he is only thinking of how giving it away might reflect on his character. Adorno, blinded by the very brilliance of his own ideological reading of *The Ring*, introduces a political-economic note into a situation which is, in reality, dominated only by Fate and the dramatist's despotic will. This will is intent, not simply on bringing about the restoration of the ring, which would resolve the moral conflict of the whole work, but on making the world end in an amoral conflagration. After all, we might say, perhaps obtusely, that Siegfried could have simply thrown the ring in the water. But he does not, and not because of the unconvincing reasons we are given, but because that would, albeit in a perfunctory way, bring the moral action of *The Ring* to an untimely end. At this point in the drama it is becoming clear that what we earlier called the drama of moral restitution will not in fact take place.

But this is not because Siegfried decides otherwise: indeed, what eventually happens seems to have nothing to do with the hero who was created to make it happen. Wagner told his friend August Röckel that he wanted Siegfried 'to represent my ideal of the perfect human being, whose highest consciousness manifests itself in the acknowledgement that all consciousness must find expression in present life and action.'[37] This does not sound like Siegfried at all. What consciousness, we ask? What action? Indeed, what life? When does Siegfried acknowledge anything so complex as Wagner credits him with? In his 1848 prose sketch Wagner described how Siegfried 'has taken the guilt of the gods upon himself [and] later atones for their wrong by his defiance, his independence'[38]. But atonement and defiance are conscious acts: you must know what you atone for, or whom you defy. Siegfried has no knowledge of such things. Yet even a critic of Adorno's formidable powers of perception can write about Siegfried submitting to the fate that Wotan wills. But the fact is that Siegfried does not submit to anything because he is not aware that there is any fate or will to submit to.

Non-consciousness is one of Siegfried's most noticeable qualities, especially as it expresses itself in action — or rather as it does not, since he never knows the real significance of anything he does. As we have seen, his ignorance of fear is simply a form of ignorance as a condition of existence; he never realises the value or the significance of the treasure he takes from Fafner; he derives no benefit from its possession; and his encounter with the Rhinemaidens only shows that he has learnt nothing about its value. His morality is that of a heroic zombie. It is both difficult and preposterous to imagine, as we might in open drama, what Siegfried would have done if he had survived the events of *The Ring*, or what 'he' might do in various extra-dramatic situations.

Siegfried has a completeness which belongs not so much to a person as to a force. He is not the only such character in *The Ring* — which is why it invites such analyses as that of Robert Donington who has interpreted it as a Jungian work of *animus* and *anima*, good and evil shadow. Such an interpretation is obviously not 'accurate' in the elementary sense that Wagner could not have read Jung. But it may be accurate in a different way: it may imply that Wagner himself may have been a suitable subject for Jungian analysis, and that the creation of *The Ring* may have been, for him, an unconscious act of inner integration, a finding of his true Self. It could also imply that we, who read *The Ring* in this way, are also unconsciously responding to some psychological or spiritual conflict within ourselves: the kind of conflict which it was Jung's life-work to try to heal. But such a reading always depends on a sense of incompleteness in the characters of the drama. If Siegfried and Brünnhilde are *animus* and *anima*, then they are not so much characters as forces; only together do they make up a 'person'.

Unlike Donington, I am tempted to read *The Ring* as if it had been inspired by Freud. Take the character of Erda. She is based on the northern epic tradition of wise women, especially Wala of the Icelandic Sagas. But only in Wagner does she appear as the embodiment of conscience: she emerges, in moments of crisis, from endless

subterranean sleep and delivers moral warning and advice to Wotan.
It is as if she were playing Superego to his troubled Ego; and
Wotan's qualities of self-consciousness, self-questioning and anxiety
are very like the qualities of the human Ego as Freud describes them.
Or take Brünnhilde's confrontation with Wotan in Act II of *The
Valkyrie*:

> You are speaking to your will,
> when you tell me your will:
> who am I
> if not your will?

And Wotan to Brünnhilde:

> What else are you but my wish's
> blindly approving instrument?[39]

It is as if Wotan were talking to a part of himself; as if both he and
Brünnhilde were part of the same troubled mind. And the entire
moral conflict of the first two parts of *The Ring* could be seen as the
dilemma of Wotan responding both to the moral warnings of Erda
and the emotional force of Brünnhilde: much like the Freudian Ego,
besieged by the Superego and the Id.[40]

A moment's thought will show that, as an interpretation, this is
both inaccurate and incomplete, and not, again, for the elementary
reason that it could not have been intended by Wagner. For if we call
Brünnhilde the Id, we ignore that very quality of passionate independence, combined with a need to be loved, which defines her
relationship to Wotan, both as her ruler and as her father. And if to
be an instrument of Wotan's will means to be his Id, is Siegfried his
Id too? To call Erda the Superego in this scheme sounds attractive
too, until we remember that the Freudian Superego is a moral
authority which the mind itself creates: it is not only the Ego's judge
but also its helpful representative towards the outside world. Erda,
by contrast, is the very voice of that outside world: she brings news
of Necessity and Fate.

Again, Freud's formulation for the healthy mind was that it was
ruled by the Ego, not the Id; and we might say that the disastrous
events of *The Ring* show what happens when the Ego (i.e. Wotan)
acts badly and abdicates its rule. But this, too, would be an inadequate
reading in the end: for what follows Wotan's abdication is not the
rule of any kind of Id, whatever we take the Id to be, but a
destruction far more complete. As with Donington's Jungian reading,

so with my own Freudian one: we may be reading, between the lines, the composer's unconscious attempt to understand the world as if it were a single mind, perhaps his own, in conflict with itself; and we may well be admitting such an inclination in ourselves. It is one of the most striking results of Wagnerian characterisation, of his peopling his stage with characters who are both more and less than people and both more and less than forces, that we can respond in this way to his work. Such characters are not open to our questioning in the way that characters of open drama are: we recognise them not only as creatures similar to ourselves but also as elemental forces that are part of us. Thus we read our own minds into Wagner's drama, which is also a drama of the world. In this sense, *The Ring* becomes Wagner's picture of the world, and our response shows, in a way that is by now perhaps familiar, to what extent we recognise it as our own.

Wagner's characters are at once overpowering and elusive. This is because they are rooted in myth, and for Wagner myth was the source of truth. In his essay *Opera and Drama* (1851), he defined myth as a 'poem of a life-view held in common'[41]. The phrase may be read as one of the earliest definitions of closed art: myth, for Wagner, is a work that confirms what we already know. But what Wagner had in mind was not mere fairy-tales. In *A Communication to My Friends* (1851) he makes clear that for him the idea of anything that was 'not bound by time and place, nor portrayed given men in given circumstances, for the understanding of equally definite human beings' was 'an utter nothing, a chimera of aesthetic phantasy.'[42] We sense that Wagner is in search of some fundamental human truth, some essential thing that we might perceive beyond the mere phenomena of a narrative. Myth, he thought, was 'mostly juster to the essence of Individuality'[43] than the elaboration of it by poets; indeed Wagner thought that ordinary people could see things, even in myth, only with the superficial clarity of the physical eye, and not 'as in themselves they really are'[44]. The Wagnerian myth is the result of what he thought was a unique perception. Wagner believed that at the heart of the mythical narrative he could see what he called 'the purely human': not the 'Figure of conventional history . . . but the real naked *Man* . . . the type of the true *human being.*'[45]

Like Schopenhauer before him, Wagner mistrusted history, and had a Romantic's dislike of what he considered its pedantry and superfluous detail. History, for Wagner, held no truth: all he could see, he said, were

> *relations*, and nothing but relations; the *human being* I could only see in so far as the relations ordered him, and not as he had power to order *them*.[46]

When Wagner considered what he called a historical-political subject, he found that

> the mere intellectual exposition of *relations* made impossible ... the presentation of the purely human individuality.[47]

Myth, by contrast, had a 'plastic unity'; and it held, for Wagner, a special advantage. When he arranged the scenes of mythological stories for his own purposes, he found that

> all those minor details, which the modern playwright finds so indispensable for the elucidation of involved historical occurrences [became] quite unnecessary, and the whole strength of the portrayal could be concentrated upon a few weighty and decisive moments of development.[48]

We can sense Wagner's impatience. He wanted to show life and Man in their essential purity, but tiresome facts, details and *relations* kept getting in his way. This is vital if we want to understand Wagner's handling of character and dramatic situation. His technique was based on concentration. He began by hewing out massive structural blocks. He told Cosima how he had 'decided to reduce *Tristan* to three love scenes'[49]; and when he was brooding over *Parsifal* he wrote to Mathilde Wesendonck about the way he was going to 'compress the whole into *three* main situations of drastic intent[50]'. Wagner's problem as a dramatist lay buried in the word 'development'. How much development could he show, or imply, in these massive, single scenes? How could he tell a story, and at the same time reveal essential, unchanging truths?

The solution to this problem is what we now think of as the typical Wagnerian scene, which is both static and fluctuating, both spare and complex. In relation to the length of these scenes, very little actual physical action takes place: the drama is largely psychological and it maintains, as we have seen, a constant sense of the past within the present. It is also a drama of tense intimacy. The typical Wagnerian mode is the dialogue: a confrontation between two people. The scale and intensity of Wagnerian orchestration can make us forget how very few scenes there are in his mature operas where more than two characters utter anything as independent, self-contained beings. We do not experience here the complex pull and pressure of the simultaneous thoughts, feelings and utterances of several people at once — which is among the finest dramatic and psychological achievements of the mature Mozart (and Verdi and Ibsen). Their art is the interplay of several 'relations' at once; the essence of Wagnerian drama is that it achieves a special intensity by concentrating the action on only one set of relations at a time. The Rhinemaidens, the Valkyries and the Norns are distinguishable but not individualised: they are not operatic choruses, and yet they have no personalities either. Indeed, except for *The Mastersingers*, the one completely open drama in Wagner's mature output, it is remarkable how small the amount of choral writing is in his operas in relation to their bulk. In *Tristan* the Chorus features only briefly in Act I: its dramatic function is little more than lyrical or decorative. In *The Ring* we have only Hagen's vassals in *The Twilight of the Gods*.

Now from the strictly dramatic point of view the chorus in opera is a thoroughly artificial device, even in relation to the operatic form; but it can be put to surprisingly realistic use. That was not always the case. At the beginnings of opera, in seventeenth-century Venice, the chorus was sometimes thought to be unnecessary and dramatically tedious; and its use often depended on money being available. This is a large subject: the history of the chorus in opera still needs to be written. But if we see Wagner in the context of opera as it developed since Gluck, then his sparing use of the chorus takes on a special significance. We might hazard a generalisation and say that opera composers have used the chorus, in varying degrees, to enlarge, emphasise or even create the setting and the social sense of the action. The formal, impersonal grandeur of the choruses in *Aida* underlines the rigidly hierarchic nature of Egyptian society; the courtiers in *Rigoletto*, the party guests in *La Traviata*, the villagers in *The Marriage of Figaro*, and, in a very special sense, the prisoners in *Fidelio*, have precise social and emotional functions. They define the social milieu of the drama, and they help to provide a context in which we can see and judge the principal characters.

Now take Hagen's vassals in *The Twilight of the Gods*. Dramatically their origin lies in Wagner's principal source, the *Niebelungenlied*. Here the intrigues of Brünnhilde and Hagen against Kriemhilde and

Siegfried are motivated by social resentments, which are precisely defined, and deeply rooted in the feudal laws of allegiance. The Hagen of the *Niebelungenlied* resents Siegfried because his presence is an implied affront to his overlord Gunther. Hagen's vassals share this resentment as all feudal vassals must; and when the time comes they fight and die to defend their lord's honour. In *The Ring* Hagen is out to destroy Siegfried for quite different reasons, and it is quite unnecessary for him to warn his men to be loyal to their new mistress and avenge her if she is wronged. And indeed, this chorus plays an entirely passive part. When Siegfried comes under suspicion their words ('What? Did he break faith?') are almost Gilbertian, and they call, somewhat feebly, on the god Donner for help. But when Siegfried appears to justify himself, the vassals are quickly pacified: all Siegfried has to do is to say a few cheering words and they happily follow him to the wedding feast.

It is a quaint spectacle: the ending of Wagner's vast cosmic drama draws near its climax in scenes of tense, almost thriller-like domestic conflict, and its vocal background is little more than a formal grand-opera chorus. And, accordingly, it is not the vassals who 'take revenge' on Siegfried at the end, but Hagen himself. Far from giving loyal support, the men do nothing. Having brought in the day's bag, they recline in a picturesque manner, and when Hagen strikes Siegfried down, four of them try to restrain him, somewhat tardily, with the words, 'Hagen, what are you doing?' They get no answer, and two of them cry out in helpless indignation: 'Hagen, what have you done?' It might be tempting to take this as the outrage felt by decent feudal subjects; but these men have been given no such reality in the action. Their presence is little more than decorative, and it only emphasises that the social context of what is happening is relatively unimportant. The real drama is beyond 'relations'.

If 'relations' have any importance in drama, then *Parsifal* is Wagner's most problematic work. If they have not, then *Parsifal* is Wagner's crowning achievement. This may be why it provokes, more even than any other of his operas, extremes of admiration and dislike. Liszt wrote to Hans von Wolzogen about it in terms which will by now be familiar:

There is nothing that can be said about this miraculous work. Silence is the only possible response to so deeply moving a work; the solemn beat of its pendulum is from the sublime to the most sublime.[51]

Nietzsche called it '*the stroke of genius* as seduction', an 'alliance of beauty and sickness', with a tendency to enervate the spirit and to 'indulge every cowardice of the modern soul'[52]. Debussy found it altogether ludicrous except for the score. One of the opera's most persuasive modern champions, Michael Tanner, has summed up the matter by saying that *Parsifal* is not so much a religious work as a work '*about* religion'; it is 'the most penetrating study we have of the psychopathology of religious belief in artistic terms'[53].

But whose belief? Dr Tanner's remark reveals the profound affinity between *Parsifal* and *The Ring*. If we bring to it the tools of a psychological approach, *Parsifal* reveals itself as another drama of the mind. It is not about the religious belief of any one of its characters: they are all there to enact a drama of religious belief within which their qualities as individuals are relatively unimportant. Approach these people as if they were characters in open drama, and we will soon find ourselves in difficulties. Writing about Kundry, Ernest Newman commented that 'her complete nature is difficult to analyse in words — it is defined for us mostly in her music.'[54] Now Newman is not usually at a loss for words to define anything, and when someone as lucid and levelheaded as he is writes in this way we have reason to be watchful. The problem is not new. In 1885 Edouard Schuré contributed an article to the *Revue Wagnérienne*, in which not only was he critical of the opera as a whole, commenting acidly on its atmosphere of 'languid and declining virility', but also of the credibility of Kundry's character. He noted the lack of any apparent connection between the two sides of her nature, and asked:

> Where does she come from? How does she live during the long intervals which separate her life of sin from her life of repentance?[55]

The article provoked a plaintive editorial footnote, obviously intended to pacify irate Wagnerites, to the effect that contributors bore sole responsibility for their opinions. But of course from Wagner's point of view Schuré's comments are not offensive so much as fatuous: our experience of the opera would gain nothing from any answers to his questions. Kundry is Wagner's embodiment of female sexuality, alternating between the extremes of voracious appetite and chaste humility. If her effect as a dramatic character is sometimes ludicrous or repulsive, as it tends to be in performance, this is for two reasons. One is that she is always seen from Parsifal's point of view: she is a problem that has to be dealt with, a force that has to be tamed. Their first encounter is a crucial moment in the drama. Kundry's kiss is Parsifal's first erotic experience, and its effect on him, according to Wagner's meticulous stage directions, is convulsive. He 'starts up with a gesture of extreme fear', 'clutches his heart, as though to overcome a rending pain', and cries out:

> Amfortas! The wound! The wound!
> It burns within my heart!

The moment is of great psychological insight. Wagner understands the kind of impact that the first erotic experience can have on a sensitive nature: how it can inspire a vague sense of terror, how it can suddenly expand the horizons of the mind and alter the range and depth of one's feelings and sympathies. And yet this passage is improbable in print and can be comical in performance.

What has happened, and this is the second reason why Kundry does not have the effect on us that Wagner intended, is that Wagner has compressed a long, complex mental and emotional process into a short, intense moment. The change from utter incomprehension to unspecific adolescent terror, and then to specific personal pity for a wounded man who is not even present, is too sudden. Wagner is not telling us how Parsifal's emotions were changed: he makes a statement about it. His problem is still the problem of development: how to give us a picture of the world and, at the same time, tell a story. Drama moves forward as action; and action implies characters who act. Kundry and Parsifal stand before us as characters, and unless we can understand them as characters we shall not be able to grasp what Wagner is saying to us. And to understand them as characters means that we constantly ask, what have they done? Why have they done it? What will they do next? And whatever they will do next, it will be in the context of their relationship to each other as characters.

I make no apologies for the pedestrian nature of these observations. We are dealing with a dramatist who is communicating the personal vision of closed art, but uses the dramatic, impersonal means of open art. The fact that he is a dramatist constantly lays him open to our questions: for character is by definition open. But Wagner uses his characters with a sense of majestic evasion: our questions are frustrated and made to seem irrelevant because his people do not have the perspective of a past. They have the density of suggestive ideas but not of characters who are accountable. Hence our sense of impatience, sometimes even of ludicrousness. For, in so far as Kundry is a character, her attempted seduction of Parsifal is rejected by him (and by Wagner) as impure and sinful; yet it endows Parsifal with an experience which is pure and holy. As for Kundry, the encounter turns her into an asexual penitent; and this moral transformation, which has the impact almost of beatification, is credited to Parsifal and his saintliness, whereas strictly speaking we ought to say that Parsifal's saintliness and his new apprehension of life are at least partly due to Kundry. But clearly, such arguments are beside the point in Wagner's world. Kundry has served her purpose as an instrument of redemption, Parsifal's and her own; but Wagner is not interested in the relations between people's actions, their motives, and their just or unjust deserts.

Here we have been led to the very core of *Parsifal*: we are confronting the nature of action and salvation. All the versions of the Parsifal legend that Wagner consulted had one thing in common: they were quests in which men went out to find the Holy Grail. Wagner's version is different: a holy object has been stolen and its guardians are waiting for someone to get it back for them. There is a sense of immobility about the opening scene, of being suspended between life and death. Amfortas bleeds from an incurable wound, and the Knights wait for the unknown saviour to regain the spear: only the touch of this spear, which had caused the wound, can cure it.

The spectator conditioned by the approachability of open drama might now want to ask several questions. We know, and Amfortas must have known, that other Knights of the Grail had been seduced before by Kundry and Klingsor: how could Amfortas, who, like all the Knights, had taken a vow of chastity, let go of the spear and yield to Kundry? Why are the Knights waiting for an unknown saviour instead of going in search of the spear themselves? What is Klingsor doing with the spear now? It appears now to have neither power nor function; it is merely an object whose role in the drama is that it is wanted back by its original owners. In the same way, Alberich's ring and his gold spend the greater part of the tetralogy in the possession of Fafner. Passive substances, without any active power of their own, lie at the heart of these turbulent events. Indeed, the power of the ring itself varies unpredictably according to who possesses it and who wants to take it. Similarly, the spear is powerless in Klingsor's hands: when, in Act II, he flings it at Parsifal it miraculously stops in mid-air.

Questioning the contents of *Parsifal* in this way clearly will not get us anywhere. The very meaning of the work resides in Wagner's conception that salvation is not dependent on action. Lucy Beckett has argued that

> Parsifal must not be seen as Christ, the Redeemer, but only as a man redeemed, who nevertheless carries the responsibility of revealing Christ's continuing redemptive power to the world.[56]

Parsifal was created, Miss Beckett tells us, to 'disclose the reality of Christ to others'. What reality? What redemptive power? Parsifal is carefully presented as knowing nothing of his own origins, not even his own name, and as understanding nothing about the nature or the causes of his actions. He is, we might say, the embodiment of effects without causes. The main reason why his sudden pity for Amfortas is unconvincing is that pity is a moral feeling, but here it issues from an amoral being. Wagner the visionary is telling us that pity, the salvation of the world, awakens in man when his sexuality is awakened; but Wagner the dramatist, for all the astuteness and humanity of this insight, has not created a character through whom this could be comprehended as a human experience. In drama there can be no completely blank characters any more than in life. Drama, moreover, is a form of experience created and shaped for our understanding in a specific way. Life is unbounded; drama is bounded by its form and its theme. To understand its action we need to understand the characters in it, and this we can only do if we can see them in the perspective of past events. When the mad Lear meets the disguised Edgar on the heath, he demands: 'What hast thou been?' Parsifal's lack of all qualities that would give him perspectives makes him unsatisfying as a character: the dramatisation of inexperience comes across as a case of amnesia.

In the larger sense, too, the work suffers from a sense of moral disconnection. The redemptive power of Christ lay largely in action. Christ did things; He understood a complex network of social, psychological, spiritual and religious forces in the world, and acted upon that understanding. He also consciously and with intent carried out what He saw as the will of God, and in doing so deliberately sacrificed His life. If we find no redemptive power in Parsifal it is because he, like Siegfried, is someone to whom things merely happen. His only deliberate act, the off-stage massacre of the lovers of the Flowermaidens in Act II, is little more than a panto-mime, presented as it is only through the wailing of the Flowermaidens. There is nothing in their coy wooing of him (Wag-ner specifies that they are to be scantily and colourfully clad), and nothing in their music, to convince us that there are dead bodies behind the scenes, and that these women had loved them. If we are being asked to believe that such a bloody price might have to be paid for redemption, then here Wagner fails completely. If Siegfried's heroism is the heroism of a zombie, Parsifal's morality is the morality of a neuter. In search of the purely human, Wagner has arrived at the barely human.

We may compare Parsifal with the greatest 'holy fool' in litera-ture, Dostoyevsky's Prince Myshkin, who is neither really holy nor quite a fool: it is merely that he has a different moral understanding of the world from everybody else's. Dostoyevsky lets us see very clearly what this understanding is, and why it is so difficult for others either to comprehend it or to tolerate it. He lets Myshkin loose upon an intricate fabric of social and psychological rela-tionships. Myshkin has a mind of his own, he has quite considerable courage; and through his actions we are made to question and re-assess the world. Parsifal as a moral being is nothing by compari-son. We may object that it is wrong to compare the hero of an opera to the hero of a novel; but when Wagner composed *The Mastersin-gers* he showed himself entirely capable of creating an equally complex set of social and psychological relationships. In *Parsifal*, as in *Tristan* and *The Ring*, his intentions were different. The problem of Wagner the dramatist is the problem of the inspiration of closed art expressing itself in dramatic form which is essentially open. It exists in the form of unfolding action. We approach drama most directly when we ask how the action we see, expressed through characters we can understand, is related to the subject of the drama as it reveals itself. Our sense that Wagner's operas are, in important respects, closed works of art, comes from the growing realisation that the actions we see do not fully express the subject of his dramas; and that we cannot fully question and assess his achievement by measuring the one against the other.

The closed quality of *The Ring* lay essentially in the moral disconnection between crime and redemption: the actions of the redeemer, Siegfried, had nothing to do with the crime which he had to redeem, and which had originally set the whole work in motion.

In *Parsifal* the disconnection is even greater because redemption is separated from action: to be a redeemer here is merely a condition of being which the redeemer himself is unaware of. Redemption is not a deed: it is something given which we contemplate in submission. Perlocutionary art can hardly go further.

The full title of *The Ring* is *The Ring of the Niebelung*. The Niebelung is Alberich: the first real action in the work is his theft of the gold. What happens to him in the end?

One day, while Wagner was composing *The Twilight of the Gods*, he told Cosima with satisfaction that 'today Alberich has disappeared'[57]. This can only refer to the completion of the dialogue between Alberich and Hagen in Act II. The logically minded spectator may wonder whether Hagen is being visited by Alberich or his ghost: for Hagen is asleep, yet his eyes are open. But when he asks Alberich who will inherit the world from Wotan, the dwarf replies:

> I − and you!
> We will inherit the world,
> if I am not mistaken about your loyalty;
> if you share my misery
> and rage.[58]

That does not sound like a ghost, but like someone eager to lay very real hands on very real power. But if Alberich is alive, what purpose other than atmospherics is served by introducing him as a ghost to his own son? And why, if he is not dead, does he not appear at the end to help Hagen recover the Ring? If he is dead, why have we heard nothing about how and when he died? During the prelude to *Twilight* one of the Norns sings:

> The gold of the Rhine
> was stolen by Alberich.
> Do you know what happened to him?[59]

There is no answer.

The point clearly exercised Professor Götz Friedrich, a recent producer of *The Ring* at the Royal Opera House in London. He brought Alberich on stage at the very end, looking on in grim despair as Valhalla burnt and the Rhinemaidens regained the Ring. Professor Friedrich's synopsis reads: 'Wotan's world dies out, Alberich looks on.' The implication is clear: Alberich is still here, a potential source of evil. But according to Wagner's stage directions Alberich does not appear at the end. Wagner was not writing a political drama like Brecht's *Arturo Ui*, warning us at the end that the bitch that bore the villain is on heat again: he was writing an apocalyptic music drama about the beginning and the end of the world, and Alberich disappears because he has no further role to play. When, at the end of *The Magic Flute*, the Queen of the Night sinks into the ground, her disappearance is not only clearly seen: it is also part of the opera's formal and intellectual conclusion[60]. The Queen of the Night is accounted for, morally and dramatically; Alberich is merely missing.

Alberich is also powerless to prevent the end of the tetralogy from returning to its beginning; just as Siegfried proves powerless to bring about the moral ending that Wotan had planned. In this sense, for all its moral seriousness, the drama of *The Ring* is not finally a moral event. There is a deep moral nihilism in its central argument, which is that the existing world is doomed, and that those who might have created a new and better world are powerless and will perish. It is true that this sounds like a moral argument; but, for Wagner, there is no causal link between the moral nature of the world and its destiny.

The Ring is a profoundly Schopenhauerian picture of the world: it shows that all effort, all enterprise, whether good or evil, is destined to end in nothingness. Wagner's libretto originally included a passage in Brünnhilde's farewell, in which love was held out as the redeemer of the world. Wagner soon cut this passage: the dramatist of causes and effects could see that the events of *The Ring* held out no justification for such a belief. Wagner the musician, however, felt otherwise, and ended the work with a tremendous orchestral elaboration of a *motif*, known as the *motif* of 'redemption by love'. It was first sung by Sieglinde in Act III of *The Valkyrie*, and the words were addressed to Brünnhilde:

> For him, whom we loved
> I will save the dear child.[61]

That dear child was to be Siegfried, and nothing on earth was going to save him. The lyrical impact of the ending of *The Twilight of the Gods* should not blind us (it usually does) to the fact that this music is lying: it entirely contradicts the action from beginning to end. The music tells us that love is the saviour of the world. But the fact is that love did not save even Sieglinde: if anything, it killed her.

Neither did love, hers, Brünnhilde's or Wotan's, save Siegfried; nor
indeed did anyone's love save anyone else. The world of *The Ring* is
doomed, and within this world love is as futile as greed. If Wagner is
expressing his faith in the transcendental power of love, then it is a
power which we have just seen to fail. Adorno writes solemnly that

> to die in love means also to become conscious of the limits
> imposed on the power of the property system over man.[62]

But, even more, to die in love means not to be able to live in love.
The sense of love as a transcendental force is undermined by the fact
that, dramatically, there is nothing left to transcend. The emptiness
here is even greater than at the end of *Tristan*. In plays like *Troilus
and Cressida* or *Antony and Cleopatra* love has a moral and
dramatic value, because the feeling which the lovers had for each
other is something which not only we, but also the survivors in the
play, can respect. At the end of *The Ring* there is no one left for us to
share such feelings with. This is an essential part of its quality as a
closed drama.

The naive thought, fundamental to all experience of living drama:
'And I wonder what will happen to them all?' has no place here. We
can have some idea how the world of *Hamlet* or *Macbeth* might go
on after the carnage of the ending: both Fortinbras and Malcolm
have specific political objectives. Denmark and Scotland are recognisable social structures, real countries, bleeding but still breathing:
the survivors have work to do. At the end of *The Twilight of the
Gods*, according to Wagner's stage directions, 'men and women,
terrified, crowd to the very front of the stage'[63]. Who are these
people? They say nothing; they have neither a musical nor a
dramatic role to play; their survival of such a catastrophe seems
improbable. In performance, if their presence impinges on us at all,
it is usually a source of distraction. There is no recognisable social
structure here: *The Ring* leaves nothing behind except the experience we have had of it. Wagner the moralist sees with utter clarity
the terrible logic of greed and power; Wagner the visionary tells us
that in the end nobody will hold any power at all. But, we may ask,
what power could there be where there is no one to hold it, and no
one over whom it could be held?

This is not the only difficulty about the ending of *The Ring*.
Wagner's friend Röckel was the first to ask him, after reading the
libretto: When the Rhinegold is given back to the Rhine, why do the
gods perish nevertheless?' Wagner's reply is one of his most typical-

ly opinionated and imaginative pieces of writing. He told Röckel magisterially that a good production would satisfy 'the simplest mind' on this matter. It was not, Wagner asserted, something to be explained by arguments, that is to say,

> things that can be generally explained, twisted and turned (one need only set a political jurist on the job as an advocate) — no, we feel in our inmost souls, as does Wotan, that [the gods'] destruction is of necessity.

And, Wagner concludes,

> The object was . . . to justify this necessity emotionally.[64]

This short passage is striking for its almost dictatorial tone. Why this vitriolic retort about legalistic procedure? Why this mistrust of all argument? The fact is that the shrewd Röckel was, in a sense, as fatuous about *The Ring* as Schuré had been about *Parsifal*. They both treated Wagner's work as open dramas of which logical and moral questions could be asked. If Wagner's reply to Röckel seems impatient and elusive, it is because poor Röckel asked precisely the sort of question to which Wagner's drama is most impervious and, paradoxically, the sort of question to which it is most vulnerable. *The Ring* was composed by two people: Wagner the moral thinker, who saw the world torn apart and punished by the moral logic of guilt; and Wagner the visionary who drew a picture of the world destroying itself in an amoral conflagration. To experience *The Ring* fully is to experience these two aspects of Wagner's creative nature struggling with one another. To the extent that it is the ending that sets the seal on a work, it is Wagner the visionary who wins: this is why, in the final analysis, *The Ring* may be called a closed work of art.

Perhaps the most revealing explanation of that ending comes earlier in Wagner's letter to Röckel, when Wagner describes how

> Wotan rises to the tragic dignity of willing his own destruction. This is the whole lesson we have to learn from human history — to will the thing that must be and ourselves to fulfil it.[65]

Wagner uses the word 'tragic' rather loosely. If we look at Wotan's predicament in *The Ring* we might say that there is nothing tragic about willing one's own destruction, especially if one has the means of salvation within one's power. And if these are the lessons of history, then Wotan's entire spiritual conflict has been redundant all

along: he need not have worried about guilt, punishment or restitution. Indeed, we might have sensed all this from Erda's words to him
in *The Rhinegold*. Her first warning was clear:

> Escape the curse on the ring.
> To irredeemable
> dark destruction
> its possession condemns you.[66]

This sounds as if things might all be well if only Wotan were to give
up the Ring. But what Erda says later is more ambiguous.

> All that exists will end!
> A dark day
> dawns for the gods.
> I advise you, avoid the ring.[67]

These lines speak of unconditional doom: Wotan's end will come,
regardless of what he wills and does. This, too, makes Wotan a less
than tragic figure: for there is nothing tragic in simply ceasing to be.
The tragic experience implies logic; it implies causes and effects; it
implies a sense of moral argument in which both we and the
characters of the drama can take part. There is nothing moral, and
therefore nothing tragic, in a sense of ending which is both unexplained and inevitable: it asks of us nothing but submission.

The argument in Wagner's letter to Röckel is not unlike the
Marxist view of history, and of man's role in history. Wagnerian
necessity, like Marx's historical necessity, will accomplish its work
in any case, and man's noblest self-fulfilment is to help it. Both
views are remarkable for their circularity, and the relative unimportance which they attribute to willed human action. On this account,
no exertion of the moral will can influence the world: a notion which
may be an extremely crude summary of Marxist thought, but which
is certainly borne out by the grandiose and sad futility of everything
that happens in *The Ring*.

Perhaps the fundamental contradiction of *The Ring* is that it is
driven by a moral will which is finally incompatible with the ending.
We feel that moral will cannot, by definition, issue in nothingness.
It conditions us to expect a *situation* at the end, not a disintegration;
a sense of value, not a sense of emptiness. When the end is
disintegration, all questions fail us because we know that there
cannot be an answer.

Notes

1. *The Birth of Tragedy*, tr. Walter Kaufmann, New York, 1967, pp. 126—7.
2. *The Case of Wagner*, tr. Walter Kaufmann (same volume as *The Birth of Tragedy*), p.160.
3. *ibid.*, p. 163.
4. *ibid.*
5. *Ecce Homo*, tr. Walter Kaufmann, New York, 1969, p. 250.
6. *The Case of Wagner*, p.183.
7. In *Untimely Meditations*, tr. R.J. Hollingdale, Cambridge, 1983, p. 222.
8. *ibid.*, p. 243.
9. *ibid.*, p. 232.
10. *Daybreak: Thoughts on the Prejudices of Morality*, tr. R.J. Hollingdale, Cambridge, 1982, pp. 101—3.
11. *Wagner Rehearsing the 'Ring': An Eye-Witness Account of the Stage Rehearsals of the First Bayreuth Festival*, tr. Robert L. Jacobs, Cambridge, 1983, p. 43.
12. *ibid.*, p. 109.
13. *Siegfried*, p. 49. Quotations from *The Ring* are taken from William Mann's translation, published by the Friends of Covent Garden, London, 1964. Two volumes; but each of the four operas is paginated separately.
14. *The Rhinegold*, p. 30.
15. Baudelaire, *Oeuvres Complètes*, Paris, 1954, p. 1052.
16. *The Rhinegold*, pp. 83—4.
17. *Richard Wagner's Music Dramas* by Carl Dahlhaus, tr. Mary Whittall, Cambridge, 1979, p. 26.
18. Schopenhauer, *WWI*, Vol III p. 306.
19. *Siegfried*, p. 53.
20. *T & I*, p. 87. Quotations from *Tristan* are taken from William Mann's translation, published by the Friends of Covent Garden, London, 1968.
21. Music critics of the time had no doubt about this. The anonymous reviewer of the *Allgemeine Musikalische Zeitung*, Leipzig (July 5, 1865), exclaimed: 'Not to mince words, it is *the glorification of sensual pleasure* tricked out with every titillating device . . . the most ideal of the Muses has been made to grind the colours for indecent plays!' Quoted in *Wagner: A Documentary Study*, ed. Herbert Barth, Dietrich Mack and Egon Voss, tr. P.R.J. Ford and Mary Whittall, London, 1975, p. 208.
22. *Darwin, Marx, Wagner: Critique of a Heritage* by Jacques Barzun, London, 1942, pp. 260—1.
23. *Wagner: A Biography* by Curt von Westernhagen, tr. Mary Whittall, Cambridge, 1978, p. 236.
24. *T & I*, p. 99.
25. In *Essays of Three Decades* by Thomas Mann, tr. H.T. Lowe-Porter, New York, 1971, p. 320.
26. *Opera as Drama* by Joseph Kerman, New York, 1956, pp. 202—3.
27. *T & I*, p. 119.
28. *The Total Work of Art* by Michael Tanner, in *The Wagner Companion*, ed. Peter Burbidge and Richard Sutton, London, 1979, p. 183.
29. In *The Ironic German: A Study of Thomas Mann*, London, 1958, p. 66.
30. *Correspondence of Wagner and Liszt*, tr. Francis Hueffer, London, 1888, Vol.1 p. 257.

31. *Rhinegold*, p. 29.
32. *Valkyrie*, p. 43.
33. *ibid.*, p. 34.
34. *ibid.*, pp. 43—4.
35. *Twilight*, p. 73.
36. *In Search of Wagner*, by Theodor Adorno, tr. Rodney Livingstone, London, 1981, p. 142.
37. *Richard Wagner's Letters to August Röckel*, tr. Eleanor C. Sellar, London, 1897, p. 127.
38. Quoted in Dahlhaus, *op.cit.*, p. 92.
39. *Valkyrie*, p. 40, p. 46.
40. There are other Freudian interpretations of Wagner. In *I Saw the World End* (Oxford, 1979, p. 35) Deryck Cooke considers the idea of Fricka as Wotan's Superego, only to dismiss it briskly. In Bryan Magee's excellent *Aspects of Wagner* (London, 1968, p. 59) there is a suggestive passage about the impact of the music,' . . . the singer's is the voice of the Ego, while the orchestra is the voice of the Id . . .'
41. *Opera and Drama*, Ashton Ellis, *ed. cit.*, Vol II p. 156.
42. *A Communication to My Friends, ibid.*, Vol I p. 274.
43. *Opera and Drama, ibid.*, Vol. II p. 191.
44. *ibid.*, p. 153.
45. *Communication, ibid.*, Vol. I p. 358.
46. *ibid.*, p. 358.
47. *ibid.*, p. 361.
48. *ibid.*, p. 367.
49. *Cosima Wagner's Diaries*, Vol. I p. 322.
50. *Richard Wagner's Letters to Mathilde Wesendonck*, tr. W. Ashton Ellis, London, 1905, p. 144.
51. *Wagner: A Documentary Study*, p. 241.
52. *The Case of Wagner*, p. 184.
53. Tanner, *op. cit.*, in *The Wagner Companion*, p. 206; p. 209.
54. *Wagner Nights*, by Ernest Newman, London, 1949, p. 695.
55. *Revue Wagnérienne*, Paris, 1885, p. 281.
56. *Richard Wagner: Parsifal*, by Lucy Beckett, Cambridge, 1981, p. 146.
57. *Cosima Wagner's Diaries*, Vol. I p. 388.
58. *Twilight*, p. 45.
59. *ibid.*, p. 13.
60. See *A New Metaphor for Mozart's 'Magic Flute'* by Dorothy Koenigsberger, in *European Studies Review*, Vol. 5, No. 3, July 1975, pp. 229—75.
61. *Valkyrie*, p. 72.
62. Adorno, *op. cit.*, p. 154.
63. *Twilight*, p. 92.
64. *Letters of Richard Wagner*, ed. Wilhelm Altmann, tr. M.M. Bozman, London, 1927, Vol I pp. 260—2.
65. *ibid.*, p. 262.
66. *Rhinegold*, p. 77.
67. *ibid.*, p. 78.

IV

NIETZSCHE AND FREUD
The drama of the mind

If we call the main characters of Wagner's *Ring* 'people', then we mean that they are, by definition, 'open' characters. They have a past, we can question them; they are accountable. But if we take them to represent parts of the human mind, then they elude our questioning in a specific and important way. For if we take Wotan, Brünnhilde and Erda to represent certain forces within the mind, then we would have to say that they have no choice of actions in the sense that a dramatic character has: it would be fruitless to ask what other actions they might have taken, and whether their lives and the outcome of the drama might have been different. Such mental or spiritual forces do not have a past: we cannot imagine some previous time when they could have 'decided' how to act, like Pastor Manders or Agamemnon. The Freudian Ego and the Id are always the Ego and the Id: they can make no choices except perhaps between action and inaction. This is why, compared with ordinary dramatic characters, such forces are not accountable: not having a past which might have been different, they lack a cohesive and 'question-able' moral substance. When Freud devised his tripartite model of the mind, he drew up an account of mental and spiritual forces whose moral accountability is limited and sometimes non-existent. When we give *The Ring* a Freudian interpretation, we implicitly acknowledge an inclination in ourselves to read it not so much, or not only, as a story, but rather, or partly, as if it were Wagner's 'picture of the world' which is peopled by these non-accountable forces. And to read a play (or a novel) in this way is to read it as if the work were outside the range of moral accountability. This is one of the most important legacies Freud has left to the modern imagination.

The history of Freudian psychoanalysis is not only the history of a medical and intellectual movement: it is also part of the history of the modern mind and its relation to morality. It is an uneasy and changing relationship. Freud's early psychological writings are not those of a moralist: they form a strenuous attempt to establish a science of the mind resting on the unshakeable foundations of biology. The unfinished work known to us as *A Project for a Scientific Psychology* was written in just over a fortnight in 1895, when Freud was thirty-nine, and reluctantly abandoned a year later. In this extremely difficult book, written in a language of severe condensation, Freud attempted to chart the workings of the mind, using neurobiology as his compass. A year afterwards he was still writing to his friend Wilhelm Fliess:

> Anxiety, chemical factors, etc. − perhaps you may supply me with solid ground on which I shall be able to give up explaining things psychologically and start finding a firm basis in physiology![1]

A few months later Freud described to Fliess the functioning of perception on a biological and genetic basis, echoes of which can still be heard in his writings thirty years later. He never quite gave up hope that psychology, chemistry and physics might, one day, link hands.

Wilhelm Fliess (1858−1928) was two years younger than Freud: a nose and throat specialist with a flourishing practice in Berlin. He was interested in biology, and in certain areas, some distinctly unorthodox, of psychology. At the time of their correspondence Freud was a neurologist with a respectable scientific record, including work on the nervous system of lower animals and the cerebral paralysis of children. To him, Fliess was a fellow conspirator, a source of inspiration and an intellectual and emotional safety valve: his 284 letters and notes to Fliess (he did not preserve Fliess's letters to him) are a unique record of work in progress.

In 1895, while this correspondence was still going on, Freud, jointly with the Viennese psychiatrist Josef Breuer, published *Studies in Hysteria*, in which they explored the cure of hysteria by the 'cathartic' method, that is, by tracing hysterical symptoms to their hidden source in a traumatic event in the patient's past. Freud also began to publish his own papers on hysteria and anxiety neuroses, and within a few months he began his famous self-analysis. In the following year he started writing *The Interpretation of Dreams*. Psychoanalysis was about to be born.

The correspondence with Fliess probably began at the end of 1892, and continued until May 1897, when Freud broke off the friendship. It is a correspondence of huge importance. Along with his letters, Freud also despatched to Fliess a series of fourteen Drafts. Some of these came to form the basis of important early papers; some were elaborated in the *Project*; all of them were outlines and speculations in which the principal ideas of psychoanalysis can be clearly recognised. Reading these Drafts, we sense that Freud was to spend his scientific life unrolling a complex bundle of ideas which he had outlined, or at least vaguely apprehended, in his early forties; and that, in a sense, like Schopenhauer, he wrote but one vast book. As Thomas Mann said of Schopenhauer's work, 'everywhere you open it it is all there.'

The Drafts are brief, schematic and highly concentrated attempts at understanding the workings of the human mind, and they were clearly written by a man who was trying to hold an uneasy alliance with both biology and psychology. Sexuality, for example, is treated with clinical precision, in terms of the somatic effects of practice, abstinence or exhaustion; and Freud begins to outline his theories of repression and the constancy of psychic energy within the mind. Meanwhile, his letters to Fliess are bursting with what appear to be very different speculations.

> In paranoia, compare the combination of megalomania with the creation of myths about the child's true parentage ...

> ... Can you imagine what 'endopsychic myths' are? They are the latest products of my mental labour. The dim inner perception of one's own psychical apparatus stimulates illusions, which are naturally projected outwards, and characteristically into the future and a world beyond. Immortality, retribution, the world after death, are all reflections of our inner psyche ... psycho-mythology.[2]

Shortly before he broke with Fliess, Freud sent off to him one of his most important letters. It includes a brief analysis of one of Freud's own dreams, and concludes with the words: 'The dream of course fulfils my wish to pin down a father as the originator of neurosis.' This is the earliest allusion in Freud's writings to what came to be known as the Oedipus complex. In the same letter, we read the following:

> Another presentiment tells me, as if I knew already — though I do not know anything at all — that *I am about to discover the source of morality* (my italics).[3]

The remark is casual, arrogant and profound. It is the sort of thing that justifies Freud when he describes himself as

> by temperament a *conquistador* — an adventurer if you want to translate the word — with the curiosity, the boldness and the tenacity that belong to that type of being.[4]

The tone and the scope of Freud's intention reminds one of the words with which Wagner had introduced the libretto of *The Ring* to Liszt: 'Consider well my poem: it contains the beginning and the end of the world.' For, like Schopenhauer, both Wagner and Freud set out, in their different ways, to encompass and apprehend the totality of existence. Freud began with neurological investigations into the nature of perception; but he soon found himself working towards a model of the human mind that would explain all the mental and spiritual activities in man's life. Freud always insisted that psychoanalysis was not a 'system', but it would be wrong to accept this disclaimer. The term 'metapsychology' was invented by Freud himself and used, in correspondence, as early as 1896; and when he came to define its scope nearly twenty years later, its all-inclusive nature was quite clear. Indeed, like all systems, psychoanalysis has its indispensable basic principles. Grasp these, and we have a key to the understanding of human life; reject them, and we undermine the whole edifice. Freud tolerated some developments and refinements of his theories; but on basic principles he did not give an inch. One assented to these, and one was free within the system; or one dissented and was cast out. Psychoanalysis is a system as rigid as Schopenhauer's, with the added refinement of a discipline binding together its practitioners. When, in old age, Freud acknowledged the kinship (he went no further) between psychoanalysis and Schopenhauerian philosophy, he pointed out that Schopenhauer had not only asserted 'the dominance of the emotions and the supreme importance of sexuality', but he had also been 'aware of the mechanism of repression'[5]. Those are also the indispensable cornerstones of psychoanalysis.

It will be said, and rightly, that Freud's thought does not encompass the totality of human existence, not even of mental life. Indeed, during Freud's own lifetime the work of Jung and Adler became both an extension and a critique of the original gospel. But the intention, as we have seen, was there; and the scope of Freud's thought is still remarkable. It may be held to explain the nature of conscious and unconscious thought; the mental processes of childhood; the nature of love and sexuality; the functioning of family life and of certain social organisations; the mechanics of artistic creativity; the anatomy of dreams, fear, pleasure and memory; and the terror, as well as the strange attraction, of death.

When Freud said that he was about to discover the source of morality, he made a claim which he nearly came to fulfill. He would certainly have agreed that morality was based on the principle of cause and effect. We can see this from the way he describes what he saw as the origin of human society. Freud sees the beginnings of society in a Darwinian primal horde, ruled by 'a violent and jealous father who keeps all the females for himself and drives away his sons as they grow up'. One day, Freud surmises, these brothers killed their father, and, 'cannibal savages as they were', devoured him. The act of eating him is thereafter re-enacted in a primitive totemic meal, of which the Christian communion is clearly a version: a shared ritual in which the sons find an identity with the father they had killed, and which imparts to them a portion of his strength. It is both an act of repentance and a commemoration of a glorious crime: and it becomes the basis 'of social organisation, of moral restrictions and of religion'[6]. The effect follows ineluctably on the cause:

> Society was now based on complicity in the common crime; religion was based on the same guilt and the remorse attaching to it; while morality was based partly on the exigencies of this society and partly on the penance demanded by the sense of guilt.[7]

This anthropological account of the origin of society is matched by a psychological account of the development and structure of the human mind. Here, the seat of morality is called the Superego, and its origin is similar to that of religion. For the herd-man, guilt came about because he had killed his father out of sexual jealousy, and replaced his oppressive authority with the pressure of guilt. Freud believes that our minds repeat this process: the Ego, the seat of our consciousness, needs to restrain the power of our instincts, embodied in a force which Freud calls the Id. To this end, the Ego develops an extension called ego ideal, or Superego, which becomes the agent of moral authority within the mind. The Superego is the source of what we call conscience; it arbitrates between the Ego and the instincts; it represents within us the things we associate with the higher nature of man; and it exercises the restraining, moral, and sometimes cruelly oppressive functions of the primal father, the ruler of the horde. In other words, the origin of conscience and morality is a form of inner intimidation. Nietzsche pre-figured this process when he wrote in one of his early books:

> Compulsion precedes morality; indeed morality itself is compulsion for a time, to which one submits for the avoidance of pain.[8]

The process which Freud describes calls for two observations. First, it is something that is being eternally repeated: each human mind, Freud tells us, re-enacts the distant, prehistoric event described in his anthropological speculations. Every man, we are told, will arrive where all other men had arrived before him. In this sense, the life of the mind includes an eternal recurrence of the past. Secondly, the purpose of this process is the restoration of balance. Just as the horde had got rid of the father and replaced it by shared guilt, the mind, too, will replace its inherited, subconscious subjugation to the primal father by setting up, within itself, an agency of conscience and values. The instincts will, once again, be under control — or at least under surveillance.

This does not mean that Freud found the sources of morality: he merely described the mechanism of its emergence. Freud's model of the mind contains a genealogy of conscience, but it admits defeat before its final causes. Conscience as we understand it, that is to say, the capacity to have a sense of our own wrongdoing, is shown to be the product of our Superego. But the Superego, Freud tells us elsewhere, comes into being to placate and control the deep-seated and turbulent guilt-feelings of our Id — the Id which is, as we shall see, the darkest area of our unconscious mind. It is as if a criminal were to ask that a guardian or judge be set over him, to prevent him from, or to punish him for, a crime he may or may not have committed. But, we ask, how does one know oneself to be a criminal before there are laws? Freud's answer to this holds the key to the moral ambiguity of psychoanalytical thought. Laws, he believes, are created by our guilt-feeling over a prehistoric and subconsciously remembered deed. Freudian man feels guilt before he feels consciousness. Indeed, Freud tells us,

> whether one has killed one's father or has abstained from doing so is not really the decisive thing. One is bound to feel guilty in either case, for the sense of guilt is the expression of the conflict due to ambivalence, of the eternal struggle between Eros and the instinct of destruction or death.[9]

Thus, for Freud, guilt is both relative and absolute. It is relative because it concerns a deed that may or may not have been committed; it is absolute in that it is part of the unconscious heritage of all men who had parents. In this respect psychoanalysis is like Christianity: it holds that human nature is contaminated by a deed committed in the prehistoric past. At one point Freud calls this guilt feeling a 'moral' factor: his quotation marks indicate ambiguity, or unease, or both[10]. The fact is that the moral significance of the Freudian guilt-feeling is obscure: he is merely explaining its force and effect by comparing it to what we now call morality. According to Freud, the more aggressive our Superego is, the more intense our sense of guilt will be. Conversely, the more aggressive our instincts are, and the stronger our guilt feelings, the more autocratic our Superego becomes. Mental energy responds to mental energy. The mind is a circular world. Guilt is simply a form of displaced energy: to call it guilt is to use a metaphor.

But, then, Freud had not set out to be a moralist. He may have set out to find the source of morality; but there is a difference between writing *about* moral values, and writing in order to convey and implant them. Freudian psychoanalysis is essentially a study of energies. One of its central tenets is what is known as the principle of constancy: an idea Freud assimilated from the biologist Gustav Fechner, and defined as 'the tendency to keep intracerebral excitation constant'[11]. Every need that arises in the mind takes the form of a tension and has to be relieved. When such psychic energy is blocked or misdirected, it results in a neurotic symptom; this symptom is 'a substitute for forbidden satisfactions'[12]. One of the vital tasks of the mind, Freud believed, was to avoid such a blockage, which he called unpleasure. 'Everything,' he writes, 'is harmful that hinders the occurrence of satisfaction.'[13]

At the core of Freudian psychoanalysis is the recognition that there is an implacable force within the human mind which exists only to be satisfied and appeased. All the mind's efforts at holding itself in balance spring from the energy latent in this force. This is the Id, the most inaccessible part of the mind, and Freud's most famous description of it deserves to be quoted at length. The Id, Freud says, is

> the dark, inaccessible part of our personality; what little we know of it we have learnt from our study of the dream-work and of the construction of neurotic symptoms, and most of that is of a negative character and can be described only as a contrast to the ego. We approach the Id with analogies: we call it a chaos, a cauldron full of seething excitations. We picture it as being open at its end to somatic influences, and as there taking up into itself instinctual needs which find their psychical expression in it, but we cannot say in what substratum. It is filled with energy reaching it from the instincts, but it has no organisation, produces no collective will, but only a striving to bring about the satisfaction of the instinctual needs subject to the observance of the pleasure principle. The logical laws of thought do not apply in the Id, and this is true above all of the law of contradiction. Contrary impulses exist side by side, without cancelling each other out or diminishing each other: at the most they may converge to form compromises under the dominating economic pressure towards the discharge of energy. There is nothing in the Id that could be compared with negation; and we perceive with surprise an exception to the philosophical theorem that space and time are necessary forms of our mental acts. There is nothing in the Id that corresponds to the idea of time; there is no recognition of the passage of time, and ... no alteration in its mental processes is produced by the passage of time. Wishful impulses which have never passed beyond the Id, but impressions, too, which have been sunk into the Id by repression, are virtually immortal; after the passage of decades they behave as though they have just occurred. ... The Id ... knows no judgement of value: no good and evil, no morality. The economic, or, if you prefer, the quantitative factor, which is intimately linked to the pleasure principle, dominates all its processes. Instincts seeking to discharge their energies — that, in our view, is all there is in the Id.[14]

One of the main tasks of psychoanalysis is to keep this force, so like the unknowable and amoral Will of Schopenhauer, under control. This is both a moral and an amoral enterprise. When Freud said that he was hoping to find the sources of morality, he was speaking as a biologist: he sought to identify the physical origins of moral behaviour. Instead, he succeeded in creating a descriptive theory of the instincts. Freud described instincts as being 'on the frontier between the mental and the somatic', and he admitted that

> instincts and their transformations are at the limit of what is discernible by psychoanalysis. From that point it gives place to biological research.[15]

> The theory of instincts is our mythology. Instincts are mythical entities, magnificent in their indefiniteness.[16]

> Every attempt to discover a localisation of mental processes, every endeavour to think of ideas as stored up in nerve-cells and of excitations as travelling along nerve-fibres, has miscarried completely.[17]

And so the cauldron-like thing, seething with instinctual impulses, which Freud calls the Id, is found to be unknowable. Therefore Freud's remark, that 'everything is harmful that hinders the occurrence of satisfaction', has both a moral and an amoral significance. It is a clinical statement, entirely amoral in its precision, which recognises the harm that can be done to man by damming up his instinctual forces: but it also has a moral motivation, because that very recognition implies an intention to restore the mind's mental balance, the intention to heal. Morality is thus a compromise, just as illness is a compromise. 'Ethics,' Freud writes, 'is a limitation of instinct.'[18] (Nietzsche had put the same idea in different words when he wrote in his notebooks about 'the grand economy which cannot do without evil.'[19])

To sum up: in the Freudian history of the mind, the Ego comes into being first, under the pressures and influence of the external world. It is to be a controlling agency which must save the Id from the consequences of its unruly, amoral impulses. Meanwhile, the Ego also develops the Superego, whose task is to appease, or to punish, the guilt-feelings of the Id. It is in this sense that the Superego introduces morality into the mind: it both placates and rules the troubled Id. But we must bear in mind that the Superego is also, in another sense, a *representative* of the Id: the Superego was born, we recall, partly in response to the Id's predicament, and appears to have more in common with the Id than the Ego has. To elaborate our earlier legal analogy, it is as if the Ego were a prosecutor, and the Id, like an anxious criminal, confronted him with the assistance of a sympathetic but stern defence connsel. Or, to put it differently, it is as if Wagner's Wotan has to listen both to the pleadings of Brünnhilde, in the name of a dangerous and unruly instinct (love), as well as hear the stern commands of Erda, in the name of moral law.

And so the Freudian mind appears to be a circular thing: a closed system which is designed to deal as efficiently as possible with disturbances both from without and from within. Its elements are both partners and embattled opponents. Such a mind is healthy when it is at peace: when the partners are co-operating, and the opposing forces are reconciled because they are equal. The ideal Freudian mind is in a state of stasis.

Psychoanalysis is, in one sense, a deeply moral science, both in its purpose and in its method. It is moral because all healing is moral. Medicine, both private and public, has become a commercial transaction: a fact which has obscured for us the essential morality of the Hippocratic oath. The act of healing is inherently moral because it is a benevolent act in itself, and also because it helps the sick or the injured to function within a healthy community. Yet, in relation to the whole bulk of Freud's writing, it is remarkable how little he has to say about this aspect of psychoanalysis. His earliest writings are almost entirely clinical in tone as well as in content. 'What,' he asks, for example, '... does normal repression furnish us with?' The answer is:

> Something which, free, can lead to anxiety, if psychically bound, to rejection − that is to say the affective basis for a multitude of intellectual processes of development, such as morality, shame, etc.[20]

This is the language of the Project: cool, technical, thoughtful and a trifle obscure, written with the detached expertise of someone performing a dissection. But as Freud's early researches progressed, they were leading him towards the problem of sexuality: a subject over which he was to become increasingly belligerent. In later life, Freud may have exaggerated the resistance his ideas had met with:

certainly the work of Richard von Krafft-Ebing (1840–1903), to mention only the best-known psychiatrist of the time, was already quite well known, so that Freud's early writings may not have caused as much hostility as he has led us to believe. But the fact is that he himself felt beleaguered; and this may well have been the reason for the increasingly moralistic tone of his work in the late nineties. During this period, when Freud was still striving to link psychoanalysis to biology and neurology, and when his style in general was abstract and technical, his opinions were gradually taking on a powerful and explicit moral force. In later years, as he came reluctantly to admit that psychology ended exactly where biology began, his moral fervour began to abate. Faced with the inexplicable, amoral force of the instincts, Freud's moralising urge lost much of its intensity.

But this is as yet some time away. In an early paper called *Sexuality and the Aetiology of Neuroses* (1898), Freud notes sternly that the increasing occurrence of neurasthenia as well as the psychological problems of sexuality had their origins in the state of modern civilisation:

> it would be one of the greatest triumphs of humanity, one of the most tangible liberations from the constraints of nature to which mankind is subject, if we could succeed in raising the responsible act of procreating children to the level of a deliberate and intentional activity and in freeing it from its entanglement with the necessary satisfaction of a natural need.[21]

As Freud goes on, his tone takes on the intensity of an evangelist.

> It is positively a matter of public interest that *men should enter* upon sexual relations with full potency ... we may with justice regard civilisation ... as responsible for the spread of neurasthenia. Much would have to be changed ... The resistance of generations of physicians who can no longer remember their own youth must be broken down; the pride of fathers who are unwilling to descend to the level of humanity in their children's eyes, must be overcome; and the unreasonable prudery of mothers must be combatted. ... our civilisation will have to learn to come to terms with the claims of our sexuality.[22]

When Freud wrote about the lack of sexual education among children, his tone became militant: he spoke of the impossibility of carrying out an isolated reform without altering the foundations of the whole system.[23]

And, in *'Civilised' Sexual Morality and Modern Nervous Illness* (1908; note Freud's quotation marks in the title), we read:

> Since normal intercourse has been so relentlessly persecuted by morality ... what are known as the perverse forms of intercourse ... in which other parts of the body take over the role of the genitals, have undoubtedly increased in social importance ... They are ethically objectionable, for they degrade the relationship of love between two human beings from a serious matter to a convenient game, attended by no risk and no spiritual participation.[24]

All this is a long way from saying that 'everything is harmful that hinders the occurrence of satisfaction.' Here lies one of the fundamental dilemmas of psychoanalysis. Freud was dealing with illness, which is not in itself a moral event; but the origins of the type of illness he was concerned with lay, for him, in the earliest moral encounter in people's lives, namely, in their ambiguous relationships with their parents. At the root of all neurotic illness there was, in Freud's view, a desire to kill. Admittedly, this desire had always been unconscious; but it is also one of the basic principles of psychoanalysis that the unconscious is part of our personality. We are responsible for our unconscious desires; and that ought to mean that any man who unconsciously desired, at the age of two, to destroy his father and possess his mother will carry a measure of responsibility for these desires through adult life. Freudian psychoanalysis is permeated through and through with the ambiguity and unease that follows from such a proposition, and Freud was well aware of this. He briefly discusses 'the ethical significance of suppressed wishes' at the end of *The Interpretation of Dreams*, but only to evade it. He thinks it best 'to acquit dreams' of the wickedness which is sometimes expressed in them; but he professes to be unable to say whether 'we are to attribute *reality* to unconscious wishes'. And yet, he goes on,

> there seems to be no justification for people's reluctance in accepting responsibility for the immorality of their dreams.

So, are we, or are we not, responsible? Freud leaves us with the caustic remark that

It is in any case instructive to get to know the much trampled soil from which our virtues proudly spring.[25]

But who had trampled the soil? What is the moral worth of a person? Where does judgement come in? The older Freud does occasionally use words like 'disgusting' about, for example, child-molesters, which is hardly a sign of excessive moral severity. But in general he is reluctant to attach moral valuations to psychological events. He accepts the elementary nature of impulses, and their tendency to aim at the satisfaction of primal needs. But, he tells us,

> These impulses in themselves are neither good nor bad. We classify them and their expressions in that way according to the needs and demands of the human community.[26]

'Good' and 'bad' are merely labels:

> the behaviour of human beings show differences, which ethics, disregarding the fact that such differences are determined, classifies as 'good' or 'bad'.[27]

These are Freud's clearest statements of moral relativity, and they show to what extent he really remained a biologist all his life. Freud had never quite lost sight of the human creature as a functioning or malfunctioning machine, which could not be held responsible, or be condemned, for cracking under too much pressure.

Psychoanalysis is also a moral activity because it is causal. Its method is logical: it treats symptoms as effects behind which the persistent questioner will eventually find the cause. Psychoanalytic practice is one of the clearest demonstrations of the essential kinship between morality and causation. It is based on the assumption that the sick mind has something to hide, and that the symptom is the lie to cover it up. Psychoanalysis moves in, like Gregers Werle in *The Wild Duck*, to find the cause of the lie and to force the mind to live without it. When Sartre says that 'psychoanalysis substitutes for the notion of bad faith, the idea of a lie without a liar',[28] he in one sense misses the point. The mind does in fact act in bad faith: for the mind includes its own liar, and the lie becomes essential for it to survive, albeit in a crippled and dishonest state. The rationalist in Sartre could not accept that the mind might be split, and that it is possible for one part of it not to know, or to be afraid to know, what the other part is or does. The Freudian analyst works in the hope that, unlike the Ekdal family in Ibsen's play, which disintegrated under the impact of Gregers's disclosures, the mind will be strong enough to survive, once its protective lie has been removed and its balance has been restored.

But even here, Freud has reservations, and they turn out to be of a moral nature. Sometimes, he admits, 'neurosis is the most harmless and socially tolerable situation' for someone who is burdened with 'real, irremovable suffering'. And he goes on:

> If we may say, then, that whenever a neurotic is faced by a conflict he takes 'flight into illness', yet we must allow that in some cases that flight is fully justified and a physician who has recognised how the situation lies will silently and solicitously withdraw. [29]

It is, Freud admits,

> a debatable point whether a certain degree of cultural hypocrisy is not indispensable for the maintenance of civilisation, because the susceptibility to culture which has hitherto been organised in the minds of present-day men would perhaps not prove sufficient for the task. [30]

This is the nearest Freud comes to Nietzsche's belief that morality, and consequently men's very existence, are based on compromise, indeed strictly speaking on error, and that truth, for most of us, might be too much to bear. Freud's moral reservations tell us that he remained undecided about the role of morality in the life of the mind; that there were occasions when the lie of illness seemed more tolerable to him than the reality brought about by the cure. Freud believed profoundly in the value of truth, in a very specific way. He held that

> Psychoanalytic treatment is based on truthfulness. In this fact lies a great part of its educative effect and its ethical value. [31]

At the same time, he remained sceptical about the worth of that ethical value.

> Whenever we go to sleep, we throw off our hard-won morality like a garment, and put it on again the next morning. [32]

If this is so, is it the sleeping or the waking man who is a suitable case for judgement? Freudian psychoanalysis does not tell us what right we have, if any, to praise or condemn, nor how we are to determine the moral worth, if any, of human actions. The very use of moral terms is questionable, and not only because Freud himself has told us that our impulses are, in themselves, neither good nor bad. In one of his papers he describes how the strange distortions of the events in our dreams are the work of our own unconscious, which performs them in order to protect our peace of mind while we sleep. This activity of our unconscious derives, Freud tells us,

> from an internal conflict, *a kind of* inner dishonesty (my italics).[33]

Whenever Freud, who is remarkable for the crispness and clarity of his writing, uses a phrase like 'a kind of', it is well to be watchful. *Dishonesty* is a moral term, but Freud does not use it in a straightforward moral sense. He uses it as a metaphor with moral connotations, but to describe an essentially amoral process.

Metaphor is an imaginative device which presents one thing but also implies another. In the previous chapter we found this to be a characteristic quality of Wagnerian drama: we saw that we could regard the mature operas as vast dramatic metaphors, with an outer action telling us one thing and the inner action something quite different. Morality in Freudian psychoanalysis has a quality similar to the Wagnerian narrative. The healing process is a moral action, but at bottom it is involved in the recognition, the acceptance, and the adjustment of amoral forces. Freud's use of the word *moral* or *ethical* increasingly comes to acquire a metaphorical significance. Just as the sleeping man's 'dishonesty' was a metaphor for the functioning of his mental defences in order to help him sleep, *moral* is a metaphor for the way we accept the guidance of certain words signifying values in order that they should help us to live with other men.

Bruno Bettelheim has written about how,

> Because of repression and the influence of censorship, the unconscious reveals itself in symbols or metaphors.[34]

This leads us on to say that a metaphor is also a kind of compromise. When Freud speaks of 'a kind of inner dishonesty', he brings into focus an essentially amoral act (the evasive action of an unconscious mind) by explaining it through the use of a moral term. But when he does so, he also compromises: the action he has described takes on a quasi-moral significance from the word he used to describe it. This sense of compromise expressed in metaphorical discourse pervades the whole of psychoanalysis and is part of its method and purpose. Freud once defined his task as

> putting at the disposal of [the patient's] ego those energies which, owing to repression, are inaccessibly confined in his unconscious, as well as those which his ego is obliged to squander in the fruitless task of maintaining these repressions. *Such activity as this is pastoral work in the best sense of the word* (my italics).[35]

That defines the aim of psychoanalysis as a strenuous moral attempt to recognise, and to redress, an amoral imbalance in the mind.[36]

Morality is not the only metaphor in psychoanalysis. It sees the human condition largely in terms of such metaphors – which are also compromises. A neurotic symptom is one such metaphor. The paralysed arm of a girl actually represents her remorse over having been, as she believes, a negligent nurse at her father's sickbed. She regards herself as worthless, but, we might say that instead of following this self-judgement to its logical conclusion and doing away with herself, she compromises by having a paralysed arm which thus becomes a metaphor of what she has done and what she, in her own view, deserves. Freud himself translated all this into the language of anthropology when he said that

> the obsessional act is *ostensibly* a protection against the prohibited act; but *actually* ... it is a representation of it.[37]

The phenomenon called transference also presents itself as one thing, but is in fact another: the patient treats the analyst as if he were a father or a lover, and what appears to be his intense love or hate for him is merely a stage in understanding the real nature of his own loves and hates. Thus transference is metaphor in action. Free association seems to be a release of random thoughts; in reality it is a coded language which the analyst will decipher to find the disguised story of the illness, often in the face of the patient's resistance and disbelief. That same resistance appears to be a denial of unacceptable facts; in reality it is the patient's insidious way of hanging on to the metaphor of his illness. Sublimation is also a form of metaphor in action: in psychoanalytic terms, artistic creation, for example, is merely one way of releasing pent-up energies. (One of

Nietzsche's notes states brusquely: 'Making music is another way of making children; chastity is merely the economy of the artist.'[38] One wonders what he would have thought if he could have read Valéry's summing-up of him as a case of 'creative syphilis'.)[39]

Dreams are metaphors that are within most people's experience: conscise representations of diffuse, unconscious thoughts, conscious or unconscious wishes, but almost always of something other than what they appear. The extraordinary dreams and hallucinations of Freud's patients, the Wolf Man and the Rat Man, are compromises, expressed in pictures, between the torment of their unconscious experience and their deep-seated need to forget about it. To analyse these metaphors is to identify the forces that made them, and to uncover the real statement which the mind is making through them. Steven Marcus has recently shown how, in Freud's account of the mind,

> a coherent story is in some manner connected with mental health ... (and that) inversely, illness amounts at least in part to suffering from an incoherent story or an inadequate narrative account of oneself.[40]

Few things written about Freud are so crucial to the subject of this book. Marcus suggests the profound connection between causality and open art, and explains why our imagination needs to re-orient itself when we sense that we do not 'understand' someone's 'story'. The sick mind is like a 'closed' play: it is not telling us a story. On the contrary, its purpose is to hide from us what had really happened, and to mislead us with a metaphor. Similarly, if we think of the characters in *Waiting for Godot* as amnesiacs, it is because Beckett's play, with its incompleteness and its contradictions, makes us think that they are giving an inadequate account of themselves.

The most difficult of the metaphors of psychoanalysis is to be found in one of Freud's most controversial essays, *Beyond the Pleasure Principle* (1920). Quite clearly the little boy whom Freud describes here is doing something much more significant than just throwing a piece of wood out of his cot and pulling it back again with his string. This dotty action 'stands for' something; but what? Before Freud explains he reminds us of something we are already familiar with, namely that

> the mental apparatus endeavours to keep the quantity of excitation present in it as low as possible or at least to keep it constant.[41]

This is, once again, the principle of constancy: it means, as we have seen, that the mind strives always to be at peace. It is also at the basis of the pleasure principle: for the mind strives for a state in which nothing disturbs its satisfaction. Now the little boy in Freud's book liked to throw his piece of wood out of his cot and then pull it back again; but what he liked doing most was simply picking up small objects and throwing them away.

> As he did this, he gave vent to a loud, long-drawn-out 'o-o-o-o', accompanied by an expression of interest and satisfaction. [42]

Watching this, Freud realised that this

> was a game and that the only use he made of any of his toys was to play 'gone' with them. [43]

Here, in this innocent but compulsive little ritual, was something that seemed to go beyond the pleasure principle: this action, Freud surmised, represented something that was independent of it and also more primitive. Here Freud identified the source of what he came to call the death instinct:

> *an urge inherent in organic life to restore an earlier state of things ...*
>
> the expression of inertia inherent in organic life. [44]

This famous essay is important because it subordinates the pleasure principle, with its clear logic of cause and effect, demand and satisfaction, to something much more elusive. The pleasure principle, it turns out, is but a servant of another function within us, whose business is not merely to keep our mind in a state of static satisfaction, but to still entirely and forever the turmoil of the spirit. And Freud concludes that this mysterious function, to which the all-important pleasure principle is subordinate, is

> concerned with the most universal endeavour of all living substance — namely to return to the quiescence of the inorganic world. [45]

With the formulation of the death instinct Freud gave his thought an element of finality which justifies us in calling it his picture of the world. With this idea as their backdrop, Freud's writings begin to appear as if they were not only a description of the world, but also a summing up of his personal feelings about it. Behind his account of the formation and functioning of the mind, an account which is

causal, sequential, and open to our questioning, he reveals a preoc-
cupation with an instinctual drive which, he claims, determines the
entire pattern of human life, and which is beyond inquiry. Lionel
Trilling recognises this when he writes that

> even if we reject the theory [of the death instinct] as not fitting
> the facts in any operatively useful way, we still cannot miss its
> grandeur, its ultimate tragic courage in acquiescence to fate.[46]

Of course Freud's argument can be questioned, and it has been:
most specifically on the grounds that he appears to equate the
compulsion to repeat with the death instinct. The former, it is said,
is in the service of satisfaction, and depends on our notion of time;
the latter appears to deny the satisfaction of recognisable human
needs, and has a sense of finality to which the notion of time is
irrelevant. The very basic nature of such a challenge underlines the
unquestion-able nature of Freud's insight: we can see that we
submit to his vision despite the strictures of logic.

Years later, Freud warned that he should not be understood as
saying that 'death is the only aim of life'; there was, he said, 'life as
well as death. We recognise two basic instincts and give each of them
its own aim.'[47] But this sober warning cannot redress the balance;
Freud cannot obliterate the picture he had called up, of living things
gravitating purposefully towards their end. In retrospect, this is the
background against which his drama of man's mental and spiritual
life is played out. When Freud says that instincts of self-
preservation and mastery are merely

> component instincts whose function it is to assure us that the
> organism shall follow its own path to death, [48]

he describes a pattern of existence which moves, against the logical
demands and needs of instinctual life, inevitably, wilfully even,
towards a negation and extinction of itself.

Freud was notoriously reticent about authors who influenced him;
but he himself noted that the recognition of the death instinct had
'unwittingly' steered his course 'into the harbour of Schopenhauer's
philosophy'[49]. And when he describes how the germ-cells of the
body

> work against the death of the living substance and succeed in
> winning for it what we can only regard as potential immortal-
> ity, though that may mean no more than a lengthening of the
> road to death,[50]

it is impossible not to recall Schopenhauer's picture of the world striving everlastingly, but ultimately only for dissolution into nothingness. Nor is it fanciful to recall how the world of Wagner's *Ring* comes to an end, with all its warring forces destroyed or self-destroyed, and how the moral tensions of the drama dissolve in the placid serenity and stasis of a primeval world. Seeing it in this context, we can say that Freud, too, created a closed world: for there is nothing so closed, nothing placed so completely beyond our questioning, as something that has ceased to live and has dissolved itself for ever.

What the little boy in *Beyond the Pleasure Principle* liked to do most was, as we saw, to throw things away into corners and under beds: to play 'gone' with them. Another thing he liked to do, Freud observed, though not quite so much, was to have a wooden reel with a piece of string tied round it. He threw the reel into his curtained cot so that it disappeared from view, uttered his usual cry of satisfaction,

> then pulled the reel out of the cot again by the string and hailed its reappearance with a joyful '*da*' (there). This, then, was the complete game — disappearance and return.[51]

The little boy, it seems, wanted to deprive himself of his wooden reel in order to repeat the experience of possessing it. He was demonstrating, in his simple way, what Freud called the compulsion to repeat. This compulsion, Freud tells us, 'expresses the *conservative nature* of the instincts'[52]: we want to re-experience events that have happened before. It is this compulsion that lies behind the death instinct: for all living, organic things are driven to return to where they had been before — the condition of dead, inorganic matter.

But to Freud the psychoanalyst the compulsion to repeat was important also because of what it told him about the behaviour of the mind. Children, he explained, repeated unpleasant experiences because they could

> master a powerful impression far more thoroughly by being active than they could by merely experiencing it passively. Each fresh repetition seems to strengthen *the mastery* they are in search of (my italics).[53]

This same mastery is the purpose of dreams in adults who suffer from traumatic neuroses. Traumatic dreams are not the same as anxiety dreams. In the latter, the dreamer provides his own punishment for his forbidden unconscious wishes. For example, when we dream that someone we love is dead, it means, according to Freud, that in our unconscious thoughts we really do wish them dead, and the pain and anxiety we feel when we dream this is our self-inflicted punishment for those thoughts. Traumatic neurosis, by contrast, means that something terrible had actually happened to the patient; and this event appears to him in dreams or hallucinations because, unconsciously, he wants to heal himself through repetition. The mind repeats the traumatic event because it hopes that repetition will help it to master the thing that tortures it. What this tells us is that mental and spiritual healing consists, in part, in resurrecting the past, so that it exists alongside the present. In a healthy mind,

> the mental past ... unlike the historic past, is not absorbed by its derivations; it persists ... alongside what has proceeded from it.[54]

On this reading, the mind has a longing to possess that which is past, in order to master it, in order not to be tormented by it. Our unconscious is beyond the computations of time because it holds its past within itself. In this sense, the Freudian mind exists in a timeless permanence.

Freud's arguments in *Beyond the Pleasure Principle* might be read as a psychoanalytical commentary on Nietzsche. The philosopher is not mentioned by name. Freud was, as we have seen, not usually forthcoming about people who might have influenced his thought; and references to both Schopenhauer and Nietzsche in his writings are few in number and oblique in tone. As far as Nietzsche is concerned, Freud was well into his thirties when the philosopher's writings began to be at all widely known. Knowing, as we do, how much Nietzsche's ideas were 'in the air' at this time, it is hard to imagine that Freud did not have a fairly clear awareness of them. On the other hand, we have also seen to what extent Freud's ideas had already been formed during his early years in psychiatry; and we may assume that Nietzsche's influence on him was not formative and essential as was, for example, that of Darwin. In any case, my concern here, and throughout this book, is not to demonstrate influences, nor to trace who had read whom and when, but to look at similarities of thought and vision, which, taken together, might trace a pattern and tell us something about the modern mind, and how it responded to literature and art.

Nietzsche interests us at this point because one of his theories, that of the eternal recurrence of all things, exemplifies one of Freud's theories. Nietzsche first announced the idea in *The Gay Science* (1882).

> What if some day or night a demon were to steal after you into your loneliest loneliness and say to you: 'This life as you now live it and have lived it, you will have to live once more and innumerable times more; and there will be nothing new in it, but every pain and every joy and every thought and sigh and everything unutterably small or great in your life will have to return to you, all in the same succession and sequence — even this spider and this moonlight between the trees, and even this moment and I myself. The eternal hourglass of existence is turned upside down again and again, and you with it, speck of dust!'
>
> Would you not throw yourself down and gnash your teeth and curse the demon who spoke thus? Or have you once experienced a tremendous moment when you would have answered him: 'You are a god and never have I heard anything more divine.' If this thought gained possession of you, it would change you as you are or perhaps crush you. The question in each and every thing, 'Do you desire this once more and innumerable times more?' would lie upon your actions as the greatest weight. Or how well disposed would you have to become to yourself and to life *to crave nothing more frequently* than this ultimate eternal confirmation and seal?[55]

Nietzsche's tone is lyrical, excited, and anxious to the point of torment: we sense that the excitement might be a cover, or perhaps a compensation, for the anxiety. It is the openness to such observations that makes Nietzsche's writings both accessible and engrossing. It has been called into question whether he was, technically speaking, a philosopher at all; but most of what he wrote, whether it is philosophy or not, has a sense of fierce personal commitment and intellectual availability: we can approach him with the same inquiring attitude, the same awareness of conscious and unconscious intention behind the actual utterance, as we bring to literature. And it is this same sense of personal commitment that will call forth from

Nietzsche those ideas which may more properly be called visions: his pictures of the world, so to speak, which make questioning and analysis superfluous, even presumptuous. His idea of the eternal recurrence of all things is one of these.

Nietzsche never thought that eternal recurrence would take place within historical time; and his vision is not subject to inquiry either in terms of philosophy or of physics. Both have been attempted; but J.P. Stern is more realistic by simply stating that this vision is 'ineffable and thus unassailable'[56]; and so is Mary Warnock, when she writes that

> Nietzsche felt it as a passion, and therefore asserted it: [that] he could not, and therefore did not wish to, apply his own critical apparatus to this assertion.[57]

The value of Nietzsche's assertion is therefore emotional: it draws on that elusive personal experience, which many of us have had, of sensing that 'we have been here before'; that 'we have felt this before'. The private and elusive nature of such sensations should not deny their validity: the commonness of this experience may mean that there is a wish in our subconscious mind to re-live or re-experience past events. The philosophical or scientific formulation of such experiences may show them to be, strictly speaking, unverifiable; but then we might say the same about Aristophanes' famous speech about the origin of sexual love in Plato's *Symposium*. What Plato, through his fictional Aristophanes, is surmising here can have no valid formulation in biology or genetics; but anyone who has felt intense love for another will respond to it as to a vision which is 'ineffable and thus unassailable'.

If Freud had written a psychoanalytic study of Nietzsche, as he had of Leonardo and Dostoyevsky, he might have regarded the idea of eternal recurrence, and Nietzsche's insistence upon it, as a symptom in a traumatic neurosis. In the collection of notes and drafts which was posthumously published as *The Will to Power*, we find the following:

> Duration 'in vain', without end or aim, is the most paralysing idea, particularly when one understands that one is being fooled and yet lacks the power not to be fooled.

> Let us think this thought in its most terrible form: existence as it is, without meaning or aim, yet recurring inevitably without any finale of nothingness: '*the eternal recurrence.*'[58]

Once again, the tone is both committed and anguished: Nietzsche is subjecting himself to a 'terrible' thought in order to master the feeling that paralyses him. The result is a vision which heals the anguished mind by the idea of repetition. For Nietzsche, every moment in time gains in significance because it is a potential future. (It follows that it is also a potential past.) And as each moment gains in significance, so does the mind which experiences the moment. Accordingly, Nietzsche came to see himself as

> the ideal of the most exuberant, most living and most world-affirming man, who has not only learned to get on and treat with all that was and is but who wants to have it again *as it was and is* to all eternity, insatiably calling out *da capo* not only to himself but to the whole piece and play, and not only to a play but fundamentally to him who needs precisely this play — and who makes it necessary: because he needs himself again and again — and makes himself necessary — What? And would this not be — *circulus vitiosus deus?*[59]

Once again, it is not at all fanciful to gloss this extraordinary passage as a response to some traumatic spiritual experience. Perhaps Nietzsche had sensed what seemed to him the futility of existence: the passage is taken from a section which is partly an attack on Schopenhauerian resignation as the 'most world-denying of all possible modes of thought'. Nietzsche cannot accept that the world can be denied; and he is scared of an existence which seems meaningless because it issues in nothing. In such a world he himself would be a creature of no significance, and his life would lack all meaning. We might re-phrase Mary Warnock's remark and say that Nietzsche felt his theory of eternal recurrence *as a fear*, and therefore asserted it as a passion: terrified by the meaninglessness of existence, he wanted to turn himself into someone who was by definition above feeling such terror: someone who could make existence necessary rather than meaningless. It is a unilateral declaration of significance, both personal and cosmic. Nietzsche is engaged in a *perlocutionary act*[60], which is also an act of intellectual dictatorship: reading him here is an act of communion which requires assent and rejects questioning.

Behind the idea of eternal recurrence lies, also, Nietzsche's mistrust of history and time. He analysed the rise of morality in human society with the causal passion of a historian, yet he regarded conventional history as 'the idolatry of the factual'. His social and psychological analyses would be meaningless without a concept of time in which event followed event and effect followed cause; yet one way of reading him is to witness a constant battle between time and the human will, usually his own. His Zarathustra tells us that the will is

> sullenly wrathful that time does not run back; [and that the past is] a stone which it cannot roll away.

Zarathustra says that he wants the world to be 'dancing on the feet of chance'; but he also wants to be a redeemer of chance and wants

> to transform every 'It was' into an 'I wanted it thus' − this alone I call redemption.[61]

J.P. Stern sums this up eloquently as an attempt to turn 'chance into intention'[62]. But, we may still ask, what does Nietzsche mean by being a redeemer of chance? He makes us wonder, as Wagner did in *Parsifal*, what redemption means here: what is being redeemed, and why by such means? There is no comprehensible connection between the great disease of the world, which for Nietzsche is the passing of time, and the remedy that he brings to it. At one point Zarathustra calls revenge the will's antipathy to time: an aphoristic phrase which not only signifies the perception that we want our deeds to undo and annihilate earlier deeds: it also sums up an urge in Nietzsche's thought which is both personal and cosmic. He is attempting nothing less than a reversal of the law of cause and effect: he wants *to will backwards*. This is more even than wanting to turn chance into intention: Nietzsche pits the caused thing which is a human mind against the very causal pressure of time. His picture of the world includes both that pressure and an arbitrary resistance to it: time, as in *Waiting for Godot* or in Proust, is both passing and being held, unmoving, a captive of the mind.

In so far as the concrete details of eternal recurrence are open to questions, we must ask whether it is possible that all the particles of the universe can, in an infinity of time, re-assemble, more than once, to create absolutely identical worlds. The problem is that an identical universe, for us, excludes by definition the memory of any previous identical universes. This is because our memory is part of our existence as we are now; and we have no memory of any previous existence, let alone one that is identical to this one. It follows that if our present existence recurs identically, we shall, in the same way, have no memory of it. This leaves us with an

existence even more meaningless than it seemed before we encountered Nietzsche. It makes no sense for him to strike a moral note and
exhort us 'so to live that you must desire to live again'[63]: for by his
own definition we cannot do any better than last time, and our lack
of memory of that last time precludes any moral improvement. We
cannot learn any lessons from a life which we do not remember.
Nietzsche makes it sound as though we had a choice; whereas his
own hypothesis means that we do the things we do because, in a
previous existence, we have done them already. The idea of eternal
recurrence is without moral significance essentially because, as
Nietzsche imagines it, it is an event which is *not caused*. It is a vision
of life which is end-less in a double sense: it has neither purpose nor
conclusion. We are, once again, in a no man's land of the mind.[64]

The nature and origin of morality is crucial to both Nietzsche and
Freud. For Nietzsche, the essence of morality is a question of rank:

> a concept denoting political superiority always resolves itself
> into a concept denoting superiority of the soul.[65]

'Good' is the way in which the high-ranking and the powerful define
themselves. 'Bad' is merely its grammatical antithesis: it is how the
high-ranking and the powerful describe the low-ranking and the
weak who are their subjects. That is to say, rulers create morality by
naming its terms. Part of the superiority of the rulers lies in the fact
that they are high-minded by nature: they are incapable of taking
either their subjects and enemies, or their misdeeds, seriously for
very long. By contrast, the low-born become men of *ressentiment*:
they begin to think of their superiors, not as 'bad' but as 'evil'. In
other words, 'good' and 'bad' are descriptive terms of very limited
moral value, while 'evil' is a word which has moral connotations
only for those who invented it. *Ressentiment*, too, may only be a
moral feeling for the low-born, but it has no other moral value: it is
merely what *they* must inevitably feel against the high-born, and
'evil' is simply the word they use to express it. Thus, for Nietzsche,
there is something inherently amoral at the root of what we call
morality: it comes from something felt by inferior people when they
rage with resentment against their betters.

This is a futile confrontation, and Nietzsche views it with both
distaste and relish. He sees quite clearly that high-born rulers need
someone on whom they can exercise their power. He believed in

the spiritualisation of *enmity* . . . the value of having enemies[66]

— a need shared, incidentally, by all totalitarian states. This condition of intellectual and spiritual belligerence is essential both to Nietzsche's politics and to his psychology. He defines the noble soul as one that 'has reverence for itself'[67]. Virtue, for him, is the 'self-rejoicing'[68] of powerful souls and beautiful bodies. Nietzsche had long believed that egoism was

not evil, because the idea of the 'neighbour' . . . is very weak in us.[69]

In other words, egoism is not evil because we are all egoists by nature: an argument which Nietzsche accepts without criticism or regret. In his last years, he took this idea a good deal further.

The value of egoism depends on the physiological value of him who possesses it . . . Every individual may be regarded as representing the ascending or descending line of life. When one has decided which, one has thereby established a canon for the value of his egoism.[70]

On this reading, virtue, which is merely another name for egoism, is entirely self-referential. If you say that you possess it, then you possess it. Those who do are called, in *Thus Spoke Zarathustra*, the Higher Men: it is they who should rule the world. Their task is also to create new worlds — but for themselves, not their neighbours: indeed not for any socially definable 'purpose'.

Unlearn this 'for' [Zarathustra demands], you creators. Your very virtue wants you to have nothing to do with 'for' and 'for the sake of' and 'because'.[71]

Nietzschean morality rises not only above social purpose, but also above the shackles of grammar. The moral world is entirely relative, and its priorities are established by its self-created rulers, much in the way the legality of a regime is established after a military coup. It has nothing external to measure itself against: hence the fact that the very words denoting purpose, comparison, and therefore, by implication, questioning, are superfluous. Morality is merely 'herd instinct in the individual'[72]. Men who possess virtue are forever separated from those who do not, by 'the pathos of distance'[73]. The phrase has no suggestion of pity or disapproval. The high-born can forever harass and punish the low-born; and what our decadent age calls justice is merely an aberration.

Nobody is responsible for his actions, nobody for his nature; *to judge is identical with being unjust* (my italics).[74]

Such a society is rigidly stratified. Nietzsche's insistence on the absolute value of rank and breeding creates a social world entirely without mobility. Aristocratic condescension and resentful hostility are its eternally frozen shapes of action. Such a society is essentially static, especially since, as we have seen, the rulers need the low-born for the sake of their mental and physical health: they need people at their disposal on whom they can vent their surplus energy.

He who lives by fighting with an enemy, has an interest in the preservation of the enemy's life.[75]

Conflict is thus permanent, almost undynamic: a condition of life as lived by Lucky and Pozzo in the first act of *Waiting for Godot*.

Here Nietzsche's view of society links up with his view of the human mind. One of the crucial passages is near the opening of *The Anti-Christ*.

What is good? — All that heightens the feeling of power, the will to power, power in itself in man.
What is bad? — All that proceeds from weakness. What is happiness? — The feeling that power *increases* — that a resistance is overcome.
Not contentment, but more power; *not* peace at all, but war; *not* virtue, but proficiency (virtue in the Renaissance style, *virtu*, virtue free of moralic acid).
The weak and the ill-constituted shall perish: first principle of *our* philanthropy. And one shall help them to do so.
What is more harmful than any vice? — Active sympathy for the ill-constituted and weak — Christianity . . . [76]

The core of this credo lies in the first two questions and the answers to them. The Nietzschean mind, in its ideal state, is overcharged with energy. If the Freudian ideal is a balance of mental and spiritual forces, Nietzsche's is that of superfluity. Still, he realises that power also has to discharge itself.

To demand of strength that it should *not* express itself as strength . . . a desire to become master, a thirst for enemies and resistances and triumphs is just as absurd as to demand of weakness that it should express itself as strength. A quantum of force is equivalent to a quantum of drive, will, effect.[77]

This is why Nietzsche's original moral legislators are plunderers, 'not much better than uncaged beasts of prey'. Faced with strangers, such creatures

> savour a freedom from all social constraints ... they go *back* to the innocent conscience of the beast of prey, as triumphant monsters who perhaps emerge from a disgusting procession of murder, arson, rape and torture, exhilarated and undisturbed of soul, as if it were no more than a students' prank, convinced they have provided the poets with a lot more material for song and praise.[78]

The tone is one of amoral intoxication; the literary flourish at the end of the passage gives it a touch of sadistic self-indulgence. Nietzsche is writing about the process of discharging power regardless of direction, and he is writing with enormous pleasure. The key word is *innocent*: these ravages are an amoral, and therefore blameless, release of pent-up energy. Freud wrote that

> civilisation is built upon a renunciation of instinct [and] presupposes ... the non-satisfaction of powerful instincts.[79]

Nietzsche would have angrily agreed. And he also pondered about the fate of such instincts when they are not satisfied. If the murderous instincts of his aristocratic marauders could not 'discharge themselves outwardly', then these instincts would '*turn inward*'. Nietzsche calls this process 'the *internalisation* of man'. This sounds very like Freud's description of repression; and indeed Nietzsche goes on to derive from this damming up of instincts the origin of what he calls bad conscience:

> an animal soul turned against itself, taking sides against itself.[80]

This internalised spiritual conflict is reflected in the birth of the state. This happens through acts of violence, when

> some pack of blond beasts of prey, a conqueror and master race ... lays its terrible claws upon a populace perhaps tremendously superior in numbers but still formless and nomad.[81]

These conquerors have no sense either of guilt or of responsibility; they subdue their prey with cruel joy. Bad conscience is nothing other than the hostility of the victims: they resent those who possess such joy. Thus the formation of the state is like the formation of personal morality: joyful, natural aggression breeds, and flourishes on, contemptible resentment.

But this aggressive force does not only vent itself on inferior creatures: as we have already hinted, Nietzsche argues that it can also turn upon the powerful man's own 'ancient animal self', and create within him another form of bad conscience which Nietzsche calls 'the instinct *for freedom*'. The soul of a man in this condition is 'a soul voluntarily at odds with itself'; it 'makes itself suffer out of joy in making suffer.' This is *active* bad conscience: it leads to

> an abundance of strange new beauty and affirmation, and perhaps beauty itself.[82]

I do not think it is entirely clear what the last four words mean. But it is clear that in the subjugated man bad conscience is bad without qualification: it is *ressentiment*, it corrupts, it weakens, and it leads to what Nietzsche calls with hatred the 'slave morality' of religion. In the conquerors, however, bad conscience is the source of higher things. If it is dammed up, it will be dangerous only to those inferior people on whom it is vented; and if it is given a proper outlet it is a noble and creative force. Thus, bad conscience, like all moral concepts, turns out to be self-referential and amoral.

Nietzsche's meditations on 'bad conscience' reveal another affinity with Freud. His account of 'bad conscience', like Freud's account of the subconscious sense of guilt, describes an internal conflict within the mind; and, like Freud, he seeks the origin of this conflict in a violent pre-historic event which had left its mark both on human society and on the human mind. And when, in a language heated with excitement and even a sense of sadism, Nietzsche writes about the souls of superior men bringing forth beauty through suffering, he is describing that same inner balancing process of the mind which Freud was to call sublimation. And a criminal, for Nietzsche, is merely a variant of this same psychological specimen, a man whose spirit is overcharged with energy: Nietzsche defines him as

> a strong human being under unfavourable conditions, a strong human being made sick.[83]

The point is taken still further in the famous section of *Thus Spoke Zarathustra*, called 'Of the Pale Criminal', which portrays a creature in whom madness 'comes *before* the deed'.

> What is this man? A knot of savage serpents that are seldom at peace among themselves — thus they go forth alone to seek prey in the world.[84]

Forty years later, in *The Ego and the Id*, Freud, too, diagnosed the case of people who are turned into criminals by an unconscious sense of guilt. Both he and Nietzsche reverse the way in which we ordinarily see the criminal process: the effect, for them, precedes the cause. It is not only that, for Freudian man, guilt is a condition of consciousness; his guilt-feeling is also the motive for his crime.

The theme of the inner drama of the mind and its overflow in action recurs in all Nietzsche's books. He called himself a psychologist and, like Freud, conducted a study of mental energies. For him, the cause of human action is

a quantum of dammed-up energy that is waiting to be used up somehow, for something;[85]

the human body is

only a social structure composed of many souls;[86]

the mind is 'the war which we are'; human virtues are

physiological *conditions*, refined *passions* and enhanced states.[87]

Note the implication, in all these definitions, that what we regard in ordinary life as examples of moral behaviour have nothing to do with willed human action. Like the young Freud, Nietzsche sought the origins of morality in amoral causes.

In the most fundamental sense, of course, Nietzsche did see the mind in terms of cause and effect. When he writes about 'the total economy of the soul'[88], he implies a system of energies within which any alteration of balance will be followed by an appropriate reaction. All his life, Nietzsche was an investigative psychologist who peered behind human behaviour and looked for its real, as opposed to accepted, causes. And yet, all his life, he felt uneasy about things being *caused*: as if causation, and its philosophical formulation, logic, were not only useless but also curtailed his freedom of thought.

When Nietzsche, who was flattered when Georg Brandes called him an aristocratic radical, writes that 'nothing is more democratic than logic'[89], he clearly identifies causal thinking with lower human rank and values: we are meant to conclude that a man who can bear to think causally is not strong enough to be free. And, just as he reversed the ordinary human view of crime and guilt, Nietzsche deplored the way people commonly thought of crime in relation to punishment. He thought that the '*alleged* relation between cause and effect, between guilt and punishment' (my italics)[90] had a corrupting influence on true morality. He believed that when we identified those two sets of terms with one another, we 'robbed the pure accidentality of events of its innocence.'[91] The implication is that crime has its own innocence: if we implicate it in its consequence, punishment, we take away its purity as a deed. Crime, too, is self-referential.

Nietzsche's rage against the shackles of causation and logic produces some of his most intellectually exciting as well as his most difficult writing. It also forms one of the fundamental contradictions of his work as a whole. For the untrained reader the question simply is whether, without assuming that things are *caused*, we can do any thinking at all. Nietzsche believes that such an assumption is actually an obstacle to thinking properly. Here is one of his classic statements on the subject:

> One ought not to make 'cause' and 'effect' *into material things*, as natural scientists do ... in accordance with the prevailing mechanistic stupidity which has the cause press and push until it 'produces an effect'; one ought to employ 'cause' and 'effect' only as pure *concepts*, that is to say as conventional fictions for the purposes of designation, mutual understanding, *not* explanation. In the 'in itself' there is nothing of 'causal connexion', of 'necessity', of 'psychological unfreedom'; there the 'effect' *does not* 'follow the cause', there no 'law' rules. It is *we* alone who have fabricated causes, succession, reciprocity, relativity, compulsion, number, law, freedom, motive, purpose; and when we falsely introduce this world of symbols into things and mingle it with them as though this symbol-world were an 'in-itself', we once more behave as we have always behaved, namely *mythologically*. 'Unfree will' is mythology: in real life it is only a question of *strong* and *weak* wills.[92]

The last sentence of this passage undermines all that had gone before. It is beyond our scope here to go into what Nietzsche means by the 'in-itself', though we may note that its freedom from things like causal connexion, necessity and law reminds us both of Schopenhauer's Will and of the Freudian Id. But when, at the end, Nietzsche asserts the supremacy, not of an unknowable Schopenhauerian Will, but of weak and strong wills, then we must ask what the function of strong or weak wills can be except to express themselves in energy, in action. And to talk of wills expressing themselves in action — is that not the same as talking in terms of cause and effect?

> A living thing desires above all to *vent* its strength — life as such is will to power-: self-preservation is only one of the indirect and most frequent *consequences* of it.[93]

In this encapsulation of his psychology, is not Nietzsche using the language of causation? It would seem that when Nietzsche scrutinises the nature of thinking he pits himself against its very instrument, the pattern-making mind. As R.J. Hollingdale puts it, he 'retained a love of gambling but rejected the rules of poker.'[94]

But Nietzsche goes further still.

> There are still harmless self-observers who believe 'immediate certainties' exist, for example 'I think' or, as was Schopenhauer's superstition, 'I will': as though knowledge here got hold of its object pure and naked, as 'thing in itself', and no falsification occurred either on the side of the subject or on that of the object. But I shall reiterate a hundred times that 'immediate certainty', like 'absolute knowledge' and 'thing in itself', contains a *contradictio in adjecto*: we really ought to get free from the seduction of words! ... When I analyse the event expressed in the sentence 'I think', I acquire a set of rash assertions which are difficult, perhaps impossible, to prove — for example, that it is *I* who think, that it has to be something at all which thinks, that thinking is an activity and operation on the part of an entity thought of as a cause, that an 'I' exists, finally that what is designated by 'thinking' has already been determined — that I *know* what thinking is. For if I had not already decided that matter within myself, by what standard could I determine that what is happening is not perhaps 'willing' or 'feeling'?[95]

There is nothing frivolous in responding to this thrilling passage by saying: When you say you analyse an event, you acquire a series of rash assertions. What is an analysis? What is an event? Can the former be applied to the latter? For if you had not already decided the matter within yourself, how do you determine that what you are doing is not 'inventing' or 'wishing'? And is it you who analyses? Is what I call 'you' the same thing as what you call 'I'? It might be thought frivolous to ask why one should have read a dozen books by a man, 'someone', who seems uncertain of their authorship, and why one should set any store by 'his' opinions. And there is nothing frivolous in wondering what an opinion is, and on what basis it can be held, let alone shared. If all the elements of discourse, namely speaker or thinker, listener, subject, are called in doubt, what is the reality of discourse? If we cannot establish reality or identity, can there be action or purpose? Without causation, can these very arguments be understood? We are in Existentialist country here, faced with the familiar dilemmas about the nature of individuality, will and action, of which the most famous encapsulation is Sartre's phrase, 'On est parlé'. But, for Nietzsche, there seems to be no getting away from the chains of cause and effect: he is trapped.

If we look at the human mind in this way, we also have to ask what responsibility means. Freud's tripartite model of the mind, like Nietzsche's analysis of 'thinking', can undermine our sense of identity. For if our 'I' consists of an Ego, an Id and a Superego, who is the 'I' that does the things we do? Nietzsche is unequivocal on the subject.

> The decisive value of an action resides precisely in that which is *not intentional* in it.[96]

The phrase recalls the romantic notion of the superior value of spontaneous actions: a notion which can be traced in Sartre's existentialism, and even in the automatic writing of the early Surrealists. Nietzsche is laying the foundations of a belief in action without responsibility, action that is not *willed*, not *caused*.

Freud was not so certain. He once argued that we must take the responsibility for evil impulses even in our dreams, since such impulses, too, were part of our being. 'What else is one to do with them?' Freud asks.

> Experience shows . . . that I . . . *do* take that responsibility, that I am *somehow* compelled to do so (my italics).[97]

As in that earlier phrase of Freud's, '*a kind of* inner dishonesty', the tone here is uneasy: the word '*somehow*' is unlike Freud's usually crisp and decisive utterance. It reminds us, once again, that Freud never really came to terms with the amorality implicit in his model of the mind. Psychoanalysis does not moralise; it accepts the amoral forces within the spirit of man; but it strives for health within that spirit, and that health lies in a moral balance. When Freud said,

'Where the Id was, there the I shall be'[98], he meant that the reasoning and evaluating faculty of the mind should have supremacy over the unreasoning, amoral faculty. Those famous words contain a moral statement of healing. It is entirely typical of the two men that Nietzsche described the ideal stance of the philosopher as 'an attitude of hostile calm'[99], while the stance of the ideal analyst, for Freud, was 'evenly suspended attention'[100].

When we undermine our sense of personality, we also undermine the value and reliability of language. When I call myself 'I', and someone else 'you', I implicitly accept that language has to do with causes and effects: if it had not, the other person would not know that I was addressing him. But if I am uncertain as to whether there is such a thing as an 'I', then I am also uncertain about what the word 'I' actually means: it might be no more than an arbitrary sound, indicating the existence of something, my 'self', which the word 'I' might turn out to be quite inadequate to describe. There might be much more to 'me' than that: a notion which leads, among other things, to the mistrust of language. This is what Nietzsche means when he says that 'words block our way'; and that, by using words, we merely touch on a problem and then, instead of solving it, create 'an obstacle to its solution'[101]. He is resentful that thinking is trammelled up in the consequence of words. Grammar, he asserts, is merely 'the metaphysics of the people'[102]. To philosophers, grammar acts as a governess, and, Nietzsche demands, 'is it not time that philosophy renounced the beliefs of governesses?'[103]

Nietzsche's attitude to language is intimately bound up with what philosophers call his *perspectivism*. Perspectivism means here that, for Nietzsche, all perception is relative, because it takes in only the surface of things, their appearance, their apparent meaning. This is not because he thought, like Plato, that things were only pale representatives, or copies, of remote, 'ideal' things: he is simply saying that what we see and understand is not all there is to see and to understand. But he also knows that we are made the way we are made; that the way we see things is, in practice, defined by perspectives. But this way of seeing is by definition limited, and therefore we have to 'recognise untruth as a condition of life.'[104] And this is one of the reasons why Nietzsche thinks that words are not to be trusted: they can only describe what little of the world we can understand. Words exist merely for a social purpose, and therefore they express not what is individual but what is average. This is where Nietzsche's thought begins to move beyond the boundaries of questioning. Words, and what we understand by them are, for him, of very limited value.

> The world of which we can become conscious is only a surface-and-sign-world, a world that is made common and meaner; whatever becomes conscious *becomes* by the same token shallow, thin, relatively stupid, general, sign, herd signal; all becoming conscious involves a great and thorough corruption, falsification, reduction to superficialities, and generalisation. Ultimately, the growth of consciousness becomes a danger; and anyone who lives among the most conscious Europeans even knows that it is a disease.[105]

> We have already grown beyond whatever we have words for. In all talking there lies a grain of contempt.[106]

Nietzsche has gone a good deal further than the Romantic idea that certain experiences are beyond words: for him speech itself is a perlocutionary act because it is devoid of real communication. It is also a form of deception: it demonstrates that the common exchange of life is error and untruth.

If we follow these arguments to their logical conclusions, we find ourselves in a world which we can only contemplate in terror and incomprehension; and this will hardly be lessened by the fact that one part of Nietzsche does not really believe in the validity of logical conclusions. Nietzsche's own linguistics is a type of perlocutionary act: it is not open to the give-and-take of argument.

Of course, all Nietzsche's arguments, involving as they do the meaning of communication, of existence, indeed the meaning of *meaning*, raise such fundamental problems that it is not surprising to find Nietzsche himself having reservations about them. One of his notes in *The Will to Power* is typical in the way it articulates the problem and then briskly despatches it.

> The most strongly believed a priori 'truths' are for me — *provisional assumptions*; e.g., the law of causality, a very well acquired habit of belief, so much a part of us that not to believe in it would destroy the race. But are they for that reason truths? What a conclusion! As if the preservation of man were a proof of truth![107]

The passage combines clear thinking with intellectual recklessness.

Nietzsche leaves us wondering whether such a price is worth paying, and whether it makes sense that it should be paid. For Nietzsche's thought here is as apocalyptic as the ending of Wagner's *Ring*: at the end of this stupendous intellectual effort, truth will be left without any valid, practical meaning, because he envisages that there might be no people to perceive it.

These cursory remarks are not a full analysis of Nietzsche's linguistics and perspectivism: such things are beyond the scope of this book. From our point of view, the importance of what has been said here is that all Nietzsche's theories were, for him, ultimately more than philosophy: he felt them like a passion, and to that extent we respond to him either by submission or refusal.

Nietzsche's perspectivism implies that illusion is something we actually rely on: in his notes he was pondering whether we might not have 'a will to illusion'[108]. Indeed, he came to believe that existence as a whole had a perspective character: by this he meant that it consisted in being 'essentially actively engaged in *interpretation*'. The human intellect, in other words, can only see things, including itself, in the perspectives it is used to. 'We cannot look around our own corner,' Nietzsche concludes simply but profoundly; but then goes on to add that at least we are no longer so limited as to claim

> that perspectives are permitted only from this corner. Rather has the world become 'infinite' for us all over again ... *it may include infinite interpretations.*[109]

Nietzsche's meditations assume a visual character here, which is unusual for him: he has, on the whole, little to say about landscape, people's appearance, or the visual arts in general. But his remarks prompt the thought that there is perhaps a deep-lying connection between a causal view of the world (which Nietzsche would like to be able to reject) and the methods of representational painting. Such paintings tell us that, whoever painted them, painted something he had seen: the painting could be referred to, or even checked against, the thing it depicts. In this sense, such pictures are open to our questions. (Giotto or Claude had not, of course, seen the religious or mythological events they painted; but the way in which they represented and interpreted those events is always open to argument.) Conversely, when Nietzsche accepts the possibility that other perspectives may exist, he encapsulates what, only two decades later, the Cubist painters were to put into practice. They, too, assumed that there were perspectives other than their own; that there was more to the world than the apparent causality of surface which it represented to the eye. They painted their pictures as if they had been able to look around their own corner and see what other people might have seen from theirs; and by doing so they imposed their own vision on the perceived world which was both liberating and dictatorial. They might have declared, with Nietzsche, that 'to grasp everything would mean to do away with all perspective relations'[110], and conversely, that to rid themselves of perspective would help them to grasp everything.

But this is to forestall the contents of a later chapter. Nietzsche's perspectivism, as we have seen, was bound up with his thoughts about the relative value of language. And so it may not be surprising that he not only rebelled against language, but allowed language, as it were, to rebel against him. It became a disobedient tool in his hands, and this was to have disastrous consequences on his reputation.

We know that Nietzsche disliked the militarism of the new German Reich, as well as the growing anti-semitism of his time; and yet he was to be hijacked by the Nazi movement and used as their philosophical mascot. The facts of his changing allegiances are not in doubt. As a young man, overpowered by Wagner's coruscating personality, he also came to share some of his ideas. Thus, aged twenty-five, he writes to Wagner about

> the world which we poor Germans lost ... by virtue of wretched political conditions, philosophical mischief and inso-lent Jewry.[111]

Sixteen years later he saw things differently.

> May it be forgiven me that I too, during a daring brief sojourn in a highly infected area, did not remain wholly free of the disease and began, like the rest of the world, to entertain ideas about things that were none of my business: the first symptom of political infection.[112]

This is a manly recantation, and it is followed by an analysis of the Jewish question, sometimes shrewd and always compassionate, including the remark that most politicians who repudiate anti-semitism do not condemn the feeling itself but merely its immoderation; and the suggestion that 'the strongest and purest race now living in Europe' should at long last be allowed to be 'settled, permitted, respected'. We may add here that Nietzsche's close relationship with his sister Elisabeth came to be permanently damaged by her anti-semitism, and even more by her marriage to one Bernhard Förster, a leading figure in the German anti-semitic movement. She was, of all people, the closest to him; yet he came to describe her as 'a vengeful antisemitic goose'[113].

Yet Nietzsche remained capable of attributing what he saw as the pernicious moral influence of Christianity to its Jewish origins.

> ... in Rome the Jews stood *convicted* of hatred for the whole human race; and rightly, provided one has a right to link the salvation and future of the human race with the unconditional dominance of aristocratic values, Roman values.[114]

Knowing what we know of Nietzsche's views on aristocratic values, it is clear whom he favours here: the Jews are clearly the contemptible people of *ressentiment*. The new God, Nietzsche writes,

> remained a Jew, he has remained the God of the nook, the God of all the dark corners and places ... His empire is as before ... a ghetto-empire.[115]

St Paul, we read, carried the process of moral decay to its conclusion with 'the cynical logic of a rabbi'.

> In Christianity, as the art of holy lying, the whole of Judaism ... attains its ultimate perfection. The Christian, that *ultima ratio* of the lie, is the Jew once more.[116]

Christianity has behind it, among other things,

> an ill-smelling Jewish acidity compounded of Rabbinism and superstition ...[117]

> One would no more choose to associate with 'first Christians' than one would with Polish Jews: not that one would need to prove so much as a single point against them ... Neither of them smell very pleasant.[118]

Nietzsche's analysis of Judaism as the religion of a 'ghetto-empire' may or may not have psychological or theological validity; but the tone and the vocabulary of his argument are those of invective, bordering on incitement. What does Nietzsche's dislike of anti-semitism matter after what we have just read? Even in a much earlier book, Nietzsche wrote an eloquent condemnation of anti-semitism, only to add that, of course, all nations could have unpleasant qualities: they

> may even be dangerous and revolting . . . to an unusual degree; and perhaps the young stock exchange Jew is the most disgusting invention of mankind.[119]

The vicious generalisation of that last remark completely undermines the liberal fervour of the context in which it is made. Nietzsche appears not to notice. In *The Genealogy of Morals* he describes how 'the morality of the common man' has become victorious in the world, and how it resulted in the blood-poisoning of mankind:

> everything is visibly becoming Judaized, Christian-ized, mob-ized (what do words matter!)[120]

The answer is that words matter very much indeed. Nietzsche was hijacked by the Nazis because he had given them hostages. Like many people who are liberal by conviction but bullies by temperament, he felt righteous to the point where he regarded himself as being free to say anything. Indeed, we might say that he suffered from a sense of superiority towards words; and that this is profoundly bound up with his moral relativism. He also spent his best creative years almost entirely in solitude, without the restraining and disciplining give-and-take of argument, of teaching, or of social obligations. He himself seems to have felt that something was amiss. Some of the evidence is in his letters.

> I no longer know with which of my views I am pleasing people and with which I am causing injury.[121]

> . . . the whole of my philosophy totters after one hour's sympathetic intercourse even with total strangers.[122]

Some of his friends, too, sensed an unhealthy alienation from the world. After reading *Beyond Good and Evil*, his friend Erwin Rohde noted briskly: 'What Nietzsche needs is to get a proper job.'[123] We are dealing with an extraordinary phenomenon here: the failure of an exceptional intellect to estimate correctly the nature and the impact of his own language. There is a vital relationship of cause and effect between writer and reader; and Nietzsche largely misunderstood his own effect. Towards the end of his sane life he began to sense this. When, in 1886, he sent off his new preface to *The Birth of Tragedy* to his publisher, he wrote:

> Quite seriously, if I do not offer a couple of hints how I am to be understood, the worst stupidities are bound to happen.[124]

The phrase, 'Am I being understood?' occurs more than once in his last writings, like the cry of a drowning man.

In one of his notes on his theory of the will to power, Nietzsche wonders whether this phrase might turn out to be 'a metaphor that can mislead'[125]. The fact is that Nietzsche's writings are full of metaphors that can and do mislead. 'Will to Power' certainly means something different to him from what it has come to mean to the non-philosophical posterity. But we must remember, too, that Nietzsche had always been fascinated by the idea of man's fighting instinct and especially its role in ancient Greek civilisation; and in his writings he was much inclined to the use of metaphors of belligerence. Erich Fromm has noted how Freud's language often took on a political or military tone when he was writing about the psychoanalytic movement, as opposed to practice; but Fromm himself admits that when Freud talks about 'the conquest of the Id', he is expressing 'a religious-ethical aim, the conquest of passion by reason'[126]. And the general tone of Freud's writing is certainly not bellicose. It is different with Nietzsche. When he means passionate and committed intellectual confrontation he writes about 'war to the knife'. Theories he opposes have to be 'finished off'. He calls tragedy moral because it is 'warlike'. Military metaphors tend to describe philosophical activity with a violence of expression that came to have a profound appeal to an age whose make-up included social instability, national and racial resentment, impatience, an obsession with virility, and a profound respect for soldierly values.

But this was not all: in Nietzsche's final writings it is as if the belligerence of his language had begun to influence his thinking.

> The *sick* ... are man's greatest danger ... Those who are failures from the start, downtrodden, crushed — it is they, the *weakest*, who must undermine life among men.[127]

> The invalid is a parasite on society. In a certain state it is indecent to go on living. To vegetate on in cowardly dependence on physicians and medicaments after the meaning of life, the *right* to life, has been lost ought to entail the profound contempt of society.[128]

Note the insidious ease with which Nietzsche, himself a chronic invalid, moves from the meaning of life to the right to life: the argument for a right to a dignified death turns into a very different one for a duty to die. Who might be the custodians of such a duty? Doctors, Nietzsche believes, should now have a new responsibility: that of

> the most ruthless suppression and sequestration of degenerating life — for example in determining the right to reproduce, the right to be born, the right to live.[129]

> The weak and ill-constituted should perish: first principle of *our* philanthropy. And one shall help them to do so.[130]

We have come a long way from 'aristocratic radicalism'; or even from a happy belief that it is right for a muscular community to vent its energies in casual bloodletting. This is the language of autocratic malevolence, indiscriminate, despotic and ruthless. Nietzsche transcends mere words with a vengeance. On a stupendous scale, and largely without knowing it, Nietzsche attempted one thing and achieved another: he set out to free men's minds from rigid intellectual and moral manacles, and to enable them to think as free beings; but in the event he helped to intoxicate them, so that they submitted to bonds more fearful than he could ever have imagined. His purpose was 'the re-valuation of values': a heady phrase which eludes analysis; and Nietzsche sensed the enormity of his task, and diagnosed his own intellectual impasse, when he wrote:

> Even to be permitted to touch on the problem of the *value* of life at all, one would have to be situated *outside* life; and on the other hand know it as thoroughly as any, as many, as all who have experienced it.[131]

We might say that only God would have qualified for this; and that Nietzsche's solution to his dilemma was an act of God-like imposition of will. He wrote *Thus Spoke Zarathustra*, and in its 'hero' created a messianic figure who would free mankind of their oppressive values.

Zarathustra is a moral teacher who preaches an amoral sermon. For him virtue, for example, is something we have in common with no one: which means that it is individual to the point of being unique, and therefore beyond comparison and questioning. 'Let your virtue be too exalted for the familiarity of names,'[132] he exhorts his disciples; and yet, later on, he tells them that virtue has its origin in a state where people are 'the willers of a single will'[133]. Thus virtue, the quality of moral excellence, is both uniquely personal and impersonally shared; it is at once above mere sharing and naming, and a product of obliterating oneself in common willing. Both descriptions put virtue beyond factual inquisition and questioning. This is the moral core of a closed world.

It is also the world of Zarathustra, who is Nietzsche's great self-referential prophet. He deplores contempt, but pours it freely on others. Lust for power, selfishness and sensual pleasure are, according to him, the privilege of the elect, those who declare that the Ego is healthy and selfishness is glorious. He announces that he loves mankind, but we soon find him admonishing his disciples that their neighbours 'will always be poisonous flies'[134]. Evil, for him, is justified through its enjoyment:

> In laughter all evil is present, but sanctified and absolved through its own happiness. [135]

This arrogant and self-indulgent book echoes with Zarathustra's ambiguous laughter: a sound both ecstatic and nasty. The section called 'Of Old and New Law Tables' is one of the passages most richly laden with Nietzschean motifs. Its finale, one of the high points of the book, reaches its climax in ecstatic self-denial: Zarathustra sees himself as the sun, and as 'an inexorable sun-will, ready for annihilation in victory!'[136] This is a sunset of the self in a state of passionate self-indulgence and cosmic emotion, not unlike the ending of *Tristan*. Indeed, we find that Zarathustra utters some of his most important sayings in a state of exhaustion, after having fasted, fainted, or both. The effect is an atmosphere of shaman-like clairvoyance: we see the supreme explicator and law-giver in a trance.

Should *Zarathustra* be treated as if it were fiction? It is written in a narrative form, and, in a basic sense, Nietzsche was telling a story: indeed, he wanted to continue it, as story-tellers often do, until Zarathustra's death, but could not think of a suitable way of bringing it about. (Books by Nietzsche do not 'end': they come to a halt, or lead into another book.) Of Zarathustra as a character in fiction we know nothing except that he has a beard and that his hair turns grey. His disciples and enemies have virtually no individuality: they are hardly more than the furniture of his thoughts. He often speaks not to them but to himself, 'to his heart', or 'to his conscience'.

But all such comments about the book are really irrelevant. Nietzsche may appear to be telling a story, but his narrative lacks the causal organisation of fiction; and it neither contains nor implies a past which could have been different, or which might in any way have changed the story we are reading. It is held together by the cogency of its imagery, and at the core of it there is an ecstatic statement: it is felt like a passion. If we consider its episodes as events, things that really happened, they appear ludicrous. Events are clearly not the point here: indeed, throughout the book we experience a stillness, a feverish immobility. The phrase 'the great noontide' recurs like a *leitmotiv*, suggesting a sense of high achievement and a sense of potent peacefulness, poised unmoving for action, like the energy in Nietzsche's model of the mind. Zarathustra's vision of the perfect future is an insubstantial, slightly bizarre dream, both roseate and lofty, of dancing gods:

> eternally fleeing and re-seeking one another ... blissfully self-contradicting, communing again and belonging again to one another — where all time seemed to me a blissful mockery of moments, where necessity was freedom itself, which blissfully played with the goad of freedom ...[137]

This is the Nietzschean paradise: silent, distant and self-communing, and static with endless, aimless movement.

We might say of certain aspects of Nietzsche's philosophy, as we might have been inclined to say of Beckett's *Waiting for Godot*, that we do not understand them. Actually, we recall, we *understood* Beckett's narrative; but we sensed that he was using it for some purpose other than telling us a story. We found that this was partly because Beckett's narrative was like a surrealist image: it did not have that specific logical, sequential coherence which we expect from stories, and by which we recognise stories. And when Nietzsche develops his theory of Eternal Recurrence, we find, in the end, that we understand what this theory says but not really what it means, because it is not argued like a theory. Theories, like narratives, can be understood, but they do not always 'make sense'. In the case of

Nietzsche's theory, we can identify the point at which we lose touch with it: it is when he attributes a moral significance to Recurrence. We have seen that, if Recurrence is as Nietzsche describes it, then it cannot have such a significance because without remembering our previous lives we could not learn from them.

This is not a question of Nietzsche having 'slipped up'. It is rather that he wants two incompatible things at once. One side of him wants to develop a scientifically viable theory of the physical reappearance of the known world, identically re-formed molecule by molecule, while another side of him wants this idea to have a bearing on our moral lives. The excitement with which the idea is expressed, the sense of yearning which fills Nietzsche's writing when he addresses himself to it, are signs of a moral motivation: he longs for Eternal Recurrence as a challenge and a salvation. It is this longing that he communicates most strongly to us; and it is this longing for freedom from the shackles of time and the purposelessness of existence that lies at the heart of his philosophy. And such a longing is, to use J.P. Stern's words again, 'ineffable and therefore unassailable'.

The same is true of the Nietzschean Superman, whose existence is essential to Eternal Recurrence. For, in Nietzsche's view, only an exceptional being can face such a prospect. R.J. Hollingdale defines Nietzsche's need for Superman by saying that if every moment is an eternity, then every individual must become a God[138]. But Nietzsche is not at all clear on how this is to come about. One way would be by evolution. At least, this is implied by Nietzsche's view that 'Man is a bridge and not a goal'[139]; and that 'Man is a rope fastened between animal and superman.'[140] On this quasi-Darwinian reading, we have to imagine that man as we know him will go on improving until he evolves into Superman. The idea of 'breeding' higher types of human beings occurs frequently in Nietzsche's books. One of his notes in *The Will to Power* reads:

In place of 'metaphysics' and religion, the theory of eternal recurrence (this as a means of breeding and selection).[141]

However, we find, Nietzsche also says that man is a species that does not evolve. 'Man,' Zarathustra asserts, '*was* an experiment' (my italics).[142] 'Man as a species is not progressing.'[143] Zarathustra also tells us that 'There has never yet been a Superman.'[144] This last assertion undermines the entire idea of Superman: for, according to the theory of Eternal Recurrence, what exists now will not only exist again, but has already existed in the past. And so, if there has never yet been a Superman, he cannot appear in any theoretical future either.

Superman's function is as obscure as his origins. It would be fatuous to inquire, as we might for example about Plato's Guardians, what tasks he will perform in human society. He is defined for us entirely in terms of Nietzsche's own emotions: a lyrical picture of nobility, generosity, and immense, smiling strength, with a powerful undertone of innocent, almost kindly brutality. There is no account, in any of Nietzsche's writing, of any contact between Superman and ordinary mortals. And at this point we are compelled to stop and ask why Nietzsche needs him at all. If it is only to create a being who can endure Eternal Recurrence, then why have Eternal Recurrence? What philosophical, psychological or social problems would it solve? Why should Nietzsche's fearsome intellect want to find the cure for his life's inner anguish, and for the moral stalemate of the world, in a chimera which is beyond real human experience, based on contradictions, and open to devastating attacks from philosophy, physics and genetics?

Here I should like to offer a psychoanalytical explanation. I have suggested earlier that Freud might have diagnosed Nietzsche's insistence on this theory as a symptom in traumatic neurosis; that is to say, that Nietzsche wanted everything to recur (or as Freud might have put it, showed symptoms of the compulsion to repeat), because his imagination had suffered a traumatic shock when he comprehended that human life was merely 'Duration "in vain", without end or aim'. But this is not all. There had in fact been a traumatic event in Nietzsche's early life which is well documented. When he was four years old, his father suffered a fall, and the little boy was attracted to the scene by the barking of a dog. Ludwig Nietzsche died insane the following year, aged thirty-five, and his autopsy revealed softening of the brain. It is not thought that Nietzsche's own eventual insanity was inherited (it would seem that his father suffered brain damage from his fall); but there is reason to think that he feared such an inheritance. One way or another, finding his father in such a state has all the makings of a traumatic event for a four-year-old boy.

Now one of the classic formulations of the theory of Eternal Recurrence comes in part three of *Zarathustra*: the prophet is addressing the mocking dwarf who sits on his shoulder. It is worth quoting this famous passage at some length.

'Behold this moment!' I went on. 'From this gateway Moment a long, eternal lane runs *back*: an eternity lies behind us.

'Must not all things that *can* run have already run along this lane? Must not all things that *can* happen *have* already happened, been done, run past?

'And if all things have been here before: what do you think of this moment, dwarf? Must not this gateway, too, have been here – before?

'And this slow spider that creeps along in the moonlight, and this moonlight itself, and I and you at this gateway whispering together, whispering of eternal things – must we not all have been here before?

'–and must we not return and run down that other lane out before us, down that long, terrible lane – must we not return eternally?'

Thus I spoke, and I spoke more and more softly: for I was afraid of my own thoughts and reservations. Then, suddenly, I heard a dog *howling* nearby.

Had I ever heard a dog howling in that way? My thoughts ran back. Yes! When I was a child, in my most distant childhood:

– then I heard a dog howling in that way. And I saw it, too, bristling, its head raised, trembling in the stillest midnight, when even dogs believe in ghosts:

– so that it moved me to pity.

Where had the dwarf now gone? And the gateway? And the spider? And all the whispering? Had I been dreaming? Had I awoken? All at once I was standing between wild cliffs, alone, desolate in the most desolate moonlight.

But there was a man lying! And there! The dog, leaping, bristling, whining; then it saw me coming – then it howled again, then it *cried out* – had I ever heard a dog cry so for help?[145]

Nietzsche's English translator, R.J. Hollingdale, explains in a note the childhood episode associated with the barking of a dog and a man lying on the ground, and adds, 'It is not entirely clear why the scene should have been evoked at this point.'[146]

I want to suggest that it is entirely clear, and that it might throw light on Nietzsche's theory of Eternal Recurrence. I surmise that the episode occurs here because that had been precisely the traumatic event to which Nietzsche's otherwise elusive theory is a subconscious reaction[147]. He had evolved a theory that all things should recur, because his own mind kept bringing back to him an event which had filled him with terror, and he wanted to 'master' this terror. If this hypothesis is correct, it may also explain why Superman is necessary to Eternal Recurrence: it is as if Nietzsche's mind had sensed that it needed great spiritual strength to 'master' such an experience.

In other words, this hypothesis requires us to regard Nietzsche's theory of Eternal Recurrence as a neurotic symptom: the result of a subconscious compulsion to re-live a past event which expresses itself as a philosophical obsession. This would explain the intensity with which the theory is described, as well as the difficulty we have in grasping its meaning. And it is worth noting here that the theory does not form an organic part of Nietzsche's central enterprise as a philosopher, which was to re-value all values, that is to say, to re-assess and re-organise the moral and psychological premises on which human life is conducted. That enterprise may have been doomed to failure, albeit for different reasons; but it does not need the theory of Eternal Recurrence. The re-valuation of all values is clearly not a feasible project in an essentially unalterable world, which has already been the same as we know it now, and will become the same again and again.

If we are to regard Nietzsche's theory as a neurotic symptom, how will that help us to understand it? We said earlier that neurotic symptoms were like metaphors: a paralysed arm represents a past act, real or imaginary, of spiritual failure, and can be cured if the analyst explains the connection. In other words, such a metaphor is open to our questions. A metaphor is, by nature, an imaginative compromise in words, but one in which the two parties enrich one another. When Blake spoke of 'mind-forg'd manacles', he was not talking about human minds making chains, but of a process of spiritual self-enslavement which we understand more vividly because we temporarily suspend our notions of what human minds can perform and how manacles are manufactured. We knowingly compromise with the poet, just as he achieves a compromise between the two words, so that he could argue his case.

Our engagement with Blake's argument, indeed the very fact that we understand it, depends on understanding his words and the context in which he had placed them. The reason why we cannot grasp the meaning of Nietzsche's theory of Eternal Recurrence is that it is an incomplete metaphor, in the sense that neurotic symptoms, like a numb arm or a nightmare, are in themselves incomplete metaphors until the analyst finds the explanation. Without that explanation, the neurotic symptom may signify something, but we do not know what: it is telling us a story which we cannot understand. The reader may respond that if our hypothesis about the subconscious theory of Nietzsche's theory is correct, then we ourselves have just supplied the missing half of the metaphor. But we must remember that analysts want to find the missing halves of their clinical metaphors so that the numb arms may be cured and the nightmares may cease. And so, if we accept the truth of this hypothesis about Nietzsche, then we imply that if only he could have been analysed, and the connection between the traumatic event in his childhood and his untenable theory explained to him, he might have abandoned his theory of Eternal Recurrence along with Superman, and been 'cured'.

Now we can see why it is that our hypothesis has only served to elucidate the essential weakness of Nietzsche's theory. This theory serves a purpose other than that of the philosophy of which it is a part. This theory is not properly *caused*, in the sense that it was not brought into being by the philosophical and spiritual problems which it was, it seemed, created to solve. It is beyond our scope of argument and questioning: it can only be contemplated with a sense of unreserved admiration or complete rejection. Nietzsche's idea of Superman, subverted and distorted, came to have a tangible influence on human society more horrible than he could ever have believed; but the idea of Eternal Recurrence, the unending repetition of all things, amoral because unchanging, is merely a 'picture of the world'.

Nietzsche's writings contain a conception of the human mind not unlike Freud's. It is a seat of warring forces where psychic energy builds up and has to be contained or discharged to safeguard the health of the individual. In certain cases this energy is discharged, as it were, inwards, and becomes the source of spiritual or artistic creation. In this sense, Nietzsche's psychology, like Freud's psychoanalysis, is a study of energies. But, as we have seen,

Nietzsche, in the few creative years left to him, was not able to clarify whether mental and spiritual health was a matter of accumulating or discharging these energies.

Freud's tripartite model of the mind possesses far greater clarity. Its essence lies in the recognition of an amoral force within the human spirit, and the purpose of psychoanalysis is the moral desire to contain it. The healthy mind contains it without the help of analysis: its life is an unceasing drama, and we can describe Freud's picture of it as a dramatisation of the mind. It is true that whenever we describe any collision or conflict of forces, however mechanical, we are bound to use active verbs, which gives our description a semblance of action. But Freud's dramatisation of mental and spiritual forces goes beyond this. The quasi-dramatic quality of his theory of the mind's structure has recently been noted[148]; but what I call his dramatisation of the mind is bound up with the way in which he evolved and envisaged his tripartite model of it.

Freud's early writings lack all dramatic quality. In one of his early papers, for example, he describes drily how, in the mind,

> compromise is brought about somewhat on the analogy of the resultant in a parallelogram of forces.[149]

In another early paper Freud writes:

> The Ego seeks to fend off the deviations of the initially repressed memory, and in this defensive struggle it creates symptoms which might be classed together as 'secondary defence'.[150]

Despite 'fend off' and 'defensive struggle', this dense passage still has a flat, clinical tone. But in *The Ego and the Id*, where the tripartite structure of the mind is fully developed, Freud's presentation is quite different. He describes the Ego, for example, as

> a poor creature owing service to three masters and consequently menaced by three dangers

and as being like someone who 'tries to mediate between the world and the Id'. This Ego

> is not only a helper to the Id; it is also a submissive slave who courts his master's love ...

> it only too often yields to the temptation to become sycophantic, opportunist and lying, like a politician who sees the truth but wants to keep his place in popular favour.[151]

Elsewhere in Freud's late works we read how, for example, in a melancholic patient,

> his Superego becomes over-severe, abuses the poor Ego, humiliates it and ill-treats it, threatens it with the direst punishments, reproaches it for actions in the remotest past which had been taken lightly at the time — as though it had spent the whole interval in collecting accusations . . .

The passage, whose sense of arbitrary legality has the remorselessness of Kafka, concludes that, when all this blows over,

> the Ego is rehabilitated and again enjoys all the rights of man until the next attack.[152]

Freud describes the Superego as an agency watching over the mind 'like a garrison in a conquered city'; it 'torments the sinful Ego with anxiety'[153]. Of course, he knew that he was using what he himself called 'the figurative language peculiar to psychology'[154]. But these quotations add up to something more than figurative language, and the difference between early and late Freud is more than merely an improvement in style. There is a real sense of drama here.

Freud himself provided part of the explanation when he said that 'it is . . . natural to man to personify everything that he wants to understand.'[155] But figurative language such as we have been reading is peculiar to Freudian psychology precisely because there is a deep affinity between psychoanalysis and drama. An analytical session is a dialogue whose purpose is to establish the truth about the past and the present. Even in primitive societies mental healing often took dramatic forms. In modern medicine, one of the earliest champions of the human treatment of patients, Johann Christian Reil (1759—1813), used the method of therapeutic theatre in which employees of his institution shared the roles with his patients. Enactment and re-enactment are among the most basic ways of approaching mental and spiritual life.

Finally, drama as an art form turns out to have had a special attraction for Freud. He was widely read, and his writings abound in literary quotations. What we know of his reading shows that he read novels, essays and biographies in preference to plays. And yet, in the entire body of his psychological writings, more than two-thirds of the literary quotations are taken from plays, from *Oedipus Rex* and *Hamlet* to the Viennese comedies of Nestroy. It is as if psychoanalysis had found in drama, the art of impersonation, dialogue and enactment, its most suitable imaginative material. Drama, much more than the novel, relies on implication: on the significance of the unspoken which needs to be heard behind the text. When Freud explained that the essence of drama was conflict, and that 'it must include an effort of will together with resistance,'[156] he also summed up the dramatic nature of the confrontation between analyst and patient. Freud thought that watching a play involved 'the more or less conscious recognition of a repressed impulse.'[157]

A sense of theatre permeates all Freud's work. In 'The Moses of Michelangelo' the marble figure is treated as a dramatic character whose motives and past actions unfold, as in a play. Only two of Freud's short papers were devoted to novels (one of these, about *The Brothers Karamazov*, is more about Dostoyevsky than about his novel); but he wrote papers on *The Merchant of Venice* and *King Lear*; a paper on Lady Macbeth; and one of his most remarkable shorter works is on *Rosmersholm* and the character of Rebecca West. His definition of the Oedipus complex springs from an interpretation of Sophocles' tragedy, and the subject is also frequently illustrated with quotations from *Hamlet*. And when Freud wanted to show how deeply the idea of killing the primal father was embedded in the human mind, he cited Greek drama: its hero and its chorus represented, in his view, the 'same rebellious hero and company of brothers'.[158]

Such an interpretation of Greek drama may or may not have historical or anthropological validity; what matters to us here is that when Freud dramatised the mind he was extending to his enterprise an imaginative habit which was a pervasive quality of his writing and his thought. But the drama we witness in Freud is essentially internal. The purpose of the mind's activity, as he sees it, is to satisfy the instincts within. It is a protective activity: its aim is to render harmless the pressures of the external world, and to calm the anxieties within the mind by the memories of a distant pre-historic past. Alfred Adler said that 'we cannot imagine a psychic life which is isolated'[159] and that

there is a strict corollary between movement and psychic life.[160]

By contrast, the Freudian mind bends its energies on preventing movement; it strives towards the condition of being a closed system; it enacts the ceaseless drama of inertia.

But in this drama the warring forces have no autonomy: they could not exist on their own, without the others, any more than we could imagine a mind that was all Ego or all Id. Yet the idea of our mental and spiritual forces having a personal identity is not without appeal. This is reflected both in plays and in the way we read them. There is, for example, a scene in *Methusalem*, by the German Expressionist playwright Ivan Goll, in which a man's Ego, Superego and Id become 'characters'. Such post-Freudian extravagance is rare: in Goll's play the result is certainly tedious and undramatic. Medieval Morality plays, too, have characters such as Envy or Pride; but these are simply concentrated embodiments of envious or proud people. It is true that we could not imagine a man who was nothing but envy or pride; but Envy and Pride can remind us of envious or proud people we know.

Still, to identify dramatic characters with such qualities or forces is to restrict them: large areas of their nature, and their past, become unavailable to us, as if they did not exist. When Ben Jonson calls his characters Subtle, or Zeal-of-the-Land Busy, he draws our attention to one aspect of their natures, usually at the expense of all the others. When Vanbrugh and Congreve call people Brute and Constant, Sir Paul Plyant and Lady Wishfort, they do their own typecasting and commentary.

Now both Jonson and the post-Restoration dramatists wrote what we call open plays: their works are remarkable for the depth and wealth of their social background and their psychological insight. And yet, when these playwrights typecast their characters in this way, they restrict them: these people lose some of their possible depth and variety by carrying a label. We know very little more about Sir John Brute in *The Provok'd Wife* than that he is brutish; whereas Lady Brute was not born a Brute, and she is a more complex character partly because she is not, in the way her husband is, burdened by a name. In this sense the play really is about her, as its title says: Sir John is largely an abstraction who is there to help Vanbrugh make his point and of whom no further questions need be asked.

It is also true that Congreve, Vanburgh, Jonson, and the anonymous authors of the Morality plays wrote plays that were invariably moral in import, and their personifications and 'humours' always represent moral qualities: we meet no characters called Wistfulness or Clumsiness (though Jonson will amuse himself with gaolers called Shackles or clerks called Metaphor). Dramatists who label their characters in this way are usually out to make a moral point of their own, and to pre-empt the audience making theirs.[161]

The 'characters' in Freud's drama of the mind have no moral connotations of their own, because they have no character of their own. They are forces, not to be analysed or argued with. They are derived from, and dependent upon, each other: they have no independent, autonomous life. When we read the central conflict in Wagner's *Ring* in terms of a Freudian drama, we mean that Wagner had imposed his will upon his characters and turned them, to some extent, into representatives of spiritual forces; and that we can sometimes make a fuller and clearer sense of these characters by likening them to the impersonal forces of the human psyche. Like these forces, some of Wagner's characters come into their own, and acquire their full significance, only in relation to each other. Wotan or Brünnhilde do not have the same autonomy, the same resonance of personal existence, as Agamemnon or Mrs Alving. They do have a past; they have motives for action; and yet they represent less of an individual history, of personal decisions and moral outcome, of cause and effect in action. They form patterns more than they live lives. This is why the destruction of everyone at the end of *The Ring*, leaving no real living world behind, is a natural ending to Wagner's drama; and this is why this ending both transcends and falls short of our sense of individual guilt or communal responsibility. It would be both frivolous and inappropriate to consider how individual characters might have averted Wagner's closing holocaust, or to analyse their personal responsibility for it. Such speculations would be irrelevant to Wagner's overriding design, which hinges on the inevitability of what is fated. In the face of that, personal guilt, or indeed willed personal action, is insignificant. To this extent, Wagner, too, pre-empts our judgement; and to liken his characters to un-analysable spiritual forces is to emphasise how much they are beyond our factual and moral questioning.

When we read any drama in terms of Freud's drama of the mind, we accept such pre-empting: we accept the domination of the supra-personal and the beyond-personal over the human, and of the amoral and the unapproachable over the moral and the accountable. Freud's influence on our imagination is therefore both profound and contradictory. He has taught us to read life as if it were an open drama, and to read plays as if they were life. At the same time he encouraged in us, as spectators of drama and readers of literature, an inclination to refrain from questioning, and to submit to someone else's picture of the world.

Notes

1. *The Complete Letters of Sigmund Freud to Wilhelm Fliess, 1887–1904*, tr. & ed. Jeffrey M. Masson, Harvard, 1985, p. 193.
2. *ibid.*, p. 228, p. 286.
3. *ibid.*, p. 249.
4. *ibid.*, p. 398.
5. *Standard Edition* (*SE*), Vol. 20 pp. 59–60. I have used *The Standard Edition of the Complete Psychological Works of Sigmund Freud*, 24 vols, ed. & tr. James Strachey, London, 1953–74.
6. *SE*, Vol. 13 pp. 141–2.
7. *ibid.*, p. 146.
8. *Human, All Too Human*, tr. Helen Zimmern, London, 1909, Section 99.
9. *SE*, Vol. 21 p. 132.
10. *SE*, Vol. 19 p. 49.
11. *SE*, Vol. 2 p. 197.
12. *SE*, Vol. 19 p. 197.
13. *SE*, Vol. 3 p. 277.
14. *SE*, Vol. 22 pp. 73–5. For those who, like myself, read Freud in English, Bruno Bettelheim's short book, *Freud and Man's Soul* (New York, 1983), is important reading. It reminds us that Freud's language, in the original, lacks the scientific tone it often has in translation: he writes about 'the I', not 'the Ego', and when, in English, we read about 'mental life', Freud also means spiritual life, the life of the soul. I have attempted to take this into account. Thus, where I give 'instincts seeking to discharge their energies', *SE* has 'instinctual cathexes seeking discharge'.
15. In 'Leonardo da Vinci and a Memory of his Childhood', *SE*, Vol. II p. 136.
16. In 'Anxiety and Instinctual Life', *SE*, Vol. 22 p. 95.
17. In 'The Unconscious', *SE*, Vol. 14 p. 175.
18. In 'Moses and Monotheism', *SE*, Vol. 23 p. 118.
19. In *The Will to Power*, tr. Walter Kaufmann and R.J. Hollingdale, New York, 1968, p. 164.
20. Letter to Fliess, in *Origin*, p. 232.
21. *SE*, Vol. 3 p. 277.
22. *ibid.*, p. 278.
23. In 'The Sexual Enlightenment of Children', *SE*, Vol. 9 p. 137.
24. *SE*, Vol. 9 p. 200.
25. *SE*, Vols 4–5 pp. 620–1.
26. In 'Thoughts for the Times on War and Death', *SE*, Vol. 14 p. 281.
27. In 'Civilisation and its Discontents', *SE*, Vol. 21 p. 111.
28. *Being and Nothingness*, tr. Hazel E. Barnes, London, 1969, p. 51. In an essay entitled 'Freud's Autonomies of the Self', Irving Thalberg questions the very meaning of the Freudian model of the mind. The argument is strictly literal. For example: '. . . things you can say about the interpersonal goings-on seem to make no sense when the protagonists [*sic*] are inside your mental apparatus.' See *Philosophical Essays on Freud*, ed. Richard Wollheim and James Hopkins, Cambridge, 1982, pp. 241–63.
29. In 'Introductory Lectures on Psychoanalysis', *SE*, Vol. 16 p. 382.
30. In 'Thoughts for the Times', *SE*, Vol. 14 pp. 284–5.

31. In 'Observations on Transference Love', *SE*, Vol. 16 p. 164.

32. In 'Thoughts for the Times', *SE*, Vol. 14 p. 286.

33. In 'On the History of the Psycho-Analytic Movement', *SE*, Vol. 14 p. 20.

34. Bettelheim, *op. cit.*, pp. 37–8.

35. In 'The Question of Lay Analysis', *SE*, Vol. 20 p. 256.

36. Jung, was, on the whole, much less troubled by the problem of morality in psychoanalysis. While he was still Freud's disciple, he held that psychoanalysis stood 'outside traditional morality; for the present it should adhere to no general moral standard.' (*The Collected Works of C.G. Jung*, ed. Herbert Read, Michael Fordham, Gerhard Adler, London, 1953–71. For the above, see *CW*, Vol. 4 p. 196.) 'Moral law', he observed in the same essay, 'is nothing other than an outward manifestation of man's innate urge to dominate and control himself' (*ibid.*, p. 213.). Later, while it was not Jung's belief that people should be held morally responsible for the causes of their neuroses, he was quite capable of expressing himself strongly to that effect. Thus, during his famous series of Tavistock Lectures in London, in 1935, given in English, he told his audience how he had dealt with a patient whose symptoms apparently originated in his uneasy conscience over living on a woman's money. Jung said he had told the patient:

> You are pretending to yourself that it is not her money, but you live by it, and that is immoral. That is the cause of your compulsion neurosis. It is a compensation and a punishment for an immoral attitude.

In case his audience missed the point, Jung added that his patient

> deserves his compulsion neurosis and will have it to the last day of his life if he behaves like a pig. (*CW*, Vol. 18 p. 1.)

37. In 'Totem and Taboo', *SE*, Vol. 13 p. 50.

38. In *The Will to Power* (*WP*), Section 800 p. 421.

39. *WP*, p. 421. For Valéry, see *Collected Works*, Vol. 9: *Masters and Friends*, tr. Martin Turnell, London, 1968, p. 337.

40. *Freud and the Culture of Psychoanalysis*, London, 1984, p. 61. The same point is made by Oliver Sacks in *The Man who Mistook his Wife for a Hat* (London, 1986) p. 105: 'If we wish to know about a man, we ask, "What is his story – his real, inmost story?" – for each of us *is* a biography, a story. Each of us *is* a singular narrative, which is constructed ... through ... our discourse, our spoken narratives.'

41. *SE*, Vol. 18 p. 9.

42. *ibid.*, p. 15.

43. *ibid.*

44. *ibid.*, p. 36.

45. *ibid.*, p. 62.

46. *The Liberal Imagination*, London, 1961, p. 56.

47. In 'New Introductory Lectures on Psychoanalysis', *SE*, Vol. 22 pp. 107–8.

48. *SE*, Vol. 18 p. 39.

49. *ibid.*, p. 50.

50. *ibid.*, p. 40.

51. *ibid.*, p. 15.

52. *SE*, Vol. 22 p. 106.

53. *SE*, Vol. 18 p. 35.

54. In 'The Claims of Psychoanalysis to Scientific interest', *SE*, Vol. 13 p. 184.
55. *The Gay Science*, tr. Walter Kaufmann, New York, 1974, Section 341 p. 273.
56. In *Nietzsche*, London, 1978, p. 110.
57. In 'Nietzsche's Conception of Truth', in *Nietzsche: Imagery and Thought*, ed. Malcolm Pasley, London, 1978, p. 62.
58. *WP*, Section 55 p. 35.
59. *Beyond Good and Evil*, (*BGE*), tr. R.J. Hollingdale, Harmondsworth, 1973, Section 56 p. 64.
60. See Chapter I p. 19.
61. *Thus Spoke Zarathustra*, tr. R.J. Hollingdale, Harmondsworth, 1961, p. 161.
62. *Nietzsche*, p. 105.
63. See Arthur Danto: 'The Eternal Recurrence', in *Nietzsche: A Collection of Critical Essays*, ed. Robert C. Solomon, New York, 1973, p. 321.
64. Milan Kundera's novel, *The Unbearable Lightness of Being* (tr. Michael Henry Heim, London, 1984), applies Nietzsche's dilemma to the problem of moral survival under tyranny. If, Kundera argues, we regard our life as something unique and unrepeatable, it will be 'like a shadow, without weight, dead in advance'. In such a life, we need not care what we do. But if we think of life as something that might recur, it becomes a responsibility, a moral burden: it is hard to bear, heavy. Or, in Nietzsche's phrase, the idea 'would lie upon your actions as the greatest weight' (*The Gay Science*, Section 341). And if that is how we see life, then we are impelled to act nobly, so that life, when it recurs, might be better. I think Kundera knows perfectly well that Nietzsche's idea is hopeless. His hero Tomas solves the problem by imagining another planet where everyone would be born again, fully aware of their previous earthly life; and then another and another planet where a second and third rebirth would take place. Kundera concludes, with pessimistic realism, that this is the vision of an optimist. His novel illustrates how potent Nietzsche's agonised vision can still be, and how deeply personal it finally must remain: some people are impelled to act nobly, but as far as we can see they achieve nothing. Ultimately, they act as if they only believe in themselves.
65. In *The Genealogy of Morals*, tr. Walter Kaufmann and R.J. Hollingdale, New York, 1969, Essay l, Section 6 p. 31.
66. In *Twilight of the Idols*, with *The Anti-Christ*, tr. R.J. Hollingdale, Harmondsworth, 1968, p. 43.
67. In *BGE*, Section 287 p. 196.
68. In *Zarathustra*, p. 208.
69. In *Human, All too Human*, Section 101.
70. In *Twilight*, p. 85.
71. *Zarathustra*, p. 301.
72. In *GS*, Section 116 p. 175.
73. In *GM*, Essay l, Section 2 p. 26.
74. In *Human All too Human*, Section 39.
75. *ibid.*, Section 531.
76. *The Anti-Christ*, Section 2 pp. 115–6.
77. In *GM*, Essay l, Section 13 p. 45.
78. *ibid.*, Section ll p. 40.
79. In 'Civilisation and its discontents', *SE*, Vol. 21 p. 97.
80. In *GM*, Essay 2, Section 16 pp. 84–5.

81. *ibid.*, Section 17 p. 86.
82. *ibid.*, Section 18 pp. 87−8.
83. In *Twilight*, p. 98.
84. *Zarathustra*, pp. 65−7.
85. In *GS*, Section 360 p. 315.
86. In *BGE*, Section 19 p. 31.
87. In *WP*, Section 255 p. 148.
88. In *BGE*, Section 193 p. 98.
89. In *GS*, Section 348 p. 291.
90. In *Daybreak*, tr. R.J. Hollingdale, Cambridge, 1982, p. 12.
91. ibid., Section 13 p. 14.
92. In *BGE*, Section 21 p. 33.
93. *ibid.*, Section 13 p. 26.
94. In *Nietzsche*, London, 1973, p. 35.
95. In *BGE*, Section 16 pp. 27−8.
96. *ibid.*, Section 32 p. 45.
97. In 'Some Additional Notes on Dream-interpretation as a Whole', *SE*, Vol. 19 pp. 133−4.
98. In 'New Introductory Lectures', *SE*, Vol. 20 p. 80.
99. In *Twilight*, p. 65.
100. In 'Psycho-analysis', *SE*, Vol. 18 p. 239.
101. In *Daybreak*, Section 47 p. 32.
102. In *GS*, Section 354 p. 300.
103. In *BGE*, Section 34 p. 48.
104. *ibid.*, Section 4 p. 17.
105. In *GS*, Section 354 pp. 299−300.
106. In *Twilight*, pp. 82−3.
107. *WP*, Section 497 p. 273.
108. Quoted by Hans Vaihinger in 'Nietzsche and his Doctrine of Conscious Illusion', in Solomon, *ed. cit.*, p. 97.
109. In *GS*, Section 374 p. 336.
110. Quoted in Karl Jaspers: *Nietzsche*, tr. C.S. Wallraff and F.J. Schmitz, Indiana, 1965.
111. *Unpublished Letters*, tr. & ed. Karl F. Leidecker, London, 1960, p. 52.
112. In *BGE*, Section 251 P. 162.
113. Quoted in Walter Kaufmann: *Nietzsche*, Princeton, 1974, p. 63.
114. In *GM*, Essay 1, Section 16 pp. 52−3.
115. In *Anti-Christ*, Section 17 p. 128.
116. *ibid.*, Section 44 p. 157.
117. *ibid.*, Section 56 p. 175.
118. *ibid.*, Section 46 p. 161.
119. *Human, All too Human*, Section 475. The remark is no less offensive for the sentences that follow, on the painful history of the Jews, and civilisation's debt to them.
120. In *GM*, Essay 1, Section 9 p. 36.
121. *Unpublished Letters*, p. 80.
122. In *Selected Letters of Friedrich Nietzsche*, ed. Oscar Levy, p. 130.
123. Quoted in Hollingdale, *Nietzsche, op. cit.*, p. 46.
124. Quoted in Kaufmann, *op. cit.*, p. 466.
125. Quoted in J.P. Stern: *Nietzsche*, p. 87.

126. Erich Fromm: *Sigmund Freud's Mission*, Massachusets, 1978, p. 93.
127. In *GM*, Essay 3, Section 14 p. 122.
128. In *Twilight*, p. 88.
129. *ibid.*
130. *Anti-Christ*, Section 2 p. 116.
131. In *Twilight*, p. 45.
132. *Zarathustra*, p. 63.
133. *ibid.*, p. 101.
134. *ibid.*, p. 40; p. 80.
135. *ibid.*, p. 247.
136. *ibid.*, p. 232.
137. *ibid.*, p. 215.
138. Introduction to *Zarathustra*, p. 25.
139. *Zarathustra*, p. 215.
140. *ibid.*, p. 43.
141. *WP*, p. 255.
142. *Zarathustra*, p. 102.
143. *WP*, p. 363.
144. *Zarathustra*, p. 117.
145. *ibid.*, pp. 178–9.
146. *ibid.*, p. 341.
147. The passage in *Zarathustra* goes on:
     And truly, I had never seen the like of what I then saw. I saw a young
     shepherd writhing, choking, convulsed, his face distorted; and a heavy black
     snake was hanging out of his mouth.
     The 'young shepherd' then bites off the head of the snake. This extraordinary
     image may perhaps have its origin in the same event, if Nietzsche's father was
     bleeding from the mouth.
148. In Wollheim and Hopkins, *ed. cit.*, p. 247.
149. In 'Screen Memories', *SE*, Vol. 3 p. 307.
150. In 'Heredity and the Aetiology of Neuroses', *SE*, Vol. 3 p. 172.
151. *SE*, Vol. 19 p. 56.
152. In 'New Introductory Lectures', *SE*, Vol. 22 p. 61.
153. In 'Civilization and its Discontents', *SE*, Vol. 21 pp. 124–5.
154. In 'Beyond the Pleasure Principle', *SE*, Vol. 18 p. 60.
155. In 'The Future of an Illusion', *SE*, Vol. 21 p. 22.
156. In 'Psychopathological Characters on the Stage', *SE*, Vol. 7 p. 307.
157. *ibid.*, p. 309.
158. In 'Moses and Monotheism', *SE*, Vol. 23 p. 87.
159. Alfred Adler: *Understanding Human Nature*, tr. Walter Beran Wolfe,
     London, 1929, p. 18.
160. *ibid.*, p. 17.
161. In *Ben Jonson, Dramatist* (Cambridge, 1984), Anne Barton warns against
     over-simplifying Jonson's characterisation (pp. 107–8), and analyses the
     significance of the characters' names (pp. 166 ff.).

V

KAFKA AND PROUST
The doors of salvation

During the dangerous summer of 1940 in Paris André Gide was re-reading Kafka's *The Trial*. He noted in his Journal that he read it with 'even greater admiration, if that is possible, than when I discovered that amazing book'. Gide noted, too, that the novel 'eludes all rational explanation'; remarked on its '"naturalistic" notation of a fantastic universe', and the 'unerring audacity of the lurches into the strange'. The entry concludes:

> The anguish this book gives off is, at moments, almost unbearable, for how can one fail to repeat to oneself constantly: that hunted creature is I.[1]

To Jean-Paul Sartre it was clear that Kafka 'wanted to describe the human condition'; and that, in the abrupt, evil and absurd trial of his world, 'we recognise history and ourselves in history'[2].

One of Proust's most undogmatic critics, Roger Shattuck, urges newcomers to approach *A la Recherche du Temps Perdu*

> as if it were a long-term cure, or an initiation to unfamiliar mental and physical movements evolved by another culture.[3]

This is almost like an invitation to enter a retreat for mystics. Such meetings between a work and its audience are perhaps familiar by now. These are descriptions of encountering closed art.

Should Kafka and Proust be discussed together, especially in such a context? Are they not 'open' artists? We usually think of Kafka's work as being steeped in moral intensity. Proust's analysis of his

Narrator's life amounts to one long tussle with time as it steadily advances upon human life. Both writers ponder and dissect, with obsessional exactitude, the physical and spiritual operations of causes and effects. And, in the most elementary sense, both Kafka and Proust are telling stories: their narratives have, overall, a forward drive, a linear character. And yet it is true that reading them, and especially reading them for the first time, we often experience a peculiar blend of precision and obscurity: words, sentences and single events are clear in themselves, but are linked to each other in ways which we cannot always grasp. We might begin to wonder whether they are after all not, or at least not principally, telling a story.

The famous opening sentence of *The Trial* contains the most important fact about the book, which is that its hero, Joseph K., is arrested for no reason that he knows or that anyone, in the course of the novel, will tell him. This has always seemed hard to accept, and commentators have tried to find some offence, legal or metaphysical, with which he could be burdened: his solitary life, his ambitions at the bank, his weekly visits to a prostitute, or even his very existence. The American critic Philip Rahv, for example, thought that Kafka had meant Joseph K. to be guilty of bachelorhood:

> A projection of that side of his [i.e. Kafka's] personality which Kafka wished to punish, K. concentrates within himself some of the faults of his author's condition and character, including the absence of family ties.[4]

Now it is true, as Rahv says later, that it is not difficult to recognise, in the author of *The Trial*, the symptoms of compulsion neurosis. But that is not the same thing as reading the book as if it were a case history. Most novels could be read in that way; but the remarkable thing about Kafka is not that he suffered from compulsion neurosis, but that he wrote *The Trial*. And even if *The Trial* could be proved to be a product of a neurosis, it would still have to account for itself as fiction. The problem with Kafka is that his fiction needs interpretation: in terms of everyday life, which many of his settings painstakingly and painfully resemble, some of his narratives are either incomprehensible or improbable. It has been suggested that Kafka's work showed similarities to certain symptoms of mental illness[5]. This does not mean that Kafka was insane: it means that he has created a world of which no fully coherent narrative account can be given. In other words, Kafka sees the world as Freud sees the sick mind: it suffers from an incoherent story. Kafka may have been a deeply neurotic human being, but he was utterly sane as an artist; and to judge his work is to judge the control he had over his elusive and inherently incoherent material.

In *The Trial* this material consists mainly in the relationship between Joseph K. and the obscure forces that persecute him: a profoundly illogical relationship, which is portrayed with the greatest exactitude. Its main feature is Joseph K.'s total ignorance of why he is arrested and what he is being charged with. When, half-way through the novel, he wonders whether he should send in a written defence to the Court, he decides that

In this defence he would give a short account of his life.[6]

That might sound as if Joseph K. thought that he stood accused of being alive at all; but this written defence is never sent off, and the idea seems to me no more than an attempt by him to show how unblemished his life had been. One way or the other, we hear no more of it; and a close and objective reading of the book shows up all attempts to identify his offence as being utterly futile. Kafka himself may have suffered from a sense of guilt, but Joseph K. is entirely guiltless − if guilt be the responsibility for a deed knowingly or unknowingly committed. There is an entry in Kafka's diaries which implies that K. is guilty[7]: I can find no justification for this in the events of the novel. The entire action hinges on his innocence and his ignorance of the charges against him: here lies the core of the illogical world of which *The Trial* is a picture.

In the seven decades since it was written, *The Trial*, like *Waiting for Godot*, has become a classic; its theme, that life is like being accused by an unknown authority without having done anything at all, has become part of our mental landscape; and the word Kafkaesque has entered the language as the most familiar novelist-adjective since Dickensian. But imagine coming to it for the first time. The beginning is abrupt and preposterous to the point of being shocking. The first few pages reveal that Joseph K. is thirty, lives in rented accommodation, and holds a responsible position in a bank. He is fairly well off (he has quite a large number of suits), and has settled, if not altogether attractive habits. What is bewildering is the way events follow one another, from the very first sentence. J.P. Stern has rightly pointed out the hideous similarities between some of

Kafka's fictional events and the 'legal' procedures in totalitarian states[8], where it would not be at all unusual for two oddly dressed men to arrest you as you woke up. The difference is that Joseph K. has no idea who the men are.

> Who could these men be? What were they talking about? What authority could they represent? K. lived in a country with a legal constitution, there was universal peace, all the laws were in force; who dared seize him in his own dwelling?[9]

The questions are briskly pertinent; the answers chillingly imprecise. Identification papers are of no interest now. The men, we are told, represent 'high authorities', and claim that these authorities order arrests only on the basis of reliable information. These high officials 'never go hunting for crime', but,

> as the Law decrees, are drawn towards the guilty and must then send out us warders. That is the law. How could there be a mistake in that?[10]

Joseph K. does not notice the crucial piece of illogicality in all this. For how can a Law decree that officials should be *drawn* towards the guilty? How can you have legally enforceable intuition? But Joseph K.'s reply is stolidly uncomprehending. 'I don't,' he says, 'know this Law.'[11]

Our response to these pages has been both sharpened and blunted by the intervening decades. We know all about arbitrary arrests; about notions of official omniscience used to justify them; but we also know who is behind them. If Joseph K. had lived in Prague twenty-five years later, he would have known who his sinister visitors were, and why they had come for him; and they would not have offered to bring him breakfast from the coffee-house across the street. The passage is by now so familiar that we are liable to overlook its essential features. Joseph K. not only has no idea who the two men are: he shows no sign that he had ever heard of anyone else being arrested in this way before; and he is ignorant of the law which is said to make his arrest legal. And yet he acquiesces in a situation which seems both preposterous and sinister. If we follow the story sentence by sentence, then what happens and what is being said are perfectly clear; taken as a whole it is utterly perplexing. Perhaps the dialogue between Kafka and ourselves has broken down? The narrative, like all narratives, can be understood; but it has taken us, step by step, into an inexplicable world.

It is extremely tempting, when confronting Kafka, to attempt rational explanations. One of his most distinguished commentators, Professor Walter Sokel, has stated, for example, that 'a close reading' of *The Castle*

> reveals that K. has no legitimate claim on the castle because he was never appointed Land Surveyor.[12]

At first sight, Professor Sokel would seem to be right. But what the Superintendent actually tells K. is that he *had* been

> taken on as Land Surveyor . . . but, unfortunately, we have no need of a Land Surveyor.[13]

It turns out that, many years earlier, indeed so far back that it could not have had anything to do with K., the Superintendent had indeed received an order, he cannot now remember from which Department, that a Land Surveyor was to be called in. His reply, that they did not need one, went to the wrong Department, but without the original order; a particularly diligent official sent the Superintendent's letter back to him for completion; and a massive correspondence ensued. After immense complications, involving the Control Authority, the Head Bureau, and the Town Council (Kafka knew the labyrinthine ways of bureaucracy), it was decided that there was no need for a Land Surveyor.

What neither Kafka, nor K., nor the Superintendent tells us, however, is how K. came to be here nevertheless. K. himself says at the beginning that the Count is expecting him. This is *confirmed*, after first being denied, by the Castle. Yet K. never once claims that he had a letter, a contract, or any other form of invitation; and the narrative is thoroughly ambiguous about his purposes. It is entirely unclear, and remains so to the end, whether he had been called here or come of his own free will. His appearance (the Castellan's son describes him as 'a disreputable-looking man in his thirties', who possesses only 'a minute rucksack' and 'a knotty stick'[14]) certainly speaks against him being a Land Surveyor who is travelling on business. On the other hand, once he has arrived, he receives a letter from an official called Klamm, who is 'Chief of Department X', saying: 'As you know, you have been engaged for the Count's service . . .', etc.[15]

As you know? But it is not at all clear that K. knew anything until he had this letter; and though he endlessly puzzles over its phrasing, its forms of courtesy and its nuances of officialese, one thing he never notices is that it does not say what he has been engaged *as*.

Where does all this leave him, and where does it leave us? I think Professor Sokel makes the same mistake as August Röckel did when he questioned Wagner about the ending of *The Ring*: he treats Kafka as the creator of an 'open' work of art, of whom logical questions may be asked. But where Wagner proceeds by a series of majestic evasions, Kafka overwhelms us with vivid details. One of his earliest published collections, *Meditations*, includes a piece of some three hundred words called 'On the Tram'.

> I stand on the end platform of the tram and am completely unsure of my footing in this world, in this town, in my family. Not even casually could I indicate any claims that I might rightly advance in any direction. I have not even any defence to offer for standing on this platform, holding on to this strap, letting myself be carried along by this tram, nor for the people who give way to the tram or walk quietly along or stand gazing into shop-windows. Nobody asks me to put up a defence, but that is irrelevant.
>
> The tram approaches a stopping-place and a girl takes up her position near the step, ready to alight. She is as distinct to me as if I had run my hands over her. She is dressed in black, the pleats of her skirt hang almost still, her blouse is tight and has a collar of white fine-meshed lace, her left hand is braced flat against the side of the tram, the umbrella in her right hand rests on the second top step. Her face is brown, her nose, slightly pinched at the sides, has a broad round tip. She has a lot of brown hair and stray little tendrils on the right temple. Her small ear is close-set, but since I am near her I can see the whole ridge of the whorl of her right ear and the shadow at the root of it.
>
> At that point I ask myself: how is it that she is not amazed at herself, that she keeps her lips closed and makes no such remark?[16]

Under all the physical detail, the short text is tense with a sense of insecurity. It begins with a note of uncertainty, and ends with a question to which there is no answer. It is as if Kafka had been seized by the minute details of the girl's physical being because, for some reason, he was fearful for his own: he gazes at her face like a giant eye seeking proof of its own existence. And yet, if this girl were to step off this tram in front of us, we would not recognise her. Kafka's description is sharply defined but disconnected. Perhaps this is because he does not describe the girl's eyes (Kafka seldom does so). His description is compulsive, meticulous, and finally insubstantial: the picture does not contain a person.

The fact is that Kafka is interested in physical details not because they help him to describe the person or the thing they belong to, but because he is trying to map out a world in which he feels ill-at-ease. Nor, again, does he write narratives because he wants to tell stories, or not chiefly: he wants to give an account of the world, which he finds both incomprehensible and frightening. For if you can give an account of something then, to some extent, you have mastered it. Physical detail and narrative are thus both functions of the way in which Kafka felt about the world. This explains why detail is so important in his work, and also why it takes second place. One way of describing his development as a writer is to say that he learned how to make his obsessional powers of observation serve both his vision as a maker of pictures of the world, and his technique as a teller of stories.

For, to go back to K., with or without his letter of appointment: in Kafka, it is with visual details as with administrative details. K. both had and had not been appointed Land Surveyor; and the only value of asking the question is to see the unimportance of a precise answer. And yet we can see the reason for Professor Sokel's inquiry: Kafka himself provokes it by endlessly dissecting the helpless corpse of the mystery, as if there might be an answer. Half-way through the long tale the Superintendent asks K:

> 'Doesn't the story bore you?' 'No,' said K., 'it amuses me.' Thereupon the Superintendent said: 'I'm not telling it to amuse you.'[17]

He is not, in the event, telling it to amuse us, either; Kafka's quizzical humour about bureaucracy is almost lost under the mountain of description which he needs to ridicule it. In his biography, Max Brod quotes at length from one of the reports Kafka wrote, when he worked for the Workers' Accident Insurance Company, on the risk of accidents in a timber works. Kafka had clearly watched men operate these fearsome machines: his observation is meticulous, his tone matter-of-fact, almost chilling. The horrendous details of possible injuries are coolly described. And we might say that Kafka went on to spend his life as a writer compiling just such reports on the world as, with frail but purposeful fingers, he operated the frightful machine of his life. Some of his long passages, describing motives and counter-motives, intentions and their frustrations, might have been written by an obsessive engineer.

Investigations of a Dog is a masterpiece of compulsive ratiocination functioning in an irrational world. There is something spellbinding about the way the dog-narrator keeps returning to the attack, as if hypnotised by detail, trying to unravel the mysteries of doghood which, for him, are the mysteries of the world. ('All knowledge, the totality of all questions, is contained in the canine race,'[18] he says: clearly a Schopenhauerian dog.) *The Burrow* is a prolonged meditation on the possibilities and counter-possibilities of attack and survival, set in an animal's dwelling which is both rationally designed and grotesquely labyrinthine. Similarly, the heroes of Kafka's two mature novels confront the world as if it were a mysterious structure or machine: to understand its workings is to be saved. But the most famous of Kafka's machines is the apparatus for the execution of criminals in the story *In the Penal Settlement*. A substantial part of the text is devoted to its description; yet it is virtually impossible to visualise. If we read these passages as if they were a do-it-yourself handbook and try to draw the machine, we find that it cannot be done. First we are told that it consists of a 'Designer' on top, a 'Harrow' in the middle, and a 'Bed' at the bottom; a paragraph later there is another description which gives us the 'Designer' on top, the 'Bed' in the middle, and the 'Harrow' at the bottom. It is hard to see what we are to imagine when Kafka tells us that the Harrow 'shuttled . . . on a ribbon of steel'. And when we read that the Harrow 'quivers' as it inscribes the sentence on the victim's body, how are we to imagine the Harrow combining the two motions of shuttling and quivering?

How, again, are the three parts of the apparatus attached to each other? Kafka tells us that a battery in the Designer (which is at the top) operates the Harrow (which may be in the middle, or at the bottom). And we read, too, that the Designer and the Bed are '. . . each . . . fastened at the corners by four rods of brass.' Are they fastened individually, or do these rods also hold the parts together? How is the battery charge communicated downwards? Is the Harrow, assuming it is in the middle, also fixed to those rods? If it is, how can it shuttle and quiver? If it is at the bottom, how are the Designer and the Bed held up above it? How can the Officer slide down on one of the rods, all the way from the top, unless the rods are free-standing? We are told that the victim, as he lies face down, strapped on by his hands, feet and neck, has a protruding gag of felt in his mouth to stop him screaming, which he is forced to take, 'for otherwise his neck would be broken by the strap'. How, then, after the gag is taken away ('for he has no longer strength to scream'), can he lap rice from a bowl at the head of the Bed without moving his head? Finally, we are told that, as the Harrow inscribes the sentence, the layer of cotton-wool on which the victim lies 'begins to roll and slowly turns the body over to give the Harrow fresh space for writing'. How can this be done when the victim is firmly strapped to the Bed?[19]

By now, the reader will be in a state of nausea aggravated by tedium. This is not what Kafka intended, and it is not what we experience when we read the actual story. The point about this machine, as about the confusion over the Land Surveyor's appointment, is that the contradictions do not matter. The pedantic exercise we have just conducted is ultimately beside the point. Such close reading of these passages does not harm Kafka's story: if we re-read it in the light of what has just been said, we will find that it does not weaken its impact at all. The description of the machine is like certain types of narrative we have encountered: each individual part makes sense, but together they do not add up to a coherent account. But then, the point about these obsessionally detailed descriptions is not that they should suggest mechanical feasibility, but that they should convey an impression of fiendish ingenuity, elaborately contrived and methodically operated.

Once again, we have come a long way from K., who may or may not have been appointed Land Surveyor. ('Oh, yes,' someone from the Castle says on the telephone, 'that everlasting Land Surveyor.'[20]) Where does all this leave K.? The answer is, with very little, if we were tempted to regard him as an ordinary 'character' in fiction. If we did, we might be wondering where he had come from and why: was it to carry out a surveying job, or indeed any other job; or had he intended, from the very first, simply to settle down here? Could it ever have been in his power to decide not to come? All we know about his past is that he comes from a town which he has not re-visited for a long time. Like Proust's Narrator in *A la Recherche du Temps Perdu*, but for very different reasons, he remembers chiefly the church tower which, for him, has 'a clearer meaning than the muddle of everyday life'[21]. (It is typical of Kafka, as it would be entirely untypical of Proust, that the church tower is never mentioned again.) K. lacks the qualities of a conventional fictional character because he lacks the psychological density given to such figures by past actions and past decisions. As a person, he has an imaginative thinness which creates one of the main problems of *The Castle*: he lacks the mental and emotional substance to carry Kafka's meaning. His function is merely to support the narrative line and the mood of the novel. And yet, the pararox is that if Kafka had put more flesh on him he would have been at odds with his creator's design. As he is, he blends into the wintry landscapes and claustrophobic interiors which make up Kafka's picture of the world.

It is a deeply Schopenhauerian picture. Kafka knew his Schopenhauer: indeed, it is hard to think that he had not read the philosopher's description of man's search for truth as being 'like a man who goes round a castle seeking in vain for an entrance and sometimes sketching the facade'. Kafka's characters are propelled (or kept in a hectic suspension) by something as mysterious and blindly striving as Schopenhauer's Will; and they are opposed or pursued by forces, or people, equally obscure, adamant and unseeing. The Court pursues Joseph K. in *The Trial*, the authorities resist K. in *The Castle*, with the same implacable force. The Dog investigates endlessly; the creature in *The Burrow* is ever on the watch, guarding against an equally determined, though unidentified, intruder. In this sense, these fictions are both quest and pursuit, attack and defence: this is one of the things that gives them their sense of restless, fretful immobility.

At the same time Kafka's writings stalk death, or gravitate towards it with irresistible, Schopenhauerian force. Some of his Aphorisms bring this out with a bleak and burnished clarity.

> Martyrs do not underrate the body, they allow it to be elevated on the cross, in this they are one with their antagonists.

> There is no having, only a being, only a state of being that craves suffocation.[22]

These might have been uttered by Joseph K. at the end of *The Trial*, as he grimly co-operates with his executioners.

At the same time, there is in Kafka a longing for stasis, for the security of inertia. Note that the creature in *The Burrow* is not really afraid: indeed, he gives a fairly bloody idea of what he would do if he were attacked. No, he builds and guards his burrow with ferocious determination, simply in order to be sealed off from the outside world. The burrow is like a closed system: a subterranean version of the untroubled immobility of the Freudian mind. (Similarly, as we draw near the end of Proust's *Recherche*, we find the Narrator bleakly admitting that happiness consists not in 'the satisfaction but in the gradual reduction and eventual extinction of desire'[23].) The acquittal of Joseph K. in *The Trial* never seems a real possibility: a fact which robs the novel of any real sense of forward movement, and gives it its characteristic atmosphere of aimless agitation, and of an unending but doomed present. In 1910, Kafka wrote in his diary:

> Zeno, pressed as to whether anything is at rest, replied: Yes, the flying arrow rests.[24]

Another of his Aphorisms reads:

> The fact that there is nothing else but the spiritual world deprives us of our hope and gives us our certainty.[25]

Kafka is describing a static world which lacks the obligations imposed by hope, and has only the hopeless conviction of a vision: a vision of a spiritual life which is clearly unattainable through action, and which is possibly also beyond the grasp of the mind.

There is another reason why the novels have this sense of fretful stillness. It is that, apart from their protagonists, there are no real characters in them who stay with us for any length of time, or who are in any hurry to achieve anything. People in Kafka are functions. The Advocate in *The Trial* has no existence apart from the Law; the Officer of the Penal Settlement is nothing without his machine (a fact which he proceeds, irrevocably, to demonstrate). The Whipper in *The Trial* informs Joseph K.: 'I am here to whip people and whip them I shall'[26] (rather like Fafner in *Siegfried*, who tells Wotan: 'Here I lie,/And possess'). This also explains why there are relatively few people altogether in Kafka's books. There is a revealing passage in one of his letters, about a story now lost:

> At the very beginning four characters are supposed to talk and be vigorously involved in everything. But I can fully visualise as many characters as that only when they come into being and develop in the course, and from the flow, of the story. Right at the beginning I unfortunately mastered only two, but if four people are pressing forward, trying to take the floor, and the writer has eyes only for two, the result is a sad, an almost social embarrassment. These two refuse to be unmasked. But because my eyes stray all over the place, they might catch some shadows of these two, but then the two solid characters, being

temporarily abandoned, become uncertain, and finally it all collapses. A pity![27]

The passage defines the nature and limitations of Kafka's talent: he seems to have been unable to cope with the complex interrelations of several people, the causes and effects of shifting, unpredictable social and psychological behaviour. It also makes one realise how few pages there are in the whole of Kafka's work where more than two people are involved with each other. And perhaps one of the reasons why he finally abandoned *The Castle* was that he could not handle so many characters. Unlike Joseph K. of *The Trial*, who spends the novel moving from person to person and place to place, K., in *The Castle*, finds himself in a settled community where everyone seems to know everyone else: a close-knit village where people, unlike K. himself, have a past; a village obscurely but vitally linked with the Castle itself. The situation implies a sense of multiplicity which was alien to Kafka's talent and seems also to have been beyond his powers.

Now nothing might seem more far-fetched than to compare Kafka with Wagner; but we found precisely this to be a characteristic of all Wagner's mature operas, with the exception of *The Mastersingers*: most of their crucial scenes are scored for two voices. Both Kafka's major novels are made up, like Wagner's operas, of long, static, meditative passages linked by abrupt outbursts of action. What brings Kafka and Wagner into this improbable proximity is that they were both creating closed art. And closed art, we can see more and more, is unfriendly to the 'relations' of history and living society, and to the complex interreaction of characters. It prefers to reveal its meaning by way of inner drama; and it is difficult to unfold inner drama in a crowd, for too many characters, clamouring for attention, simply get in the way. Closed art lacks the ethical curiosity and the moral reserves that would sustain too many different characters in conflict. It is a despotic art, and despotic art is also a tyrant of character.

One subject Kafka hardly explores at all is childhood. There are very few children in his writings; those that there are tend to come in groups, with little sense of being individuals, and none of them have an important part to play. When K., in *The Castle*, recalls a childhood scene, it is to remind himself, in order to cheer himself up, of how he had once climbed a wall in a graveyard. This moment of infant pride is related casually, almost sadly, and it communicates no sense of childhood whatever. And when Kafka writes about families, their children are usually grown up: he has nothing to say about a child's relationship with its parents and the adult world, or about theirs with the child. These are relationships of growth and change; of shifting and unpredictable intimacies and hostilities: *relations* of the most vital kind. The same description applies to marriage: another area of experience to which Kafka's writing is virtually a stranger.

The three pages of *Children on a Country Road* (1904–5), published in *Meditation*, is Kafka's only piece entirely written about childhood, and its fragile, elusive ending, like an early picture by Chagall, places it firmly in fantasy land. At the end of a rumbustious day the little narrator runs off into the forest and towards a strange city, where folks never sleep because they never get tired. The whole thing is quizzical, yet precise. Kafka is still in his workshop, trying to weld together physical observation, static psychological fantasy, dream images and linear narrative form. It is as if he were undecided about whether he wanted to tell stories or produce some personal notation of the world. In these early writings closed art has not yet found its confident, despotic mastery. But the description of the child's view of nightfall, his uncomfortable, frugal supper, and of a wild, almost demonic romp in the open air, are piercing in their physical immediacy. Compare this with the opening pages of the *Recherche*, where the Narrator describes going to bed at night as a small boy. He is using his younger self as a focus round which his family and acquaintances slowly materialise in ever widening circles. But at their centre the little boy is all agony of mind: there is almost nothing in these pages to define him as a small body. Proust is evoking childhood as the fountainhead and prototype of all life's sufferings; Kafka evokes it as a dream-like paradise of energy, fleshed out with physical awareness, but entirely remote. The piece contains no reflection: it is, like the little boy who narrates it, all body.

With this short piece childhood disappears from Kafka's fiction. From Proust it receives its agonised apotheosis. But it is an apotheosis of a very special kind. E.M. Forster said about Proust, with prissy accuracy, that 'as to babies, they are quite outside his imaginative scope.'[28] Indeed, from the beginning, the little Narrator is all mind, all observation: there is no sense about him of the physical pains and hilarities of childhood. There is a smelly intimacy about being a small child; but Proust has little time for intimacy, physical or any other. Indeed, the greatest work of subjective literature takes place almost entirely in public. The *Recherche* contains almost no description of family life. We never see the Duc and Duchesse de Guermantes at home, except in the presence of guests. They have no children, and neither has anyone else while the Narrator is acquainted with them. Children in Proust are born off-stage; parents are remote. We witness the relationships of Robert Saint-Loup with his mother, his mistress and his wife only in public places, mostly parties. The Narrator's sexual awakening takes place in a hotel. He visits M. de Charlus in the latter's own house, but his extraordinary reception is, he surmises and probably rightly, organised like some bizarre theatrical performance, and the Baron comments on the contents of his home as if it were a museum. The Narrator tells us, sometimes to the point of tedium, that in loving Albertine he loves something he himself has created, his idea of her; and it is worth noting how very seldom we actually see them together, still less on their own, and that what they actually say to each other would fill only a few pages. Their 'affair' takes place in his parents' flat, in the parents' absence, and in conditions of secrecy, as if they were in quarantine, or staying in a hotel of dubious repute.

Combray is the nearest we get to Proust writing about family life; and it is quite clear that he would have been prefectly capable of writing an intimate and realistic family novel if that had been his intention. But of course even Combray is not *home*: it is where the grandmother and the great-aunts live, and where the family go on holiday. Even Combray is only temporary: it does not have all the associations, delightful or exasperating or both, of permanence. And so, it is a place of temporary residence which becomes the most solid point of reference in a world of deceptive and fugitive things. The point about Combray is that here everything is known and account-able for. We know where everyone has been and where everyone is going. No one can be a stranger, because sooner or later someone finds out where everyone comes from; and it is always some place someone knows about, so that everyone turns out to be someone's relation or acquaintance. Everyone, in other words, has a coherent 'story'. And yet we soon realise that even this paradise of certainty has its flaws. Combray society turns out to be entirely wrong about the pivotal character in the Narrator's life, Charles Swann: some of Proust's finest social comedy is contained in those pages where the Narrator's two great-aunts treat the faint echoes of Swann's immense social prestige with kindly incredulity and provincial condescension.

At the same time, Combray also has its mysteries, which are not to be penetrated until the end of the book. There are the famous two Ways, one towards Swann's house, the other towards that of the Guermantes', where the family take their daily walk. 'Swann's Way' has the fascination, for the little boy, of offering a glimpse of Swann's wife, whom Combray society will not receive, and also of their provocative little daughter; the 'Guermantes' Way' has the allure of an unapproachable aristocratic family, whose ancestors are buried in the local church, and whose glamorous historical name haunts the boy's imagination. At the end of the novel, the ageing Narrator will find that the two Ways are in reality one, but by then neither will matter to him very much. For Proust has written a deeply Schopenhauerian novel. Swann's Way and the Guermantes' Way are, we find, only images and names, and the quest to find their true nature will end in disappointment: a sense of recognition in which maturity is combined with a perception of insubstantiality, of a nothingness at the end of the search. Indeed, the title of the novel is something of a misnomer. The story we read is not the story of a search: it is a voyage of fulfilments and frustrations which is vague and directionless, not unlike the striving of Schopenhauer's amoral Will. And what is found at the end is not time as we ordinarily understand it, but a mysterious capacity to understand and value things in the face of time. When, at the end of the novel, the Narrator sets out on his search, it is a search for something he has already found. And so, strictly speaking, Proust's title tells us one thing, but the action of his novel is about something else. Indeed, the pernickety reader might even ask why, if the two Ways really were the same, the Narrator's father, whose sense of direction never ceased to astonish his wife, had not realised this. One answer is that this is one of those questions, usually provoked by 'open' art, but which does not enrich our reading of Proust's book. Another, which is not nearly as frivolous as it sounds, is that if the Narrator's father had made the discovery we would not have had the book at all.

Kafka's writing reminds one of Schopenhauer's remark that 'all original thinking takes place in images'[29]. Kafka appears to think, to imagine, almost entirely in terms of pictures: vivid, sharply defined, self-contained. His writing, Walter Sokel notes, 'confirms to or repeats the activity of the dreaming mind.'[30] In 1911 Max Brod noted in his diary that 'nothing but Kafka's dreams seem to interest him any more'[31]. His writing can be seen as a series of images such as one sees in dreams: haunting, abrupt, and full of details that do not always fit together. Perhaps the secret of his best early stories (*The Metamorphosis, In the Penal Settlement*) is that they were transcriptions and developments of specific dreams. On this reading, *The Metamorphosis* would have sprung from a monstrous anxiety dream, a masochistic fantasy which included the dreamer's own extinction. This is why the ending of the story, though it is, on the face of it, an assertion of relief, optimism and reassuring normality, is in fact so desolating: under the cool discipline of the writing we sense the anguished mind tormenting itself with a vision of life which would be all the better for its own departure, and in which he would leave neither memory nor trace. Kafka's imagination worked essentially with single pictures, and it was a question of whether a picture had narrative potential. *The Bridge* (1916) did not.

I was stiff and cold, I was a bridge, I lay over an abyss; my toes buried deep on one side, my hands on the other, I had fastened my teeth in crumbling clay. The tails of my coat fluttered at my sides. Far below brawled the icy trout stream. No tourist strayed to this impassable height, the bridge was not yet marked on the maps. Thus I lay and waited; I had to wait; without falling no bridge, once erected, can cease to be a bridge. One day towards evening, whether it was the first, whether it was the thousandth, I cannot tell — my thoughts were always in confusion, and always, always moving in a circle — towards evening in summer, the roar of the stream grown deeper, I heard the footsteps of a man! Towards me, towards me. Stretch yourself, bridge, make yourself ready, beam without rail, hold up the one who is entrusted to you. If his steps are uncertain steady them unobtrusively, but if he staggers then make your-self known and like a mountain god hurl him to the bank. He came, he tapped me with the iron spike of his stick, then with it he lifted my coat-tails and folded them upon me; he plunged his spike into my bushy hair, and for a good while he let it rest there, no doubt as he gazed far round him into the distance. But then — I was just following him in thought over mountain and valley — he leapt with both feet on to the middle of my body. I shuddered with wild pain, quite uncomprehending. Who was it? A child? A gymnast? A daredevil? A suicide? A tempter? A destroyer? And I turned over to look at him. A bridge turns over! And before I fully turned I was already falling, I fell, and in a moment I was ripped apart and impaled on the sharp stones that had always gazed up at me so peacefully out of the rushing waters.[32]

It is hard to read this text and not guess its source and inspiration to be a dream picture. It combines utter improbability with fearsome accuracy of detail: the coat-tails, the iron spike of the stick, the bushy hair. Note the inevitability of destruction, which Kafka is quick to state: '. . . without falling no bridge . . . can *cease to be* a bridge'. The reader has no time (almost no right) to ask: who says you have to cease? This is narrative in the form of instant flash and extinction; and it combines the heady excitement of Nietzsche (the being apart, the sense of being chosen, the sense of danger) with the obsessional watchfulness of the characters in the novels of Samuel Beckett. It is the essential illogicality of such writing, and the way it issues in nothingness, that puts it beyond questioning. The piece is short, vivid, violent: it reminds one of the paintings of Salvador Dali, in which a sadistic imagination combines with a passion for uncanny detail to create images of terrifying calm. The four fragments, under the title *The Hunter Gracchus* are probably different attempts to turn one short dream sequence into narrative form. The first, with its harbour, bell-tower and pillared doorways, its empty window and its monument, together with its oddly detached human figures, recalls the paintings of de Chirico: it has the same atmosphere of unnatural calm and self-absorbed activity.

Just as, in *The Bridge*, each single detail is clear, in *The Castle* the individual episodes are clear too: it is the way the details cohere, the way the episodes follow one another, that is beyond causation as we understand it. Note, in *The Castle*, how soon it gets dark every day; how quickly, almost to his own surprise, K. gets from one place to another. In this sense, 'dream-like' writing, and indeed dreams themselves, resemble narratives that had 'broken down': each segment is comprehensible, but the whole they form is obscure and discontinuous, as if concealing rather than revealing a meaning. But fictions are not dreams; and one effect of Kafka's 'dream-like' writing is that it can undermine the reader's confidence in his control of his stories. We do not always know where we are, but in a way which makes us suspect that Kafka does not know either.

And this sense of a succession of pictures, pregnant with imminent disaster, tense with obscurity, still, almost as if framed, is another thing that gives Kafka's work a sense of being always in a timeless present. What we might call the Proustian peep-show has a similar effect. The most shocking and important revelations which the Narrator experiences in the *Recherche* (the lesbian embrace of Mlle Vinteuil and her friend, the first encounter of Charlus and Jupien, Charlus in the male brothel) are events he witnesses through windows, as a concealed observer. These moments are and remain, for him and for us, like framed pictures; Marcel recalls them in that way; and they translate into pictorial terms two of Proust's most important themes: the revelation of hidden realities, and the arrest of things in time.

The *Recherche* begins with not being able to sleep, and ends in a great metaphorical awakening. The time that passes in between has fascinated readers and critics, more than in any other work of fiction, mostly because of a vagueness about time in a novel which has time for its subject. The narrative progresses in huge spans, but each actually deals with only a short period of time. Thus, the first 370 pages of volume three describe the Narrator's life with Albertine by reflecting on a specific day of their lives, during which she goes out without him and returns; then he goes out for an evening at the Verdurins and returns; then they quarrel, and the next morning he finds her gone. But this section also includes news of, and reflections on, the deaths of Swann and of the novelist Bergotte: two men whom the Narrator admired, who had influenced his life, and whose values, it is beginning to be intimated, he is about to outgrow. And so this long span of narrative brings with it several important 'endings' in the Narrator's life. The actual time-span Proust covers is little more than twenty-four hours; but the narrative intimates a spiritual time-span of immense scope and significance.

But, throughout several such long stretches of narrative, there is virtually no reference to actual length of time, to dates, or to anyone's age. The first date occurs some nine hundred pages into the novel, and even this comes from the past: the Narrator sees the date 1872 on one of Elstir's early watercolours. It had clearly been painted some years before, and gives but the vaguest notion of what the date of the narrative might be. And so, when the Duchesse de Guermantes suddenly exclaims that she had not seen Swann for fifteen years, the reader is jolted by the unaccustomed factuality of it into an awareness of time which seems both to have been, and not to have been, passing.

Some critics have been worried by the occasional discrepancies of fictional and historical time in the *Recherche*. It has been pointed out, for example, that Françoise suggests X-ray treatment for Aunt Leonie in Combray; that the Combray period cannot be placed, on the basis of other internal historical evidence, later than the early 1890s; but that Röntgen did not discover the X-ray until 1895[33]. But this has no effect on the way we experience the passing of time as we read, any more than does the appearance of the Princess Sherbatoff, who claims to be in exile from her native Russia, even though the time in the narrative is well before the Great War and the Bolshevik Revolution. It is right to compare the time scheme of Proust's novel to a creeper growing against the wall, which is 'organically complete in itself, but innumerable points of contact and support explain its upright position'[34]. But the reason for this has nothing to do with conflicting dates or with people's ages: it has to do with the way these are placed in the narrative. It is the irrelevance of accuracy which conveys the sense of Proustian time.

Kafka's novels affect us in a similar way. His narrative combines a sense of timelessness with the rigidity of a calendar. *The Trial* takes place over a period of precisely one year, as we gather from its beginning and its end; but in the intervening chapters time becomes increasingly vague. This sense of timelessness is reinforced by the nature of Kafka's characters, who appear to live in a time-less present, without the density of a clear fictional past. We encounter them in positions and situations of almost frozen immobility. It is not surprising that Kafka abandoned a chapter about Joseph K.'s visit to his mother: such a relationship would have involved a sense of a past as well as a sense of intimate kinship, and both would have been alien elements in Kafka's world.

Proust's novel is a voyage of discovery, and his Narrator suffers, all along, from the anguish of appearances. He meditates on how we ourselves clothe the faces of those we love 'with a loving and mendacious likeness'[35], so that when, after an absence, we come upon them unawares, we feel shattered by what we perceive as a change. Lying, he ponders, 'is the basis of all conversation'[36]; indeed, life is a 'perpetual error' which does not bestow its countless forms merely upon the visible and the audible universe, but upon the social universe, the sentimental universe, the historical universe, and so forth.[37]

Behind the pompous and melancholy tone, there is an unmistakeably Nietzschean edge to all this: when Nietzsche talks about people who 'read off the facts naively from the surface'[38], he might be describing Proust's young Narrator, as he begins his journey, irresistibly drawn by the fascination of names and social surfaces. The novel is the story of how the surface cracks, and what Marcel finds underneath. This is a matter of experiencing both art and life. When the Narrator achieves one of his greatest social ambitions and gets invited to the Duc de Guermantes' dinner party, the evening becomes an aesthetic as well as a social revelation. Before dinner, he asks to see his host's collection of paintings by Elstir, and he meditates on how the painter

> recreated those optical illusions which prove to us that we should never succeed in identifying objects if we did not bring some process of reasoning to bear on them.[39]

And he goes on for another four dense sentences, which deserve to be quoted in full:

> How often, when driving, do we not come upon a bright street beginning a few feet away from us, when what we have actually before our eyes is merely a patch of wall glaringly lit which has given us the mirage of depth. This being the case, it is surely logical, not from any artifice of symbolism but from a sincere desire to return to the very root of the impression, to represent one thing by that other for which, in the flash of first illusion, we mistook it. Surfaces and volumes are in reality independent of the names of objects which our memory imposes on them after we have recognised them. Elstir sought to wrest from what he had just felt what he already knew; he had often been at pains to break up that medley of impressions which we call vision.

There is something heroic about this description of the painter wrestling with visual illusion and the preconceptions of intelligence in order to arrive at what, for him, is true knowledge; and something intense and deeply felt about the Narrator's respect for his example. Then, when Marcel enters the dinner party, the experience is repeated on the social plane. He is crushed by his discovery that

the Duc d'Agrigente is a 'vulgar drone' with 'a ponderous noncha-
lance which he considered elegant'; that his personality is 'as
independent of his name as of a work of art that he might have
owned;' and that 'his name, entirely distinct from himself, bound by
no ties to himself,'[40] probably contained in itself all the poetry that it
had suggested to Marcel. At the same time, he finds that these
people retain their fascination for him, for to him they are still
enveloped in an air of history.

To the very end, Marcel struggles with a terror of relativity, a
terror of how the surface of life relates to the substance beneath. For
him, the world is 'the psychopathological universe'[41]. As in Nietzsche, the matter is not merely a question of optics or linguistics.
Proust, too, regards the problem of vision and perception as a
problem of moral value. Are objects and people what they appear to
be? Do they deceive us? Do we decide what they are before they tell
us themselves? The visual and aesthetic dilemma is also a moral
dilemma.

Looking at the Duc de Guermantes and his guests with Marcel's
eyes, we find that the past is present in these people in a manner
which also contributes to our sense of the novel's immobility. The
past in Proust is not so much the past of individual people as The
Past; not the life of the Guermantes brothers as children, but the
existence of Geneviève de Brabant and Gilbert the Bad. The past is
what people stand for, what they remind Marcel of, rather than the
people they had been or the things they had done. Proust's people do
not have a past in the sense of having done things which, like
accretions, enrich and complicate their personalities: rather, we
become familiar with them as they keep on doing much the same
things all the time. Theirs is a past of repetitions, not of change and
diversity.

Another thing that strikes Marcel about society is its systematic
unpredictability. He makes desperate efforts to gain admittance to
the Guermantes' salon, not only because he is mesmerised by the
glamour of their name, but also because he is in the throes of
adolescent love for the Duchesse. No sooner does he stop being in
love and haunting her on her daily walks, but he is befriended by her
and receives his long-coveted invitation. And the elusiveness of
others is complemented by a consistent social short-sightedness of
Marcel's own: note how often he actually fails to recognise people,
or is unsure that they really are who he had thought they were. The
warmth of Marcel's welcome at the Guermantes is as inexplicable to

us as it is to him. Just as we never find out what exactly he said to Bergotte to captivate him, we never know what it is that makes him a social asset. Equally, the things he says to Saint-Loup at Doncières hardly justify the latter in calling him 'the cleverest man I know'[42]. But this is probably deliberate. Saint-Loup is not particularly intelligent, and probably not used to mixing with 'clever' people. Marcel solemnly informs him that

> the influence we ascribe to environment is particularly true of an intellectual environment;

that each of us is conditioned by an idea; and that, since an idea

> is a thing that cannot partake of human interests and would be incapable of deriving any benefit from them, the men who are governed by an idea are not governed by self-interest.

Saint-Loup, who is not used to such conversation, may well be impressed. Actually, the irony of Marcel's pompous little speech is that the whole book is designed to contradict it. Marcel's life has been conditioned, and his vocation is to be decided, not by an idea but by sensations. And, in any case, we do not even know where he was educated, or when he read the books he appears to know. When, at the end, enlightenment comes to him, it has nothing to do with intellect.

Marcel is wrong, too, about men who are governed by an idea — though it is far from clear whether this irony was intended by Proust. For it is during this same Doncières episode that the Dreyfus Case is fully introduced into the novel: it is to become one of the moral cornerstones of the *Recherche*. And it becomes evident that the anti-Dreyfusards, who were governed by ideas, such as the sacredness of the army, were swayed by self-interest in the deepest sense. Finally, the Doncières episode is interesting because this is where Marcel and his military friends have a long conversation about the art of war. The discussion is passionately theoretical; and the upshot of it all is general agreement between the young men that if there should be another war, which they consider most unlikely, it is bound to be a very short one. All this is taking place in the first decade of the century; and the irony of this complacent prophecy is all too clear. Indeed, the whole Doncières episode is an elaborate example of how everything in the book, hopes and intentions, opinions and beliefs, is cancelled and undermined as the narrative progresses.

Proust's world is one in which things are *not caused*. Marcel gains acceptance into high society when he stops seeking it. Swann drifts into an affair with Odette almost unwillingly, falls passionately in love with her when, indeed because, he is unsure of her, becomes obsessionally jealous when he possesses her, and indifferent to her in marriage. Marcel's own affair with Albertine follows a similar pattern. For him love is merely a matter of acquisition: he can love only when he does not possess. When he is jealous, he suffers; when he is not, he is bored. And what he loves is not so much another person as a representation: what he calls a showcase for the perishable collections of his own mind. 'The bonds between ourselves and another person,' he observes, 'exist only in our minds.'[43] Proust makes a gesture towards characterisation when he makes Marcel say:

> I was too inclined to believe that, once I was in love, I could not be loved in return, and that pecuniary interest alone could attach a woman to me.[44]

But we are not convinced that Marcel is in any way a special case, for love takes the same predatory form for almost everyone. There is no real portrait of a marriage in the whole of the *Recherche*. The Verdurins seem only to be married so that they can give their Wednesday parties. The Guermantes' marriage takes place almost entirely in public: we never see them on their own. Saint-Loup becomes unfaithful to Gilberte almost at once after their marriage. 'Ignominious marriages,' Marcel reflects gloomily, 'are the most estimable of all.'[45] We long, in vain, to see one such marriage in action. Marcel's parents are the merest sketch. Marcel's relationship to his mother is entirely one-sided: she might almost not be a sentient person. Between him and his father no relationship seems to exist at all. Eventually, just as Alberich had disappeared from *The Ring*, both parents disappear from the novel: they have served their purpose, and Proust writes no more about them.

The love affairs of the book are all fashioned in the same predatory manner: men always love their social inferiors; women prey on men's money, their peace of mind, or both. Marriage is never the intention: Swann marries Odette only when a child is on the way and love has gone. Love in Proust is sterile, not merely in the sense of seldom producing children, but also in the sense of not producing any joy, any increase in one's knowledge of others, any sense of permanence, any lasting human value. Love is merely a matter of inflicting and enduring pain: it reaches its height in the scene of Charlus's flagellation. In this sense, homosexual love is the same as love between the sexes. Charlus is a homosexual predator until Morel arrives to prey on him in turn. All love in Proust is a matter of pursuit and destruction, and it is usually seen from the point of view of the pursuer. We never really know what Odette thinks of Swann, what Rachel thinks of Saint-Loup, what Albertine thinks of Marcel — and neither do the men themselves. Love is a one-way relationship in which cause and effect have no role: it is always the person you love who is most elusive. People are not loved for their qualities, not really even for their looks or their sexual allure. It is entirely typical of him to feel that Albertine belongs to him most completely in the unconsciousness of sleep; and his anguish at losing her is not grief for someone whose personality and daily doings were a part of the fabric of his life, but merely the obsessional self-pity, dignified by philosophical reflections, of a vain man.

In Kafka's world love is abrupt, savage and desperate. (Not surprisingly, he was a passionate admirer of Strindberg.) In *The Trial* Joseph K. kisses Fräulein Bürstner

> first on the lips, then all over the face, like some thirsty animal lapping greedily at a spring of long-sought fresh water. Finally he kissed her on the neck, right on the throat, and kept his lips there for a long time.[46]

They never meet again.

His affair with Leni, consummated, like the other K.'s in *The Castle*, on the floor, is simply a ravenous meeting of two different needs. He needs security and comfort, while Leni, in any case, as the Advocate explains, finds 'nearly all accused men attractive'[47]. In *The Castle*, too, Frieda seems to sense the supplicant in K., from a distance:

> As soon as her eye met K.'s it seemed to him that her look decided something concerning himself, something which he had not known to exist, but which her look assured him did exist.[48]

In both affairs love is almost pathological: a matter of persecuted men being singled out by women who are solitary, anxious, ill-used, protective and ultimately unknowable. And both affairs are doomed to helpless mutual incomprehension.

In Proust, as Jean-François Revel has noted, no one is ever seen at

work except domestic servants and expensive doctors[49]. To these, we
may add artists, for we see Berma act and Morel play the violin; and
Elstir paints during Marcel's first visit to his studio. But, apart from
these exceptions, professions simply label people: they give them a
social reference without a social function. Proust praised Flaubert's
work for being free of

> all parasitic growth of anecdote and historical scavenging,[50]

and sought to free his own work of what he thought might be such
parasitic growths. In *Jean Santeuil*, his first attempt to write the
kind of novel that the *Recherche* was to become, people's jobs and
professions are much more important to the story; and there is also
a realistic and quite intense atmosphere of family life.

Most of this, as we know, has gone from the *Recherche*; and yet
much of its strength still lies in its episodic nature. The crushing of
Charlus by the Verdurins, or the Guermantes' heartless treatment
of the mortally sick Swann are deeply conventional, realistic narrative episodes, and they stand out with huge human force. The entire
social structure of the book is made up of what, in someone else's
work, Proust might have called parasitic growths of anecdote. Indeed
we may say of Proust what Nietzsche said of Wagner: that he was a
miniaturist. Proust himself said, in an unguarded moment, that the
'sole merit' of his books lay 'in the solidity of their tiniest parts'[51].
And when readers say (with some justice) that Proust is 'difficult', or
(also with some justice) that he is 'boring', they are describing the
experience of reading a work of enormous length, whose huge
structural spans are made up of 'tiny parts'. The type of concentration that such writing requires is different from what we need when
we read eighteenth- or nineteenth-century novels. There, episodes
usually have a forward drive: they have a dynamic role in a linear
structure. Proust's 'tiny parts' have that function too, but they also
have another: they act as *leitmotivs*. If we read the *Recherche*
attentively, we gradually find ourselves, as we do with Wagner's
operas, in touch with all its parts. Proust told his friend Lucien
Daudet that the various parts of the novel would be

> like those pieces which, when played separately at a concert, we
> fail to recognise as *leitmotivs* until later when we are able to
> place them in the work as a whole.[52]

Thus our reading of Proust is forward and backward at the same
time. These may be elementary observations; but they tell us
something essential about the novelist's relationship to his readers.

This is not merely a question of the *Recherche* being a long novel. Kafka, too, noted mournfully in his Diary that Max Brod had warned him

> against writing such long passages and regards the effect of such writing as somewhat jelly-like.[53]

Brod's warning, quite clearly, had no effect; and all readers of Kafka will be familiar with the simultaneous sensations of pellucid clarity and closely packed density which his writing gives. It is often as if the text resisted us, unwilling to be read except at the cost of considerable effort. This is more than merely a matter of writing in long paragraphs, or, in Proust's case, in complex sentences as well, and using imagery elaborately deployed as *leitmotivs*. It raises the question of whether either Kafka or Proust gave much conscious thought to what the experience of reading them was going to be like; and if they did, what sort of experience they envisaged. For the fact is that this experience can be despotic as the effect of Wagner's operas is despotic: not only the visionary content of closed art, but also its manner of presentation demands the kind of total attention which is close to submission. Nietzsche diagnosed the essential quality of such art when he wrote about artists who had the 'will to *immortalize*':

> the tyrannic will of someone who suffers deeply, who struggles, is tormented, and would like to turn what is most personal, singular and narrow, the real idiosyncrasy of his suffering, into a binding law and compulsion.[54]

Nietzsche's analysis was inspired by the Romantic pessimism of Schopenhauer and Wagner; but we know enough about both Kafka and Proust to realise how accurate the diagnosis has turned out to be, and how much the first two great creators of closed art in fiction have in common with their forerunners. The implication of their style, and of their presentation of their texts, is that those who do not read them properly do not really read them at all, and that therefore there is a sense in which the writer does not wholly care whether he is read or not. It is a question, as Nietzsche put it, of whether your work is created

> from the point of view of the witness, or whether [the artist] has forgotten about the world.

If he has, he is the creator of what Nietzsche calls 'monological art'. This is of the utmost importance for the understanding of closed art, one of whose vital ingredients is a profound and despotic solipsism. Nietzsche's definition of 'monological art' and J. P. Stern's concept of the 'perlocutionary act' spring from the same source. Both describe an urge to communicate and assert something essentially personal, singular and irrefutable: an urge which is so intense that the receiving audience is diminished to being part of a near-ceremonial act. The irony of Nietzsche's definition is that he himself came to succumb to what he had diagnosed: it is not surprising to find the author of *Zarathustra* asserting that 'whatever is perfect suffers no witnesses.'[55]

One of the most important things that the worlds of Kafka and Proust have in common is that in them things are *not caused*. We never find out the reason for Joseph K.'s arrest, nor, in *The Castle*, whether K. had been sent for or not. The investigating Dog can see food on the ground and small dogs in the air, but not the human hands that scatter the former and cuddle the latter. The dying Chinese Emperor's last message will never reach its destination, any more than Zeno's flying arrow will hit its target: for in Kafka's world, if there is a cause, there is likely to be no effect.

One of the most crucial examples of this is the story *In the Penal Settlement*. The Traveller tells the Officer: 'I do not approve of your procedure.' The Officer seems stunned, and mutters to himself: 'So you did not find the procedure convincing.'[56] But that is not what the Traveller had said: he said he did not approve of it, which is that rare thing in Kafka, an open moral comment. Or is it? The Officer seems to treat it as such: he clearly considers that he has been accused of injustice, because he now sets the machine to engrave the words 'BE JUST!'; lies down on the Bed, and is duly executed. But it is an execution with a difference. The machine does not inscribe the sentence on his body: it simply stabs him to death. It also breaks down and disintegrates in the process (and its breaking down is as difficult to visualise as its functioning). Nor does the Officer experience that 'enlightenment', that 'transfiguration on the face of the sufferer'[57], that 'radiance of justice'[58], which he had described to the Traveller. The Officer's face remains exactly as it was in life: 'no sign was visible of the promised redemption.'[59]

In the Penal Settlement is probably the most amoral work of literature created by a painfully moral imagination. It seems to me wrong to interpret it as prophetic of the Nazi death camps: to do so is

to deal with only half the story. For the world which created the
machine is already crumbling; the Officer seems to be the machine's
last remaining champion; and he destroys himself because of the
moral disapproval of someone from the outside world. But then, the
manner of his dying may also make us doubt whether he had been
telling the truth about the machine: whether it really used to bring
enlightenment to its victims. Because, if enlightenment is a function
of justice, then the one thing the machine was unable to carry out
was precisely what it had been designed for: we see it perform the
act of justice upon the Officer's body, but without any enlightenment. And, in any case, if it really was an act of justice to kill the
Officer, then Kafka is telling us that justice, by definition, does *not*
bring enlightenment. Moreover, when the machine is made to
operate according to its essential function ('BE JUST'), it can only
destroy itself. Finally, it is possible that the Officer does not regard
the Traveller's words as moral comment, but simply as an observation on the machine's inefficiency, namely, that it is not just.
Therefore both the machine and the Officer have to be punished, and
the idea of justice is reduced to a question of efficient industrial
design.

So did we witness justice without a moral lesson, or murder with a
just cause? What Kafka is describing here is the murderousness, the
futility, and finally the impossibility, of justice: we can analyse the
meaning of the story until we find the very word emptied of content.
The fiendish tale leaves us with a feeling of horrified detachment: a
feeling which is re-inforced by the Traveller's hasty departure, with
a menacing gesture towards those he leaves behind. The legend,
current in the settlement and engraved on the tombstone of the Old
Commandant who had invented the machine, signals the possibility,
however vague, that one day the machine might work again. It is as
if Kafka were threatening us with a particularly terrifying form of
Eternal Recurrence. And it is entirely typical of his closed art that,
while ordinary questions about the story are irrelevant (it never
occurs to us to wonder where the Traveller comes from), the
questions as to its actual meaning multiply. It is also typical that
only one answer can be correct. Closed art may face the reader with
several alternative meanings, but will only accept one of them as
valid. In this sense, Kafka's stories are miniature Schopenhauerian
structures: loosen one stone and the whole edifice crumbles. The
way we interpret the functioning of the machine in the penal
settlement will determine our reading of the story as a whole. The

details do not matter. If we try to prove the psychological or mechanical consistency of a Kafka story, we end up with something both elusive and bizarre. Perhaps the best way to the heart of these works is to expose their crucial contradictions, their essential, discontinuities. Kafka is one of the very few writers who are best understood in the light of their own darkness.

At one time Kafka considered publishing *In the Penal Settlement*, together with *The Judgement* and *The Metamorphosis*, under the joint title *Punishments*. One can only suppose that some horrendous sense of irony, or anxiety, lurked behind this idea. Punishments for what offence? Few things are more nagging in Kafka's works than the sense of disproportion between the things that are visited upon his characters and the deeds, if any, that could be said to cause them. This monstrous sense of disproportion puts in question the moral value of everything Kafka tells us about the world. We saw how the beginning of Wagner's *Ring* was permeated by a sense of unspecific anxiety. That constitutes the very air of Kafka's universe: here things can never really be known. Nietzsche wrote that logic was

> the conceptual understandability of existence — for logic calms and gives confidence.[60]

That is precisely the calm and confidence Kafka's people lack: they are troubled by the profound illogicality of the world they live in. It is a discomfort of the mind. But it is not real guilt. Kafka's characters do not feel guilty, any more than they really are: it is the 'law' that confronts them with accusations. Kafka's world is one in which punishment is threatened irrespective of guilt. Anxiety is not something his characters feel: it is the principle of existence which informs the fictions as a whole. Freud held that man felt guilt irrespective of a deed; and Kafka's world is, in yet another sense, like Freud's picture of the sick mind: it is inflicted with a sense of guilt whose source is unknown.

And there is something deeply Schopenhauerian in Kafka's sense that things cannot ultimately be known, as well as in the relentless and inexplicable striving of his characters to know them. The same applies to Proust. Marcel's heartrending question about Albertine, 'In her heart of hearts, what was she?'[61] never receives an answer. There is a fundamental difference here between Kafka and Proust on one hand and novelists like Jane Austen or Henry James on the other. *Emma* and *The Portrait of a Lady* both have heroines with illusions about the world and entirely mistaken opinions about people. But, in the end, Emma and Isabel are enlightened, for their authors created a world in which things can be known. Emma's ignorance about people and things tells us something about her which is both concrete and moral. Her discovery of the truth is therefore a process of growth, of maturing. She may have been misled, mystified or ignorant, but that does not make unknowability the basic principle of the world she lives in.

The works of Kafka and Proust share a monstrous sense of disproportion between guilt and suffering. Morally speaking, the *Recherche* is held together by a sense of guilt which is largely imaginary. When little Marcel's mother decides to spend the night in his room she is clearly doing it against her principles, and the little boy is quick to note that his unhappiness has now been recognised as something for which he is not responsible. At the same time, the event has somehow raised him to the dignity of a grown-up: his demands have to be taken into account. And yet he also feels guilty for defeating his mother.

> It was the first abdication on her part from the ideal she had formed for me ... I felt that I had with an impious and secret finger traced the first wrinkle upon her soul and brought out the first white hair upon her head.[62]

The subject returns at the end of the long novel. Marcel still remembers

> the night that was perhaps the sweetest and the saddest of my life, when I had alas! ... won from my parents that first abdication of their authority from which, later, I was to date the decline of my health and my will, and my renunciation, each day disastrously confirmed, of a task i.e., to write books that daily became more difficult ...[63]

> Was not that evening when my mother abdicated her authority, the evening from which dated, together with the slow death of my grandmother, the decline of my health and will?[64]

There is something obsessional and confusing about all this. What has any of it to do with Marcel's ill health? The fact that he is an invalid is first announced, with characteristic vagueness, in volume two: 'For some time now I had been liable to fits of breathlessness ...'[65] And right up to the very end of the book, there is no hint that

Marcel's illness was in any way connected with the episode of the goodnight kiss. In any case, the reader might ask, why should someone's willpower begin to decline just when, by having asserted it, they have won a concession? Perhaps Marcel had already felt guilty, even before this, simply about his own unhappiness? We are not told. In this sense the whole of Proust's book is a vast elaboration of childhood anxiety, in which the feeling of guilt existed before the child had done anything at all.

Perhaps the unconscious reason for Marcel's desire to recapture the lost time of childhood is a need to resolve this monstrous discrepancy. It is important to note here how Proust identifies with Marcel. He often shows him up for being vain, insensitive, or cowardly; but there is nothing to suggest that he finds his Narrator's lifelong sense of guilt excessive. Even Marcel's extraordinary remark, that the pain of remembering the lesbian scene he had witnessed in his childhood was a punishment for allowing his grandmother to die — even this is presented at its face value, without any indication that Proust is aware of its hysterical illogicality. No, Marcel's anxiety is essential to the mood which dominates the novel and makes up Proust's picture of the world. It is one of the things that make the *Recherche* a closed work of art: for this anxiety is entirely beyond our questioning. Its function in Proust's plot is to feed Marcel's nostalgia, and ours, for the past. In this respect the *Recherche* is a novel for neurotics. It tells them that all events in life are like psychological symptoms: sources of pain, until they resolve them by looking back far enough into the past. It relies on a sense of loss and nostalgia towards the past in general and childhood in particular. People who lack such a sense usually do not like Proust. For the one question which would render the whole novel almost meaningless, is *why*? Why the longing, why the irreparable sense of loss? To ask such questions is not to question the novel as we might an open work of art: it is to call into question its very existence. And it is an unanswerable question: for who can argue with anxiety or nostalgia? But the neurosis, both in the novel and in the reader, is (at least temporarily) healed by Proust: he tells himself and his reader that by looking within oneself the past may be found again.

It is an elusive solution to this immense enterprise, because it is both personal and unrepeatable. But it is comforting for the neurotic reader, because what Proust is telling him is what he wants to hear. In this limited sense, the *Recherche*, too, is a perlocutionary act. Like a psychoanalyst of the self, Marcel resurrects his own past: as the narrative moves forward, his memories keep tugging us backwards, until past and present meet at the end. And yet, we may recall, even that past was a time of need, of lack, of an aimless search. In this sense, throughout the whole novel, until the very end, nothing changes: it portrays not so much action and change as a persistent state of mind.

Part of this time-less quality of Proust's narrative comes from his use of mythological images. When Marcel describes how, as a boy, he used to see Mme de Guermantes on the banks of the Vivonne,

> taking the place of my shattered dream, like a swan or a willow into which a god or a nymph has been changed;[66]

when he compares her and the Princesse de Guermantes in their box at the opera to

> the assembly of the gods in the act of contemplating the spectacle of mankind;[67]

when he compares Albertine to 'a young bacchante';[68] he is doing more than evaluating human life in terms of art. He is also making us feel that these people are safe from the ravages of time. For Marcel suffers from an incurable need to arrest time: we might say that, like Nietzsche, he wanted to *will backwards*.

Marcel's fondness for universal laws is born of the same desire to create a sense of permanence and stability in the world. The result is not always successful. Marcel, observing how Swann's values have changed since his marriage, comments sagely:

> Thus it is superfluous to make a study of social mores, since we can deduce them from psychological laws.[69]

What psychological laws? Where and when had Marcel learned them? The trouble with the remark is that Proust seems not to realise how it invalidates the entire social aspect of his novel, which reveals to us precisely that we deduce psychological laws from the observation of social mores. Proust's 'laws' also turn, occasionally, into meditations entirely out of proportion to the events which prompt them. Marcel's reflections on the true reality of emotions and perceptions, after he misses a chance to be introduced to Albertine on the street, only underlines the triviality of the event: the narrative weakens its hold on us as we wonder how so much mental activity can be caused by something so trifling. But, at their best, Proust's 'laws' are much more than a pose or a stylistic device: they, too, are part of an attempt at creating cohesion in an unstable and fragmentary world. This fragmentary and elusive quality, which underlay, for Proust, the apparent stability of life, receives its imaginative incarnation in Marcel's meditation on the fountain, designed by Hubert Robert, in the garden of the Prince de Guermantes. The passage deserves to be quoted at length.

> It could be seen from a distance, slender, motionless, rigid, set apart in a clearing surrounded by fine trees, several of which were as old as itself, only the lighter fall of its pale and quivering plume stirring in the breeze. The eighteenth century had refined the elegance of its lines, but, by fixing the style of the jet, seemed to have arrested its life; at this distance one had the impression of art rather than the sensation of water. Even the moist cloud that was perpetually gathering at its summit preserved the character of the period like those that assemble in the sky round the palaces of Versailles. But from a closer view one realised that, while it respected, like the stones of an ancient palace, the design traced for it beforehand, it was a constantly changing stream of water that, springing upwards and seeking to obey the architect's original orders, performed them to the letter only by seeming to infringe them, its thousand separate bursts succeeding only from afar in giving the impression of a single thrust. This was in reality as often interrupted as the scattering of the fall, whereas from a distance it had appeared to me dense, inflexible, unbroken in its continuity. From a little nearer, one saw that this continuity, apparently complete, was assured, at every point in the ascent of the jet where it must otherwise have been broken, by the entering into line, by the lateral incorporation of a parallel jet which mounted higher than the first and was itself, at a greater altitude which was however already a strain upon its endurance, relieved by a third. From close to, exhausted drops could be seen falling back from the column of water, passing their sisters on the way up, and at times, torn and scattered, caught in an eddy of the night air, disturbed by this unremitting surge, floating awhile before being drowned in the basin.[70]

This elaborate image is one of apparent solidity: the water of the fountain appears unmoving from the distance, yet it is made up of unceasing motion. The description is lyrical and clinical at the same time: it sums up the transitory nature, as well as the permanence, of both society and life. It is an image of both movement and stasis, discontinuity and cohesion. It sums up Proust's desire to impose unity and form, as it were by an act of imaginative will, on the stuff of life, which is recalcitrant and perishable, insistent but fugitive.

This need, to confer permanence on what is fleeting, is the counterpart of Marcel's fear that a real knowledge of things, and especially of people, is impossible. Take his description of Albertine, when he meditates on how she had entered

> upon that lamentable period in which a person, scattered in space and time, is no longer a woman but a series of events on which we can throw no light, a series of insoluble problems, a sea which, like Xerxes, we scourge with rods in an absurd attempt to punish it for what it has engulfed. Once this period has begun, we are perforce vanquished.[71]

Once again, Proust invokes the apparent solidity of water to describe the utter elusiveness of other people. The passage also recalls Nietzsche's analysis of the thinking mind: Marcel takes his idea of Albertine to pieces until she seems to have no recognisable identity left. This is both the cause and the effect of his own anguish. The closer people are to Marcel, the truer this is. Mme Verdurin, Françoise, Norpois and Charlus achieve the majestic roundedness of the greatest creations in fiction: they belong to the world of open art, where people have both the burden and the freedom of their past and their future. This is why, in the novel's present, they move with the fleshy unpredictability of real people, and, at the same time, enact the dance-like patterns of art. But Albertine, like Kafka's girl on the tram, is ultimately featureless: when we unwind the cocoon of Marcel's meditations about her, we find no identifiable person. The woman Proust created lacks the mental and emotional substance that could carry the immense burden of Marcel's questioning anguish. She is to the fictional world of the *Recherche* what the spear is to the world of *Parsifal* or the ring to the world of *The Ring*: a passive object of contention that can, in the end, only inflict suffering. While Marcel has her, he watches with terror how her identity disintegrates in his mind; after he has lost her he suffers until he becomes desolated by the fact that even his grief for her is gone. He is trapped between apathy and agony. His spiritual solution is entirely appropriate to one who believes that 'the experience of

oneself ... is the only true experience.'[72] The only way left for
Marcel is inwards. At the end of the novel he is utterly alone

The *Recherche* is unique among novels in that there is serious
critical debate about how it really ends. Edmund Wilson thought it
was 'one of the gloomiest books ever written'[73]; after the affair with
Albertine the novel has, for him, 'nothing but demoralisation and
decay'[74] until the Narrator integrates his experience into literature.
By contrast, Germaine Brée thinks that the novel ends on a note of
triumph, of a destination achieved[75]. Both critics treat the book as a
moral work; and so, in a sense, it is. But, like the mature operas of
Wagner, the *Recherche* seems to have been written by two people: a
moralist and a visionary. Proust the moralist is Proust the open
novelist. Not only has he created a critical portrait of a society, with
a large number of characters who can all be 'questioned' by us: the
entire novel is, in a profound and vital sense, an act of questioning.
    Marcel is deeply engaged with his past, his surroundings, and his
own personality. The novel seeks to unravel the causes that shaped
the Marcel we see at the end: its purpose is to codify the logic of his
existence. Proust also approached society and politics in a spirit of
impassioned inquiry. He wanted to analyse how people and society
shape one another. The way he portrays society has its specific
limitations; but it is clear that Proust attached an unmistakeably
moral value to social action and behaviour. This is worth stating so
crudely because we shall find Marcel asserting at the end of the novel
that art is 'the most austere school of life, the true last judgement;'[76]
whereas the novel delivers its own last judgements on people in the
context of moral conduct. We assess the worth of the Duc and
Duchesse de Guermantes, finally, not on the basis of their resemblance to historical figures, not on the basis of her sense of dress or his
understanding of painting, but on the basis of how they treat the
mortally sick Swann.
    But the *Recherche* has two endings. The one is public and moral;
the other is private and amoral. The happiness that finally comes to
Marcel is a private experience: it is attained through the sensuous
joy he finds in apprehending 'the essence of things'[77]. And the
important thing about this apprehension is that it is experienced
without the participation of Marcel's will or his intellect. The writer
who reasons, he observes, goes astray. 'A work in which there are
theories,' he asserts, 'is like an object which still has its price-tag on

it.'[78] These two sentences seriously undermine the value of the social and public novel we have read so far. Marcel has been trying to make sense of the world, to unravel its meaning: what else is that but a form of reasoning? He has tried to clarify and codify his understanding and his experience by formulating general laws. To talk about 'the general law of oblivion'[79]: what is that but an attempt to sum up experience in a theory and attach a price-tag to it? And yet all this is now denied in the 'private' conclusion of the book: Marcel experiences his revelations, like Nietzsche's Zarathustra, almost in a state of unconsciousness.

> It is sometimes just at the moment when we think that everything is lost that the intimation arrives which may save us; one has knocked at all the doors which lead nowhere, and then one stumbles without knowing it on *the only door through which one can enter* — which one might have sought in vain for a hundred years — and it opens of its own accord (my italics).[80]

One is irresistibly reminded of the priest's parable in Kafka's *The Trial*. It is about the man from the country who waits all his life by the open door leading to the Law, only to be told by the Door-keeper:

> 'No one but you could gain admittance through this door, since this door was intended for you. I am now going to shut it.'[81]

Few passages in literature communicate to us with such force the futility of all endeavour. And we can see that, in the last analysis, there is no difference between the bleak ending of Kafka's novel and the apparently optimistic one of Proust's. Both Marcel and the man from the country have been standing by a door, one closed, the other open, but both leading to the only salvation possible for each one of them alone. They are both ignorant of the nature of this salvation. One of them, in the end, is locked out, though he wanted to be admitted all his life; the other is admitted, though he only dimly sensed that he had been locked out of somewhere. Their will, their actions and their intentions play no part in whether they enter, or are turned away from, the doors of salvation. Marcel talks about having knocked on doors which lead nowhere as if, throughout the novel we have just read, he had been searching for enlightenment. But the truth is that this is only how it seems to him now: in reality, he spent his life pursuing women and social success. It is in this sense that the novel has not been a search at all. It is only now, at the very end, that the search begins — except that, with the revelations Marcel has just had, it is virtually over.

Of course, in an elementary sense, if Proust had made Marcel talk constantly about looking for his salvation, we might have had a tedious novel and no real revelation at the end: from this point of view, Germaine Brée is right to call the *Recherche* a detective story. But actually, she calls it 'a moral detective story'[82]; and that is a very different thing indeed. For what Marcel and the man from the country have in common is that the salvation of the one and the damnation of the other come to them irrespective of will, action or merit. Like so many other things in Kafka and Proust, their fates are *not caused*. When Proust chooses involuntary memory as the road to salvation he confirms, like Nietzsche, the supreme value of the unintentional. This is why salvation and damnation in Kafka and Proust are essentially amoral. They are merely effect without cause: this is why they have not, and do not express, value. Camus praised the moral value of lucidity in Kafka, and went on to add that this moral value could not be 'diminished in his eyes by pronouncing it as sterile as all pride.'[83] It really is extraordinary to see one of the most fiercely moral spirits of twentieth-century literature justifying his amoral submission to someone else's work with such a hollow and self-indulgent argument. If you call literature moral when you admit that it is sterile, what does 'moral' mean? What can be moral that is not productive of something; that is not dynamic, purposeful?

It is not a question of mere optimism. If we find the conclusion of the *Recherche*, for all the exaltation of its language, pessimistic and bleak, it is because of the totally fortuitous nature of the happiness that has come to Marcel. We know, and he knows, that but for the incident of the uneven paving-stone he would still be as apathetic, disappointed and unfulfilled as before. If Proust really thought, as he told his friend Mme Straus, that he had written 'a breviary of joys'[84], he was quite mistaken. All closed art is pessimistic, because it gives stagnation a sense of achievement, and deprives movement and energy of their possibility of fulfilment. If the reader replies that this is to beg the question, because by saying this we approach Kafka and Proust from a moral and dynamic point if view, the answer must be that both novelists demand such an approach. Kafka's best work raises questions of guilt, punishment and justice, all moral matters, only to reveal them to be empty of meaning. Proust, in his turn, presented the social and moral portrait of an age; and he also made his Narrator assert that

> There is in the human body a certain instinct for what is beneficial to us, as there is in the heart for what is our moral duty.[85]

From the philosophical point of view, this is neither more nor less satisfactory than Kant's moral imperatives, or Socrates' assertion that evil-doing proceeds only from ignorance. But Proust was a novelist; and what concerns us here is that he created a fictional world, with a hero who went around believing in moral duty but whose salvation came to him without his doing anything to achieve it. Kafka and Proust, like Wagner, created a moral and an amoral world at the same time.

Like Wagner, too, they created heroes who possess a curious innocence. Kafka and Proust shared a problem which had, until then, been unusual for novelists: how to write narrative which is objective, linear and causal, and communicate a picture of the world which is subjective, circular and self-contained. In other words, how to tell a story and, at the same time, create a vision. Do you write as an omniscient narrator who both knows and shapes everything and everybody he describes, or as a suffering creature to whom it all happens?

In the last analysis, we all know that novels are written by somebody, usually novelists, and that all fiction-reading is a suspension of some kind of disbelief: we read, and temporarily treat as truth, a text which we know to have been wholly or partly invented by somebody. We know perfectly well that Conrad's novels were written by Conrad: the fact that he presents them as tales told to him, a fictional Conrad, by a fictional narrator called Marlow, gives these narratives a temporary, haunting sense of reality, as if we had found an old document in a trunk. The fact that Sartre presents the narrative of *Nausea* as someone's diary does not make the novel authentic in a factual sense: it is a literary gesture, whose artificial reality we provisionally accept. We recognise the trick and at the same time connive at it: this degree of complicity is part of the essence of all literary and artistic experience. Roland Barthes wonders about who it might be that utters the narrative generalisations in Balzac's novels: is it the hero of the novel, is it Balzac the person, or Balzac the novelist?[86] The distinctions have their value; but, in the final analysis, all that matters is that we are addressed by a fictional consciousness. It is not so much a question of whether the story is told by a novelist as a citizen, a novelist posing as an omniscient narrator, or a fictional spokesman of his whom we call the hero: it is, rather, a question of what is being told.

Flaubert's *Sentimental Education*, for example, is written by an apparently omniscient narrator; and yet virtually the whole novel could be reprinted in the first person singular, without altering anything but the personal pronouns, since not only does almost the whole action take place in Frédéric's presence, but it is also experienced from his point of view. Meanwhile, the novel as a whole leaves us in no doubt as to what we should think of Frédéric: his view of people and events is presented in such a way that we are able to judge him as well as the other characters. His eyes are at once his, Flaubert's and ours: through him, we can see more, and see it better, than he can.

Now the central concern of both Kafka and Proust is nothing less than to comprehend the meaning, the spiritual essence, of life. Accordingly, their heroes are people who lack such a comprehension. The subject of the novels is, to put it simply, the way in which truth is or is not grasped by human beings; and Marcel and the two K.s are used to show us how this happens. This is why all three of them are rather innocent people, hamfisted, sometimes even dim. These are the most important characteristics which distinguish them from their authors. Thus Joseph K., in *The Trial*, reflects that 'it was not usual for him to learn from experience'[87]. The Landlady in *The Castle* tells K. that his

> ignorance of the local situation is appalling ... it's the kind of ignorance which can't be enlightened at one attempt and perhaps never can be.[88]

He is told that he talks 'like a child'[89], and that he is 'incapable of understanding'[90] why he cannot procure an interview with Klamm. The Landlady seems to have sized K. up correctly: he proves this by actually falling asleep during his potentially very useful meeting with the official Bürgel.

Similarly, when, in the *Recherche*, Marcel reads a passage in the (pastiche) Journal of the Goncourts about the Verdurins' evenings, he is astonished to find that these evenings, which he had thought tedious and vulgar, are described as stimulating social and intellectual experiences. Marcel is depressed, and comments sadly to himself:

> Certainly I had never concealed from myself that I knew neither how to listen nor, once I was not alone, how to look.[91]

But this strikes us as utterly preposterous: how could such a person have accumulated the mass of physical, social and psychological detail which fills the 2900 pages we have read so far? And yet it is clear that Proust has taken considerable trouble to define Marcel's character in precisely this way. It is not merely that the older Marcel, who is telling the story, is more mature than the younger self he is describing: we are asked to believe that, all along, he had been incapable of observation and timorous of experience. Thus, he tells us that he could not say what Mme Verdurin had been wearing one evening because 'I have not an observant mind'[92]. When Marcel was a child, we are told, he used to be so cowardly that he would run away in order not to witness a family conflict; and he is just as cowardly much later, when the Verdurins are preparing to humiliate Charlus:

> I had but one thought, which was to leave the Verdurins' house before the execution of M. de Charlus occurred.[93]

Marcel reflects, too, that, in the past, he knew 'more books than people and literature better than life'.[94] But it is far from clear that, by the end of the novel, Marcel knows either people or life any better. He is constantly astonished by everything that happens to him: at the very end he is shaken to the core by the spectacle of other people getting old.

One is reminded of a passage in Dostoyevsky's *The Idiot*: Radomsky tells Prince Myshkin that all the disastrous events in the story had been caused by Myshkin's 'inherent inexperience'[95]. This is a curious phrase. Strictly speaking, inexperience is not inherent: it is merely a condition which precedes experience. The Russian word Dostoyevsky uses here has connotations of 'ineffectualness', that is, not simple inexperience in the ways of the world, but a quality which is the opposite of 'practical'. What Radomsky is saying is that Myshkin is inherently unable to absorb and master experience, or to learn from it. Now Radomsky is far from being an objective witness, and his judgement of Myshkin is only partly accurate. Dostoyevsky's point, to put it very simply, is that Myshkin's uncorrupted innocence enables him to perceive and understand certain things better than other people with their more sophisticated, but possibly more blunted, sensibilities. And yet Radomsky is throwing light on an important aspect of Myshkin's character: there are certain experiences, certain traits in people as revealed by their actions, to which Myshkin's understanding is impervious.

The same kind of 'inherent inexperience' may serve as a definition of something crucial to the characters of both Marcel and the two K.s. In Kafka's novels this is part of the imperviousness of everything and everyone to events: his heroes remain as unchanged by experience as anyone else – as indeed Kafka's entire world. Kafka underlines this by making the two K.s persistent, bellicose, sometimes even remarkably self-centred. They are far from being passive victims: Gide was wrong when he thought of Joseph K. as simply a 'hunted creature'. In fact, he is quite often on the attack; and when, for example, he keeps his anxious clients waiting at the bank, he may well appear as unapproachable and unpredictable to them as the Law and its officers appear to him. When he takes initiatives they tend to turn out to be disastrous ones: his 'inherent inexperience' defines both him and the world he moves in.

One of Marcel's functions in the *Recherche* is to think a great deal: an activity in which the two K.s hardly engage at all. Indeed, they may be said to have virtually no mental life. By contrast, Marcel has more mental life than most characters in fiction. When he tells us that

> what we call experience is merely the revelation to our own eyes of a trait in our character,[96]

he is diagnosing the unchanging nature of the self, the subjective nature of experience, and the mind's capacity for analysing both. And it is precisely this kind of reflection that makes Marcel's 'inherent inexperience' at odds with the novel as a whole. This is the essential discontinuity in the *Recherche*. It is hard to believe that anyone as obtuse and remote as he is made to appear could have given us his descriptions and analyses of life and experience. Critics who believe that the Narrator and Marcel are two different fictional persons are covering over, with interpretative ingenuity, a profound rift in Proust's work. The fact is that Marcel simply does not have the intelligence of his own narrative voice. And, because of the retrospective nature of the story, this voice remains much the same from childhood to middle age. Marcel relates all his childish joys and fears, all his adolescent apprehensions, with the complex understanding of an adult mind which both remembers and evaluates them. And yet the novel never communicates the experience of acquiring that understanding. But such is the steady consistency of the narrative voice that, combined with the sheer length of the novel, Marcel's inadequacies are swallowed up in its flow. Like our inquiry into Proustian time, or into the mechanical feasibility of Kafka's execution machine, our observations about Marcel's intelligence are finally irrelevant to Proust's vast design, which is to create a picture of the world as a search for the past within the self. Critics who regard novels as artefacts, things that simply exist rather than imitate other things, may be right about the *Recherche*, to the extent that it finally matters little whether its narrative voice is Proust's or Marcel's. In our experience of reading it, it is, in the end, simply a story which is *being told*.

> He who, by virtue of the strength of his memory and imagination, can most clearly call up what is long past in his own life will be more conscious than others of the *identity of all present moments throughout the whole of time*. Through this consciousness of the identity of all present moments one apprehends that which is most fleeting of all, the moment, as that alone which persists. And he who, in such intuitive fashion, becomes aware that the *present*, which is in the strictest sense the sole form of reality, has its source *in us*, and thus arises from within and not from without, cannot doubt the indestructibility of his own being.[97]

This comes, not from the *Recherche*, but from one of Schopenhauer's essays, 'On the Indestructibility of Our Essential Being by Death'. Like Nietzsche and Proust after him, Schopenhauer wanted to resist the passing of time by imposing his will upon it. Like Proust, he believed that reality had its source in ourselves; and that this enabled us to unite the past with the present and to say a defiant No to time, and therefore also to death. It is a private vision, self-sufficient because unquestion-able, of timelessness. Marcel, too, records that when he tasted the *madeleine* he also stopped being afraid of death. How, he wonders, was this possible? He now surmises that it was because his inner being found something in common between a past and a present moment. This something had to be, by definition, 'extra-temporal'[98], and by finding it Marcel placed himself, too, outside time. He calls such timeless moments 'fragments of essence withdrawn from Time'[99]; and they contain he tells us, the only true joys he had ever known. His spiritual objective is to 'immobilise' such moments[100], and to get to know them. It is by doing this that Marcel launches himself on his vast journey of literature as introspection. He is about to initiate himself into the magic of the self.

Proust makes a polite nod in the general direction of mankind by telling us that if we should consider this a form of egotism, then 'it was an egotism that could be put to work for the benefit of other people.'[101]

This sudden outburst of literary altrusim is unconvincing. By now we know perfectly well that Marcel's journey is inwards. He has already reflected that art could not tell him anything about the lives of other people, and he has told us, too, that the essence of the past which he would try to express 'is, in part, subjective and incommunicable'[102]. We have reached here the pure air of blissful, self-contained amorality familiar to us, in different guises, from Schopenhauer, Nietzsche and Wagner. The outside world gradually drifts away. As Marcel begins to concentrate on his 'inner book of unknown symbols', he also begins to see 'every public event, be it the Dreyfus case, be it the war,'[103] as nothing more than an idle writer's excuse to delay his great task of deciphering the self.

Those words simply annihilate the moral core of the novel. Samuel Beckett, quick to recognise a fellow spirit, was quite right to point out (he was the first to do so) that 'Proust is completely detached from all moral considerations,'[104] And so, though the novel ends on a note of confirmation and joy, its ending is actually bleak. I do not think that this was what Proust intended. But the fact is that Marcel has reached a desolate, almost barren maturity. Like Wagner's operas, the *Recherche* has an inner and an outer story. The outer story is one of movement, progress and change; of deepening perceptions; of moral growth. The inner story, by comparison, is one of stasis. Marcel has not been anywhere: he has merely found himself. This is not to belittle either his achievement or Proust's: finding oneself is a moral achievement which not many people are capable of. But Marcel finds himself by renouncing the moral: the fulfilment achieved by Proust's inner story seems lesser, more etiolated, less shareable, than the social and moral aspirations which his outer story proclaims.

When Kafka's books end we experience an even greater feeling of desolation. His world, in any case, is exhausted from the start. In

The Castle K. is, for reasons that are never explained, so tired, even at the beginning, that he cannot walk without leaning on Barnabas. The Superintendent does not file things any more. Gregor Samsa in *The Metamorphosis* becomes less and less capable of movement. The investigating Dog tells us that by now he is almost entirely inactive. Joseph K. in *The Trial* becomes less and less efficient at his job. Everywhere, there is an air of things running down. Kafka's works gravitate towards annihilation: he recorded what he saw as the slow ticking of extinction at the heart of the world. In his Diaries he described his hope

to raise the world into the pure, the true and the immutable.[105]

In his fictions he achieved the purity of darkness, the truth of unknowability, and the immutability of the void.

This is as near as we can get to truly closed art in fiction. In the end there are no questions to ask at all. Erich Heller summed this up when he said that there was 'no *answerable* question to be found anywhere in the works of Kafka'[106]. And it is in this respect that Kafka's affinity with Nietzsche is closest. Nietzsche apprehended the world as a lie; Joseph K. in *The Trial* complains that the Priest turns lying into a universal principle. Nietzsche tried to cheer himself up (though he failed to do it for us) when he devised his gigantic intellectual enterprise of revaluating all values. He hoped, in this way, to reveal the true reality of existence behind its apparent reality which he believed to be false. Both he and Kafka perceived the same lie at the core of the world. Kafka recorded his terror of it in his Diaries; but in his fiction, far from being, as Erich Heller would have us believe, the victim of the curse of the Nietzschean world, he is its true citizen and devoted cartographer.

And the important point about the dreamlike structure and texture of Kafka's stories is that, for all the nightmarish conviction they give us as we read them, the experience of them can, in the end, feel hallucinatory to the point of being unreal. The nature of so many of Kafka's characters as mere functions, at once insubstantial and stolidly immobile, weakens our belief both in them and in the tales that contain them. His imagination strikes us as more authentic than the worlds it produces.

When Emma Bovary dies she leaves a real world behind: we know what happens to the people in it, and such was the open nature of Flaubert's world that if he had not told us we would feel impelled to ask. But what is there to ask about the woman Joseph K. sees a moment before his execution? Does it matter, to him or to us, whether she is or is not Fräulein Bürstner? Can we imagine K.'s landlady, Frau Grubach, wondering what happened to her nice, quiet lodger? Does anyone ever wonder where the Traveller is going after leaving the penal settlement? Such questions are irrelevant: these people cease to exist when the story ends. The family of Gregor Samsa survive him as figures in a picture rather than real people: Kafka's masochistic imagination deprives them of the consolation of memory, and the moral burden of remorse.

For Marcel, in the *Recherche*, there is a private salvation in art. His path is prepared through his exposure to acting and his experience of painting and music, reaching its Schopenhauerian peak with the performance of Vinteuil's Septet in which Marcel senses 'some definite spiritual reality'. Vinteuil, he thinks, must have '"heard" the universe and projected it far beyond himself.'[107] Kafka's world offers no such consolation. Art, like people, is a function. Titorelli, the Court Painter in *The Trial*, paints grim, identical landscapes, and portraits of judges that are all more or less alike. There is nothing individual about his work: the post is hereditary, and 'new people', he explains briskly, 'are of no use for it'[108]. He paints the judges as they want to be painted: as the Whipper whips, Titorelli paints. Technically, he is a representational painter, but he is denied the chance to 'represent' anything, and seems not to miss it. Nothing could be more unlike the passionate engagement of mind and heart which Proust attributes to Elstir. 'There are always people like yourself,' Titorelli cheerfully informs Joseph K., 'who prefer depressing pictures.'[109] Here, if anywhere, Kafka may have been prophetic: it is as if he had foreseen the official art of totalitarian societies: the art of the sanctioned and predictable likeness, which is impersonal and ultimately meaningless.

Music in Kafka has, at first sight, no Schopenhauerian urge or significance. When, in *The Metamorphosis*, Gregor's sister plays the violin, we are not told anything about the music except that she is 'playing so beautifully'[110]. Kafka seems not to be interested in the sound of music: indeed he hardly ever writes about people's voices. Here the description is entirely pictorial: looking through the doorway into the living room, Gregor sees a picture of stillness and peace — an image of an unattainable spiritual life. Gregor is promptly expelled. When the peasants in *The Castle* sing, their voices blend 'into one continuous howl'[111]. The seven mysterious dogs in *Investigations* produce 'a terrible clamour': their music, the narrating Dog tells us, robbed him of his senses. And yet he also tells us:

> They did not speak, they did not sing, for the most part they kept almost stubbornly silent, but from the empty air they conjured music. All was music.[112]

What sort of music, then? What kind of sound? The description of the dogs is purely visual, as they form 'dance-like patterns' in canine perfection. I think that Kafka is simply writing about pure spiritual experience, and it is remote and almost painfully unspecific because he regarded it as unattainable. We realise that Kafka is profoundly Schopenhauerian: music illustrates the unattainable spiritual essence of life, even though the world in which Kafka's people live is no place for harmony.

The mice in *Josephine* do have an inkling of what singing is, and they admit that Josephine's art does not really correspond to it. So is it singing, really? Is it not perhaps just a sort of piping or whistling? For the mice, in any case, it does not matter what or how she sings: they know her voice, such as it is, and want to hear it. Her singing, then, is a kind of perlocutionary act, entirely appropriate to the closed world of Kafka's books. And with this singing we approach a world of pure noise: like the whistling sound which the narrating animal thinks he hears in *The Burrow*, or the noise K. hears when he telephones the Castle:

> The receiver gave out a buzz of a kind that K. had never before heard on a telephone. It was like the hum of countless children's voices — but yet not a hum, the echo rather of voices singing at an infinite distance — blended by sheer impossibility into one high but resonant sound which vibrated on the ear as if it were trying to penetrate beyond mere hearing.[113]

If the inexorable Castle is an image of the Will, then this is its true copy: unknowable, beyond hearing, almost as if beyond experience. We are in the world of anti-music.

Germaine Brée has said that it was impossible to imagine Proust finishing the *Recherche* and then going on to write something quite different. This is true; and the reason for it is that there could not have been anything more for him to write. All his previous work had been a rehearsal for this book: a rehearsal to find out whether it was possible for him to write the Book that was in him. The *Recherche*, as we have it, is among other things an act of faith which states that the writer's task is to explore and express the timeless essence of his own innermost being. Once a writer has done that, his life's work is complete. On the other hand, the novel can be said to be unfinishable, to the extent that the self is inexhaustible — and also because Proust framed his great structure in a way that makes it infinitely expandable. From what we know of his working methods, it is not at all frivolous to wonder how much longer the novel might have become if Proust had lived longer, and in better health, and could have corrected and elaborated even more of his proofs. Nor is it merely frivolous to imagine him still alive in 1941, a frail but active seventy-year-old, scorning the safety of Vichy, and still tinkering with his book while the descendants of General Boisdeffre and Colonel Henry helped to round up French Jews for the German death camps. It might have shaken his faith in art as the true last judgement.

If Kafka's novels are unfinished it is perhaps because they, too, are unfinishable. Partly, this is a problem of technique: how do you bring to linear conclusion narratives which resemble, and were probably inspired by, the abrupt and often non-linear images one sees in dreams? But it is also one of the paradoxes of closed art that, rigidly structured and framed as it is, it can expand infinitely. *The Trial* is defined and enclosed by its beginning and its end even more firmly than the *Recherche*; yet, in between, how many more episodes might this structure not have been able to bear? The same applies to *The Castle* and to *Amerika*, whose vaguely outlined endings, as reported to us by Max Brod, might have taken endless numbers of further chapters to reach. It is the most profound discontinuity in Kafka's work, and one which he cannot have intended, that the 'cause' in his major fictions, which is the narrative unfolding of a dream image, remains forever out of reach of the 'effect', which is the conclusion.

If Kafka can be said to have written but one work all his life, that, too, is more than a metaphorical statement. His recurring visions of annihilation, and his visions of eternally suspended action which is barely distinguishable from inaction, are far more closely related than what we usually recognise as the recurring themes and preoc-cupations of novelists. We may say that Henry James's novels are concerned with the problems of maturity and moral duplicity; or that William Golding is preoccupied with obsessions and the nature of evil. But these themes and preoccupations intermingle with others; and they also change in depth and emphasis, and they grow (or diminish) in subtlety or intensity from book to book. But Kafka sought, during his short creative life of some twenty years, to cast and re-cast his great central metaphor of existence as a meaningless and inexplicable configuration of events in indeterminate time. Malcolm Pasley has noted the almost total absence of metaphor and imagery in Kafka's writings[114]: an absence which throws into sharp relief the nature of his individual works as metaphors. If metaphor is a compromise between a thing and its description, then Kafka strove to find just such a compromise when he tried to express a static vision in narrative form. In the end the vision usually overpowers the narrative; and this is why the end of each 'story' is the total fading out, or the eternal and unchanging survival (the two are hardly distinguishable) of each picture of the world.

In this sense, Kafka's books may be thought of as self-sufficient objects, or self-contained machines creating themselves as the product, which is how some critics approach fiction. But this view of novels is in itself a 'closed' view. It questions a work, not in reference to a world which the work creates, and which may or may not resemble the world which we know; rather, it submits to a work as a world in itself, which has more in common with other such worlds than with ours. This is not intended as a value judgement, but only as a definition of two different approaches. The type of criticism I have just described is essentially a philosophy of reading, while this book remains within the confines of a study of ourselves and what we read, and how the two reflect each other.

Proust's version of finality is different from Kafka's: it is a finality of endlessness. Marcel meets his own past: those lost parts of his self which had given him joy. He is, he tells us, stepping outside time; outside the causes and effects of ordinary existence. The solution is as private and arbitrary, as magniloquent and despotic, as that which Nietzsche had found. Like him, Marcel seeks to arrest time and replay it: he, too, 'wills backwards'. Some of Proust's provisional titles for the novel (*The Past Prolonged, The Past Delayed*) bear this out[115]. And one of the reasons why the idea of 'time regained' is difficult to understand is that, like Nietzsche's Eternal Recurrence, it is an incomplete metaphor: *a metaphor of desire*, which expresses a profound need, but which cannot, in the very nature of that need, give it a fulfilment that the mind can grasp.

Marcel sounds very like Nietzsche, too, when he talks about

making an 'attempt to transcribe a universe which had to be totally redrawn.'[116] This is his personal transvaluation of values; and just as Nietzsche both wanted to and dreaded to, he sets out on his life's journey all over again. For what follows Marcel's revelations at the end is that he sets out to write the novel we have just read: if we were to follow the logic of the narrative we would have to begin to read it again. Nor is this entirely fanciful: Proust planted references to people and places in the early sections of the book which can only be understood on second reading. And if the *Recherche* is a fictional version of Nietzsche's Eternal Recurrence, then Marcel is its Super-man. Mysteriously enlightened, possessing obscure powers of understanding and imagination, and about to enact in public some great act of private confirmation, he is, like Superman, ecstatic, arrogant and remote as he sets out on the journey we have just travelled with him. Harold Pinter was right when he ended the film-script he based on the novel with a passage, taken not from the end, but from some twenty pages earlier: 'It was time to begin.'[117]

Notes

1. *Journals 1889–1949*, tr. and ed. Justin O'Brien, London, 1967, p. 655.
2. In *What is Literature?* tr. Bernard Frechtman, New York, 1965, p. 221.
3. In *Proust*, London, 1974, p. 33.
4. In *Literature and the Sixth Sense*, London, 1970, p. 41.
5. Anthony Storr in the *Spectator*, October 31, 1981, pp. 21–2.
6. *The Trial*, tr. Willa and Edwin Muir, London, 1953, p. 126.
7. *Diaries 1914–1923*, tr. Martin Greenberg, New York, 1965, Vol 2 p. 132 (Vol. 1: 1910–1913, tr. Joseph Kresh). The entry reads as follows: 'Rossman [the hero of *Amerika*] and K., the innocent and the guilty, both executed without distinction at the end, the guilty one with the gentler hand, more pushed aside than struck down.' The way Joseph K.'s executioner 'thrust the knife into his heart and turned it there twice' does not strike me as being done with a gentle hand.
8. 'The Law of *The Trial*', in *On Kafka: Semi-Centenary Perspectives*, London, 1976, pp. 26 ff.
9. *T*, p. 10.
10. *ibid.*, p. 12.
11. *ibid.*, p. 13.
12. In *Franz Kafka*, Columbia, 1966, p. 40.
13. *The Castle*, tr. Willa and Edwin Muir, London, 1957, p. 61.
14. *ibid.*, p. 11.
15. *ibid.*, p. 28.
16. In *Wedding Preparations in the Country and Other Stories*, tr. Ernst Kaiser and Eithne Wilkins, Willa and Edwin Muir, London, 1978, p. 98.

17. *C*, p. 65.
18. In *Shorter Works*, Vol. 1, tr. & ed. Malcolm Pasley, London, 1973, p. 159.
19. In *Metamorphosis and Other Stories*, tr. Willa and Edwin Muir, London, 1961, pp. 171−179.
20. *C*, p. 26.
21. *ibid.*, p. 15.
22. In *Shorter Works*, p. 89.
23. *Recherche*, III, p. 458. References are to the translation by C.K. Scott Moncrieff and Terence Kilmartin, 3 vols, London, 1981.
24. *Diaries*, I, p. 34.
25. *Shorter Works*, p. 93.
26. *T*, p. 95.
27. In *Letters to Felice*, tr. James Stern and Elisabeth Duckworth, London, 1974, p. 124.
28. In *Abinger Harvest*, London, 1967, p. 112.
29. *WWI*, II p. 245.
30. *op. cit.*, p. 4.
31. *K: A Biography of Kafka* by Ronald Hayman, London, 1981, p. 1.
32. *Shorter Works*, pp. 50−51.
33. See Gareth H. Steel: *Chronology and Time in 'A la Recherche du Temps Perdu'*, Geneva, 1979, p. 68.
34. *ibid.*, p. 157.
35. II p. 142.
36. III p. 203.
37. III p. 585.
38. *The Will to Power*, ed. cit., p. 333.
39. II p. 435.
40. II p. 449.
41. III p. 466.
42. II p. 106.
43. III p. 459.
44. II p. 1161.
45. I. p. 507.
46. *T*, pp. 37−38.
47. *ibid.*, p. 203.
48. *C*, p. 40.
49. In *On Proust*, tr. Martin Turnell, London, 1970, p. 40.
50. In *Proust: A Selection from his Miscellaneous Writings*, tr. Gerard Hopkins, London, 1948, p. 235.
51. Quoted in *The Quest for Proust*, by André Maurois, tr. Gerard Hopkins, London, 1950, p. 183.
52. *Letters of Marcel Proust*, tr. Minna Curtis, London, 1950, pp. 211−212.
53. *Diaries* I, p. 170.
54. *The Gay Science*, ed. cit., pp. 329−330.
55. In *Nietzsche contra Wagner*, in *The Portable Nietzsche*, tr. Walter Kaufmann, New York, 1976, p. 665.
56. In *Metamorphosis, &c.*, pp. 190−191.
57. *ibid.*, p. 180.
58. *ibid.*, p. 184.
59. *ibid.*, p. 197.

60. *GS*, p. 328.
61. III p. 527.
62. I p. 41.
63. III pp. 922–923.
64. III p. 1102.
65. II p. 534.
66. II p. 24.
67. II p. 54.
68. III p. 622.
69. I pp. 552.
70. II pp. 680–81.
71. III pp. 99–100.
72. II p. 952.
73. In *Axel's Castle*, London, 1961, p. 135.
74. *ibid.*, pp. 150–51.
75. In *The World of Marcel Proust*, London, 1967, p. 237.
76. III p. 914.
77. III p. 905.
78. III p. 916.
79. III p. 659.
80. III p. 898.
81. *T*, p. 237.
82. In *Marcel Proust and Deliverance from Time*, London, 1956, p. 222.
83. In an essay, Hope and Lucidity, in *The Kafka Problem*, ed. Angel Flores, New York, 1946, p. 259.
84. In Curtiss, *ed. cit.*, p. 187.
85. III p. 184.
86. In 'The Death of the Author', *Image-Music-Text*, tr. Stephen Heath, London, 1977, p. 142.
87. *T*, p. 11.
88. *C*, p. 58.
89. *ibid.*, p. 113.
90. *ibid.*, p. 53.
91. III p. 737.
92. II p. 981.
93. III p. 312–13.
94. II p. 487.
95. *The Idiot*, tr. David Magarshack, London, 1955, p. 623.
96. II p. 935.
97. Schopenhauer: *Essays and Aphorisms*, tr. R.J. Hollingdale, London, 1970, p. 69.
98. III p. 904.
99. III p. 908.
100. III p. 905.
101. III p. 1093.
102. III pp. 393–94.
103. III p. 913.
104. In Samuel Beckett: *Proust & Three Dialogues*, London, 1965, p. 66.
105. Diaries, II p. 187.
106. In *Kafka*, London, 1974, p. 31.

107. III pp. 381–82.
108. *T*, p. 168.
109. *ibid.*, p. 181.
110. *Metamorphosis*, p. 53.
111. *C*, p. 43.
112. *Shorter Works*, pp. 151–52.
113. *C*, p. 26.
114. In his Introduction to Franz Kafka: *Der Heizer*, Cambridge, 1966, p. 7.
115. See Bree: *The World of Marcel Proust*, p. 96.
116. III p. 1104.
117. III p. 1088.

VI

PICASSO AND BRAQUE
The silent beholder

In the beginning, all pictures were pictures of worlds. And yet, to some extent, they were also pictures *of* the world, in the sense in which the phrase has been used in this book: for all paintings tell us something about how the artist felt about the life and the world around him.

This is partly a question of what the painter chooses to paint. The fact that most of Constable's works are landscapes, and that his portraits are simply not in the same category of excellence, tells us that nature, in the sense of open country and preferably in summer, was what, as an artist, he found the most significant and absorbing thing in life. Conversely, the fact that some ten per cent of Rembrandt's entire output consisted of self-portraits, and that portraiture in general accounts for about two-thirds of his paintings and a quarter of his graphic art, tells us that for him as an artist the most important thing was human nature and behaviour: he told us what he felt about the passing of time by showing how it traced its passage on human faces, especially his own.

This is all the more striking because Rembrandt painted mostly what he wanted to, whereas his contemporaries usually worked for commissions. Not only that: painting at that time was divided up into specialised areas. Hobbema, for example, was best known for wooded scenes, and the Willem van de Veldes, both father and son, for seascapes. This was not because they had passionate feelings about the sea: but having both been professional sailors, and being astonishingly good at drawing and painting anything to do with ships and the sea (the elder Van de Velde's work is still being used as source material by naval historians), they were able to corner lucrative markets both in Amsterdam and in London. Therefore what they painted were pictures of worlds but not, in our sense, pictures of the world: the van de Veldes do not suggest to us, as sometimes Goya, Van Gogh, Gauguin or the young Derain do, that behind their pictures, and in all their different subjects, there is a personal world, consistent, private and passionately felt, which is both the source and the goal of their inspiration. Again, the great Italian masters from Duccio to Raphael no doubt believed in God and the teachings of the Church; but the fact that they painted almost exclusively religious pictures was partly a consequence of what their patrons wanted from them. Their picture of the world was a reflection of the world's picture of itself.

The period we are concerned with here is remarkable, among other things, for the fact that the older types of patronage were disappearing. The Salons in Paris and the Academy in London were still, to some extent, arbiters of official taste, and they brought painters commissions; but their hold was weakening, mostly through the influence of buccaneering dealers, and the increasing tendency of the painters themselves to paint what they wanted to. Picasso is on record as speaking with horror of the idea of a painter being commissioned; and the Braque who quoted what he thought were Nietzsche's words, 'An aim is a servitude'[1], was clearly very much his own man. One of the remarkable things about the Cubist painters is that they went on creating a body of work which was not only, like the work of the Impressionists, greeted with ridicule and accusations of incompetence, but also met with incomprehension. Most of Picasso's friends were bewildered and dismayed when, in 1907, they were allowed a glimpse of *Les Demoiselles d'Avignon* in his studio (it was not to be properly exhibited in public for another thirty years). Even Braque was puzzled and appalled: he told Picasso that looking at the painting felt like drinking petrol or eating old rope. Braque's dismay was shortlived; but real understanding as well as full enjoyment of Cubist art is still restricted to a relatively narrow circle of experts and connoisseurs. *Legible* is a crucial term in its vast critical literature. When a cultivated but untrained person looks at a Cubist painting he is liable to ask, first, *what it is,* and then to say that he does not understand it.

To the reader who recalls the opening pages of this book, these words may sound familiar. For what do we mean when we say that we do not understand a painting? Until the beginning of the twentieth century, representation was to painting what narrative was to a play: it enabled people to see what a picture was *about*. Pictures could be poorly painted, ill-constructed, confusing or sacrilegeous, but, like narratives, they could be understood. There was nothing one could not understand about a picture of the Last Supper, or the Crucifixion, a still life or a landscape. Complaints about the incomprehensibility of the Impressionists or the Fauves were short-lived, and were essentially concerned with technique. People like Pissarro and Monet were told that it was absurd to represent frock-coated gentlemen in the street with little daubs of paint like black tongue lickings. August Strindberg, from whom one would expect enlightened ideas on contemporary painting, wrote solemnly of Manet that he

> must have something wrong with his eyes or be touched in the head. He has employed colours which do not exist in nature and is consequently, in my opinion, a bad painter.[2]

What the public and the critics were saying, in effect, was: we can see quite clearly that you are painting frock-coated gentlemen, but we know what frock-coated gentlemen look like and it is not like this. We recognise your houses and your lakes, but they are not lilac and mauve in real life. You either cannot or will not do your job as a painter properly: you are either incompetent or mad.

The untrained beholder's reaction to Cubist paintings is entirely different. Picasso's work in 1907 and 1908 includes experiments in distortion which are extremely puzzling (though not very much to anyone who knows the late work of Cézanne), but they are legible, they can be understood. But a painting from the height of the Analytic Cubist period, such as *Woman with a Guitar* (1911; Museum of Modern Art, New York), known as *Ma Jolie*, is, at first sight, incomprehensible. When we are told that, at the time of painting it, Picasso had just found a new mistress, Eva, whom he called, after a popular song of the day, Ma Jolie, we are little the wiser. The picture includes the painted words Ma Jolie; but it is not clear whether they are painted on a songsheet, and if so, why the songsheet appears as two separate pieces of paper. What, in any case, are these pieces lying on? Or leaning against? Indeed, are they pieces of paper? The title tells us that we should look for a woman and a violin: an enterprise which might appear impossible. The untrained beholder's reaction might be summed up by saying that, for him, the narrative of representation has broken down.

What is the narrative of representation? When Rembrandt painted one of his portraits of his mistress Hendrickje, certain events took place: we can assume that he must have decided on a pose, placed her in a certain way in relation to the light, decided what aspect of her character to reveal. We can 'read' all this in the picture: it is part of its narrative. Over and above its literal content, it tells us something about the simple, factual, physical relationship between it and the artist who painted it. If *Ma Jolie* implies such a relationship, we certainly cannot 'read' it. Again, Rembrandt's self-portraits at Kenwood and in Washington tell us, without the aid of biographical knowledge, a good deal about what happened, over the years, to Rembrandt the painter and Rembrandt the man. To those who look at them with historical knowledge, they may also suggest something about whom, if anyone, they were painted for. And so pictures can contain yet another narrative: the nature and the story of their relationship to their original beholders.

Because, to paraphrase E.M. Forster again, oh dear, yes, a picture also tells a story; and when we say that we cannot understand a painting, we mean that we cannot follow this story, and that the dialogue between the picture and ourselves has broken down. For looking at pictures, too, is a kind of dialogue. We seek and we find. One of the oldest metaphors about paintings is that they are windows opening out on to the world. Paintings are also like theatres: we are witnessing something that has just happened or is happening or is about to happen. Some painters seem to have known this perfectly well: there are striking similarities between certain types of Renaissance group paintings and the techniques of contemporary stagecraft[3]. A picture like Matisse's *Le Thé* (1919; Los Angeles County Museum) has the atmosphere of a Chekhov play, as if an intimate moment in a family gathering had been interrupted by an intruder: the dog, lying on the grass in the foreground, has raised its head, in greeting or in suspicion.

One way or another, when we look at a picture we see an event, and this implies a past and a future. Christ is being lowered from the Cross, which implies that He had been crucified and will now be buried. Even a still life has a story, such as Fantin-Latour's in the National Gallery in Washington: someone had put a vase of flowers on the table, with a basket of fruit, a cup and saucer on a tray, and a book. The quality of the china and the presence of the book on the highly polished table tells us that we are in a prosperous home; the fact that the basket is of coarse wickerwork, the kind that would not normally be brought into a drawing room, and the fact that one of the tangerines has been peeled and both rind and segments are still on the elegant little tray, may indicate that Fantin-Latour did not just find these things but put them there himself because he was interested in their contrasting textures and colours. He quite possibly peeled the tangerine himself, so that he could show how well he could paint the pearly flesh of the segments.

Portraits, too, contain narratives. Cézanne's youthful self-portrait (1865–6) shows him as a turbulent young misfit, almost demonic in the way his dark eyes, with hardly any whites visible, glower from under the huge forehead. He looks back at us over his shoulder, as if telling us that we have just met someone both interesting and dangerous. But his much later *Self-Portrait with a Beret* (1900; Boston Museum of Fine Arts) is clearly by a man who is no longer interested much in his own appearance, except as an assemblage of planes and volumes. The curved back of the chair on the right is echoed by his rounded shoulder, and by his majestic beret which dominates the painting. His body is abruptly cut short just above the waist, making him look almost like a clumsily carved bust. The brooding gaze suggests both that Cézanne had a quiet and unshakeable confidence in himself, but also that, at the same time, he had no illusions about being old and unsuccessful. But there is no hint that he is dwelling on this with the sense of loss, pain, and contemplative maturity which infuse Rembrandt's late self-portraits. The brushwork, thinning out towards the bottom of the painting, tells us quite plainly that the painter has said all he has to say about himself.

Now if, through the window of a picture, we look at a story, we also assume that there is a narrator; and we can engage both of them, painter and picture, in a dialogue. Was Cézanne given to brooding about himself? Perhaps that, after all, is what the melancholy droop of his moustache indicates. Did Fantin-Latour really peel the tangerine himself? If he did, that would explain the faint air of contrivance that, for all their homeliness, hangs over these objects. If Fantin-Latour's aim was to show off by giving himself an extra object to paint, then this contrivance is as much part of the resulting picture as the objects in it and his skill in painting them.

All this means that we can ask Cézanne and Fantin-Latour questions. Such questions make sense because there are answers to them, explicit or implicit, in their paintings; and when we know these answers we look at the paintings in a new and enriched way. The reason is that these pictures belong to open art. They are accountable. It makes sense for us to ask, as it did with Ibsen's *Ghosts*, whether this or that could or should have been done differently. And this implies time, too: there was a time, now past, when Fantin-Latour might have decided that the gardener's basket looked incongruous in this setting, and painted an ornamental clock instead. And his still life has an inner world of visual logic, too: the objects are reflected on the highly polished surface of the table, telling us that this is a home where the furniture is properly looked after; and we may assume that there is a window on the right, because that is where the light appears to come from. In other words, we are in a little world where things are *caused*.

So what exactly happens when we say that we do not understand a painting? Do we suspect, as with plays, that the dialogue between painter and beholder has broken down? Or that the painter is concerned with something other than telling a story?

The first such reaction is recorded in Giorgio Vasari's *Lives of the Artists*. Writing about certain frescoes, now lost, by Giorgione, Vasari is showing distinct signs of impatience. He complains that there are

> no scenes to be found ... with any order or representing the deeds of any distinguished person, of either the ancient or the modern world. And I for my part have never been able to understand his figures ...
>
> ... one sees, in various attitudes, a man in one place, a woman standing in another, one figure accompanied by the head of a lion, another by an angel in the guise of a cupid; and heaven knows what it all means.[4]

Having read this, one would like to have Vasari's comments on Giorgione's *La Tempesta* (Accademia, Venice). This extraordinary painting is, in one sense, perfectly clear and 'legible', containing as it does some of the most basic elements of representational art: a man, a woman, a baby, buildings and a landscape. And yet there has been considerable debate about what it 'means'. The first description we have dates from 1530, by which time Giorgione had been dead for twenty years. It is by the Italian traveller and connoisseur Michiel, who describes it as a landscape with a soldier and a gipsy. This is remarkable, because landscape painting was then a very young art indeed; and yet the landscape in the background, with its approaching storm, made a greater impression on Michiel than the human figures in the foreground. In our own time, Edgar Wind has written a brilliant interpretation of the picture as an allegory of *Fortuna*, in which the human figures

> display the martial confidence and maternal affection that befit 'a soldier and a gipsy' — characters whose unsettled mode of life has made them familiars of *Fortuna*[5].

The difficulty here is that the 'soldier' carries no weapon, nor does he look martial enough to be a soldier; and the woman is certainly not a gipsy. Some commentators think that the man is a shepherd, but he looks too like a gentleman for that; and if G.M. Richter is right, and the painting represents the childhood of Paris[6] (two earlier works, *The Finding of Paris* and *The Judgement of Paris*, have been attributed to Giorgione), then who are the man and the woman, since they are clearly not Priam and Hecuba? And why, in any case, is the woman clad, or rather half-clad, in a large sheet? One commentator attempted to solve the mystery by saying that Giorgione may have belonged to one of the many secret societies of the time, and painted the picture for initiates[7].

Not only are these questions unlikely to find an answer; they also relate to things which are secondary to the most essential quality of *La Tempesta*. This is its mood: mysterious, menacing, beguiling. An immense stillness embraces the whole scene. Walter Pater said about Giorgione's paintings that

> they belong to a sort of poetry which tells itself *without an articulated story* (my italics).

He saw in these pictures

> some brief and wholly concrete moment — into which, how-ever, all the motives, all the interests and effects of a long history have condensed themselves, and which seem to absorb past and future in an intense consciousness of the present . . .

> . . . exquisite pauses in time in which, arrested thus, we seem to be spectators of all the fullness of existence, and which are like some consummate extract or quintessence of life[8].

These lines, meditating on an event captured in stillness, and on time which both progresses and is arrested, could have been written by Proust — who certainly read Pater. In any case, they were clearly written by a beholder who was subjugated by, above all else, the mood of the picture. And nearly eighty years later Kenneth Clark, neither a sentimental critic nor a mystic, admitted that he could not say how *La Tempesta* achieved 'its magical power over our minds'. Part of its 'incantatory power', Clark writes, 'lies in its defiance of logic'. Its force, he believes, can only be fully felt 'by those who are prepared to surrender themselves to its mood[9]'.

Such reactions to a work of art will by now be familiar. *La Tempesta* may well be the first work of closed art in painting, its simple and easily recognisable contents firmly subordinated to its subtle and elusive mood. The human figures are as unaware of each other as they are of the storm: this is a world in which things do not seem to be *caused*. The painting is representational and yet it is not open to our questioning. It represents figures and a landscape we recognise, but an event which we do not understand. The painter imposed on the contents of his picture a personal vision. In other words Giorgione broke down the dialogue between his painting and us. It speaks to us but we are silent. From our vantage point today this may not seem sensational; but it went against all the accepted criteria of painting as they were understood in Giorgione's time.

Leon Baptista Alberti (1404–72), in his treatise *On Painting*, published nearly a century earlier (1436), asserted that 'The greatest work of the painter is the *istoria*'[10]. For Alberti, this did not mean that the most important thing for a painter was to tell a story: *istoria* included the idea of narrative content, but it also carried a more complex meaning. It meant composition:

Bodies ought to harmonize together in the *istoria* in both size and function;[11]

it meant content:

The *istoria* will move the soul of the beholder when each man painted there clearly shows the movement in his own soul;[12]

and it meant moral significance:

whatever the painted persons do among themselves or with the beholder, all is pointed toward ornamenting or teaching the *istoria*.[13]

Clearly, *event* is an important part of Alberti's *istoria*: it is meant to have a narrative as well as a moral impact on the beholder. As if to clinch this point, Alberti states:

> I strongly approve in an *istoria* that which I see observed by
> tragic and comic poets. They tell a story with as few characters
> as possible.[14]

The vital thing to grasp here is that the event is not self-contained or
self-referential. Alberti's emphasis is on *relations*: between parts of
the painting, and between the painting and ourselves. If the painter
gets them right, the beholder can let loose his critical faculties on the
painting, and he will then find that everything he sees in it has a
reason for its existence.

Alberti's precept, that figures in paintings should reflect the
movements of their souls, found its echo later in Leonardo da Vinci,
who asserted that motion should be

> expressive of what passes in the mind of the living figure.[15]

For Leonardo, too, it was a question of traditional representational
skills. A figure, he warned,

> which does not express by its position the sentiments and
> passions, by which we suppose it animated, will appear to
> indicate that its muscles are not obedient to its will, and the
> painter very deficient in judgement.[16]

This sums up both the logic of representation and the relationship
between the picture and the beholder. The entire enterprise of
Leonardo's writings on art presupposes people who will look at
paintings with critical eyes. Pictures must be open to questions, and
the answers must be correct. Leonardo's *Treatise*, as it has come
down to us, is not a metaphysical document, as the Surrealists
almost came to believe: it is a practical guide to painters on how to
paint pictures which would satisfy the critical beholder.

This relationship between pictures and their public remained
essentially the same until the end of the nineteenth century. Joshua
Reynolds held that painting was possible only because

> there will be necessarily an agreement in the imaginations as in
> the senses of men.[17]

'It is in vain,' Reynolds warned,

> for painters or poets to endeavour to invent without materials
> on which the mind may work, and from which invention must
> originate. Nothing can come of nothing.

When Blake got to this passage, he scribbled furiously on the margin: 'Is the Mind Nothing?'[18]

That defiant question is one of the first indications of the way in which Western painting was going to go.

Now let us return to *Les Demoiselles d'Avignon*. The first thing that strikes us when we come face to face with this large picture (it is about eight feet high and almost as wide) is a sense of bodies without a sense of weight. The second is the eyes. These women look at us, and yet do not look at us. The two in the middle appear to have the same kind of astigmatism: their right eyes stare at us, but their left eyes, bulging slightly out of their heads, look away somewhere to our right. The left-hand figure is painted in profile: her left eyelid is just visible, while her right eye faces us with a flat, stylised, almost Egyptian look. This eye looks nowhere, unless we block out the rest of the face: then the disembodied eye will gaze at us like an ancient divine symbol, all-seeing, and detached from its owner. The top right-hand figure has unseeing eye-sockets rather than eyes. Finally, the squatting figure has curiously dislocated eyes, each of which looks at us; but because they are painted at an odd angle to each other, they give a cross-eyed, almost unseeing impression. The Demoiselles both see us and do not see us; we communicate and yet we do not.

There is the same equivocal quality about their bodies. The lower right-hand figure squats solidly, but it is not clear on what; the left-hand figure has one foot, probably though not certainly its right, on the ground. These two equivocal resting points give the painting a sense of physical gravity, and balance the composition in a surprisingly conventional manner. And yet there is a weightlessness about the group. The two women in the middle look like reclining nudes placed upright: perhaps it is because we cannot see their feet that they seem to be suspended in mid-air. The woman on the left is holding up what may be a curtain: but her fingers are straight, they do not *grasp*. This hand looks as if resting against something solid. The bodies are painted in flat planes: there is only the most minimal modelling, and only abrupt white and dark lines serve to indicate their female curves.

It is hard to know how far a knowledge of the picture's biographical background has influenced its critics (the Carrer d'Avinyo was a Barcelona street where Picasso bought stationery, and where there was also a brothel); but its description as 'a tidal wave of female aggression'[19] matches nothing that we actually see on the canvas. These women communicate no erotic charge; and the ponderous size of their bodies seems only to emphasise their impassivity. Compare them with Ingres's women, obviously enjoying their nakedness, their indolence, and the heat of the Turkish bath; or with Manet's Olympia, whose body shows its weight by the way it imprints itself on the sheets, and around whom final preparations have clearly just been completed for the reception of a lover, and the impassive quality of Picasso's Demoiselles becomes obvious. Part of the reason why they have no physical charge is that they do not have a cause-and-effect background to explain their existence. We have no idea, and it would add nothing to our experience of the painting to know, what they might have been doing before we came on the scene: the most we might say is that they had been sitting and standing together, and that the woman on the right had just come in. To compare these women to the characters in Velazquez's *Las Meninas* is to miss the point. Something has just happened in Velazquez's painting: either the King and the Queen have unexpectedly walked into his studio, or the Infanta is being restless, as small children often are. One way or another, a specific event has just been interrupted by something equally specific; and everything in this elaborately frozen yet utterly natural moment speaks of a world beyond and around the canvas, and of a world that existed before the canvas was set up. People and objects are interrelated socially, psychologically and aesthetically: even the pictures on the rear wall have been identified by scholars[20].

By contrast, Picasso's Demoiselles form a composition, but they lack a world. Where has the right-hand woman just come from? The question is preposterous. Who had bought the fruit? It hardly seems to matter; it is difficult to associate the figures in this picture with anything as specific as eating. Technically, the fruit is important, because it holds up the middle of the composition; but it rests on a perilously up-tilted table and looks as if it might be about to slide off the bottom of the picture. In other words, the fruit has an artistic function, but it lacks the full substantiality of a real thing.

Again, it is hard to know how far the knowledge of Picasso's time influences his critics; but to describe this picture as being 'almost . . . an example of "propaganda by deed"'[21], is to read into it something that simply is not there. *Les Demoiselles d'Avignon* has no moral content whatever. In fact, it is precisely any moral content it might have had that Picasso discarded. In his early sketches for the painting there are two men as well, both fully dressed, one sitting in the midst of naked women, the other entering from the left, carrying first a book and, in later sketches, a skull. This is clearly a scene with a moral import: and accordingly, the women have a strong physical and sexual presence, while the men are clearly there to remind them, and us, of the transience of all physical things. It has been said that Picasso originally planned

> a kind of *memento mori* allegory or charade though probably with no very fervid moral intent.[22]

And why not? The man who painted *The Burial of Casagemas*, *La Vie*, and *Woman Ironing* respectively six, four and three years earlier, was perfectly capable of fervid moral intent, sometimes indeed to the point of lugubriousness or sentimentality. But whatever Picasso's intentions may have been to begin with, he ended up with a picture which has almost no moral, social or psychological context. His earlier paintings of dreamy, melancholy circus folk, detached from their working surroundings and usually shown against pale, neutral backgrounds, had clearly been leading him in this direction. With *Les Demoiselles* he arrived at one of the first great works of closed art in modern painting.

Seeing it is a spellbinding experience, but it is disconcerting too, precisely because this impact is not related to a specific context. *Les Demoiselles* implies no world beyond its canvas; whereas, up to now, it had been just such an implied world that held a large part of the moral content of paintings. Manet's Olympia is lying in a very real apartment: the painting has clues as to its period, its price, and the possibility that the occupant we see may not be paying her own rent. The way her maid looks at her defines a specific personal and social relationship. All of this is suffused with a moral significance, even though Manet is not openly moralising: he may or may not have been interested in whether sexual relationships based on money are right or wrong, but he shows us enough to make us think about the subject. In other words, Manet operates in an aesthetic, social and moral context; his *istoria* is clear and eloquent; and *Olympia* may be approached with questions that can, with varying degrees of precision, be answered. *Les Demoiselles d'Avignon* is not without an *istoria*, but with one that is very much narrower. How little we know about these massive figures. A touch of sadness in the faces of the two women in the middle, and an expression of aimless savagery in that of the woman on the right is registered, but remains part of the grandiose impersonality of the whole group. Picasso is experimenting: how far can he go in reducing painterly depth and physical and psychological context, and yet paint something that still contains recognisable life?

It is this, rather than the distortions in the faces of the two women on the right, that links this picture to Cubism and makes it its forerunner. For Cubism was an experiment which remained, at all times, a representational, not an abstract art. Its essence, and its dilemma, was a passionate attachment to the visible world, especially the objects in that world. The physical object was the Cubist subject *par excellence*: objects are less likely to overwhelm a painter than a landscape (though Cézanne seems to have been obsessed by certain objects), and they do not have the unpredictable, elusive, unique and 'question-able' life of human beings. Objects are, simply, more amenable to being manipulated. The rebellion against conventional perspective, which was implied in the final works of Monet and came into the open with Cézanne, Gauguin and the Fauves, had its origin in the desire to assert the primacy of the object, and not to allow it to be diminished by the protecting, and concealing, structure of perspective.

Indeed, modern painters came to regard this structure as oppressive: a form of deception and hindrance. When Alberti and his followers worked out the scientific theory of perspective they had, of course, no such purposes: for them it was a solution to the problem of representing three-dimensional space on a two-dimensional surface. It was essentially a technical matter; but we can see that it also had a moral significance. For the Renaissance artist it meant that, in a world which had been divinely organised and ordained, he found his own place. He understood how the world 'worked', to such an extent that he could make representations of it for other people. When, in Shakespeare's *Troilus and Cressida*, Ulysses explains the moral order of the world to the Greeks, he uses a visual language partly determined by the achievements of the Renaissance painters. For him, the heavens and the planets

> Observe degree, priority and place,
> Insisture, course, proportion, season, form,
> Office and custom, all in line of order.[23]

This, for Shakespeare, is the *istoria* of the world.

Modern painters became impatient with that 'line of order'. Braque complained that

> scientific perspective ... forces the objects in a picture to disappear away from the beholder instead of bringing them within his reach *as a painting should* (my italics).[24]

We may recall, at this point, how Nietzsche had expressed his impatience with the perspectival view of the world; how he regarded 'interpretations' as something that man was forced to accept as standing between him and the world, like a necessary lie. He was convinced that

> to grasp everything would mean to do away with all perspective relations.[25]

Like Schopenhauer before him, Nietzsche was in search, not of real things, but of Reality: both thought that, beyond all we see and sense, there is some essential Reality which it is the business of the human mind to identify and attain.

The origin of modern painting lies precisely here: in the urge to seize on something, be it colour, space, structure, or sense of movement, that would hold the key to that hidden reality. The problem was that there was always something standing in the way. When Van Gogh exclaimed that 'It isn't possible to get values and colour'[26], he expressed a problem that was both technical and spiritual. Van Gogh's great desire was to express himself in pure colours; but he realised that that was not how we saw objects in the world. Their shapes, their volume, the changes of light and shade to which their appearance is subject, all impinge on their own, local, colour. Therefore colour had to be modulated, that is, given 'values', to represent more realistically what we actually see. On the spiritual level, Van Gogh was wrestling with the obdurate facts of the physical world which seemed to stand in the way of his self-expression. Matisse, whose feelings about colour were just as passionate (he actually believed that if he left one of his paintings in someone's sickroom, the impact of the colours would cure the patient), crashed through the barrier that had held Van Gogh back, and learnt to use unmodulated colour to express both volume and space. What he and the Fauve painters have in common with Picasso and the Cubists is a search for the essential beyond the accidental, and a personal decision as to what that essential is.

To repeat: scientific perspective was not an invention, but a method of painting pictures that would reproduce, as closely as possible, the ordinary experience of actually seeing things. By reproducing ordinary vision, the Renaissance painter found a way of holding visual dialogue with the visible world. This reciprocal relationship (my painting is like this *because* the world is like this) is fundamental to open art. When modern painters broke with perspective, they also broke with cause and effect as a creative principle. Logic became their greatest enemy, just as it had been Nietzsche's. Closed art in painting is the product of the painter despotically imposing himself on the logical web of the visible world. Braque summed up the matter majestically when he said:

> Traditional perspective failed to satisfy me. Mechanised as it is, it never puts one *in full possession of things* (my italics).[27]

Of course the very choice of subject is, as we said at the beginning, a decision and self-assertion, and thus a form of imposition, by the painter. He must decide to put his easel down somewhere. But even if Fantin-Latour arranged the objects before he painted them in his *Still Life*, the effect remained natural: everything looks as if it had just been left there by somebody. By contrast, Cézanne's still lifes tell us quite clearly that the hands of the master had done more than merely arrange and paint. Inconsistencies in Cézanne's paintings have frequently been pointed out: the most famous being his *Kitchen Table* (Jeu de Paume, Paris), in which, if we follow the edge of the table under the tablecloth, it does not meet the edge at the other end. But in the extraordinary *Still Life with a Gingerjar and Eggplant* (Metropolitan Museum, New York), we are dealing with more than such simple inconsistencies. The familiar objects contain a powerful and paradoxical visual tension. There is a sense of incipient movement caused by the angle of the plate from which the pears, one feels, ought really to roll off at any moment. The lemon is so perilously balanced that it seems as if it were not really supporting the melon above it. And yet how solid it all looks, how heavy with substance. The turbulent folds of the napkin contrast dramatically with the serene, self-contained look of the fruit.

The whole assembly seems quite deliberately to have been arranged. It tells us that Cézanne was passionately interested in surfaces and textures as essential qualities of things; but also that, in order to reveal these qualities, he was prepared to invade the world of the objects and rearrange their relationship to the natural physical world. It mattered not a jot to Cézanne that if you hold a plate at a certain angle everything will roll off it: he used an improbable angle, painted on the fruit, and created a sense of balance which is perilous, and yet heavy with a sense of substance and compositionally stable. This was the sort of thing Kandinsky meant when he wrote of

> that principle of subordinating drawing ... to internal aims that was so clearly, so definitely resurrected from the dead by Cézanne![28]

And Cézanne's lordly way with objects found appropriate praise from a critic as level-headed as Meyer Schapiro, whom we find extolling Cézanne's *'creative will'*, and who, faced with one of Cézanne's most typical late still lifes, wrote almost humbly that, with all its distortions, it was

> so powerfully coherent that we cannot (*do not wish to*) imagine an alternative (my italics).[29]

But of course we know perfectly well that there is an alternative, and that it had been ignored for a specific purpose. There is a constant, brooding tension in these late still lifes between Cézanne's sense of the real, the physically touchable, and his majestic sense of composition and pattern. They bear the mark of a despotic artist, who imposed himself upon reality. This is the sense in which Cézanne is the true forerunner of Cubist painting, with its pervasive conflict between representation and despotic design, between sensation and aggressive intellect.

The Fauve painters, too, approached ordinary reality like intruders. They had a perfectly respectable ancestor in Leonardo, who observed that

> colours will appear what they are not, according to the ground that surrounds them.[30]

This principle was carried furthest by Claude in such twilit landscapes as his *Seaport* (Duke of Northumberland's Collection). Here the setting sun throws a delicate pink-mauve glow on the sky, the clouds, the water and the stonework of the building on the left. But this glow combines subtly and pervasively with the local colour of everything; and in the right foreground the blue and terracotta clothes of the two boatmen, echoed by the clothes of the two women on the left, stand out in all their natural freshness. Local colour never completely disappears in Claude: that only really happens with Gauguin, and Fauve painters like Derain, Vlaminck, and the young Braque. In Derain's *London Bridge* (Museum of Modern Art, New York) the thin strip of red sky at the top asserts itself boisterously on the bases of the pillars, and is echoed on the bridge itself in red patches which may or may not be vehicles crossing. The blue of the buildings, in turn, envelops the underside of the arches, and finally spends itself in blue patches on the water. Thus, for Derain, the local colour of the underside of the arches had disappeared entirely, whereas that of the vehicles on the bridge has, if anything, become more intense. The point is that the kind of evening light which would throw a tinge of blue on the stonework would, in the ordinary act of seeing, also affect and perhaps transmute the red of the vehicles. But Derain was not concerned with the ordinary act of seeing: his picture is a visionary re-creation of what he had seen. What he has done is to disrupt the reciprocal relationship between his picture and the world and, therefore, between his picture and us.

Such disruption can come about in other ways, too. Let me record here, in perhaps not strictly technical terms, my experience of seeing, for the first time, Matisse's *Landscape at Collioure* (1905) in a private collection. The picture is quite small: about 15" × 18". I perceived it, as it were, in two stages. First I registered a seemingly random arrangement of vivid patches of flat, unmodulated colour, often separated by unpainted areas of canvas. Then it was as if my eyes had altered their focus, trying to peer at something further away: they registered a sense of depth which had not been there before. Only then did I make out the landscape: the overhanging trees on the left, the smaller ones, with red and mauve trunks, on the right, the pale mauve pathway leading to the left, past the blue clearing in the middle. Pink and gold hills glowed in the background. The flatness of individual elements in the picture was re-interpreted by my eyes as being the surface of things with volumes.

What happened was like the movement of a camera when it focuses from something near to something distant — except that I had not changed my position. It was simply that the picture existed on two planes. It could be perceived either as flat patches of colour signifying nothing; or as a landscape with depth and distances; but it was not possible, even after prolonged viewing, to combine the two visual experiences and hold them together. Matisse had done two things. First, like Derain in *London Bridge*, he disrupted the ordinary logic of the way we see things and expect to see them reproduced: it is simply not true that tree trunks are tomato red and dark mauve, or that the ground is lilac or blue. Secondly, Matisse disrupted the ordinary logic of the way we see pictures. When I saw his landscape, it was *despite* its component parts. A tree painted by Claude remains a tree when you focus on it; we still sense around it the unchanging depth and structure of the landscape; the tree lives on for us in its own context. But if we focus on one of Matisse's trees, the context will disappear, and the thing will no longer look like a tree with space behind it, but like a flat surface. If ordinary seeing, including seeing pictures, is an act of organising visual sensations, then Matisse disrupted it, and established dissociation as a way of pictorial perception.

This ambiguity of vision preoccupied Matisse all his life. *View of Notre Dame* (1914; Museum of Modern Art, New York) can be seen, depending on one's focus, either as the image of the cathedral, shimmering yet substantial, in unspecific blue space, or as a U-shaped window carved into a thick blue wall. The pictures on the wall in *Large Interior in Red* (1948; Musée National d'Art Moderne, Paris) may be pictures; or they may be views of other rooms. It is as if Matisse were out to prove that pictures were not simply windows on the world, but enigmatic worlds in themselves, which contain either windows or pictures. Through such paintings, we look at an ungraspable reality beyond. Uncertainty of vision here becomes a way of seeing. In *French Windows in Collioure* (1914; private collection) the ambiguity between exterior and interior is complete. What is 'inside'? What is 'outside'? The blue-grey, black, olive-brown and green verticals, solid but translucent slabs of paint, might have been painted by Rothko.

Derain once said that 'where there is temperament there can be no imitation'[31] – the perfect credo for the despotic artist whom the passion for the visual has made impatient with the visible. But the tyranny Derain practised still needed the subject: his pictorial world owed its existence, and was a passionate response, to the visible world. But perhaps he sensed that the intensity of his vision might not, finally, be able to contain the things which inspired it. This may be what he meant when he wrote to Vlaminck:

> I see myself in the future painting compositions, because when I work from nature, I am the slave of such stupid things that my emotions are on the rebound.[32]

Thus the visionary in Derain was still haunted by the humble landscape painter. The same thing seems to have bothered Juan Gris, too, when he told the dealer Daniel-Henri Kahnweiler:

> I never seem to be able to find any room in my pictures for that
> sensitive, sensuous side which I feel ought always to be there.
> Maybe I am wrong to look for the pictorial qualities of an
> earlier age in a new form of art. At all events I find my pictures
> excessively cold ... Oh, how I wish that I had the freedom and
> the charm of the unfinished![33]

Gris may not have had such reservations about his final pictures; but
his words remind us of how Nietzsche feared that his entire thought
might collapse after an hour's sympathetic conversation with a
stranger. In both the painter and the philosopher, the quest for
Reality seems to have left behind an abiding thirst for the simplicity
of real things.

The fact is, and it may sound startling at first, that the Fauves and
the Cubists painted pictures much in the way Wagner composed
operas and Proust wrote his novel: a despotic inspiration pulled
them towards a visionary art, and yet this went hand in hand with a
passion for observation and for the rendering of the solid realities of
life. Analysing Cubist paintings from the point of view of verisimili-
tude is understandable and sometimes illuminating, but also, in the
end, futile. One of Picasso's friends, the sculptor Manolo, once asked
him:

> What would you say if your parents came to meet you at
> Barcelona station with such faces?[34]

The question is as well founded and ultimately as fatuous as August
Röckel worrying Wagner about the ending of The Ring. Picasso did
not want to do visual imitations of faces: he sought a new kind of
visual experience, inspired by faces, and he needed faces (and figures,
bottles and guitars) to signpost his experience for the beholder. He
knew perfectly well that the two sets of things were different.
Matisse was characteristically clear and matter-of-fact about all this.
When someone solemnly asked him whether a tomato looked to
him, when he ate it, the same as it did when he painted it, he replied
imperturbably: 'No, when I eat it I see it like everybody else.'[35]

It is often said that Cubism is a realistic art because the objects in
the paintings — newspapers, bottles, musical instruments, cigarette
packets — are the sort of things that would be found on café tables or
in painters' studios in Paris at the time. There is a certain amount of
aesthetic theorising in such a view, even though it would be quite

clear to anyone seeing one of these Cubist paintings for the first time that it could only be a twentieth-century work. And yet there is very little sense of lived life in a Cubist still life: we do not feel that someone has left or placed certain objects in a place where you or I could walk by or sit down. Again, John Berger has written that the Cubists celebrated a new kind of value in art: 'the value of the manufactured'[36]. But the fact is that there is no sense, about Cubist objects, of having been *made*, like Van Gogh's chair or his boots; or of their being used. It has been shown that even an ornate piece of furniture in a painting by Carpaccio can be manufactured today, given good powers of observation and suitable tools, but that a piece of furniture painted by Picasso, if imitated by a skilled craftsman, will turn into an object which could not have been designed by anybody[37]. The actual object-ness of Cubist objects is always in some doubt. A Cubist glass is neither full nor empty, neither dirty nor clean, and nobody ever drinks from it. It does not appear to have been accidentally left or deliberately placed. By contrast, the wicker-work basket on Fantin-Latour's table hints at a garden outside; the fruit in it speaks of the time of the year; the presence of the book, which looks real enough to be in Mrs Alving's drawing-room, hints at a certain social ambience.

All this means, too, that Fantin-Latour's *Still Life* does not need a title: indeed, what it has is not a title so much as a description. By contrast, let us take Picasso's *The Architect's Table* (1912; Museum of Modern Art, New York). Like many of his and Braque's paintings, it was given its title by Kahnweiler, who noticed what looks like a T-square lying diagonally across the picture from left to right. On the left we can make out two wine glasses and a bottle of Marc. If we were like Picasso's friend Manolo, we might ask what kind of architect keeps bottles of drink, glasses, and a pipe on his working table; and then we notice that there is also a fragment of tasselled tablecloth, which is not what architects cover their tables with either. Christian Zervos, who possibly did not notice the T-square, or thought it less important, called the picture *The Bottle of Marc*. Picasso himself, who personally sold it to Gertrude Stein, told her that it was 'your still life Ma Jolie' — the familiar words referring to Eva being painted on the left of the canvas.

A whole history of art and its appreciation could be written by investigating how pictures acquire their titles. Until the nineteenth century few pictures needed them: portraits were painted for their sitters or their relations, and most religious and historical painting

assumed a shared body of knowledge. A picture of the Last Supper
or the Fall of Icarus hardly needed identifying by a title. But with
the more recondite mythological pictures of the eighteenth and
nineteenth centuries the spectator began to need some guidance.
Some of the historical paintings of David and Géricault clearly
required titles if their content was to be understood; and even
Breughel's *The Conversion of Paul* (Kunsthistorisches Museum,
Vienna), with its complex narrative structure, needs a title to help
the inexperienced viewer to identify its central action. In other
words, the *istoria* of such pictures needs pointing up. This is
increasingly so with modern painting. The titles of some of Gauguin's Tahitian pictures are moral messages, and the painter made
sure they were understood by writing them on the canvas. When
Whistler called his famous portrait of his mother in the Louvre
Arrangement in Grey and Black, he was drawing attention to the
fact that the picture contained something beyond what was legible in
it.

So far, all this is part of the dialogue between paintings and their
beholders. But who gave Monet's late landscapes their titles? In one
sense, with such works, titles begin once more to be superfluous: the
painter's single-minded exploration of light, shape or texture becomes more important than the object he is painting. Adolphe
Appia, the Swiss theatre designer and theoretician, whose tastes
were formed by Schopenhauer, Wagner and Nietzsche, thought that
pictures did not need titles: he wrote that 'it should be unnecessary
to identify title with subject'. Every work, Appia argued, supplied its
own title; and if one were to judge by the insistence of artists on
titles, one might believe that

they seriously doubt the import or the interest of their work.

Such an argument assumes that the subject of a picture is obvious,
but at the same time regards it as subordinate: Appia implies that
our sense of communion with a picture does not depend on what the
artist is painting but on the quality of our experience as beholders.
Yet he cannot entirely dismiss the factuality of paintings: he adds
that the title to the artist is what the pen is to the thinker:

it enables the work to be developed ...; its worth is not
intellectual but moral.[38]

Appia's distinction is entirely in keeping with our argument. What
he is saying is that the title interposes itself between the artist and

his work as a criterion and a means of judgement: it tells us what the artist paints so that we can judge how well he paints it. The title is thus a norm, aesthetic as well as moral: it enables us to assess the artist's truthfulness as well as his skill. It follows from this that artists who communicate with us over the heads, as it were, of their subjects, appeal to us in a way which is supra-moral: they offer us an immediacy of artistic experience which asks not to be judged but to be accepted. Abstract artists emphasise this when they give their pictures titles like 'Composition II': they remind us in this way that their visual purity is untainted by factuality or 'anecdote'. And when a painter like Barnett Newman calls a work of pure abstraction *Ajax*, he is asserting a near-mystical connection between the artist's inspiration and his subject which is free of the shackles of identification. Kandinsky, for whom abstraction was very much a moral issue, was never able to settle the matter of titles to his lasting satisfaction.

The interesting thing about Cubist painting is how arbitrary the titles often seem to be; how many alternative titles some of the pictures could have; and how, at the same time, they need their titles. These works may not be about one particular object any more than about another; but they are still about objects, and the painters clearly wished us to recognise them. Their titles, mostly given by dealers, sometimes by friends, list the contents like a catalogue. And yet any one item would do: indeed, *The Architect's Table* might also have been called 'The Visiting Card', because it includes a copy of a card Gertrude Stein once left on Picasso. Might this give the picture a documentary significance, recording as it does, however obliquely, a now defunct social practice? No, such a reading would seem discordant with the rest of the painting, just as, to anyone seeing it for the first time, its present title might seem to be. The other objects in this painting have no obvious connections either with the card or with the T-square — indeed they have no reference to anything beyond themselves. The fact is that Cubist objects are visual pretexts magnificently usurped for a purpose which has little to do with life, or with their ordinary use — just as Wagner's *Ring* is not an opera about jewellery, and the *Recherche* is not a novel about biscuits.

Meanwhile it would be both glib and untrue to say that Cubist paintings are simply about themselves. Yet this idea has been the source of much critical and analytical commentary, not all of which has much to do with the ordinary experience of seeing either things or pictures. When, during the winter of 1909–10, Braque painted a *trompe l'oeil* nail, with its own conventional shadow, at the top of *Violin and Palette* (Guggenheim Museum, New York) and *Violin and Jug* (Kunstmuseum, Basle), he provoked a good deal of comment about the way he had shown up the contrast between old-fashioned imitation or representation of objects on the one hand, and presentation, the creation of a new reality on the other. He himself, much later, described the introduction of lettering into his pictures, saying that he did this because of his

usual desire to get as near the reality of things as possible.

The letters he had painted were, he said,

forms which could not be deformed, because being two-dimensional, they existed outside three-dimensional space; their inclusion in the picture allowed one to distinguish between objects situated in space and those which belonged outside space.[39]

Now on the face of it it is hard for us to conceive of an object which is outside space. But Braque was working his way towards a way of painting that would defy the accepted notions of pictorial space. His *Man with Guitar* (1914; Musée d'Art Moderne, Paris) contains a figure, a guitar, an armchair, and the wall behind them. The painting, especially the left-hand side, has about it a sense of receding volumes, but without a sense of that which has volume. The receding effect is produced by the shading of each plane; this, and the absence of perspective, combine into an effect of depth without space: of things being visible and yet beyond reach. It is a curious sense of reality, being both deeply personal and ungraspable. Braque wanted to be 'in full possession of things' by liberating them from perspective: hence his implication that anything three-dimensional is in danger of being 'deformed', as if the ordinary act of seeing were an act of corruption. A Renaissance painter would have found this incomprehensible; Nietzsche, for whom a perspectival view of the world implied an essential misrepresentation, would have agreed. To us, it might seem that Braque's brilliant technique has given the objects in his pictures a liberty which is like a different kind of bondage. His attempt to situate objects outside space is not unlike Proust's to situate events outside time. Both are ways of 'willing backwards'; of trying to preserve objects and experiences from corruption by relativity and time: acts of illogical despotism of the mind to justify a private, and closed, vision.

In fact, when we actually see *Violin and Palette*, the famous nail turns out to look little more real than anything else in the picture; and there is actually something not quite real about the nail in *Violin and Jug*, with its odd, ring-like head: it is hard to imagine anyone hammering it into the wall. When Picasso painted the words 'Ma Jolie' into a picture, he may have been thinking of Eva; but a knowledge of this fact will give the painting precisely the kind of 'anecdotal' significance that Picasso was least interested in. As part of the picture's surface, however, those letters are as real as anything else — which is not 'real' at all. A shop sign saying CAFÉ does not mean it is a café: it only indicates that there is a café there somewhere. The problem is not unlike that of the omnipresent author, which was discussed in the previous chapter. We all know that pictures are not real in the sense that the world we walk about in is real: they are painted by people, usually painters, and everything in them is their contrivance. Braque's nail does not make his painting less of a painting and more of an object, just as Dürer's elaborately calligraphed initials do not, by themselves, suddenly make us realise that this is not, after all, a real scene but an artefact created by Dürer. When Veronese painted himself as one of the musicians in *The Marriage at Cana*, it did not, by itself, suddenly disabuse his contemporaries and make them realise that this was a painting and not a real supper.

These are elementary observations; but they are worth making here, because they might help us to distinguish where the Cubists broke with the conventions of painting and where they did not. Braque's nail does not make his painting any more or less like a real thing, because its use and its appearance are as arbitrary as the fragmentation of the violin underneath. The nail is made to throw a shadow, the violin is not: both are parts of the same a-logical visual scheme imposed by Braque, just as, in Chirico's *The Serenity of the Scholar* (1914; private collection), and *The Philosopher's Conquest* (1914; Art Institute of Chicago), both the unmoving clouds of smoke and the flags briskly fluttering in the wind are part of the same sky, windy or wind-less, in an a-logical visual scheme imposed by Chirico. Both pictures are fractured visions; they are patterns of dissociation.

When Picasso and Braque started making *papiers collés*, they took this sense of dissociation to a new level of sophistication and complexity. These deceptively simple looking works play on the same Cubist paradox of indicating volumes without showing any pictorial depth; and their use of strips of paper of different kinds, combined with pencil and charcoal drawings, give them a sense of both substantiality and weightlessness. In a well-lit gallery they can look like airy ships floating on an invisible sea. But behind the visual beauty a strenuous aesthetic game is going on. Braque's *Glass, Clarinet and Newspaper* (1913; Museum of Modern Art, New York) has an almost vertical clarinet drawn in charcoal, its end nearly circular as befits a good Cubist instrument; and across it, almost horizontal, a broad brown paper strip of imitation wood. We might say that the drawing gives us the clarinet's shape, and the paper its colour and texture. Our job as beholders is to put the brown-ness and the wood-ness together with the clarinet-ness in our minds, and so make up Braque's object ourselves. It is a kind of cerebral Impressionism: we are given visual hints of objects and their qualities, like dissociated clues, and only if we understand Cubist iconography will they cohere into a whole.

Picasso's and Braque's use of newspapers in their *papiers collés* has produced a good deal of literature relating the contents of these cuttings to the picture. It is true that some of the cuttings, announcing an interview with the Governor of Indochina, or advertising a cure for impotence, are hilarious in this unexpected context: part of their effect is to take the solemnity out of the business of looking at pictures. But when we read them, we focus entirely on their content, not on their shape or their place in the composition, for the simple reason that we have to stand too close to them to see the picture as a whole. And the very act of contorting ourselves, trying to read cuttings that are frequently upside down or sideways, distracts from any sense of looking at a picture: for one thing, it makes us feel faintly ridiculous, which was probably part of the intention. Then, when we stand back, we see the composition as a whole, and the newspaper cuttings become part of a pictorial texture which is both spatial and un-spatial. One thing they are no longer, is newspaper cuttings. As with Matisse's little Fauve landscape, the ordinary process of looking has been disrupted: we can only see the composition as a whole when we allow some parts of it to lose entirely their original meaning, identity or function. Arcimboldo's fantastic heads, so admired by the Surrealists, work on us in the same way: either we see a pear and a cucumber, or a chin and a nose, but not both simultaneously.

Schwitters's collages have the same effect. It is beyond the scope of this study to examine the complex imaginative structures of Surrealism; we should only note here briefly that a great deal of Surrealist art makes its impact by emphasising the original identity of its component parts, thus creating that important Surrealist paradox, the composition that does not cohere. We might say that Surrealist art is closed art because the *istoria* of the works defies logical questioning, or, as in the case of Dali, is open to only one, usually deeply personal interpretation to which we may or may not have the clue. Another fundamental aspect of Surrealism, its belief in the accidental and the dreamlike, also makes it a type of closed art because it signals the artist's rejection of responsibility for his work. Responsibility is, of course, the moral and causal relationship *par excellence*; and when the Surrealists undermined it, they did not only take the idea of the artist as an inspired but unconscious vessel further than ever before: they excluded the beholder from questioning it in a specific and fundamental way.

One way or another, all closed art in painting begins with dissociation: this was the first and fundamental innovation of the Fauves and the Cubists. Until the end of the nineteenth century, painting relied on our need for association: our need to perceive *relations* between things. It is the internal dissociation in the pictures of the Fauves, the Cubists and their followers, the abrupt alienation of the objects from each other, their surroundings, and their corresponding originals in the known world, that make their work closed to us. It is unrewarding, sometimes impossible, to 'question' these pictures because they correspond less and less to the associative world which has conditioned us, and on whose workings and coherence we pattern our perception and our questions. Braque said that a picture was 'made up of disaffected objects'[40]. What he meant by this was that the objects in his paintings were not dependent on their 'relations' to each other; and to make sense of his pictures we have to submit to a view of the visible world which regards these relations as being, to a large extent, beside the point.

Braque also described how, when he turned a patch of white on the canvas into a napkin, that patch of white would have been 'conceived in advance without knowing what it will become'.[41] Gris, too, described how, when he painted, he began with a cylinder and turned it into 'a bottle — a particular bottle'[42]. He is describing an imperious geometrical imagination creating shapes of recognisable objects. But this had nothing to do with mere imitation. 'My aim,' Gris told Kahnweiler,

> is to create new objects which cannot be compared with any object in reality ... These new objects therefore *avoid distortion*. My *Violin*, being a creation, need fear no comparison.[43]

What Gris does not explain is how his violin will be recognised by you or me without mentally comparing it with other violins. (Essentially, Gris is using the same language as Malevich, who asserts that '*the Suprematist does not observe and does not touch — he feels.*'[44]) Note the severely Platonic tone of Gris's words: he clearly believes that he has painted a kind of super-violin, and he takes pride in severing the causal links of resemblance between his painting and the objects that are like it. In this sense, for the Cubist painter, the whole world is made up of disaffected objects.

This dissociation between the objects within the picture, combined with the dissociation between the picture and the world it represents, means that we cannot 'read' such paintings as a guide to the world that produced them. If we compare *The Architect's Table* with Fantin-Latour's *Still Life*, we will see how little Picasso tells us about the lifestyle and tastes of anyone who might have owned the objects in his painting, or indeed the painting itself. We can tell from Raphael's pictures that he worked for a more sophisticated religious public than Duccio; and we can tell, without much extra-pictorial knowledge, that Manet's *Déjeuner sur l'herbe* was meant to entertain the worldly and shock the old-fashioned. Such pictures can be seen, from the evidence of their style and content, to belong within the context of a specific world, of a specific setting within a specific culture. Both the pictures and the cultures can thus be questioned by us: they open into and illuminate each other.

 Cubist paintings, by contrast, open largely inward. Their social content is severely limited. The objects in them do not suggest their makers and barely indicate their users. At most, they hint at a world or at an ambiance. There is nothing to indicate, in Picasso's work between 1914 and 1916, that this was the time of the Great War, or indeed that anything was happening outside his studio at all. This is partly why Cubist paintings lack all moral content. By the time Picasso came to make a moral statement in *Guernica*, he had returned to clearly legible, strongly representational images, whose language owes as much to the dream world of the Surrealists as to his own Cubist techniques. The point is that *Guernica* was painted *in a context*: it expressed outrage in response to a known event. The vocabulary of Cubism is not equipped for such a reciprocal act.

This vocabulary is one of autocratic visual experiment, best suited to deal with lifeless objects — which is probably why Braque painted no portraits at all and why Picasso, who did but few in his Cubist period, brought his own vision to dominate them. After Gertrude Stein had sat innumerable times for her portrait, Picasso lost patience and painted out the whole head, saying: 'I can't see you any more when I look.' This proved to be more than the usual impatience that comes from concentrating too long: months later, when Picasso returned from Spain, he re-painted the portrait with great speed, and it bore the visible influence of the ancient Iberian sculptures which he had been seeing both in Spain, and in Paris before his trip home. Yet Picasso was haunted by the idea of art as imitation all his life. He produced a large number of pictures which show people being painted, but the image on the canvas is either quite different from the sitter, or cannot be seen at all. Painting, Picasso seems to be saying, is a self-referential act: it has little to do with what people look like.

Take, for example, the great portrait of the dealer Ambroise Vollard. The intricate orchestration of pale brown and ochre planes draws our eyes to the sitter's domed head; then, following the contours of the lowered eyelids, we slide down the face as it dissolves, with its tightly closed lips, into the network of densely overlapping planes suggesting a chin sinking into a capacious collar like a strange sunset. The lower half of the picture is lit up in the middle by an area of pale brown-grey, touched with silver, its glow answering the pink-brown glow of the head. Now when we turn to Picasso's meticulously detailed drawing of Vollard, done five years later, we can see how much likeness had actually emerged from the scaffolding of the painting. At the same time we realise, too, that the face and its likeness had served only as tools for Picasso's experiment: how to indicate the volume of a head without directly indicating the space it occupies. The face emerges like a ghostly presence from the fragmented substance that covers the canvas. We can only tell that the subject is a man of mature years and possibly bald. The drawing, by contrast, is all specific life: here is an ample French *bourgeois*, stubborn, shrewd and extremely self-possessed, and well but not ostentatiously dressed (note the stout, not very elegant boots).

Picasso was not interested in any of this when he executed the

painting. And just as Henry Moore chooses to hollow out the parts
of the body that are most bulky, Picasso, after 1910, leaves out the
most important part of the human portrait: the eyes, or at least a
sense of *looking*. It is through its gaze, whether it is directed at us or
not, that a portrait defines and confirms its relation to the world, and
to us. But the eyes disappear in Picasso's armoured Cubist faces: the
human head becomes a withdrawn mask, glimpsed through broken,
opaque glass. Things went even further with *Girl with a Mandolin*
(1910; Museum of Modern Art, New York), for which a model
called Fanny Tellier gave numerous sittings. She need not have
bothered. Picasso was to say later that he had let her pose for him

> because she asked to do so and I didn't want to say no. But in
> the end I found her a terrible nuisance. Her presence prevented
> me from painting what I wanted to.[45]

The resulting picture is more an object than a person. It marks an
early stage in a crucial development of Cubist art, and its relative
clarity makes it easy to see what Picasso is doing. He has not yet
quite given up 'looking around his own corner', to use Nietzsche's
phrase: he makes us see the underside of the mandolin, which ought
not to be visible from our viewpoint, and we see more of the girl's
shoulders and left elbow than we would in life. But it is clear that the
rendering of solid bodies, complete with parts of them that are not
usually visible, was no longer enough. Parts of the figure begin
ambiguously to fuse into each other. The girl's left hand is barely
indicated; the right is partly one with the instrument she is holding.
The head is little more than an outline, and it is not clear where the
profile ends and the background begins. Just as parts of the subject
begin to dissolve into each other, the subject itself begins to dissolve
into its background. Or rather, it sometimes seems, in the complex
works of Analytic Cubism, as if objects and figures were being
invaded by whatever surrounds them.

At this stage, as Gertrude Stein shrewdly commented, 'each thing
was as important as any other thing'[46]. Or, we might add, as
unimportant. We are embarking here on a style where objects
virtually disappear behind an intricate network of fragmented surfaces. The impression these paintings give is of the co-existence, but
not the mutual dependence, of its objects and their encasing scaffolding: rather like the Proustian time-scheme, which has a parallel
existence with the story without being quite dependent on it. We
still have a powerful and recognisable sense of composition: these

pictures would make no sense if we were to turn them upside down. But within them a process of profound dissociation is taking place. Objects become less and less legible, more and more lost in the spreading, dense network of scaffolding.

There is no obvious reason, either, why this inner fragmentation should not continue and become even more elaborate. In this sense, too, to use another startling comparison, these paintings remind us of the novels of Kafka and Proust: they appear to be both infinitely expandable and severely enclosed. This may explain Picasso's and Braque's increasing tendency to give their compositions oval forms: they provide a frame of ostentatious artificiality, which both contains and draws attention to the savage visual conflict within. And as objects and their surroundings invade one another, Cubist painting loses all sense of pictorial depth. We perceive only warring volumes, but without any sense of space enclosing them. Inside these haunting compositions there is nowhere to go. Looking at them — and looking means organising and co-ordinating what we see — can give us a sense of being constantly thwarted. Hence the immense stillness of Cubist canvases, which is one of their fundamental paradoxes. The furiously intersecting lines and volumes finally cancel each other out; and as the compositions spread to the edge of their canvases, all movement is extinguished.

Now movement can only be expressed in space: indeed, there can be no movement without space. In his essay *Moment and Movement in Art*, to which the next few pages are greatly indebted, E.H.Gombrich associates the sense of movement with what he calls 'the primacy of meaning' and 'the effort after meaning'[47]. We need, when we look at a picture, to see what it 'means': that is, to judge the size and the position of the things in its space. We must be able to 'understand' that the smallness of a house in the background of a picture 'means' that it is further away from us. In other words, we expect a picture to have a coherent narrative, and we expect to be able to follow it: in this instance, we must be able to conclude, from looking at the picture, that whoever painted it was further away from the house than from the things in the foreground of the picture. We unconsciously work these things out; and any sense of movement the painting gives us will depend on how well we have worked them out. Thus, when we look at Constable's *Wivenhoe Park* (National Gallery of Art, Washington), we think of the birds in his sky as flying, though we know perfectly well that they are painted. But in the ordinary act of looking at the picture, we have a sense of soaring, of distant flutters in the air. This is because we recognise the things Constable painted as birds, and we know that birds fly. When Magritte paints a tuba and a chair in the sky, we experience no sense of movement, because we know that tubas and chairs do not fly. Constable's birds are also placed in a perspective structure: we register their 'bird-ness', because their size, and their position in relation to the clouds and trees, fits them into the picture's 'meaning'. Constable also painted his birds against bulging clouds, in a wide landscape, with space all around them, into which and out of which they might have flown. And we sense, too, that the sky does not end at the frame; that the birds must have come into Constable's view from somewhere beyond the area which he was painting, and probably flew off out of his view again, long before he had time to paint even one of them.

In other words, a sense of pictorial movement depends on what Professor Gombrich calls the picture's meaning. Now pictures, like narratives, can be understood in a simple sense: we can 'read' *Wivenhoe Park* as containing birds, sky, clouds and trees. But if the picture is to 'tell a story', we must be able to grasp the spatial relations between its parts: to understand that, and to understand why, the house in the background is smaller than the black cow in the foreground. That is how we recognise what the picture 'means': its ability to tell a story depends on our being able to grasp these *relations*. This is the painting's *istoria*. And so, a sense of movement in pictures does not mean that our eyes move over its surface: it means that we recognise both things that can move, and pictorial depth which gives such movement scope. And this pictorial depth always implies, not only the world which we see on the canvas, but also a world beyond the picture plane: a world of things we might be able to walk around, a world of causes and effects, of *relations*.

This, in turn, is why pictorial movement depends both on representation and on context. Magritte's tuba does not fly. Malevich's Suprematist works and Lissitsky's intricate Prouns, which do not represent anything, are entirely static, except when their parts are grouped arrow-like together, as if to suggest cosmic traffic signals. Kandinsky, too, sometimes introduces a sense of movement into an abstract canvas, but only by using arrow-like patterns, or speed-lines such as draughtsmen and cartoonists employ to indicate movement. Delauney's great orange discs can suggest a pulsating movement, as if they were vast planets. Bridget Riley's paintings, whose lines do actually seem to move, are carefully structured optical experiments in which the artist addresses herself through the retina to the nervous system, rather than through the retina to the mind. In other words, such non-representational paintings do not suggest movement except by purely optical means, or with the aid of graphical associations which relate their contents, in our minds, to things or objects we know, such as pulsating lights or rotating wheels. And if pictorial movement depends on representation, representation, in turn, depends on pictorial depth. A cube lives in a geometrical depth only. Alter its surface by turning it into a sugar lump, a dice, a brick or a house, and you put pictorial depth around it.

And it is only when we look at true pictorial depth that the idea of time in painting has any real meaning. All pictures, including Cubist ones, imply time in the simple sense that we need time to 'take them in'. But, as we have seen, representational paintings also imply time in the more subtle and internal sense that they 'tell a story': we sense that something had passed before the picture itself 'happened', and that other things may happen in an implied but definable future. And only pictorial depth contains objects that can imply such an existence in time: objects that have a past and a future. The paradox of Cubist objects is that they have little of either. When we say that these objects do not look as if they had been made or used, we mean, too, that it is not easy to imagine ourselves taking hold of them. We cannot grasp an object that is not surrounded by space; and Picasso's and Braque's treatment of space diminishes the sense of physical actuality, the graspability, which their objects have. Braque's experiments with space, his flattening it out around objects, may, as he had hoped, have given him complete possession of these objects; but by imposing his vision on their surrounding depth, he took away some of their graspable reality, as well as their sense of having come from somewhere, of having, at some time in the past, been *made*. These objects are held in an unmoving present. We can question these objects to as little purpose as Beckett's clowns: they may be said to suffer from whatever might be, for objects, the equivalent of amnesia.

It is because Cubist paintings do not imply a before or an after that they have no moral content either. Of course, Cubism as an enterprise, defying both the poverty of the artists and the initial incomprehension and hostility of the public, did have a moral quality. It was a heroic period, as Braque recalled in his old age:

> The things Picasso and I said to one another during those years
> will never be said again. Nobody could say them, and even if
> they were said, nobody would understand them ... But what
> joy we had from them! ... It was rather as if we were two
> climbers roped together.[48]

There is something intense and heady about all this: a sense of
apartness, uniqueness, and exaltation. The simile of the climbers
charges Braque's words with a sense, not only of being at a great
height, but also in great peril. The whole passage has a Nietzschean
tone, and this is more than fortuitous. We have seen Braque
paraphrasing Nietzsche, as he thought; and we know that the young
Picasso lived and worked, in Barcelona and Madrid, among intellec-
tuals for whom Nietzsche's writings were part of their daily bread[49].
The Nietzschean idea of unhindered self-expression would have
appealed powerfully to the temperament of both painters. And
indeed there is something heroic, arbitrary and ultimately incomprehensible about the entire Cubist enterprise, just as there was
something heroic, arbitrary and ultimately futile about Nietzsche's
rejection of logic and perspective.

Of course, when we call Cubism incomprehensible, we apply the
language of engagement and questioning to closed art. A mind
accustomed to the give-and-take of open art is puzzled in front of
Cubist paintings, which represent objects wilfully distorted by a
despotic imagination. Nietzsche objected to the tyranny of perspectival vision for the reason, among others, that it needed interpretation; but it may be argued that a Cubist painting, created in defiance
of perspective, needs interpretration in an even more fundamental
sense. We do not ask what social background the girl in *Girl with a
Mandolin* comes from: we ask why she is painted like this. We do
not question the inner relations of Picasso's painting: we question
the very nature of his inspiration. When Gris said that his violin
needed to fear no comparison, he spoke with the creative pride of an
artist who needed to fear no judgement. Now open art is moral in
that it communicates with the world and allows itself to be judged by
its standards. In this sense representation is essentially moral: for to
imitate correctly and to be truthful about experience is a moral
enterprise. This does not mean that all representational art is moral.
Giorgione's *La Tempesta* is a work of representational art; but we
call it a closed work because we do not know what event is being

imitated in it; it does not offer us a coherent narrative. (If it really has a hermetic meaning, and if we knew what it was, we could give a moral account of it.) Nor does this mean that anything more 'like' is also more moral: that would make Raphael's portrait of Castiglione in all probability more moral than Graham Sutherland's portrait of Winston Churchill. In fact, the contrary may well be the case, since Sutherland's painting included an element of moral judgement on his sitter, whereas Raphael's is redolent of the civilised admiration of an equal. Not having photographs of Castiglione, we shall never know. But the important point is that both painters gave us latitude to judge the matter: we can judge both portraits in the light of our experience of people, and according to our ability to judge characters from faces. By contrast, Picasso tells us very little about Vollard in his portrait painting of the great art dealer, and even less about what he, Picasso, thought of him.

Landscape painting, too, has a moral aspect. It had begun as a means of providing background to human events in paintings, and its history could be written in terms of its handling of the human figure. Painters like Altdorfer and Claude came to use the human figure, in their different ways, to underline the grandeur of their religious or lyrical conception of landscape; but at all times the human presence is there as a kind of norm. It might disappear in Turner at his most tempestuous, and in some of the more contemplative works of the Barbizon painters. But the unpopulated landscape still remained a rarity. Even Richard Wilson includes people in his most grandiose landscapes (the tiny figures usually seem impressed with their surroundings); and there is one solitary human creature crossing the torrent even in James Ward's *The Gordale Scar*.

In one sense, it is a matter of simple experience. Constable was told by his friend 'Antiquity' Smith not to

> set about inventing figures for a landscape taken from nature; for you cannot remain an hour in any spot, however solitary, without the appearance of some living thing that will in all probability accord better with the scene and the time of day than any invention of your own.[50]

This is exactly the kind of realistic professional advice that Leonardo was giving to his contemporaries. Smith had no doubt what sort of landscapes most people normally saw around them, and in his view the painter's task was to make sure that they recognised them in his pictures. It is only with the late works of Monet, with Cézanne, and the Fauves that unpopulated landscape becomes the rule rather than the exception. Moreover, Monet's visionary series of Rouen Cathedral, of the rocks at Etrétat, of haystacks and water lilies, are not only empty of human presence but even begin to blur the identity of their actual content. Landscape becomes the expression of pure personal vision. When the young Kandinsky first saw one of the *Haystacks* in Moscow, he was exhilarated by its beauty before he could see what it represented[51]; and when we look at a painting like *The Thaw* (Metropolitan Museum, New York), we find that Monet's wintry whites blend into each other with such chromatic subtlety that they make the actual landscape difficult to perceive, and make us think of the stark elusiveness of Malevich's *White on White*. Monet himself, in his old age, told an American pupil that he wished he had been born blind and suddenly gained his sight, so that he might have begun to paint without knowing what the objects were before him. This is the language of pure vision; and it signals to us that, as modern landscape developed into an art of motifs passionately contemplated but bereft of human content, it took the first step towards closed art. For the human figure links the landscape to organised, populated life, to values we created and understand. By leaving it out, painters have deprived their pictures of one point of contact between them and us, one point of engagement and assessment. It may have been an aesthetic decision; it may have been an artistic gain; but it is also a moral loss.

Now Cubist painting was, as we saw, a moral activity. In this context it is far from naive to remind ourselves that Picasso was also a considerable representational artist: it tells us that he could have achieved instant conventional success, but that he painted differently because he was interested in something different. Picasso was working towards something that was essentially amoral. His and Braque's despotic acts of vision took their art ever further out of the reach of people who expect their pictures to be 'legible'; and in the end nothing can be moral that cannot be shared and understood. Morality depends on interlocking causes and effects; it is defined by mutual relations between people. No one can be moral on his own. Equally, if a picture (or a play or a novel) can be understood, then it can, by definition, be understood by more than one person, because understanding depends on things having features and qualities which can be defined, described — and, therefore communicated. To Alberti and Leonardo all this would have seemed obvious. But what we *feel* about a picture is a different matter: feelings are not always communicable. We all feel something about works which we understand; but this feeling depends on their 'stories'. What we feel about *Ghosts, The Trial* or *Wivenhoe Park* depends on first understanding what happens in them. The most subjective and incommunicable sense of identification with Mrs Alving depends on first knowing her story and understanding Ibsen's *istoria*. We may share Van Gogh's touching pantheism, but only because we can see what he made of things we are familiar with, such as sunflowers and boots.

But reading modern art criticism we often find ourselves in the presence of feelings of an entirely different kind. For example, writing about the great American Abstract Expressionists, Robert Rosenblum compares Rothko's *Light Earth Over Blue* with Caspar David Friedrich's *Monk by the Sea* and Turner's *Evening Star*, and writes that Rothko

> places us on the threshold of those shapeless infinities discussed by the aestheticians of the Sublime.[52]

Rothko may or may not have liked to be compared to aestheticians; but as for the Sublime, its treatment in Romantic literature itself is firmly rooted in *things*: waterfalls, clouds, mountains. The feelings of sublimity or terror are firmly anchored in these physical presences. Little William Wordsworth, who felt himself a trouble to the place when he wandered around the lakes, was a very real boy who was very frightened indeed. Similarly, both Friedrich and Turner have a human presence in their landscapes: hints of sentient creatures, whose presence is the key to what the painters felt about their pictures and how they wanted us to feel. In the case of Friedrich, it is precisely the monk who makes the picture what it is. Rosenblum is not unaware of this: he notes that these figures (he calls them 'literal detail'[53]) form an emotional link between the picture and the spectator. But he thinks that when we stand before Rothko's painting we do not need such links any more: they are 'no longer necessary; we ourselves are the monk by the sea'[54]. We may recollect how Gide re-read *The Trial*, and wrote: 'that hunted creature is I'. Rosenblum's attitude, like Gide's, is one of identification amounting to submission. Only this could have caused him to write:

> These infinite, glowing voids carry us *beyond reason* to the Sublime; we can only *submit* to them in an act of faith and let ourselves be absorbed in their radiant depths (my italics).[55]

We must not doubt the genuineness of Rosenblum's feelings; but they have certainly nothing to do with questioning, with engagement. The passage reminds one of Cosima Wagner's diary entry about listening to Wagner playing *Tristan*. It is the swooning of the intellect.

This is far from being a solitary example. Here is Leo Steinberg, writing about Jackson Pollock:

> Questions as to the validity of Pollock's art, though they remain perfectly good in theory, are simply *blasted out of relevance* by these manifestations of Herculean effort ... *How good these pictures are I cannot tell*, but know that they have something of the barbarism of an ancient epic. Does anybody ask whether the Song of Gilgamesh is any good? (my italics).[56]

Why, yes, any ordinary reader, who bought the Penguin edition, certainly would, and Sumerian scholars must be asking it all the time. Asking whether a thing is any good is not merely an act of cerebral dissection: it is the mind's response to the way we respond to a work of art. When a critic prefaces his views by saying he does not know how good a picture (or a play, or a novel) is, he is not practising criticism so much as expressing his feelings, and expressing them in such a way as to rule out critical engagement with the work. And if there is something reverential in his tone, then that, we ought to see by now, is an appropriate response to closed art, which has had something quasi-religious about it from the beginning. Miró spoke of Mondrian arriving, through the purity of his painting, at 'saintliness'[57]. Antonin Artaud thought that in the paintings of Picasso's Cubist period 'the soul was re-discovered in its entirety'[58]. Kafka, it is said, believed that Picasso was not wilfully distorting things so much as registering

> the deformities which have not yet penetrated our consciousness[59]

– a notion which puts Picasso's art beyond questioning or argument, for it is seen to be dealing with things of which we can have no experience. André Salmon wrote of Picasso that he stood

> immortal at the centre of a transfigured universe ... Art present and Art to come derive from his benevolent tyranny.[60]

Critical language such as this grows up naturally in response to art that offers little or nothing to engagement or argument. We cannot 'question' a painting by Rothko the way we can question one by Friedrich: it does not have the interrelation of parts which implies a narrative, a life before and after and beyond the canvas — which, in other words, constitutes an *istoria*. It has a harmony of colours: but colours are open only to analysis which is purely optical, and not to questioning. What would we question them about? I myself have sometimes felt in front of some of Rothko's canvases that they were like massive architectural structures, translucent but impenetrable, solid but weightless, glimpsed as if from an immense distance through mists. This may be what Rothko intended; or I may have been reading a kind of *istoria* into what is a pure expression of feeling.

One of the central paradoxes of Cubist painting is that it was a moral pursuit which produced amoral art. Another is that its intense concentration on the essence of objects deprived these objects of so much of their actual object-ness. The solidity of things dissolved under the painters' analytical gaze. Like Schopenhauer's thought, like Wagner's operas and Kafka's novels, Cubist painting is the result of the deepest personal commitment issuing in magnificently impersonal works. The short period during Picasso's and Braque's careers, when some of their canvases looked virtually identical and neither would sign them, was for them a personal paradise of impersonal creation. It does not seem fanciful to say that Cubist painting was one great Schopenhauerian act: the artists' Will, seeking to dominate the visible world, achieved a strange objectification of that world, and of that Will, in these passionate but remote pictures, fragmented but indivisible, falling apart yet enclosed. The Cubist objects — the bottles, the glasses, the violins — became the subject of a search which was as complex, cerebral and transcendental as these objects were simple, physical and mundane. The Cubist painters, painting mostly from memory, wanted to find something eternal in them. So, instead of painting *this* bottle on *this* table, with its own particular translucency and shadow, they painted Bottles whose shape, translucency and shadow became inessential except as they contributed to an investigation of light, volume and space. In this, the true ancestor of the Cubists is Monet, whose great series were investigations of what the artist felt about light, volume and space, but especially light, in the course of which the mundane attributes of the things he painted became almost redundant. We might say that Monet was objectifying his Will; and his Series, in which he painted the same motif, in different lights, several times, is an example of a painter's impersonal but visionary identification with an object. It is the visionary nature of these paintings which makes them forerunners of closed art: Monet's haystacks are not fully open to factual questions, because, in themselves, they are far less important than what Monet has to say about light.

The small vocabulary of Cubist painting has often been remarked upon: anyone who has seen a large number of them together can easily feel that he is moving inside the same interior. Indeed, more than with any other previous style of painting, we find it easier to assess, even to understand, these works when we see a large number of them together. It is not a question of style. The paintings of the elder Pieter Breughel or Georges de la Tour, so markedly and consistently individual in style, are all vividly different. Nor is it a question of certain recurring motifs: the maps, for example, that appear on the wall in the background of so many of Vermeer's pictures, do not express a closed personal vision. Cubist paintings are related to each other because they subjugate the varied, the everyday, the unpredictable and the individual to a vision which is embodied in, and expressed through, a technique, and which dominates them like a mood. These pictures are visual statements about something more than what they represent; that is what gives them a kinship which goes beyond style. It is in this sense that, just as Schopenhauer wrote one vast book, the Cubist painters created one massive, identifiable, but elusive world.

And just as Wagner, in his search for what he called the 'purely human', arrived at something that was not quite human but also something more, just so Picasso and Braque, in their quest for what we might call the purely visual, took away from the things they painted most of the attributes on which visual recognition and moral engagement depend. Indeed, in doing so, they may have helped us to realise how closely these things, the factual, the logical and the moral, depend on one another. They may have helped us to realise, too, that to strive for the 'purely visual' is necessarily to move away from the visible physical world. For a picture which is not purely visual must, by definition, be a picture of *something*: something which exists in the world we know, and which involves the logic of recognition. In this sense, Picasso and Braque pursued an impossible quest. The increasing 'legibility' of their post-war pictures, with their greater range of colour and texture, makes one feel that they were pulling back from a precipice.

But the process that had started when the ageing Cézanne imposed his will on the arrangements of the humble objects on his table could not be stopped. Braque said that, as a painter, he wanted to be in full possession of things; he and Picasso helped to launch painting on a new course, and it has led to a new, despotic art which aspires to the full possession of its beholders.

Notes

1. 'I think it was Nietzsche who said "An aim is a servitude", and it's true.' Quoted in *Braque* by Jean Leymarie, Paris, 1961. I have not been able to trace these words in Nietzsche's writings.
2. Quoted in *Strindberg: A Biography* by Michael Meyer, London, 1985, p. 118.
3. See *Painting and Experience in Fifteenth Century Italy* by Michael Baxandall, Oxford, 1972, pp. 73 ff.
4. *Lives of the Artists*, tr. & ed. George Bull, Harmondsworth, 1965, pp. 274–5.
5. In *Giorgione's Tempesta, with Comments on Giorgione's Poetic Allegories*, Oxford, 1968, p. 3.
6. In *Giorgio da Castelfranco*, Chicago, 1937, p. 6.
7. *ibid.*, p. 50.
8. *The Renaissance*, ed. Kenneth Clark, London, 1961, pp. 140–1. Pater's famous, and deeply Schopenhauerian formulation, 'All art constantly aspires towards the condition of music', occurs in this essay.
9. In *Landscape into Art*, London, 2nd ed., 1976, p. 116.
10. *On Painting*, tr. John R. Spencer, New Haven, 1966, p. 70.
11. *ibid.*, p. 75.
12. *ibid.*, p. 77.
13. *ibid.*, p. 78.
14. *ibid.*, p. 76.
15. *Treatise on Painting*, tr. John Francis Rigaud, London, 1835, p. 3.
16. *ibid.*, p. 75.
17. *Discourses on Art*, ed. Robert R. Wark, New Haven, 1975, p. 132.
18. *Complete Writings*, ed. Geoffrey Keynes, Oxford, 1966, p. 471.
19. In 'The Philosophical Brothel', by Leo Steinberg, *Art News*, New York, September/October 1972, p. 22.
20. See 'Velazquez and *Las Meninas*' by Marilyn Millner Kahr, *Art Bulletin*, New York, June 1975, pp. 225 ff. For the comparison with Picasso, see Steinberg, *art. cit.*, p. 22.
21. John Berger in *The Success and Failure of Picasso*, Harmondsworth, 1965, p. 73.
22. By William Rubin, in *Picasso in the Collection of the Museum of Modern Art*, New York, 1972, p. 42.
23. *Troilus and Cressida*, I. 3. 96–8. The word *insisture* is controversial, this being the only example of its use in the language. Kenneth Palmer, in the Arden

edition (London, 1982, p. 127) discusses its two possible interpretations. Both could be understood in the visual sense.

24. Quoted in *Braque* by Edwin Mullins, London, 1968, p. 128.
25. See Chapter IV above, Note 110.
26. *The Letters of Vincent Van Gogh*, sel. & ed. Mark Roskill, London, 1963, p. 267.
27. Quoted in Leymarie, *op. cit.*, p. 38.
28. In 'Letters from Munich', reprinted in Kandinsky: *Complete Writings on Art*, ed. Kenneth C. Lindsay and Peter Vergo, London, 1982, Vol.I p. 69.
29. In *Paul Cézanne*, by Meyer Schapiro, London, 1952, p. 100.
30. Leonardo da Vinci: *op. cit.*, p. 145.
31. Quoted in *André Derain* by Denys Sutton, London, 1959, p. 21.
32. Quoted in *Fauvism and its Affinities*, by John Elderfield, Museum of Modern Art Exhibition Catalogue, New York, 1976, p. 108.
33. In *The Letters of Juan Gris*, tr. & ed. Douglas Cooper, privately printed, 1956, p. 212.
34. Quoted in *Cubism* by Edward Fry, London, 1966, p. 158.
35. In *Picasso*, by Gertrude Stein, London, 1938, p. 19.
36. Berger: *op. cit.*, p. 57.
37. *Master Pieces: Making Furniture from Paintings*, by Richard Ball and Peter Campbell, Poole, 1984, consists of twenty illustrated essays, with diagrams, on how to reproduce pieces of furniture in famous paintings. No. 18 is about the making of the sideboard seen in Picasso's *Still Life on a Sideboard*, (1920; Musée Picasso, Paris), pp. 125 ff.
38. See *The Work of Living Art: A Theory of the Theatre*, by Adolphe Appia, tr. H.D. Albright, Florida, 1960, pp. 45–8.
39. Quoted in *Braque*, by John Richardson, Harmondsworth, 1959, p. 10.
40. Quoted in *Georges Braque*, by John Russell, London, 1959, p. 12.
41. Quoted in *Braque: The Great Years*, by Douglas Cooper, London, 1973, p. 46.
42. Quoted in *Juan Gris*, by James Thrall Soby, New York, 1958, p. 110.
43. Quoted in *Juan Gris: His Life and Work*, by D.-H. Kahnweiler, tr. Douglas Cooper, London, 1969, p. 144.
44. In *The Non-Objective World*, tr. Howard Dearstyne, Chicago, 1959, p. 94.
45. Quoted in *Picasso: The Cubist Years. A Catalogue Raisonné of the Paintings and Related Works*, by Pierre Daix and Joan Rosselet, tr. Dorothy S. Blair, London, 1979, p. 68.
46. *op. cit.*, p. 12.
47. Reprinted in *The Image and the Eye*, Oxford, 1982, p. 51.
48. Quoted in Russell: *op. cit.*, p. 13.
49. See *Sources and Background of Picasso's Art 1900–1906*, by Phoebe Pool, Burlington Magazine, 1959, pp. 176–82.; and *Picasso: The Formative Years*, by Anthony Blunt and Phoebe Pool, London, 1962, esp. pp. 6–18.
50. Quoted in *Memoirs of the Life of John Constable Esq., R.A.*, by C.R.Leslie, London, 1949 (first publ. 1843), p. 26.
51. See *Reminiscences* in Lindsay and Vergo, *ed. cit.*, Vol. I, p. 363. Kandinsky describes seeing the picture as one of the two events 'that stamped my whole life and shook me to the depths of my being'. The other event was, significantly, a performance of Wagner's *Lohengrin* at the Bolshoi Theatre. See also the Editors' notes in Vol. II pp. 888–9.
52. In 'The Abstract Sublime', *Art News*, February 1961, p. 40.

53. *ibid.*

54. *ibid.*

55. *ibid.*, p. 56.

56. In *Pollock's First Retrospective*, repr. in *Other Criteria*, Oxford, 1972, p. 265.

57. Quoted in *Miró*, by Roland Penrose, London, 1970, p. 199.

58. See Artaud: *Collected Works*, Vol. II, tr. Victor Corti, London, 1971, p. 189.

59. See *Conversations with Kafka*, by Gustav Janouch, tr. Goronwy Rees, London, 1971, p. 143.

60. Quoted in *A Picasso Anthology: Documents, Criticism, Reminiscences*, ed. Marilyn McCully, London, 1981, p. 141.

VII

CLOSE OF PLAY

STORIES AND INTERPRETATIONS

At first sight, the very idea of closed drama might seem a contradiction in terms. After all, the simplest theatrical event is pregnant
with questions. A man appears on a stage, and we become inquisitive at once. Who is he? What brings him here? A dramatic
character carries with him, as functions of his existence, questions
about time and causation. Even in the kind of ritualistic drama that
Artaud advocated, drama which is not interested in character, time
and causation, the spectator can only identify the nature of the
ritual by asking who its personages are, what they signify, and how
they fit into the event which is unfolding before him.

A novel can spread itself more easily: it can describe the appearance of its characters, their surroundings, the time and place they
live in; they can be shown thinking things, remembering this or
that. The narrator can take care of the randomness and abruptness
of life. But a play is under a different, special kind of pressure,
because it is *an event*. In it things must, and do, happen. All
narratives tell stories, directly or indirectly; but a play is a unique
kind of narrative because it is a story which tells itself *by taking
place*.

There is no such thing as a static play. Maeterlinck believed in a
drama of stasis: he thought that 'most of the tragedies of Aeschylus were without movement', and that life in them was 'almost
motionless'. Drama, for Maeterlinck, consisted

solely and entirely in the individual, face to face with the universe.[1]

But what, we ask, happens then? What does the individual say to the universe? In Maeterlinck's own early plays the languorous, *faux-naive* dialogue is clearly meant to suggest deep spiritual stillness, a world haunted by nothingness; but underneath everything is tense with the impending melodramatic revelation. Eric Bentley has pointed out that the English title of Samuel Beckett's most famous play is innacurate. *Waiting for Godot* is not at all the same as *En attendant Godot*: the original French title tells us that what we see is 'what happens in certain human beings *while waiting*'[2].

All this means that playwrights, more than novelists, have to get on with it: they have to represent, or present, events: and events, by definition, move forward. We are used to flashbacks in films: the ease with which the past can be made to invade the present; but this should not blind us to the essentially forward-moving nature of drama in the theatre. And, of course, we make sense of flashbacks as flashbacks precisely because we place them and understand them in a sequential context: we read them, that is, with a sequential mind. Plays are linear: they are much more like real life in this respect.

Strindberg tried, in some of his late plays, to represent what he conceived to be the non-linearity of life: indeed, his plays have been described as 'petrified situations'[3]. In *To Damascus*, or *A Dream Play*, for example, things do not always happen because some other things happened first. Take Part II of *To Damascus* where Strindberg's hero, the Stranger, is waiting outside the bedroom for his child to be born. His wife sends out the maid to ask him to get a letter from the pocket of one of her dresses. The letter, which is addressed to him, has been opened and the Stranger is confirmed in his suspicions that his wife has been stealing his mail. This is something we know already: in Act I she told her mother that she was doing this because she

> wanted to know the man with whom I joined my destiny — I suppress anything that might swell his pride. I isolate him so that he may keep his electricity and perhaps blow himself up.[4]

(The Stranger is experimenting with alchemy and trying to harness lightning to make gold.) What the stolen letter contains is 'confirmation from the greatest authority living' that his experiments are scientifically valid, and he leaves at once to meet him. To his mother-in-law's protestations he replies:

> You have called my wife, your daughter, a whore, and my unborn child a bastard. Keep them. You have murdered my honour. There is nothing left for me but to seek it elsewhere.[5]

Now the mother-in-law has said no such thing, but she does not refute the accusation, any more than she did a few minutes earlier when the Stranger first made it. On that occasion he simply called her 'just about the most loathsome person' he knew. Now, letter in hand, he departs 'to save my soul from destruction'. In the next scene, one of the most bizarre and haunting in Strindberg's late work, we see him at a banquet at an inn, where academic dignitaries in full evening dress celebrate his scientific achievements. The banquet, however, gradually turns into a rowdy gathering of drunks and beggars; the Stranger is denounced as a charlatan and is taken off to jail for not paying the bill. And eventually all this turns out to have taken place in the Stranger's mind: he arrives back home to find that he had only been out of the room for a minute.

These events take up most of Acts II and III. Technically, they are a series of complex dislocations. It is probably only in the Stranger's heated imagination that his mother-in-law calls his wife a whore; just as the banquet and the subsequent humiliations all take place in his mind. Yet the mother-in-law never protests, and the nightmare seems real to us because, through it, the Stranger has learnt a few things. It is during the banquet sequence that he hears that 'the greatest authority living' has withdrawn his support. But if this is all happening in his mind, can it also be true? The Stranger becomes conscious of his spiritual poverty when he realises that he had left wife and child 'for the sake of an illusion'. But now we know that he had not really left them; so is this realisation also true in the Stranger's waking life? Is Strindberg, in other words, merely reading us a moral lesson, or is he showing us someone going through the moral process of learning from things that happened to him?

In fact what Strindberg has done is to impose the texture of a vision upon the natural narrative movement of the play. Nothing happens in the first two acts which could be seen as causing either the Stranger's nightmare or his disillusionment. The letter in his wife's pocket which triggers it all off is the clumsiest of melodramatic devices. Strindberg is telling us what *might* have happened if the Stranger had gone off to meet the eminent scientist, and what he thought, and wanted us to think, would come of such a meeting. He is saying, too, that traumatic events, such as great disappointments, or the fear of them, would haunt one's mind (or haunted his) as if they had been preposterous nightmares. One way or another, we are meant to accept the spiritual reality of these events regardless of their physical reality; indeed, part of Strindberg's point is that the spiritually real need not depend on being physically real. 'All is failure and vanity' is the import of the whole bizarre sequence, and it was in order to assert this that Strindberg interfered with the play's linear movement. This is Strindberg's picture of the world.

All this: the playwright's imposition of his message on the nature of his material and the way he undermines what seems true by presenting it illogically, will by now seem familiar. We are present at the making of closed drama. When the Stranger gets back home he finds yet another letter in the pocket of yet another dress: this one tells him that his first wife has re-married and his children now have a stepfather. This has been one of the Stranger's obsessions throughout the play and, during the preceding dream-sequence, he dreamed that it had come true. Now it has. *To Damascus* is, among other things, a demonstration of the reality of the unreal; a record of the way in which waking life is nagged and tormented by things we fear to think about. The price of this demonstration is a violation of the way a play naturally moves forward. Things happen that are not, properly speaking, caused.

Yet, in the meantime, the essential linearity of drama does assert itself after all. All three parts of *To Damascus* tell their story, such as it is, in a recognisably sequential movement. The play as story proves stronger than the play as a system of dislocations, despite the fact that Strindberg gives us a sense of a past event which may or may not have happened, and which may or may not have been, in any real meaning of the word, the past.

But usually the playwright helps us to construct the past: he draws up a blueprint and we follow his instructions. We piece together the past from the implications of present events. Sophocles' *Oedipus Rex* and the mature dramas of Ibsen are the best examples of the present and the past unfolding simultaneously. These plays are not just virtuoso pieces of construction. Their effect is not the kind of stillness we experience at the beginning of *Tristan and Isolde*, where opposing dramatic and psychological forces almost cancel one another out. In both Sophocles and Ibsen, the past we are discovering has caused the present we see. The two narratives, one turning us towards that past and the other carrying us forward, are bound together by the moral chains of cause and effect. They create a sense of movement, both complex and inevitable, which is the true dynamic of both drama and morality. It is also a forward movement: by the end of such plays the world is a different place for everyone in it. And so when we say that we understand a dramatic narrative we mean that we perceive the causes which created its forward movement. In performance, the economy of dramatic construction demands that we perceive these causes swiftly: we need to be alert, logical, questioning. In this sense plays are, by definition, open.

So is character. We said in the opening chapter that character in drama implies the possibility of a different past. A dramatic character is someone who has done certain things but who might also have done others — in which case the play might have been partly or wholly different. There is a child present in every intelligent spectator who will say that if only Othello had stopped to think and spoken to Desdemona quietly there need have been no harm done. Such an attitude to a play is naive; but it is also the source of an important perception: it recognises Othello's psychological substance, and it implies that we are questioning his actions, rather than merely accepting them. It is this same perceptive child in us who, at a good performance, hopes until the end that this time the catastrophe might be averted. A playwright as un-naive as Brecht has written in his notes on *Life of Galileo* a passage entitled 'Could Galileo have acted any differently?'[6] Brecht concludes that he could: the case of Galileo is a tragedy of the wrong decision, and Brecht pinpoints it precisely in Scene 11 and Galileo's conversation with Vanni the ironmonger. This does not mean that Brecht seriously considered an alternative Galileo who evaded the Inquisition and returned to Venice to carry on with his researches, any more than we would seriously contemplate an extra-fictional Othello who gave Desdemona a new handkerchief, dismissed Iago, and lived happily ever after. Questioning a character is not the same as giving him an extra-fictional reality: it is to recognise that, for the fictional duration, he is real.

Half a century ago L.C. Knights's essay, *How Many Children Had Lady Macbeth?* exploded the cosy nonsense of Shakespeare criticism which treated the characters as intimate friends one could invite to tea: a school of which A.C. Bradley was the most distinguished representative. Yet, behind all his excesses, Bradley had an important point: namely, that the dramatic character is the royal road to the understanding of plays. Professor Knights approvingly quotes the dictum by George Wilson Knight that

> the persons, ultimately, are not human *at all*, but purely symbols of a poetic vision (my italics).[7]

But the fact is that the poetic vision is expressed through the language these persons use and that, in a good play, they use it in a way which is appropriate to their characters. Macbeth's language, full of tormented, apocalyptic anxiety, is entirely different from, say, Banquo's. It is this language, in relation to his actions, that defines Macbeth's place in the poetic vision which is *Macbeth* the play; it is Macbeth's actions that give Shakespeare's imagery its anchor and its function – indeed, its very meaning. Language has to do with action before it can make sense as a source of imagery. The theatrical experience is, in the first place, a confrontation with character. Character expresses itself in event; the story precedes the picture. In the theatre we are all Bradleyans.

When we look at characters we hope to understand the causes of their actions, but we often find that these actions are also confirmations. In ordinary life we tend to assume, unless we are practising existentialists, that action follows from character: a man behaves in such and such a way because he is such and such a person. But in the theatre we also have to deduce character from action. Indeed, it is often a person's final act that seems to define him for us. When, at the end of *Hedda Gabler*, Tesman decides to put aside his work on domestic industries in Brabant in the Middle Ages and settle down instead to edit Lovborg's notes, he finally confirms for us that he does not have an original mind. He also enables us to compare him and his pursuits with those of Hedda, Lovborg and Brack – a comparison which is, morally speaking, strongly in poor Tesman's favour. It is Pastor Manders's last act, the burning down of the orphanage, which confirms that the moral egoism which had made him take Mrs Alving back to her husband is still stronger in him than anything else: now that he knows what Captain Alving was really like he will burn down the orphanage that bears his name rather than be associated with it. In another note on Galileo Brecht remarks tersely: 'His crime has made a criminal of him.'[8]

Yet if it is true that the dramatic character is defined by his actions, it is also true that we understand actions in the light of character. Just as in paintings we recognise shapes as things which we already know, in plays we judge people's actions in the light of what we already know of them. Such actions provide a context for our final judgement: earlier actions function as signposts for our understanding of the later ones. Looking before and after, we question the entire play through its characters in action.

That brings us back to the problem of the static play. One reason why we feel that 'nothing happens' in *Waiting for Godot* is because character, as we understand it, does not issue in appropriate action, and action does not put a satisfactory psychological seal on character. We cannot question either of them through the other: this is one of the things that defines *Godot* as a closed play. I have suggested, too, that when we say we do not understand a play we imply that it is not telling a story; and indeed criticism of such plays is often based on the assumption that it is not. It is the mutual logic of character and action that makes a story, and if we do not feel that such logic holds a play together we search for its meaning elsewhere.

One alternative is to consider the play as a poem. This seems to me an evasion. Poems have a different dynamic and a different purpose. A poem is a personal affair: it reports on a situation which is the situation of the poet, mental, spiritual or physical, at the time of writing. Even argumentative or meditative poems, like George Herbert's *The Collar*, or Philip Larkin's *Whitsun Weddings*, are written from the vantage point of feelings and thoughts understood and evaluated. (A poem of impersonation, like Eliot's *Prufrock*, is a report on an imaginary self.) In this sense a poem is a summing up. In plays, by contrast, things lead to one another. Things happen because other things have happened, and the summing up is left to us. When we do our summing up of a play we each make our own statement on its subject, based on the events the playwright unfolds before us; and we arrive at it by questioning these events and the people who enact them.

Plays are a web of utterances in context and expressed in action; and the problem of the closed play is that its characters no longer bear the same organic relation to events that we have been accustomed to. The 'character' of the Grandfather in Maeterlinck's *The Intruder* is not in any way defined by the fact that he, the only blind person present, is the only one to suspect what is happening. Maeterlinck is saying that the blind 'see' more than the sighted, and that the old understand life (and death) better than the young. These are age-old assumptions, and one could argue with them in the context of real life. What we cannot do is argue with them in the context of Maeterlinck's play, for there is nothing in this garrulous

and crotchety old gentleman *as a character* that explains his mystical
intuitions. He is Maeterlinck's principal motif, the one that sums up
his message; and he is one of many Maeterlinck characters whom
Wilson Knight would have been fully justified in calling symbols of
a poetic vision.

Arthur Symons wrote that Maeterlinck's plays were 'dramatic as
to form, by a sort of accident, but essentially mystical.'[9] In other
words, we do not so much follow Maeterlinck's plays as apprehend
them. Still, the fact remains that people do not write plays 'by a sort
of accident'. Freud said that people have a tendency to personalise
what they wish to understand – a remark which underlines both the
dramatic nature of Freud's imagination and the essentially open
nature of drama. It is a literary form of which questioning is the
inspiration and the essence, and to which questioning is the most
appropriate response. Our response to a play by Maeterlinck depends
on how much the author's mystical frame of mind is evident in, and
how much it undermines, the open form he is using. His characters
are the clue to this. He presents them in recognisable settings (the
stage directions of *The Intruder* have a solid bourgeois precision);
but do we respond to them as people or as symbols in an essentially
non-dramatic argument? Yeats summed up Maeterlinck's characters
admirably when he wrote that they were,

> instead of human beings persons who are as faint as a breath
> upon a looking-glass, symbols who can speak a language slow
> and heavy with dreams because their own life is but a dream.[10]

Yeats defines precisely that insubstantiality which is fundamentally
unrelated to action. Criticism of closed plays is often a diagnosis of
such inner dislocations.

Another way of approaching such plays is to call them myths.
Yeats, again, described in his Introduction to his play *The Resurrection*, how for years he had been 'preoccupied with a certain myth
that was in itself a reply to a myth'. And he continued:

> I do not mean fiction, but one of those statements our nature is
> compelled to make and employ as a truth though there cannot
> be sufficient evidence.

And then:

> When I was a boy everybody talked about progress, and
> rebellion against my elders took the form of aversion to that
> myth.[11]

Clearly, to Yeats, 'myth' could simply mean 'idea'.

In our own time, the Polish director Jerzy Grotowski has written about myth as an essential part of drama: for him myth holds values which modern man must confront if he is to determine his own. When theatre was still part of religion, Grotowski argues, it incorporated myth, profaning it and transcending it at the same time; and the spectator was given

> a renewed personal awareness of his personal truth in the truth of a myth.

Modern man, Grotowski goes on, cannot experience this any more. Today

> spectators are more and more individuated in their relation to the myth as corporate truth or group model, and belief is often a matter of intellectual conviction. This means that it is much more difficult to elicit the sort of shock needed to get at those psychic layers behind the life-mask. Group identification with myth — the equation of personal, individual truth with universal truth — is [Grotowski concludes] virtually impossible today.

There is a note of regret in all this; but Grotowski is not in despair. We can, he thinks, confront myth; that is to say,

> while retaining our private experiences, we can attempt to incarnate myth, putting on its ill-fitting skin to perceive the relativity of our problems, their connection to the 'roots', and the relativity of the 'roots' in the light of today's experience. If the situation is brutal, if we strip ourselves and touch an extraordinarily intimate layer, exposing it, the life-mask cracks and falls away ... The violation of the living organism, the exposure carried to outrageous excess, returns us to the concrete mythical situation, an experience of common human truth.[12]

We may pause here and wonder whether modern man is so badly off that he needs to confront myths he is sceptical about, and whether that is the easiest path to common human truth. But, what is more important, we should note Grotowski's impatience with the 'individuated' attitude of spectators who insist on intellectual conviction rather than identify themselves, as a group, with myth. Here lies Grotowski's paradox: his violently cerebral argument seeks human truth in group submission rather than in a sense of personal validity.

What is missing from both Yeats's and Grotowski's remarks about myth is any consideration of it as a narrative. Indeed, Yeats is quite explicit in calling it a statement as opposed to fiction. But a myth is not a statement; nor is it a thing, an idea, or a situation. A myth is something that happened. The myth of Prometheus consists, primarily, not in Prometheus' ideas or what he stood for, but in what he did and what was done to him. 'All myths,' Claude Lévi-Strauss reminds us, 'tell a story'.[13] Now strictly speaking you cannot have 'group identification' with a story, nor can you 'incarnate' a story. When we regard the theatrical event as something to identify with, we define it as closed drama. Wagner wrote that myth was the poem of a life-view held in common: one of the first coherent statements of the nature of myth as an idea to accept, rather than a narrative to understand. Nietzsche had something similar in mind when he wrote about '*myth* as a concentrated image of the world'[14]. Grotowski's idea of myth as 'corporate truth or group model' is close to this. He wants theatre to have something deeply rooted in the psyche of society. This is clearly essential, since if it does not have that it has nothing. But if that is all a play has, it will lose its uniqueness as an event: it will be no more than a reminder of ideas held in common.

With this in mind we should reconsider Martin Esslin's influential remark that what he defined as the Theatre of the Absurd 'is a theatre of situation as against a theatre of events in sequence'. Esslin admits that 'things do happen in *Waiting for Godot*', but argues that these happenings

> do not constitute a plot or a story; they are an image of Beckett's intuition that *nothing really ever happens* in man's existence. The whole play is a complex poetic image [making] in the spectator's mind a total, complex impression of a basic, and static, situation.[15]

But this is no more true than Vivian Mercier's witty remark, quoted at the beginning of this book, that in *Waiting for Godot* 'nothing happens, twice'. The fact is that things happen all the time. The two men meet and meet again; they discuss the New Testament, and talk about what may or may not have happened the previous day; Pozzo and Lucky come and go, twice — all these are things that happen. When Vladimir and Estragon make conversation or ritually insult each other they are making things happen, albeit only to help pass the time which, as Estragon sagely remarks, 'would have passed in any case'. Beckett's point is not that, as Estragon puts it, 'nothing happens, nobody comes, nobody goes, it's awful': that is only what Estragon thinks. Beckett's point is that when life provides no events for us, we make our own. The events Vladimir and Estragon make for themselves are also events in the play: they make up its story.

Of course, that is not the same as a plot. To quote E.M. Forster once again, a plot is

> a narrative of events, the emphasis falling on causality. 'The king died and then the queen died' is a story. 'The king died and then the queen died of grief' is a plot.[16]

In this sense *Waiting for Godot* has a story, though it does not quite have a plot. The grip of causality is relaxed, almost non-existent. Pozzo goes blind, we do not know why ('I woke up one fine day as blind as Fortune'), or when ('Don't question me. The blind have no notion of time'). We note that, while in Act I he drove Lucky, in Act II he is led by him, but that his ideas about the treatment of servants are no more attractive than before. If Estragon wants to get Lucky on his feet, Pozzo suggests,

> he should pull on the rope as hard as he likes as long as he does not strangle him. He usually responds to that. If not he should give him a taste of his boot, in the face and the guts as far as possible.

Minutes later Pozzo cries out in lyrical despair:

> Have you not done tormenting me with your accursed time? . . . They give birth astride a grave, the light gleams an instant, then it's night once more.[17]

Can this be the same man? Through what precise experience has the blind Pozzo become something of a visionary? This is not a question we can answer: Beckett provides nothing in the way of conventional characterisation. We note, however, that the passage is taken up minutes later by Vladimir in what is the final lyrical summation of the play. Soon Godot's messenger will come with his disappointing message: there is little more to happen, or to say. The text, in other words, is held together not so much by the causal pressure of events as by its rhythms. And of course describing plays like *Godot* in musical terms is yet another way of coming to grips with its elusiveness as a story.

The notion is not new: Arthur Symons had even thought that

a play of Shakespeare's, seen on stage, should give one the impression of assisting at 'a solemn music'.[18]

But, like it or not, *Waiting for Godot* is still a story: as with Strindberg's *To Damascus*, an essential linearity asserts itself. We know that the events in Act II follow those in Act I; and when the characters ponder about how much time has passed in between, it is precisely against this knowledge of ours that we measure their uncertainties. We recognise that this is a closed world because we live in an open one, and what for Vladimir and Estragon is a simple condition of existence is something we sense as an intimation of alienation from the world. We, for our part, know the world we live in to be concrete, tangible and more or less calculable. Vladimir's description of the world as 'this immense confusion'[19] has to be set both against the utter lucidity of the play, the clarity of its construction, and against the fact that we, the spectators, are not confused. Vladimir may not understand the world, but we understand what he says about it.

We can only accept *Waiting for Godot* as a static situation rather than an event if we identify ourselves with its characters and their situation to the point of taking their world on their own terms. This is, in fact, not unlike treating the play as a 'myth' in the corrupted sense of the word: that is, an archetypal situation rather than a narrative. A mythology of myth has been created in criticism, and its effect is to make us submissive. Regard a play as embodying a mythical event, and your attitude to it will be awed and unquestioning, the only alternative being total rejection. 'Myths,' Frank Kermode has written, 'call for absolute, fictions for conditional assent.'[20] This defines the aesthetic of submission.

At the beginning of this book I defined *Waiting for Godot*, in J.P. Stern's words, as a perlocutionary act: the alarming suggestion was thrown out that to watch this play might in some respects be like listening to a speech by Hitler. I hope the reader has by now realised that both more and less is at stake. Hitler's speeches, as Professor Stern points out, had no real informational content: as at all totalitarian political meetings, the audience was assumed to know what was going to be said to the point of having a sense of identity with the speaker. Also, those present would have argued back, literally, at their peril. This is where the similarity between the Nazi rally and the play ends, and not simply because the latter is not actually dangerous. For plays do tell us something. It is in the events of a play, and in what happens to its characters, that its 'informational content' lies: that is what we find out.

We go to plays in the expectation of something new. It is true that if we go to a play by a writer we know we have some idea of what to expect: indeed, that is sometimes why we go. But then, if the play seems to us a new departure we are not, for that reason, shocked. Again, when we go to a play we already know, we know that we will see different actors and a different interpretation. Quite often we think we know perfectly well how a play should be done and we go, resigned to yet another production which will not do justice to our ideas. One way or another, whatever the degree of familiarity, something unknown, and to be revealed, is the essence of the dramatic experience. The theatre is a place of revelation; a scene of action. All of this is wholly alien to the perlocutionary act, for the perlocutionary act holds no revelations for us and gives no scope to our critical faculties. When Alan Schneider, one of Beckett's best-know directors, writes about *Happy Days*:

> I accept Winnie's dominating presence in the mound, the literal absence of legs in the first act and of anything below the neck in the second act as I accept Picasso's lady with several faces or Dali's bent watch,[21]

he is describing a partial suspension of his critical faculty: he submits to closed art.

The question about closed drama will always be: how closed is it? Therefore the remainder of this book is not intended to categorise plays dogmatically into open or closed. Schopenhauer, we recollect, said that a consistent solipsist could only be found in a lunatic asylum, and we shall see that if there is such a thing as a truly closed play, it is little more than a collection of apparently demented voices. We are looking, therefore, not so much for a certain type of play, as for things that certain plays have in common. We shall cut across accepted categories of drama, and sometimes compare playwrights who are not usually mentioned in the same breath. It is an open-ended search.

SYMBOLS AND OBJECTS

The best place to begin is Ibsen's *The Wild Duck*. It was written in 1883−84, a decade or so before Villiers de l'Isle Adam's *Axël* and Jarry's *Ubu Roi*; two plays which are variously held to signal the arrival of modern twentieth-century drama. In Act Two of Ibsen's play, when Gregers Werle comes to Hjalmar Ekdal's studio, old Lieutenant Ekdal shows him the loft. At the story of the wild duck Gregers pricks up his ears. What strikes him is what he sees as the secret of the bird's survival:

she's forgotten what it's like to live the life she was born for; that's the whole trick.

Soon he is telling the family that he would really like to be

a tremendously clever dog. The sort that dives down after wild ducks when they have plunged to the bottom and gripped themselves fast in the seaweed and the mud.

Gregers is in a moral frenzy: he clearly sees himself as a liberator. But his audience does not get his drift; and when he leaves, Hedvig is puzzled enough to say:

I think when he said that he meant something else ... I felt as though he meant something different from what he was saying all the time.[22]

What strikes Hedvig as sinister might seem to us familiar: Gregers has been talking symbolism without knowing it. We are entering treacherous territory here. We must distinguish between symbols and Symbolism in drama. The former is as old as drama itself, and recalls Arthur Symons's warning that

without symbolism there can be no literature: indeed not even language. What are words themselves but symbols, almost as arbitrary as the letters which compose them ...?[23]

Taken in this general sense, the symbol is closely related to the image. A good deal of modern Shakespeare criticism, for example, which we know as the study of imagery, would have been recognised by Symons as a study of Symbolism. The function of imagery in drama is to be our guide, through the plot, towards the meaning. It is the moral and imaginative means whereby we mediate between the story the play tells us and what the play is *about*. Take Ibsen's

Ghosts: a play which is about liberty, heredity, and the nature of inherited moral standards. These ideas are not explicitly formulated in the play: they are implied by what happens and what is said in it. When *Ghosts* was written most people thought it was about syphilis. But if we take the play, as I think we should, as being about liberty, heredity and morality, then syphilis, and parenthood, acquire a significance that could be called symbolic.

Or take Shakespeare's *Macbeth*. Duncan and the court arrive outside Inverness castle, and Banquo remarks:

> This guest of summer,
> The temple-haunting martlet does approve,
> By his loved masonry, that the heaven's breath
> Smells wooingly here: no jutty, frieze,
> Buttress, nor coign of vantage, but this bird
> Hath made his pendent bed and procreant cradle:
> Where they most breed and haunt, I have observ'd
> The air is delicate.[24]

Banquo means nothing by these words except politely to echo Duncan's cheerful words about Macbeth's castle. But in the context of the play these lines hold, unknown to Banquo, a grim irony: the 'temple-haunting martlet' suggests that the castle is a sanctuary for innocent natural life. The short passage is full of 'images of love and procreation',[25] and is in monstrous contrast to the hatred and murder which is to follow. Imagery like this is symbolic in that it serves as illustration to the content of the play; it elucidates the events of the plot by manipulating our imagination. Things are said which we feel to be deeply important without their being openly stated.

Ibsen in *The Wild Duck*, goes further. The irony of the bird in its loft as a symbol is that Gregers gets it hopelessly wrong: neither Hjalmar nor Hedvig can really be equated with a wounded creature who has 'forgotten what it's like to live the life she was born for', and Gregers's idea of rescuing them is the central tragic error of the play. For *The Wild Duck* is partly about responsibilities: whom are we responsible for, and to what extent? What right does a man have to take on responsibilities for others when it is not demanded of him? The play is also about realities. For the loft and the birds may be a poor substitute for the forests of Hoydal, where the Lieutenant used to hunt; but to him they are real, and help to keep him alive.

We can talk about both symbolism and Symbolism in *The Wild*

Duck. In the first sense, Ibsen used his symbols, his imagery, to help us see into the play and into its complex moral and personal relationships. Even more than in *Macbeth* or *Ghosts*, imagery here is something through which we can question the play: it is an essential part of the way we experience it. To put it quite simply, the play would lose something essential if there were no loft and no wild duck: far more than *Ghosts* would if there were no books on Mrs Alving's table. The books are an important illustration of a theme; the loft and the bird contain part of the life of the play. Here, too, lies their power as Symbolism. For, in this second sense, Ibsen's imagery points beyond the play and makes it one of the earliest Symbolist dramas. It is no accident that *The Wild Duck* was the first of Ibsen's plays which contemporary critics and audiences greeted with incomprehension: they complained that they could not see what it was *about*. They thought, in other words, that Ibsen was doing something other than telling a story. In fact, in addition to telling a story, he was also making a statement about life. The symbolism of the wild duck and the loft, of Hedvig, Hjalmar and the Werles, is also Symbolism in action. It is saying to us that in life we are both victims and not victims; that what is real is relative, just as clear-sightedness (Gregers's, Hjalmar's, Gina's) and blindness (Hedvig's, Old Werle's) are relative matters. Such formulations are elusive because it is the essence of Symbolism to intimate things that are difficult to express. It follows that what cannot be expressed cannot be questioned. Symbolism is the first step towards closed drama.

And with closed drama itself we enter a still more elusive world. Images and symbols take on a character which is less substantial, less functional, more arbitrary. Yeats told the actress Florence Farr how he

> once cared only for images about whose necks I could cast various 'chains of office' as it were. They were so many aldermen of the ideal, whom I wished to master the city of the soul.[26]

These words, written in 1906, speak of a growing impatience with functional, accessible imagery and foreshadow the more esoteric Symbolism of Yeats's later plays. More than twenty years later we find him writing that he particularly recommends *The Cat and the Moon* for 'no audience could discover its dark, mystical secrets.'[27]

These words would have got a wholehearted response from the

young Maeterlinck, whose early Symbolist plays Yeats always admired. In *The Intruder* (first performed in 1891) the already gloomy atmosphere turns more fearful with the following exchange:

THE GRANDFATHER: I cannot hear the nightingales any longer, Ursula.

THE DAUGHTER: I think someone has come into the garden, Grandfather.

THE GRANDFATHER: Who is it?

THE DAUGHTER: I don't know; I can see no one.

THE UNCLE: Because there is no one there.

THE DAUGHTER: There must be someone in the garden; the nightingales have suddenly ceased singing.

THE GRANDFATHER: But I do not hear anyone coming.

THE DAUGHTER: Someone must be passing by the pond, because the swans are scared.

ANOTHER DAUGHTER: All the fish in the pond are rising suddenly.

THE FATHER: You cannot see anyone?

THE DAUGHTER: No one, father.

THE FATHER: But the pond lies in the moonlight.

THE DAUGHTER: Yes; I can see that the swans are scared.[28]

The pedantic spectator might object that, even if you can see the frightened swans, it must be impossible, looking out of the windows at night, to see fish rising in the pond, even in moonlight. But to say this would be as obtuse as to ask where Vladimir had got his carrot, or where Kundry spends her time between her transformations in *Parsifal*. That would be to speak the language of rational questioning, whereas Maeterlinck's characters speak the language of a mood. It is quite beside the point whether anyone can see the fish: the image is meant to convey a sense of animal terror outside, in order to express the growing human terror within. The fish become symbols of fear, like the silent nightingales or the swans that cross over to the other side of the pond. But this symbol is entirely at the service of the unspoken. Antonin Artaud noted that Maeterlinck had

a certain way of unifying — by virtue of whatever mysterious analogies — a feeling and an object, putting them on the same mental plane without recourse to metaphor.[29]

It is not surprising to see Artaud responding so strongly to Maeterlinck; but as often happens with him, he does not put his case very clearly. There is nothing 'mental' about the union of feeling and object in the passage from *The Intruder*: it takes place on an emotional plane. The object (the rising fish) is not linked to the feeling (our sense of terror) by the mental links of logic but by the emotional link of mood. Unlike Shakespeare's martlet or Ibsen's wild duck, Maeterlinck's fish are not an organic part of the dramatic event but a lyrical decoration on it. Indeed, the whole purpose of the play lies more in these lyrical decorations than in the events which prompt them: their intimations of terror define the play more precisely than its actual 'plot'. Thus we might say of Symbolist plays that the things in them which tell us what the plays are *about* are more important than the stories they tell. The picture takes over from the story, the mood from the content.

Strindberg goes even further. His closing stage directions to *A Dream Play* describe a vision of a

> burning castle, showing a wall of human faces, enquiring, grieving, despairing. As the castle burns, the bud on the roof bursts open into a gigantic chrysanthemum.[30]

The primitive eloquence of that final image conveys an ardent optimism, both spiritual and sensual, which the play itself had denied every step of the way. This is Symbolism burgeoning with a life of its own, denying the ground it grows from. It is a lie of the imagination, like Wagner's love music at the end of *The Ring*.

Beckett, too, is sometimes spoken of as a Symbolist playwright, but it is hard to see why. Vladimir's carrot, for example, symbolises nothing — if to symbolise means to point beyond both the play and the symbol to something unspoken. The apprehension we need here is not imaginative but factual: the carrot does not, for example, symbolise natural resources. It is a simple prop of life, like hats and boots. It does not 'stand for' food: it *is* food. In *Endgame* the blind Hamm demands his dog: it turns out to be a black toy dog with only three legs and no sex organ (Clov has not quite finished making it). Still, Hamm is particular about the dog's function.

HAMM: (*his hand on the dog's head*) Is he gazing at me?
CLOV: Yes.
HAMM: (*proudly*) As if he were asking me to take him for a walk?
CLOV: If you like.

HAMM: (*as before*) Or as if he were begging me for a bone. (*He withdraws his hand.*) Leave him like that, standing there imploring me.
Clov straightens up. The dog falls on its side.

Later, Hamm intones:

HAMM: Our revels now are ended. (*He gropes for the dog.*) The dog's gone.
CLOV: He's not a real dog, he can't go.[31]

Again, the dog symbolises nothing. It is an object which Hamm likes to imagine is a real animal, knowing perfectly well that it is not: it is part of his make-believe reality, a prop to sustain him on the way to extinction. It could only be called symbolic if we were to see it as signifying, for example, that we all need some such make-believe — which is like saying that everything means something. The clue to *Endgame* is Hamm's quotation from *The Tempest*: it tells us that he sees himself as a magician exercising power whereas he is an extinct volcano at the mercy of others. Prospero's renunciation is the act of a man who has asserted his values in the world, learnt a profound moral lesson and is conscious of mortality; Hamm's is an admission of defeat after an unspecified battle in which no man, and no idea, is victorious. Perhaps the entire action of *Endgame* is symbolical, which would make it an allegory: a series of events signifying another, different set of events. But this is clearly not the case: there is no other imaginary set of events into which this action could be translated.

No, *Endgame* is a statement, a summing up. Beckett is giving us a picture of human relationships: the sense of claustrophobia, the sense of mutual dependence, both real and pretended, which it is made up of. Its quality as a closed play lies in the incontrovertibility of its vision. As we said about *Waiting for Godot* at the beginning of this book, there is nothing in the play to enable us to engage with it in argument, the way we might engage with *The Tempest*. We cannot say: 'Yes, except that . . .' It is a question of being or not being able to perceive and to contrast different values within the same work, values which can be assessed in the light of their difference from each other, and of their relationship to the whole. Only think of Prospero's and Caliban's different attitudes to forgiveness, or to language: how much more such things tell us about them, and about the play, than Hamm's and Clov's attitudes to the stuffed dog.

Images and symbols, too, have different lives in different plays. Prospero's book and staff mean power to him, and the possibility of revenge; they mean liberation to Ariel, protection to Miranda, slavery to Caliban. Antonio and his friends, in turn, may be defined by the fact that they do not know that the book and the staff have any power at all. Hamm's dog, like Vladimir's carrot, is a simple function: it does not have the vital, informative and imaginative value of the martlet in *Macbeth*, or of Ibsen's wild duck; or even the eerie mood which is meant to attach to the preposterous fish in *The Intruder*. I use these rather simple examples because the life of a play is often defined by the simplest and most humble things in it. Indeed, in open drama objects have a vital part to play even when, as in Greek drama, only few of them are needed. In closed drama the role of the object is different. The most important thing about the boots in *Godot* is that they do not fit. The tree is considered only as a potential gallows (the leaves that appear on it in Act Two do not symbolise anything: they merely signal the passage of time). The fault of a belt is that it is not strong enough to hang a man (and testing it means that your trousers fall down). When the moon rises, it is, again, simply an event of nature, notifying us of the passing of time: it has none of the sinister lyricism of the red moon which is so important to the impact of several Expressionist plays and of Brecht's *Drums in the Night*; nor the erotic lyricism it has in Wilde's *Salome*. In Beckett's *Happy Days* Winnie's possessions are displayed only to demonstrate their uselessness. The pedantic spectator of *Krapp's Last Tape* might have objected that if Krapp had really owned a tape recorder thirty years earlier (the play was written in 1958), he would have had to be a man of private means: he could not have afforded one out of what sound like very meagre royalties. (Beckett told his biographer, Deirdre Bair, that he had never, until he wrote the play, seen a tape recorder, and did not know how it worked.[32]) And, while in Beckett's two *Acts Without Words* life is a battle with objects, they are not so much real objects fulfilling their normal functions, as things representing the hostility of the universe; and most of his late plays, from *Play* onward, have hardly any objects in them at all.

In Ionesco's plays objects are both useless and terrifying. In *The Lesson* the Professor demonstrates arithmetic with non-existent matches and, for the play's climax, has 'a big imaginary knife'. In *The Chairs* chairs are brought on only to show that no one comes to sit on them; and in *The New Tenant* furniture becomes the means of imprisoning a man until he is unable to move. The unquestion-able other-ness of these objects is what matters, not their function; how man feels among them is the play's concern, not what he does with them.

The attitude of many German Expressionist plays to life could be defined from the way objects are treated in them. Thus Georg Kaiser's play *The Coral* takes its title from a piece of coral the Billionaire's Secretary wears on his watch-chain to distinguish him from his employer, whose double he is. The whole thing is as improbable as the Billionaire's way of conducting his business and his sudden decision to kill the Secretary. The Billionaire comes from a poverty-stricken background and has spent his life escaping from it. His whole existence has been, he says, 'restless energy – restless flight'[33]. The Secretary had a secure and happy upbringing; and the implication is that the Billionaire, by killing him, hopes somehow to take over his past. But the killing also turns out to be his way of handing over his empire to his only son who is rebelling against his father's dictatorial attitudes. The conflict is cerebral, impassioned and improbable: Kaiser's characters have virtually no individuality, and the coral on the watch-chain as a way of distinguishing master from servant sums this up perfectly. In Act One, the Billionaire is visited by the Gentleman in Grey: a personage of whom we know nothing except that he wants the Billionaire to sign a manifesto declaring that he regards 'the enrichment of the individual as the most infamous scandal'. The Gentleman in Grey is

> of powerful build, in a loose-fitting, light-grey suit, whose pockets are stuffed with newspapers and pamphlets. Round red head, cropped hair. Sandals.

The newspapers and pamphlets turn out to be socialist literature, which the visitor brought with him only to describe them as worthless: 'Wasted effort. Pointless excursions down blind alleys'[34]. But the Billionaire's sheer energy, anxiety converted into action, confuses him and he leaves. He returns in Act Five to visit the Billionaire in jail where he is awaiting execution, having been convicted in the belief that he is the Secretary who killed the Billionaire. The Gentleman in Grey

> has obviously undergone a transformation: his suit – in colour as before – is of impeccable cut; light spats over patent leather boots, grey top hat, white kid gloves with *black chenille trim-mings* (my italics).[35]

Note the precision and the utter improbability of the whole thing. Kaiser is describing a total spiritual transformation which is as abrupt and beyond argument as the difference in the man's appearance is total: an idea has been dressed up in two different sets of clothes to make the dramatist's point more effectively and to save him time actually presenting the conversion as a psychological event. We are reminded of Strindberg's late plays where he shows us a series of emotional tableaux, preferring to display his characters in defeat or victory rather than in battle.

Finally, talking about Mrs Alving's books, we may note that people do not read books in closed plays. This may sound an eccentric observation, but it has a wider significance. For it is remarkable how often, from the Renaissance onwards, as the habit of reading gradually spread, people in plays were shown reading, possessing, or at least knowing about, books. Books are important to Hamlet, and nearly fatal to Prospero; Vanbrugh's *The Relapse* opens with Loveless reading what appears to be a book of philosophy; the books which Lydia Languish reads in Sheridan's *The Rivals* quite strain her gift for duplicity; John Tanner in Shaw's *Man and Superman* has just written a book; in Ibsen's *The Pillars of the Community* Roerlund, the schoolmaster, is discovered reading a book promisingly called *Woman as the Servant of Society*; the plot of *Hedda Gabler* partly hinges on the books Lovborg has written and the one Tesman may never write; and Allmers in *Little Eyolf* has been writing one, aptly called *The Responsibility of Man*. Miss Prism, in *The Importance of Being Earnest*, has written a vast novel, and has strong views on the nature of fiction, and Cecily Cardew is discovered with a German grammar and a volume of, of all things, Schiller.

Closed plays are different. Maeterlinck's characters might as well be illiterate. There is no room for books in the lives and minds of people in Strindberg's late plays, except for the one the Stranger has just written in *To Damascus*: and we may note how improbable it is that the Lady's mother, a simple woman living an isolated life in the Austrian mountains, should have read it already. Almost no one reads books in German Expressionist plays, though in Kaiser's *The Flight to Venice*, a play about George Sand and Musset, literature makes an inevitable appearance, if only to lead to the Nietzschean conclusion that 'Words are the death of life.'[36] Beckett's Krapp, himself a writer (though it is not clear what he writes), seems to possess only a huge dictionary, though he does hint that he may have read Theodor Fontane's *Effi Briest* (the title of which Beckett misspells). Vladimir appears to have read the New Testament, and the four men in *Godot* are the first of several Beckett characters with a wide range of literary quotations and recondite vocabulary at their disposal, neither of which can be explained from what we know of them *as characters*.

The point about books is that reading them is an act of culture: it opens up another world to people. Those who read them or talk about them, those who have or talk about pictures, are in touch with a whole system of relations which are an analysable world unto themselves, outside the world of the play we are seeing. Closed drama excludes such worlds. (Note that Hamm's room in *Endgame* contains a picture, but that it hangs face to the wall.) Such things are props for the life of the mind; and while closed drama may tell us something about mental life, it has little to say about what goes on in the minds of its characters. Hence it is almost as if they were deprived of imagination: their existence is exhausted in simply existing. No wonder we find it hard to imagine them doing other things, being in other places. Characters in closed plays have no interest in politics either — with a few significant exceptions which we shall discuss. Closed plays have little or no interest in the multifarious relations that exist between us and those other worlds which open up in art or in public affairs. They close in on the essentials; the people in them, even when they are in company, are alone.

STAGES AND DIRECTIONS

The rise of closed drama coincides with a watershed in the history of the stage. Ever since Aeschylus began to enlarge the cast of Greek tragedy, the history of Western theatre has been one of striving for what, for the sake of simplicity, we have to describe as realism. The progress was never straight or steady (we have only to think of the artificiality of Dryden's tragedies, compared with Shakespeare's); but the development of the theatre has been, in general, towards a more and more realistic representation of life. The process reached its climax with the domestic dramas of Ibsen and the rise of Naturalism at the end of the nineteenth century; and it was at the very same time, too, that the reaction set in. Arthur Symons was looking forward to

> a new art of the stage, an art no longer realistic, but convention-
> al; no longer imitative but symbolical.[37]

Note that for Symons the symbolical represents an advance on the imitative: that which cannot be known but only hinted at takes precedence over what can be grasped and compared. Note, too, his preference for what he calls conventional, as opposed to the realistic: the general, the representative, the unspecific, is gaining in author-ity over the 'merely' imitative. In the same essay, writing about *Ghosts*, Symons singles out Ibsen's stage directions for the second and third acts, noting only their descriptions of what is visible outside, with 'the room as before'. (The stage directions for Act One, with their precise description of the room and its furnishings, do not seem to excite him.) Symons then adds: 'What might not Mr Craig do with that room!'[38]

As Edward Gordon Craig never directed *Ghosts* we shall never know; but we have some idea how he approached *Rosmersholm*, from the programme note he composed to his production of it. It opened in the Teatro della Pergola in Florence, on December 5, 1906, with Duse as Rebecca West. Craig's programme note is worth quoting from at length.

> Ibsen's marked detestation for Realism is nowhere more appa-
> rent than in the two plays *Rosmersholm* and *Ghosts*. The words
> are the words of actuality, but the drift of the words something
> beyond this. There is a powerful impression of unseen forces
> closing in upon the place: we hear continually the long drawn
> out note of the horn of death ... Realism is only Exposure,
> whereas art is Revelation: and therefore in the mounting of this
> play I have tried to avoid all realism. We are not in a house of
> the nineteenth or twentieth century built by Architect this or
> Master Builder that, and filled with furniture of Scandinavian
> design. That is not the state of mind Ibsen demands we shall be
> in. Let us leave period and accuracy of detail to the museums
> and the curiosity shops. Let our common sense be left in the
> cloak room with our umbrellas and hats. We need here our
> finer senses only, the living part of us. We are in Rosmersholm,
> a house of shadows. Then consider the unimportance of custom
> and clothes — remember only the colour which flows through
> the veins of life — red or grey as the sun or the moon will it,

dark or fair as we will . . . cease to be curious — throw away all
concern, enter into the observance of this as though you were at
some ancient religious ceremony, and then perhaps you will be
aware of the value of the spirit which moves before you as
Rebecca West . . . we must, for this new poet, re-form a new
Theatre . . . the reasons are manifold and the will to remould is
irresistible. It is therefore possible now to announce that the
birth of the new Theatre, and its new Art, has begun.[39]

There is a touching arrogance about the way Craig calls Ibsen a 'new
poet': the seventy-eight-year-old dramatist had actually died six
months earlier. It is as if Craig had just discovered him, in blissful
unawareness of his reputation as a realist. Of course Ibsen's contemporaries had frequently called him a symbolist and not always, as we
have seen, without reason. But it is something entirely different to
present *Rosmersholm* as an 'ancient religious ceremony'. When
Craig writes about 'the value of the spirit that moves before you as
Rebecca West', his own spirit is that of idolatry: he is submitting to
his own reading of *Rosmersholm* as if it were a closed play. One
might never guess that Rebecca was also a murderess, and that Ibsen
is unfolding, for our questioning, her complex web of guilts and
virtues. As for the 'unimportance of custom and clothes', we have
only to remember Ibsen's meticulous description of Ulrik Brendel's
appearance; or ponder why Brendel should have thought, from Dr
Kroll's appearance, that the headmaster was a 'brother of the cloth'
— points which Ibsen took the trouble to explain meticulously to one
of the play's first directors[40].

The reason both for Craig's almost complete failure in his own
working life and for his enormous subsequent influence is that he
was an apostle of closed art at a time when closed drama was not yet
fully born. With hindsight one wonders why he never directed any
of Strindberg's late plays (he was only forty at the time of Strindberg's death); why he directed Ibsen's *The Vikings at Helgeland*,
The Pretenders and *Rosmersholm*, but not *Brand* or *Peer Gynt*;
Shakespeare's *Hamlet* and *Much Ado*, but not the late romances. It is
almost as if Craig had only been attracted to plays in which he could
display his unique talent by violating their text or their spirit. When
he directed *Hamlet* for Stanislavsky's Moscow Art Theatre he
explained to the actors that he wanted them

> to understand that the performing of Shakespeare does not
> demand great variation of pose or movement. Shakespeare's

ideas are in the words. To translate them into movement, into acting, is only possible on one condition, that there should be as *little as possible of this acting and movement* (my italics).[41]

Craig could hardly have chosen a more unsuitable place to promote such ideas. The essence of the Stanislavkian method of acting is the closest causal link between the text and the actor's behaviour on stage. Whatever its excesses then or later, the famous method strove for social, emotional, historical and psychological accuracy. Stanislavsky's famous book, *An Actor Prepares*, is a manual of open drama. When the Director tells his class that

all action in the theatre must have an inner justification, be logical, coherent and real,[42]

he treats acting as Leonardo treated painting, and assumes that the spectators will look with the same critical eye at the performance as at a picture. Quoting from Coquelin, Stanislavsky compares acting to portrait painting:

The public will say either 'That is Tartuffe', or, 'The actor has not done a good job.'[43]

The logic of representation lies at the heart of this approach, as it did at Leonardo's. At one point Stanislavsky criticises some of the Art Theatre's productions: by trying to convey spiritual content and not yet quite knowing how to do it, they burdened their plays, he thought, with too much production.

We exaggerated the outward and external side of manners ... lifeless objects, properties and sounds began to bulge out of the general scheme ... There was no spiritual darkness ... Ethnography choked literature and the art of the actor.[44]

Reading this, we could also sum up Stanislavsky's approach to the theatre by saying that he asked of a performance what Alberti had asked of paintings: a narrative impact, a sense of composition and economy, clarity of content, and moral significance. He might have paraphrased Alberti and said that the greatest work of the actor is the *istoria*. (Alberti himself had used the living theatre as his idea of *istoria* in practice.)

Stanislavskian theatre, in other words, is a theatre of relations: between actor and text, text and presentation, text and acting, performance and audience. The entire history of Western theatre is a history of understanding, projecting and exploiting these relations. This compositeness of the theatre is part of its open-ness: it is by nature an art form which we question, by considering its component parts in relation to each other. When we say that Craig was an apostle of closed art, we mean that he was impatient with these relations: he wanted to reduce the theatre to a less complex, more uniform art. One of his problems was the multiplicity of people in plays. He told his actors in Moscow how he was afraid that

> in following out the idea of seeing everything through the eyes of Hamlet we may be pedantically consistent in the execution of this idea. But on the other hand to make the characters realistic is also dangerous. They can at once lose all their symbolism, and then the play may lose very much . . .[45]

Craig seems to have felt uneasy with several characters at once: Hamlet being his mouthpiece, he had little time for the others except to reduce them to the status of symbols. Closed art requires an inspiration which is intense but limited. We have seen this in Wagner, in Kafka, and in the Cubist painters: their worlds are mostly sparsely populated. Similarly, Michael Meyer notes that 'Strindberg was often curiously weak in his subplots, as with his subordinate characters.'[46] This is not because Strindberg could not write, but because he was dramatising a concentrated vision. This is the shape of closed drama to come.

Craig's passion for marionettes is a result of a dislike of the human body and the human personality at work. He told Adolphe Appia that the human body in movement seemed to signify less and less to him. Writing in his magazine *The Mask*, under one of his many pseudonyms, Craig says of the marionette that

> if left to himself, he will do nothing wrong . . . doing nothing . . . And it is this doing nothing, this saying nothing, this meaning nothing which raises him to an altitude that is limitless.[47]

Arthur Symons wrote, less lyrically but more to the point, in his *Apology for Puppets*, that

> The living actor . . . has always what he is proud to call his temperament . . . The marionette may be *relied upon* (my italics).[48]

The point is that the marionette, sculptural, expressionless and completely manipulable, eliminates one of the essential relations inherent in the theatrical experience: the relation between the actor and his role. Through the actor and his performance we can question the play; the marionette, being the tool of a vision, is beyond such questioning. Thus Craig could write, in another article in *The Mask* called 'Gentlemen, the Marionette!'

> What the wires of the über-marionette should be, what shall guide him, who can say? I do not believe in the mechanical ... nor in the material ... The wires which stretch from Divinity to the soul of the Poet are wires which might command him; ... has God no more such threads to spare ... for one more figure? I cannot doubt it. I will never believe anything else.[49]

This lyrical passage (the punctuation is all Craig's own) is no part of the practical literature of the theatre: it is a hymn to a creed. Reading it, we can understand better why Craig should think of a performance of *Rosmersholm* as a religious ritual. The theatrical event, for Craig, aspired to the condition of a divine event. His interest in the mask, too, should be seen in this context: he saw it as part of something otherworldly in the theatre. 'It is this sense of being beyond reality,' he wrote in 'A Note on Masks',

> which permeates all great art. We see it in the little clumsily painted pictures of those periods when the true *beyond* was of more importance than the right perspective.[50]

Note the brisk dismissal of perspective in favour of the unattainable *beyond*. Craig's attitude to both play and audience was conditioned by this aesthetic otherworldliness. Denis Bablet remarks shrewdly that what really interested Craig in his famous screens 'was not so much the construction of moveable architecture as the idea of movement in the abstract.'[51] Craig's preoccupations in stage design were thus not unlike those of Malevich and Lissitsky in painting.

Craig also explained to Stanislavsky and his actors that in Hamlet's speech, 'Seems, madam? Nay, it is. I know not "seem"'', only the first two and the last two lines were important. 'These four lines,' he said,

> express an important thought and must be spoken accordingly. All the rest of the monologue [*sic*] must be pronounced more as music, so that the thought becomes so much lost in the sounds that the audience simply *does not follow* the thought except in the above-mentioned four lines.[52]

This is far from the essential openness of the theatrical experience: dramatic speech is reduced to sound which need not be followed as thought, only as music. The stage-director as musician.

Deep down, Craig wanted a theatre created and run by one man. The first volume of *The Mask* was dedicated

> to the single courageous individuality in the world of the theatre who will some day master and remould it.

One of his contributors, the French critic Edouard Schuré, who had also written in the *Revue Wagnérienne*, advocated a

> Theatre of the élite which for the sake of its essential medium one might call the Theatre of the Dream, and which I call the Theatre of the Soul on account of its inspiring element.[53]

To have a soul and dreams is, clearly, a privilege of the elect. There is an unmistakeably Nietzschean ring to all this, and indeed in a good deal of Craig's own writing, which is wholly appropriate to the creator of the Über-marionette. (Just as Nietzsche never made clear what the Superman would actually do, Craig never gives us a clear picture of how a theatre of marionettes would function.) Craig's prospectus for his school in Florence bore an epitaph from Nietzsche about discipline; and it seems in retrospect inevitable that Craig should have spent most of his active life running this school, free from the complex practical demands of the working theatre and undisturbed by audiences. He is perhaps the first practitioner in the theatre of what Nietzsche called 'monological art', or art without witnesses[54].

W.B. Yeats, who was an admirer of Craig's (he actually used Craig's famous moveable screens in the Abbey Theatre), was a kindred spirit. Part of Yeats's complexity as an artist was the coexistence in him of the hard-headed practical man of the theatre with the preening aesthete who could have stepped out of Gilbert and Sullivan's *Patience*. Here he is, writing to John Quinn about his play *At the Hawk's Well*:

> I hope to create a form of drama which may delight the best minds of my time and all the more because it can pay its expenses without the others. If when the play is perfectly performed (musicians are the devil) Balfour and Sargent and Ricketts and Sturge Moore and John and the Prime Minister and a few pretty ladies will come and see it, I shall have a success that would have pleased Sophocles.[55]

The snobbery and the effrontery of these words are astounding: it is hard to reconcile such fatuousness with Yeats's shrewdness as a manager and his intelligence as a critic. But the fact is that, like Nietzsche, Yeats was, by temperament, an aristocratic radical, and he had a clear idea of the kind of art he wanted to create for people like himself. He wrote that the discovery of the Japanese Nōh plays helped him to invent

> a form of drama, distinguished, indirect, symbolic, and having no need of mob or press to pay its way — an aristocratic form.[56]

Yeats's idea of the aristocratic was tinged with romance; what he really meant by the word was *exclusive*.

Strindberg, another aristocratic radical, had already sounded the theme. In a letter written in November 1888, shortly after the completion of *Miss Julie*, Strindberg declares:

> We don't want big spectaculars. We shall only play for the élite and don't need the bourgeoisie — who will in any case follow suit in ten years![57]

and in another letter, dated the following day:

> High prices and small houses — so that only the élite can come — we shall sell only the stalls and the dress circle — the upper galleries will be blocked off, so that we shan't get any mocking rabble.[58]

This may sound odd coming from a man who called himself 'a socialist, a nihilist, a republican, everything that is anti-reactionary'[59]; who saw the anti-feminist element in his early plays as a subject for public controversy; and who, when his supporters struck a medal for him during his blasphemy trial, wished to have the following legend engraved on it: 'You were born to provoke; you were born to strike. I am called the liberator who came too early. I am called Satan, my name is Johan August Strindberg. The truth is always audacious.'[60] (There was room only for the last five words.)

But all this is part of the same inner contradictions which made this hugely prolific author write to Bjoernson:

> My distaste for art as a falsification has taken on a quasi-religious character ... This is the dilemma. To be useful I must be read. To be read I must write 'art', but I regard art as immoral ...[61]

And again, to his publisher, Bonnier:

> Simply being an artist nauseates me. My intelligence has developed from fantasising to thinking. The conjuring of voluntary hallucinations at one's desk is like self-defilement.[62]

This is more than the routine exasperation of the writer fretting at his solitary trade: it is a case of artistic schizophrenia; of life denying itself; the showman and the monological artist locked in unending battle. All these things will be echoed later by the self-tormenting compulsion of Beckett's Unnameable to go on with his words; and echoed, too, in Beckett's plays, where Strindberg's moral-artistic dilemma is dramatised as the very stuff of life: the need to speak, to tell stories, either in order to pass the time or to offer proofs to oneself that one exists. The dialogue of Beckett's plays consists, not so much in interlocking speeches, as in the outpourings of parallel griefs: his characters are monological people.

Another important figure whose ideas imprinted themselves on the way we think about the theatre was the Swiss architect and designer Adolphe Appia (1862–1928). As with Craig, his actual output was negligible compared with his influence. The total of his productions could be counted in single figures, and he was fifty-one by the time he staged his first full-length work, Gluck's *Orpheus et Eurydice;* yet such was his reputation by then that the audience included Claudel, Diaghilev, Georges Pitoëff, Harley Granville Barker and Bernard Shaw. Like Craig, Appia steadfastly refused numerous offers from theatres and opera houses: he is said to have disliked the technical aspects of production and had a reputation for having no patience over details. His view of the theatrical event was lofty. 'When we buy a ticket,' he lamented,

> ... our unfortunate relationship to the presentation is manifest. To queue at a box office is humiliating ...[63]

Appia was a visionary, whose principal artistic influence was Wagner; and his writings show a profound kinship of mind with Nietzsche and, most especially, with Schopenhauer. 'Music,' he wrote,

> is the direct expression of our inner being; that is, its hidden life.[64]

For Appia, a stage performance was a vision. 'Ancient drama,' he declared, 'was an *act*, not a spectacle.'[65] This meant both a grand spiritual event and an occasion where performers and spectators shared the same essential experience. Or, to quote Denis Bablet, Appia wanted to regain 'the ludic power' of the theatre.

Yet he also had a strongly practical attitude to stagecraft: he was, for example, one of the earliest men of the theatre to emphasise how wrong it was to put the three-dimensional figure of the actor in front of two-dimensional flats. He grasped a vital point about *Tristan and Isolde*, which is both its core and its chief weakness *as drama*, when he wrote that

> it eludes theatrical form and will forever elude it because the dramatic action is entirely within.[66]

In *Siegfried*, he commented, Mime's smithy must be small and oppressive because 'a dwarf, furthermore a very timid one, would not reside in a spacious cave', while

> Siegfried, with his handsome, tall posture does not feel at home in such surroundings and the audience must feel vividly this uneasiness.[67]

All these remarks are full of a sense of *istoria*: Appia is aware of theatrical presentation as a logical-pictorial exercise concerned with conveying psychological reality, and the relationships, both mental and perspectival, between people and their surroundings. And, reading his famous essay, *The Staging of Tristan and Isolde*, one is struck by the fact that virtually all his remarks concern what happens, physically, on the stage rather than what goes on, musically, psychologically, or spiritually, in the orchestra pit. Appia complained all his life that the 'realistic' presentation of Wagner's operas was diametrically opposed to their spirit:

> if everything in the auditorium in Bayreuth expresses his genius, on the other side of the footlights everything contradicts it.[68]

Writing about *Tristan and Isolde*, he complains that its setting is 'completely unrelated to the inner drama'. This, in Appia's view,

> destroys the equilibrium ... and delivers the drama to the chaos of sensations ... What method [he asks] can be drawn from *a drama indifferent to its performance*? — Unquestion-

ably, the utmost reduction of decorative elements ... In emphasising ... the indifference of the stage towards the dramatic
action, we compel the spectator to *take part* in this action. The
exclusively inner function of the poetic-musical expression
becomes for him a necessity: the equilibrium is re-established
through the production ... on the one hand we are observers,
on the other, we are blind supernumeraries (my italics).[69]

With these words Appia puts his finger on an essential aspect of
closed art: the artist's ambiguous attitude to performance and to his
public. We have noted this in connection with both Nietzsche and
Kafka; we saw how Picasso kept *Les Demoiselles d'Avignon* in his
studio for decades; we observed Yeats's passionate élitism; and it is
hard not to agree with Appia that, despite Wagner's own interest
and skill in theatrical production, there is something in the overwhelming psychological impact of *Tristan and Isolde* which makes
the business of performance seem almost irrelevant. And, as Appia
indicates, it is this same impact that makes us participants rather
than spectators: we are overpowered rather than confronted by the
experience; we are overwhelmed by it rather than made to question
it. This is the source of another of Appia's important ideas: the
breaking down of the barrier between stage and auditorium. For the
man who regarded ancient drama as an act rather than a spectacle, it
was natural to believe that

> Instead of providing us with an *Environment*, the work of art
> must create a setting for itself *within us*.[70]

From this it is but a short step to saying that an audience as such is
unnecessary. The art of drama, for Appia,

> does not exist to present the human being for *others*. The
> human being is independent of the passive spectator; he is, or
> ought to be, *living* ... Our first move ... will be to place
> ourselves imaginatively in boundless space, with no witness but
> ourselves ... Shall we be creators of space? For whom? We are
> alone. Consequently it will be for ourselves alone that we will
> create space ...[71]

'A work of living art,' Appia says,

> ... needs no audience, for it implicitly contains the audience
> within itself ... *Living* art is not a representation ... from the
> moment it exists we are with it, in it ... Even though our

collaboration *in* the work be small, we shall live with it; we shall discover that we are artists.[72]

Appia is torn between the need of the artist/performer to express himself regardless of whether he is heard or seen, and the need of his ideal spectator to be a part, impersonal and ecstatic, of the artistic event. His meditations are the clearest expression of the nature and dilemma of monological art. At the same time, it is entirely in keeping with Appia's pictorial way of thinking that all this reminds us of Schopenhauer and the way the philosopher reacted to art in general and pictures in particular: namely, as a special objectification of the all-pervading Will. For, in a central but ultimately elusive sense, we are at one with a work of art. Accordingly, we find, in *Music and the Art of the Theatre*, the following Schopenhauerian thought:

> The *mise-en-scène* . . . is therefore 'ideal', in the sense that its material reality is subject to aesthetic considerations superior to its intelligible form, and this ideality is all-powerful because it imposes itself on the audience by perfectly concrete means, directly, without the intervention of thought.[73]

When Appia wrote this, he was both a man of *istoria* and an apostle of closed art. The presentation has to be truthful to the subject, but it comes to the spectator with an immediacy to which thought is irrelevant. Appia had a vision of stage and auditorium united in

> the *Salle*, cathedral of the future . . . the perfect place for dramatic art to flourish — *with or without an audience*.[74]

This implies, not a non-existent audience, but people who submit to an artistic experience at the cost of renouncing their need to question, even to think. The critical faculties are suspended: we are not far from witnessing a perlocutionary act.

Appia might have found it difficult to recognise his ideas in the Soviet theatre of the 1920s; but the work of Vsevolod Meyerhold (1874—?1940) in this period is based on a similar principle of uniting stage and auditorium in a shared atmosphere imposed by the director. For Sergei Tretyakov's play *I Want a Child*, Meyerhold got El Lissitsky to design a set which incorporated both parts of the theatre in one huge oval space. The performance was to take place all around, as well as in front of, the spectators, the aim being to give them a constant sense of being part of the event. A few years earlier Guillaume Apollinaire had imagined something similar, though for a very different kind of theatre: in the Prologue to *The Breasts of Tiresias* (1917) he complains that

> ... they wouldn't have built us a new theatre
> A circular theatre with two stages
> One in the middle the other like a ring
> Around the spectators permitting
> The full unfolding of our modern art
> Often connecting in unseen ways as in life.

This, Apollinaire thinks, is what the dramatist needs, because

> His universe is his stage
> Within it he is the creating god
> Directing at his will
> Sounds gestures movements masses colours
> Not merely with the aim
> Of photographing the so-called slice of life
> But to bring forth life itself in all its truth.[75]

In all Meyerhold's work, the most famous example of involving the audience was probably his production of Emile Verhaeren's play *The Dawn*, which was put on in 1920 to mark the third anniversary of the Bolshevik Revolution. Admission to the derelict Sohn Theatre was free; there was no heating; there were political placards on the walls; and the house-lights were left on throughout the performance. The cast wore no make-up; they spoke motionlessly, facing the audience all the time, and 'their hoarse voices, which evoked irony in experienced theatre-goers' were deliberately made to sound like voices at a political rally[76]. Some of the actors descended to where the orchestra pit used to be, and acted as a chorus. At a certain moment during the performance a Herald appeared and read out a real bulletin on the Civil War which was at its height at the time. Less than two weeks after the opening the Red Army won an important victory at Perekop, and a telegram announcing this news was immediately incorporated in the performance. The effect on the audience, consisting mostly of workers and soldiers, is said to have been tremendous. An eyewitness wrote:

A greater merging of art with reality I have never seen in the theatre either before or since.[77]

But the most famous aspect of the production was that claques of actors were placed throughout the auditorium and given the task of leading the applause when the context of the play made it necessary. This drew venomous criticism from Nadezhda Krupskaya, Lenin's wife, who wrote in *Pravda*, three days after the opening, that

> to cast the Russian proletariat as a Shakespearean crowd which any self-opinionated fool can lead wherever the urge takes him is a sheer insult.[78]

To us, ironically, Meyerhold's device sounds sinister in a different way: for it was partly by packing party meetings in just the same way, with claques of activists, that Stalin and his supporters took power over the Party machine and the State.

With *The Dawn* we are in the presence of something new: the theatre of manipulation. At its core is the desire to eliminate theatrical illusion because it was held to cast a spell over the audience and prevent it from thinking. Brecht expressed this view most clearly when he suggested that

> To prevent the spectator from 'swooning away', to combat 'free' association, small choruses can be placed in the auditorium to show him the right attitude, to invite him to form his opinions, to summon his experience to his aid, to exercise control . . .[79]

It is hard to understand, from this unpleasant and dishonest passage, how on the one hand you combat free association in people's minds, and at the same time invite them to form their own opinion. But Brecht's intention is quite clear: he is proposing to use the theatre for purposes of direct persuasion.

Of course all theatre that makes us think does this to some degree; but the difference in methods is crucial. Open drama is a private experience on a public occasion. It does not ask for audience participation in the immediate physical sense: it asks for silent confrontation and critical engagement. Open drama assumes that its audience will attend to its contents in performance as well as think about it afterwards. It is true that the spectators will still be influenced by the fact that they are members of a crowd partaking of shared emotions. But an essential freedom is left them: the freedom of personal involvement, individual interpretation and private judgement. A crowd which is made to participate is, by definition, manipulated, and skilful manipulation in public can be difficult to resist. In any case, anyone who has ever been to an 'audience participation' performance will know that real participation is hardly ever possible. If you take up the actors' offer of a dialogue they will soon begin to evade you because the performance has to proceed on lines broadly agreed beforehand and because, in the end, they will want to go home. When an audience 'participates' it is on the director's and the performers' terms.

On a more aesthetic level, to eliminate theatrical illusion is to eliminate a specific type of questioning. This does not mean that we should defend the most pernickety type of stage realism where every object is real, and real dogs walk on real grass. Indeed, such realism is only another kind of disruption: the real dog reminds us of the 'unreality' of the whole event. Theatrical illusion has its own internal consistency, which can be created by the most obviously artificial means. Every successful opera production bears this out. Or take the matter of masks. In Greek classical drama their use had a practical origin: all the characters wore masks partly because the size of the theatres demanded that they should all be seen. But when Wedekind, in *Spring Awakening*, introduces the Man in the Mask in the final scene, he is drawing attention to the fact that he has brought on a character from another world. We react like Hedvig in *The Wild Duck:* we ask what the appearance of this man *really* means. In a skilful production the effect is eerie and haunting; in less accomplished hands the device simply shatters the consistency of the play, and makes us realise that the Man in the Mask is no more than Wedekind's mouthpiece offering, as it happens, a shallow and facile solution to all the agonies we have just witnessed.

In the modern theatre the mask is usually (though not always) obtrusive: it draws attention to itself as a device. When masks are worn only by some of the actors, the intention is usually to make a point about the 'reality' represented by one or the other part of the cast, and the result tends to be to underline the unreality of all of them. We become conscious of the fact that we are being told something. When Yeats wrote that 'in the end one would write plays for certain masks'[80], he was expressing a desire for a style of hieratic unreality, which was entirely in keeping with his lofty feelings about drama, but which the practising playwright in him managed never to quite put into effect. The mask is also a director's way of telling actors precisely what to do, indeed, what to feel. Jacques Copeau said that the actor receives from this papier-maché object the reality of his part. He is controlled by it and has to obey it unreservedly ... It is not only his face that has changed, it is all his personality, it is the very nature of his reactions, so that he experiences emotions he could neither have felt nor feigned without its aid ... a being without life till [the actor] adopts it, which comes from without to seize upon him and proceeds to substitute itself for him.[81]

Seen in this way, the mask virtually excludes the actor, and finally also the spectator, from questioning the role and the performance.

The point about the consistency of the theatrical illusion is that it establishes a set of internal relations which is the material for our questioning. Text, acting, scenery, costumes, lighting, though purposefully organised, indeed manipulated, by expert hands, form a whole which we engage with by measuring its parts against each other. The theatre of manipulation disrupts these relations and tends towards a spectacle. Meyerhold's production of *The Dawn* was clearly a political spectacle; and most comments on it at the time dealt with it in non-theatrical terms.

The fact is that spectacle is a perlocutionary act. It leaves no room for engagement. We do not question a production like Meyerhold's, any more than we would question a circus act, or a dance sequence by Busby Berkeley. The comparison is far from frivolous: intellectually, technically and aesthetically the three things are entirely different, but they share a desire to enthrall and impress, and the desire to concentrate the audience's mind in one specific and predetermined direction. We do not argue: we admire or we dislike. And of course the theatre of manipulation also resembles the political rally, which is clearly the kind of impact Meyerhold wanted his production to have. He would have been appalled to have it suggested that his work might have had something in common with the Nazi rallies; but the language of mass politics and of the theatre of manipulation have common roots. Goebbels recognised this when he made overtures to Erwin Piscator, a lifelong Communist, to come back from his Moscow exile and set up a Nazi propaganda theatre. The man he asked to mediate was Gordon Craig[82].

In one sense Symbolist drama, too, could be described as a theatre of manipulation. It is a spectacle for the mind in which symbols, images, or symbolic actions direct the audience's imagination towards the recognition and acceptance of a meaning. Ibsen in *Brand* and Yeats in *At the Hawk's Well* both used the hawk as a symbol. In *Brand* it is something sinister and threatening, whose destruction brings both liberation and death. In Yeats's play it is the embodiment of supernatural forces which both tempt you to action and thwart you:

> The Woman of the Sidhe herself,
> The mountain witch, the unappeasable shadow.
> She is always flitting upon this mountain-side,
> To allure or to destroy.[83]

Yeats once wrote that birds like the heron, the hawk, the eagle or the swan were 'the natural symbols of subjectivity'[84]; but that is not the way he used the hawk in this play, though perhaps a little more like the way Ibsen used it in his. In both plays the hawk is the symbol of something eloquent but arbitrary, and it imposes itself on the text and on the texture of the play almost like a spell — sometimes to the point, as in *At the Hawk's Well*, where the meaning of the play is seen to reside in the symbol rather than in the events of the play.

Arthur Symons wrote that Symbolism was

> a literature in which the visible world is no longer a reality and the unseen world is no longer a dream.[85]

This is exemplified with appalling eloquence by Villiers de l'Isle Adam's *Axël*, a hugely influential play, whose symbolic content has been much more frequently remarked upon than its raucously melodramatic action. In performance the play would probably look like a bizarre version of *The Ring*: it consists of long, static and verbose confrontations, punctuated by brief events of hideous violence and quite remarkable improbability. Like *The Ring*, too, it relies heavily on the unravelling of past events which are equally complicated, and which the characters narrate at great length. The central symbol is, as in Wagner, treasure: here it is gold and precious stones, said to have represented virtually all of Germany's liquid assets, which Axël's father, the late Count Auersperg, a distinguished general, was charged with saving during the Napoleonic wars. Suspecting a conspiracy, the Count caused it to be buried somewhere on his vast estates in the mountains of the Black Forest, and was duly assassinated soon afterwards. No one knows now where the treasure is; nor are we told how the German banking system had recovered from the blow. The Count's wife died in childbirth, and Axël, his posthumous son, knows only that the treasure exists but not exactly where.

The treasure stands to the events of the play in much the same relationship as the gold stands to *The Ring*'s: it is its passive centre, exerting no real power except lust for its possession in some people, and a desire to transcend such lust in others. Potentially, it is a symbol of riches, power and responsibility: in sum, of the phenomenal world. Axël is an intellectual Siegfried: a student of the occult, improbably handsome (Villiers's stage directions are lyrical on this point), of incredible physical strength (he can strangle wolves with his bare hands), one of the country's most formidable swordsmen, and a virgin. Axël knows what the treasure might be worth, but will not deign to act to gain possession of it: indeed, he declares that he would only take it if it came to him 'from the depths of the Unknown', and would defend it only if it came to him

> without warning, without my having been guilty of a single effort of search — that is, having achieved for myself the status of a mere passer-by.[86]

Axël's morality is based on the simplest amorality: lack of interest. When, in a debate with his Nietzschean mentor, the mysterious Master Janus, he resists the call for the self-renouncing life of a magus, he does so in speeches of magnificent imprecision.

> And suppose I should be a man for a moment? Isn't the earth beautiful? Flaming blood courses through my young veins. The great crime of loving and living![87]

Such lyrical clichés are as close as Axël gets to telling us what he would actually do with his freedom. One way or another, none of this explains what happens when he comes face to face with Sara, Princess of Maupers. She is a stranger to him: a distant relation who, by the study of occult books, has found out the whereabouts of the treasure and, at the moment of being ordained a nun, escapes from her convent and comes to Castle Auersperg. She duly discovers the treasure in the crypt; and she and Axël play out a love confrontation which begins with the grotesque savagery of Kokoschka's *Murderer Hope of Womankind* and ends in a Wagnerian *Liebestod*. What happens between them can hardly be called an experience: it is more like a conflagration. It certainly does not involve relations, either carnal or intellectual — though it is in the mind, if anywhere, that the two respond to each other. They share an orgasm of the imagination.

Master Janus had warned Axël, in language worthy of Schopenhauer, that if he remained in the mundane world he would be 'incarnated beneath the veils of organism in a prison of relationships'[88]. Now, faced with an all-consuming relationship, Axël's intense desire is to renounce it. Rather than experience love and then its fading away, he wants to die with Sara; and they both drink poison, expiring against the

> distant murmurs of the wind in the forest vastness, vibrations of awakening space, the surge of the plain, the hum of life.[89]

These final stage directions might suggest that Villiers is, however obliquely, on the side of life, rather as Kafka seems to be, for some readers, at the end of *Metamorphosis*. But it is clear from the impassioned lyricism of the dialogue that Villiers's heart is entirely with the two suicides. Ukko, the young page whose approaching nuptials represent life going on after Axël's death, is much the most unconvincing character in the play. Villiers is clearly in favour of renunciation through death.

But renunciation to what end? This is a question to which there is no answer in *Axël*, and it is fatuous to ask it. The play urges us to apprehend and value something beyond both life and death, but it gives us no means with which to grasp that value. The fact that it takes place during Easter, ending on the morning of Easter Monday, cancels out all questioning by telling us that death is the true resurrection.

The play is a huge intellectual spectacle designed to lead us to this conclusion and to this unanswerable question. What I suggested about Symbolist drama, that the things which tell us what the play is *about* are more important than the story the play tells, is profoundly true of *Axël*. And we may perhaps see by now that such drama has something important in common with Meyerhold's theatrical event, and with the kind of performance advocated by Brecht in the twenties and thirties. In all of them, the audience is manipulated, through its senses or through its imagination, to respond to things in the play which are external to its events, and which the manipulator, be he playwright or director, rates higher than the text. Another way of saying this is that we cannot question the text and the play's events through these external things, nor these things through the text and the events, because the relationship between them is not organic, as in Shakespeare, Racine or Ibsen, but has been created and imposed upon the dramatic experience by the despotism of the political agitator or the poet. It is not fanciful to describe either kind of theatre with the words Tristan Tzara used to describe the principle of the Dada movement: the dictatorship of the spirit.

The most important representative of that dictatorship in the modern theatre was Antonin Artaud. He is usually thought of as a subversive figure, a liberator of the spirit, the artist as Messiah. That is certainly how he saw himself. The truth is more complex.

The most sober and accessible statements of Artaud's ideas occur in a series of four letters he wrote between 1931 and 1933, one to Benjamin Crémieux and three to Jean Paulhan, and now known as Letters on Language[90]. Artaud's central remark is that 'a gesture culture' also exists side by side with 'word culture'. He claims that he is 'extending stage language and potential by adding another language to speech', and that he is

> attempting to restore its ancient magic effectiveness, its spell-binding effectiveness, integral with speech and whose mysterious potential is now forgotten.

Playwrights, Artaud claims, do their work 'in the abstract, that is, on paper,' whereas the director is 'a kind of demiurge' who unleashes 'certain blind forces on a cosmic level'. Words, moreover

> because of their predetermined nature . . . stop and paralyse thought instead of fostering its development

— a remark which recalls Nietzsche's notion that everything spoken is thereby devalued. The director's task, accordingly, also consists in 'reuniting words with the physical movements from which they originated', so that words would be understood, not only for what they mean grammatically, but also as part of the sounds and movements they are associated with. The problem of the theatre, for Artaud, is rooted in the pointlessness of what is simply written down. But he has a solution:

> Rhythmic, syllabic repetition, special vocal inflection embracing the exact meaning of words, all arouse a greater number of mental images in the mind, producing a more or less hallucinatory state, obliging our sensibility and our minds to undergo a kind of anatomical deterioration.

Artaud's essential ideas are all here. The theatrical event, for him, is beyond the logic of language and reason; it is both magical and dangerous; and the director who creates it is a purifying agent, almost like a saviour. We may note, too, that Artaud's thoughts are concentrated mostly on *how* to express: he has little time for the things to be expressed. He told Louis Jouvet in a letter that he had

> something to say about the stage, something absolutely person-al, like a modern painter who contributes his own formula to other living formulae.[91]

And he went on to complain that 'no modern play ... gives the stage the equivalent of Chirico.' Artaud deplores the theatre's 'lack of imagination': it should deal, he thinks, not with

> personal life, that side of life where CHARACTER reigns supreme, but a kind of emancipated life, sweeping human personality aside, where man is only a shadow. Theatre's true purpose is to create Myths, to express life from an immense, universal aspect and to deduce imagery from this life where we would like to discover ourselves.[92]

This tells us nothing, either about 'this life', and the imagery it might supply, or about life's 'universal aspect'. When Artaud talks about creating myths he sets on his theories the seal of imprecision. Myths, for him, have neither narrative nor characters: indeed, almost no content. The Artaudian myth is simply the theatrical event, shaped by Artaud's own imagination, and overwhelming both performer and audience.

Artaud's famous essay, *The Theatre and its Double*, is a lurid intellectual poem based on the image of a plague victim's body. He explains, with growing excitement, that in such a corpse life is destroyed but without any loss of matter. The only exceptions, he claims, are the brain and the lungs, because they are both dependent on our consciousness and our will: we can, he informs us, stop both breathing and thinking whenever we wish. In other words, the plague attacks the seats of will-power and consciousness. Artaud is fascinated by the idea of 'the disease as a kind of psychic entity, not carried by a virus,'[93] and with the plague as a monstrous event which holds whole communities in its grip and makes people commit extraordinary acts of cruelty and shamelessness in public. From the plague, he tells us, come 'a mental freedom'[94].

Now the point of all this is that, for Artaud, 'stage-acting is a delirium like the plague and is communicable'[95].

The condition of a plague victim who dies without any material destruction, yet with all the stigmata of an absolute, almost abstract disease upon him, is in the same condition as an actor totally penetrated by feelings without any benefit or relation to reality. Everything in the actor's physical aspect . . . shows that life has reacted to a paroxysm, yet nothing has happened.[96]

There is 'something victorious and vengeful in the theatre'[97]; it is 'a revelation'[98], which brings out all the cruelty in us and all the perversity of which we are capable.

A few pages of such observations create an impression of sadistic excitement, no less unpleasant for being theoretical and self-admiring. We do not know how well Artaud knew Nietzsche's works; but his ideas on the nature of cruelty in art may well have derived from *Beyond Good and Evil*; and his 'Letters on Cruelty' to Jean Paulhan and André Rolland de Renéville express the deeply Nietzschean thought that all creation is essentially cruel because it imposes and consumes. Performers and spectators are both victims of the Artaudian holocaust. In its own cataclysmic way this, too, is an artistic event without an audience, though Appia, whom Artaud revered, might have found it difficult to see the kinship between his vision and Artaud's. The key to all this is a sense of possession by some huge force. What Artaud has in mind is something far more powerful than any 'spell' which the conventional bourgeois theatre can exert over its audience; indeed, it is almost irrelevant to speak of a spell where no one is meant to contemplate resistance.

When Artaud read this essay at the Sorbonne in 1933 he performed it: sweating, screaming, his face contorted, he was, in the words of Anaïs Nin who was present, 'enacting his own death, his crucifixion'. The audience began to laugh, jeer, and finally to leave. Afterwards Artaud complained to Nin that people wanted something objective, they wanted to hear *about*. 'I,' he said,

want to give them the experience itself, the plague itself, so they will be terrified and awaken.[99]

The point is echoed elsewhere: Artaud saw the theatre not as 'a game and an entertaining way of passing an evening', but as something having 'the status of therapy'[100]. But if we are to be patients, what are we to be cured of? The difficulty lies in the magniloquent vagueness of Artaud's diagnosis.

We do not see that life as it stands and as it has been made offers us much cause for exaltation. It seems as though a colossal abscess, ethical as much as social, is drained by the plague. And like the plague, theatre is collectively made to drain abscesses.[101]

This is as near as we get to being told what is wrong with us and what cure the theatre is to perform. 'Like the plague,' Artaud asserts, 'theatre is a crisis resolved either by death or cure.'[102] This is not unlike the way Nietzsche said he felt after a performance of *Tristan*, except that Artaud's imagery, laden with moral significance, actually lacks moral content. It is no good arguing with him that people do not die of exposure to drama or that the plague could not be cured, any more than to note that the plague was carried not by a virus but by a bacillus. Such factual exactitude is entirely beside the point. Artaud's analogy is a key to a tormented and sadistic imagination: his purpose is to commit an act of cruelty on our minds and to unite our spirits with his own in beneficial agony.

The spirit of all this is echoed by Artaud's famous essay on the Balinese theatre[103], whose themes, he states with satisfaction, are 'very general, indefinite and abstract'. The Balinese performance is 'a wonderful compound of pure stage imagery and a whole new language'; and all of it is 'steeped in deep intoxication'. The actors look like moving hieroglyphs, and impress him as much by the precision of their movement as by 'their knowledge of physical fear and how to unleash it'. The whole thing is ordered and impersonal,

> matching some dark, prodigious reality we have repressed once and for all here in the West.

It is also a purely *theatrical* event, by which Artaud means that it has done away with the playwright in favour of the producer, who becomes

> a kind of organiser of magic, a master of holy ceremonies ...
> What he sets in motion is MANIFEST.[104]

What Artaud communicates here is a sense of ecstatic admiration for, and union with, a huge event, superbly organised, visually stunning, and appealing to the mind but without involving the reason. I do not know another piece of writing about the theatre that reminds one so strongly of the atmosphere of a Nazi rally. The Artaudian spectacle is a truly perlocutionary act. It seems no accident that, albeit with his mind unhinged, Artaud later dedicated a copy of his apocalyptic pamphlet, *The New Revelations of Being*, to Hitler[105]. The point is not that, as Jerzy Grotowski pointed out, Artaud completely misunderstood Balinese theatre, which consisted of

> concrete expressions, specific theatrical letters in an alphabet of signs universally understood by the Balinese.[106]

It is rather that when, as Grotowski says, the performance 'brought forth a completely different performance which slumbered in [Artaud's] depths', that performance turned out to be one of brutal ecstasy, a ritual of submission, a hymn to significance without any hold on what was to be signified. In one of his notes relating to this essay Artaud writes joyfully about 'men reduced to a diagrammatic state'; and he describes the Balinese theatre as a place 'where all feelings are brought to a state of consent'[107]. Closed drama can have no better definition.

Artaud's only dramatic work of any substance is the melodrama *The Cenci*. Shelley, too, based a play on this true story of a sixteenth-century Italian aristocratic family, and it is worth glancing at the differences. Shelley, who was almost incapable of writing anything that did not have some moral import, stated in his preface that he had no intention of making his play 'subservient to what is vulgarly termed a moral purpose'. He then went on to argue that

> no person can be truly dishonoured by the act of another; and the fit return to make to the most enormous injuries is kindness and forbearance and a resolution to convert the injurer from his dark passions by peace and love. Revenge, retaliation, atonement, are pernicious mistakes. If Beatrice had thought in this manner she would have been wiser and better; but she would never have been a tragic character. The few whom such an exhibition would have interested, could never have been sufficiently interested for a dramatic purpose, from the want of finding sympathy in their interest among the mass who surround them. It is in the restless anatomising casuistry with which men seek the justification of Beatrice, yet feel that she has done what needs justification; it is in the superstitious horror with which they contemplate alike her wrongs and their revenge, that the dramatic character of what she did and suffered, consists.[108]

It is worth quoting this passage at length, because it shows us Shelley's dilemma as a dramatist. Beatrice Cenci, having been raped by her father, finally takes her revenge and thus acts in a way which Shelley morally disapproves of, but which he is perfectly content to put in his play. Those of his audience who try to justify Beatrice's action are morally wrong; and it is our contemplation (and of course Shelley's) of their dilemma which is the justification of the play. The confusion of Shelley's last sentence betrays his uneasiness: for clearly, Beatrice's 'dramatic character' cannot 'consist' in the audience's casuistry about what she has done. It is curious to see Shelley worrying about this, because the problematic character in the play is not Beatrice but Cenci himself. His entire dramatic existence consists in unmotivated hatred and an irrepressible urge to torment others. The word 'irrepressible' should not suggest any attempt on Cenci's part to control himself, for he makes none. No part of his personality expresses any opposition to his impulses; the only disapproval is expressed in other people's conventional exclamations of incredulity and horror.

Coleridge spoke of Iago's motiveless malignity; but if that is Iago's basic nature, how skilfully Shakespeare fleshed it out, both by hinting at Iago's professional discontent and sexual jealousy, and by making him credible, and therefore human and accountable, as an open-mannered, manly soldier with an acerbic sense of humour. Cenci, by contrast, is pure hatred, not far from being a wild animal, which makes Beatrice's scruples about her revenge seem not moral so much as feeble. The difference between Shelley and Artaud is that the latter is not interested in such moral niceties any more than he is interested in character: he wants to communicate an atmosphere of evil and doom to which action serves merely as illustration. His notes contain a cancelled line for Cenci which implies considerable psychological insight: 'My actions are now more afraid of me than I am of my actions.'[109] What this conveys is not only the monstrosity of the man but also a profound split between what he is and what he does. Psychologically speaking, Cenci is fuelling his own ego by telling himself that he is even more terrible than the things he might do; but for some reason Artaud cancelled the line, and what the play as a whole confirms is that Cenci is so entirely in the grip of his desires as to have no will of his own. It is God's fault, he claims, to have made him the father of a creature whom he uncontrollably desires. 'Before anyone condemns me,' he exclaims,

> let them accuse fate. Are we free? Who can maintain we are free when the heavens are ready to fall on us? I have opened the floodgate so as not to be engulfed.[110]

And Beatrice herself, as she is taken away for execution, tells us:

> Everything dies, the world consumes itself, alternating between good and evil ... Neither God, nor men, nor any of the powers that govern what we call our fate, have chosen between good and evil.

Her last words, and the play's, are:

> Who can assure me I will not meet my father after life? The thought makes my dying most bitter. In the end, I fear it will teach me I am not unlike him after all. [111]

In Artaud's picture of the world crime and punishment, criminal and avenger, merge into one. The causality of normal experience, which defines moral and immoral acts, disappears to make way for an amoral event. We are reminded of Schopenhauer's meditation on the essential identity of the tormentor and the tormented: his profoundly amoral notion that to inflict suffering on another is merely a case of the Will 'burying its teeth in its own flesh'. The same Will inhabits all of us; and when we give pain to someone else, 'the inflicter of suffering and the sufferer are one'[112]. Artaud's play, too, takes place as if under an amoral spell. The gist of Beatrice's final words is not that revenge is as evil as the crime, but that both are simply events under the same baleful influence. Cenci and Beatrice both enact Evil, which makes them both criminals as well as victims. On this reading, will and moral purpose are meaningless and so, ultimately, is character. Indeed, we might say that if character meant anything at all to Artaud it simply meant fate.

RESPONSIBILITY, DESTINY, ENDING

This is a good point at which to return to Ibsen's *The Wild Duck* and Gregers Werle. We saw that with Gregers Symbolism entered the world of modern realistic prose drama. The same play and the same character mark another important event: the arrival of the psychotic character as protagonist.

For there is clearly something psychotic in Gregers's behaviour: he seems to be in the grip of something stronger than himself, but without knowing it. The man who values truth more highly than worldly things is no stranger to us in Ibsen's work: *Brand* is the tragedy of such a man. But Brand's fanaticism involves self-sacrifice. For him belief is a matter of action because, in the play's world, God and his commandments are real. Brand's mistake is that he believes himself obliged to make inhuman sacrifices which, in the end, cancel the value of his intentions. Ibsen lets us see, too, that there is a profound kinship between the demands of satisfying one's faith and satisfying one's vanity, all the more powerful for being entirely subconscious. Moreover, both Brand's faith and his vanity are fuelled by the fact that he is really needed by others: the villagers do not want him to go away, and in his wife Agnes he satisfies a craving for renunciation and sacrifice by imposing them on her as a duty. All along, Brand walks the path of decisions, constantly challenged by those weaknesses of simple humanity, both in himself and others, which make survival possible by demanding compromises. Brand is an 'open' character because every decision he makes is a matter of clear choice: he could, and we sometimes feel he should, have decided otherwise.

Gregers Werle, by contrast, is a drawing-room Messiah whose actions entail no sacrifices. Unlike Brand, Gregers serves no God: he is the servant of some inner need which he does not fully understand. He has the temperament of an apostle, and it is fuelled by resentment towards his father. Gregers's mistake is that he thinks he can atone for his father's unfaithfulness to his mother by exposing the arrangements with which the old man had covered things up. It is a mistake because these arrangements involve not only his father, but also people who had nothing to do with Old Werle's actions. Gregers is dreaming of moral restitution and ends up with something less than revenge. His is a failure of the moral imagination: he destroys the people he wants to save by imposing on them his own salvation. The point about Gregers is that, unlike Brand, he does not know what he is doing. It is not that he is stupid: the way he questions his father and scents out the truth behind the old man's evasions shows considerable shrewdness. But there is something manic about this questioning, which Old Werle diagnoses accurately when he tells Gregers that he ought to be a little more at peace with himself. And from the moment when Gregers departs with the words, '. . . now at least I see my vocation'[113], we sense that we are in the presence, not of someone who makes decisions, but someone who is driven.

Gregers is also the driving force of *The Wild Duck*: without him, there would be no play. Such characters become crucial to Ibsen's remaining plays. *Rosmersholm* is a conflagration caused by the love of a man and a woman both of whom have a deep-seated fear of physical passion which they neither understand nor, until the end, even perceive. Freud has analysed brilliantly how Rebecca's nature, hideously bent on power, is finally thwarted by ineradicable guilt. By contrast, Rosmer's nature makes him a prey to the influence of others. The key to his character lies in two things Dr Kroll says to him: that he is 'impressionable', and that he is 'not the kind of man who can stand alone'[114]. This helps to explain his final insane challenge to Rebecca that she should prove her truthfulness to him through death: Rosmer is a man whose need to depend on others has completely undermined his confidence, in them as well as in himself. If Rosmer is a psychological suicide, Hedda Gabler is a psychological killer as well: there is something compulsive about the way she pursues Lovborg, just as there was something self-destructive about her marriage to Tesman. And once again Ibsen provides a suitable victim: Lovborg, a man obsessionally driven to unsatisfactory relationships with what he thinks are strong and protective women.

The point about such characters in Ibsen (they will reappear, especially in *The Lady from the Sea*, *The Master Builder* and *Little Eyolf*) is that they do not seem to be able to help themselves. Their effect on the plays is a sense of inevitability different from what we experience in classical tragedy. We are in the presence of compulsion. Even a character like Racine's Phèdre does not give us this precise sense of the psychologically inevitable: she finds herself in a tragic situation, but there is nothing about her to suggest, as there is about Gregers, Hedda and Rebecca, that such a situation is her natural element, and that she would, albeit subconsciously, seek it out. Part of our engagement with plays like *Phèdre* consists in our tense involvement with the decisions of their characters: our wish to know, right to the end, what they will avoid and what they will choose. The characters in Ibsen's late plays seem to be driven to what they do by something stronger than themselves, so that questions about their decisions, indeed their personal will, begin to be less important. It is not that they are incapable of decisions, or that they do not have to make them: Hedda decides to shoot herself at the end, which may surprise us, though not as much as it surprises Tesman and Brack. It is, rather, that their decisions are forced on them by something within themselves which they cannot control.

There is a sense of pressure and compulsion about Hedda, a sense
that in any situation there is only one decision she can take. This is
not a matter of hindsight: of saying at the end of the play that it all
seemed somehow inevitable. We have only to think of Pastor
Manders in *Ghosts*, weighing up the matter of insuring the orphanage; of Angelo in *Measure for Measure*, being confronted by
Isabella's moral fervour and her physical beauty. These are situations where we are aware of people applying their minds and feelings
to an act of moral choice, and where we are aware that their decision
could go either way. In Ibsen's late plays the action centres on people
who move along their paths as if largely unaccountable for their
behaviour.

These plays inaugurate what we might call the theatre of diminished responsibility. We should not confuse this with Greek
tragedy, where the pressure of necessity and the actions of the gods
form a background against which the dramatist investigates the
value of human will and choice. For Wagner, by contrast, this
confrontation between Fate and willed human action became a
problem which he was not quite able to solve: this is what lies
behind the profound moral ambiguity of Wotan and, indeed, of the
whole *Ring*. One of the main themes of *Tristan and Isolde*, summed
up in the tragic ambiguity of the love potion, is the ultimate
irrelevance of responsibility to action. The essence of Cenci, in both
Shelley's and Artaud's play, is that his viciousness is entirely
unmotivated and has the force and impact of a psychosis.

The psychotic character has something in common with some of
Molière's people, and with the 'humours' of Ben Jonson. They,
indeed, are creations of whom G. Wilson Knight could justly have
said that they are symbols of a vision rather than human beings.
'Open' characters in Shakespeare virtually make themselves before
our eyes. Someone like Jonson's Zeal-of-the-Land Busy is *given*: he
comes to us finished, closed — a function. In this sense, the more a
character is a 'type' the less we can question him. A greedy type is
there to show us what greed is like, rather than how it comes about
and what are its degrees. We do not question the background of
Jonson's Sir Epicure Mammon, his parentage, say, or his education;
nor do we wonder whether he might ever change and become a timid
recluse. He fits into a moral view of the world of which greed is a
part. We, the audience, are meant to agree with Jonson about where
we stand in relation to it. In religious drama our attitude is even
more fixed. Eric Bentley was right when he remarked that 'in the

drama of fixed morality there is no moral questioning at all.'[115]

Contemporary drama, too, has its types. But whereas in the classical theatre the type was based on vices, that is to say, on moral qualities, the modern type tends to be based on professions: there are 'typical' army officers, advertising agents, cleaning ladies or psychoanalysts. Paradoxically, the intention is not essentially moral, and yet the effect can be more open: we can question such characters more easily because their profession places them in a context.

The dramatist who committed the greatest part of his talent and imagination to the theatre of diminished responsibility was Strindberg. His early naturalistic works are closed plays precisely to the extent that their characters are psychotic. Our questioning of *The Father* is limited by the fact that both the Captain and Laura are in the grip of feelings which border on the pathological. Strindberg wrote the play after *Comrades*, but set it earlier in time because he wanted to explain the origins of its heroine, the mannish and difficult Bertha. But *The Father* no more explains what made Bertha into the woman we see in *Comrades* than the Nurse's description of the Captain as a child explains the sort of man he is now. She tells him that he was always

> a silly boy, so we had to tell you stories, because you thought we all wanted to hurt you.[116]

Earlier, the Captain broods over the fact that 'Father and Mother had me against their will, and so I was born without a will.'[117] The remark is senseless; and none of this adds up to a coherent genesis of character. For one thing, the man we see before us has plenty of will. Laura, too, tells the Doctor that the Captain has never taken a decision without reversing it: a description which clearly does not fit.

The fact is that Strindberg wrote the play to demonstrate how female ruthlessness and cunning can destroy a man's sanity, and he signposted his argument with psychological clues which carry momentary conviction but never add up to a coherent picture. This in itself does not make *The Father* a closed play, only an open play with faults. The same is true of Bertha, the Captain's daughter. In *Comrades* we see her as an unsuccessful painter and a domineering woman. In *The Father* the Captain worries that little Bertha might be trained

> for some masculine vocation that'll need years of study and be completely wasted if she does get married;

and that, what is worse,

> Bertha's future is being decided ... in there from motives of
> hatred ... Man versus woman, that's their theme, all day
> long.[118]

In his final defeat, the Captain cries out that Bertha became his
enemy because she had been forced by her mother to choose
between her parents. But this is no more than hysteria. Bertha could
just as well have become her mother's enemy: after all, it is she who
is forcing her to live at home against her will; and the fact that an
untalented painter becomes a disastrous wife cannot be explained by
the Captain's little sermon about the need to have a useful profession.

Comrades did not need *The Father* in the sense that *The Valkyrie*
needed *Rhinegold*: nothing that Strindberg put in the later play
explains or justifies what happens in the earlier one. (He planned a
third play, concluding the story with a comedy of marital reconcilia-
tion. Not surprisingly, it never got written.) One senses that in
Comrades Strindberg was more on Axel's (the husband's) side than
on Bertha's, especially when he is made to pass off Bertha's painting
at the Salon as his own, in the hope that this might gain her a prize.
This is a clumsy device, attributing to Axel a generosity which he is
not otherwise seen to possess; and, along with Bertha's own insuf-
ferable behaviour, it helps to load the dice against her. The play, like
A Doll's House, ends with a woman in a state of moral revolt leaving
her husband − except that here it is she who is in the wrong. In *A
Doll's House* we watch Torvald, not basically an objectionable
character, slowly enmeshing himself in the consequences of his
actions and his attitudes; but in *Comrades* Bertha, who is the
offending party, is put at a disadvantage all along.

Still, *Comrades* has the vigour, and almost the even-handedness,
of the best social and marital satire: no one comes out of it especially
well. I have dwelt on this play because it has some of Strindberg's
strongest qualities − his psychological insight, his mordant sense of
comedy, and his theatricality − without being what we think of as a
typical Strindberg play. Towards the end of his life he wrote, quite
plausibly, that if *The Father* were produced against an abstract set of
draperies it would be

> elevated from the heavy everyday world to the level of tragedy
> in high style. The characters [would] be sublimated, ennobled,
> and appear as from another world.[119]

This could not have been said about *Comrades*; and if *The Father* were produced in this way it would take away some of its effectiveness as a domestic tragedy. But Strindberg's remark is important because it underlines the fact that with *The Father* he embarked on something new: he started writing dramas of obsession and apocalyptic psychology.

Laura and the Captain are not so much real people as personifications of mental conditions. We are told, in Act II, that their marriage was based on his need for a mother, and that for her physical passion was

> an ecstasy followed by pangs of conscience, as though my blood was ashamed. The mother became the mistress — ugh![120]

This is a hideously brilliant piece of psychoanalysis, written nearly twenty years before Freud published a line on the subject. But it does not explain the most important thing before us, which is the almost inhuman ferocity of the confrontation. Laura is like an avenging angel against whom a great crime, called life, has been committed. Her sexuality illustrates but does not explain her all-consuming desire for power. To Strindberg, as to Artaud, character here means fate.

George Steiner has written about 'the grain of the inexplicable' in tragedy[121]: about such ultimate questions as why Macbeth should have met the witches at all, to which there is no answer. And indeed, all open plays, like the open world we live in, are closed off somewhere, by something. God, the gods, Fate and Destiny are the great ultimates of Greek, Shakespearean and French tragedy; social and psychological forces are those of the plays of Molière and Büchner, Ibsen, Brecht and Shaw. What makes these plays open is the distance between these ultimates and ourselves. We reach the end by crossing the terrain of the play. The great ultimates themselves, when we reach them, may not yield an answer; but they are the background against which we measure and question the play's events. Our progress towards them, through these events, is one of engagement and learning: this is the essential movement, as well as the moral content, of the open play.

The closed play defines itself by how much of this movement, this engagement, it excludes. The characters in Ibsen's late plays and, even more, in Strindberg's naturalistic tragedies, seem to carry the unquestionable ultimates within themselves. This is what character as fate means. Maeterlinck's characters, under the sentimentality of their presentation, exude a sense of confronting Destiny face to face. The Promethean heroes of Ernst Toller's plays are in immediate personal conflict with the mystico-political forces that shape their world.

This immediate contact between dramatic characters and the great ultimate matters raised by drama has three effects. It magnifies these characters into something superhuman, almost mystical; it limits their scope of will, decision and dramatic action; and, to the same extent, it limits the scope of our own engagement with them. When the Captain cries out:

> You didn't want it to be like this, I didn't want it, and yet it happened. Who rules our lives?[122]

— we feel that we are in the presence of people who are both more and less than human.

We have the testimony of Strindberg's own preface to the fact that a great deal of conscious effort had gone into the characters of *Miss Julie*. Strindberg worked out the relationship between Julie and Jean, their psychological make-up, their social and racial background, with almost repellent care. Yet obsession proves stronger than insight. The two characters' actual past becomes almost insignificant compared with what they stand for. Julie's story of her parents makes a powerful point, bordering on absurdity, about the evils of *mésalliance*, heredity, and the upbringing of girls; but in the end all this will have no bearing, except in the most theoretical sense, on Julie's actions. The same goes for Jean's story of how he had first caught sight of Julie in her parents' garden, and the nauseating description of his escape. The narrative and its ghastly symbolism are heavy-handed and incredible; their function is to provide a reason for Jean's treatment of Julie. In performance the device fails, partly because it is so over-wrought and improbable, and partly because Jean's character, so powerful and yet so perfunctory, needs no such socio-psychological fleshing-out. The past, instead of being a shaping force, becomes irrelevant under the pressure of the present.

Strindberg has written, somewhat pompously, about his use of what he rather oddly calls the ballet in the middle of the play, even explaining that the song the servants sing is

> circumlocutory rather than direct ... for the cunning (weakness) of servile people is not of the type that engages in direct assault.[123]

In performance the scene invariably comes across as what it basically is: a device to allow time for Julie and Jean to have intercourse offstage without the curtain having to be lowered. As for the servants, they are little more than props. They have no reality whatever as people belonging to the house; nor are we aware of them as being servile, cunning, or anything else.

The servants in *Miss Julie* point to a lack of context in the play: the context of community. The confrontation between Julie and Jean is a battle between two states of mind. Strindberg wanted to surround them with a sense of a real society, but it simply disappears in the heat of the encounter. One definition of a closed play is its limited sense of community. We have noted how unreal, as people, were the chorus of men and women at the end of Wagner's *Götterdämmerung*. In the same way, the children whom Pelléas sees going down to the beach in Act Three of Maeterlinck's *Pelléas and Mélisande* have no human reality whatever: they are described to make us think of innocence, of simple life going on despite the ominous events we are witnessing. Arkel is a king, but he has no reality as a ruler, nor the settings as a country, a place for a community, which he rules: like the King and the Queen in *Princess Maleine*, he is simply an embodiment of old age and authority. He mentions at the beginning that he had plans for a political marriage for Golaud, but the idea is never mentioned again. We have seen, too, how unconvincing are the simple loves and lives of the humble retainers in the background of Villiers's *Axël*. Axël's famous remark, 'As for living? Our servants will do that for us'[124], only reminds us that the servants in the play do very little living indeed.

The same thing can happen in plays that have an explicit social and political purpose. Bertolt Brecht's earliest plays, *Baal* and *Drums in the Night*, are Expressionistic in tone, yet they have a strongly felt social context. Baal's landlady, the literary socialites, farmers and woodcutters he encounters, have a powerful sense of reality, and Baal's progress, a perversely lyrical *Stationendrama*, is a progress through recognisable areas of a recognisable society. But with *In the Jungle of Cities* we enter a different world. Brecht is beginning to move towards his favourite means of expression, the parable; and one way of defining a parable is to say that in it the story becomes subservient to the story-teller, who relates it in order to convey a meaning of his own. Hence the make-believe background of so many of Brecht's plays: they are closed plays to the extent that their settings are unreal. We all know that the Chicago of

In the Jungle and of *St Joan of the Stockyards* is as unreal as the Far East of *Man Equals Man*; and for anyone who knows anything about the history of collective farming in the Soviet Union, the prologue and the concluding lines of *The Caucasian Chalk Circle* are a preposterous lie. But these settings are part of the Brechtian parable which it would be fatuous to question: they emphasise, by their very lack of particularity and authenticity, indeed we might say by their frank dishonesty, the universality of what Brecht wants to say.

Yet in practice the make-believe settings often undermine Brecht's intentions, precisely because his plays have such a powerful social and political drive. In performance, as well as in reading, one is conscious of the credibility gap between the hard-headedness of Brecht's politics and the *faux-naiveté* of his settings: the content is undermined by the falsity of the context. In this sense, Brecht's *Lehrstücke*, which must rank among the most unpleasant plays written in the name of *realpolitik*, are far more authentic. His greatest plays, *Life of Galileo* and *Mother Courage*, both have real historical backgrounds, and both take place in a context of community which is as important for their impact as their plot and their characters. By contrast, an important play like *The Good Person of Setzuan* is weakened by its lack of a sense of community. People appear to know each other and they tell us what their family ties are; but Setzuan never comes across as a village where life has its ways and people have their habits and social functions. The population is no more than a backdrop, and this fatally weakens the play's argument which is about the survival or otherwise of personal integrity in a community founded on greed. The English playwright who has distilled the best of Brecht into his own work is John Arden; and we have only to think of the unnamed north-country town where *Serjeant Musgrave's Dance* takes place, in a period deliberately left somewhat vague by the author, to realise what an all-pervasive sense of reality can be achieved against settings that are not completely precise.

To return to *Miss Julie*: it is with the future as it is with the past. The end of an open play, as we saw earlier in this book, is not the end of its life. I am not referring to the kind of sentimental reverie in which we think wistfully of Orsino's and Viola's married life after *Twelfth Night*. Yet the fact is that such thinking is part of our experience of a play: when it ends, we are aware of the life it has left behind, or the life it might have moved into. Mrs Alving will have to live with herself after what has happened, and so will Pastor Manders; one imagines that the latter will find it a lot easier. At the end of *The Wild Duck* we are conscious of the horror and the preposterousness of Gregers's situation, renting a room in the house of the family whom he has just destroyed. The ancestors of such characters are Angelo in *Measure for Measure* and Bertram in *All's Well That Ends Well*: one of Shakespeare's greatest innovations consisted in putting people through potentially tragic experiences, and then making them face life with those they have wronged after the humiliating agony of a comic dénouement. With such plays, their afterlife becomes an important part of our moral experience.

The end of *Miss Julie* seems to leave us with an extraordinary situation. What will happen to Jean now? Clearly, all the servants must know what happened, and it cannot be long before he is implicated in Julie's suicide, particularly as she will be found with his razor in her hand. And if this is so, why did Jean, who is far from stupid, choose this way out? The fact is that these are thoughts very much after the event, and that in performance the question simply does not arise. What Strindberg wanted to show us was the monstrosity of the encounter, and beside that the matter of consequences fades into insignificance. Once again, it seems useless to ask certain questions: they are out of key with the play's drive and its mood. Michael Meyer has commented that Strindberg's early plays 'end feebly'[125]. By contrast, his mature plays end rather as an explosion does. There is simply nothing more to happen, nowhere further to go. When Jean tells Julie that 'It's the only possible ending,' the words acquire a sense of theatricality which Strindberg may not have intended, but which nevertheless says something important about the play: how does one achieve a sense of an ending, of something appropriate and fitting, rather than just a sense of being spent, after such a volcanic eruption? There is a quality of the closed play in *Miss Julie* which is defined by both the hideous inevitability and the preposterousness of its conclusion.

If a play is a unique event, its uniqueness is confirmed by its ending. Frank Kermode has written some illuminating pages about the way fictional organisation imposes itself on our sense of the passing of time, and the way in which we need this fictional organisation to create for us that arbitrary but satisfying structure we call a novel — or, in our case, a play[126]. It is worth stating the commonplace that a different ending could mean a different novel, a different play. The ending is the key to *A la Recherche du Temps*

Perdu. The family excursion at the end of Kafka's *The Metamorph-osis* may or may not be artistically successful, but it turns the story into an entirely different kind of work from what it would have been without it. Aeschylus' *Agamemnon* is a satisfactory drama but it is a travesty to perform it on its own: without *The Eumenides* and *The Libation Bearers* it lacks a proper ending, and if we did not know the latter plays we would not know what Aeschylus wanted to say.

The ending can make a crucial difference to whether we regard a play as open or closed. Put simply, if Godot turned up at the end of Beckett's play we might find out what was the nature of the appointment and it might change Vladimir's and Estragon's lives. Of course, as we contemplate this idea we realise that the two men's lives cannot be changed for the simple reason that the play has no context within which to change. 'What exactly did we ask him to do for us?' Estragon asks[127]. Not only is there no precise answer to that: as the play goes on we realise that they may not actually know Godot at all. Within the fictional reality called *Waiting for Godot* the arrival of Godot would be senseless: it is the ending that confirms this. Indeed, it is the ending that establishes one of the crucial things about the play, which is that its action is inconclusive. Had Beckett written only the first act, the play would be merely odd. The two acts together establish inconclusiveness as one of its themes.

Now actions are by nature conclusive: that is what makes them actions. The footballer who misses the goal has still carried out an action. And until we encountered closed drama we might have said that a play, too, was by definition conclusive, simply by being an event: it has an action which takes place. The difference with plays is that they cannot, so to speak, miss the goal: they have to be seen to have set out to do something and then to have done it. The reader may retort that *Waiting for Godot* sets out to show the inconclusive-ness of life and then goes on to show it. But the fact is that there is a difference between what a play does and what a play says: which is a new way of putting into words the old difference between form and content. Beckett achieved a specific aim in the form of his play, that is to say in its organisation, its shape, the sequence of its events. These things are what the play *does*. But its contents, what it is about, what it *says*, tell us that actions do not fulfil themselves in achievement; that cause as you will, there will be no effect. In this sense the play shows us one thing and tells us another. The content denies the form.

*   *   *

To return to Strindberg: if his early plays are closed to the extent
that his characters are psychotic, his late plays are closed to the
extent that Strindberg himself is psychotic. It is not necessary to
know Strindberg's life in order to realise this. The scene between
Indra's Daughter and the Advocate in *A Dream Play*, where they
admit that their marriage has become unhappy, is an obsessional
account of obsessions. She feels suffocated in their small room
because they cannot open the window: heating is too expensive.
Their child cries too much, which puts his clients off; and they
cannot take a larger apartment because they cannot afford it. The
place is dirty, but they are both too tired to scrub the floor. She
suffers from the dirt, he from her untidiness. They eat cabbage
because it is cheap, but she hates it.

ADVOCATE: Why didn't you say so?

DAUGHTER: Because I loved you. I wanted to make a sacrifice
for you.

ADVOCATE: Then I must sacrifice for you my love of cabbage.
The sacrifice must be mutual.

DAUGHTER: Then what shall we eat? Fish? But you hate fish.

ADVOCATE: And it's dear.

DAUGHTER: This is harder than I dreamed.

ADVOCATE: (*gently*) You see how hard it is! And the child,
that was to have been our bond and blessing, is
becoming our ruin.[128]

The comedy of this is both brilliantly perceptive and unintentional.
Strindberg is a master at describing marital warfare: but in the way
he heaps detail upon detail, compressing a relentless litany of
dissatisfactions into some four minutes of playing time, he betrays
that he himself is as obsessed with the paltry things that can ruin
marriages as his characters are. The same is true of *To Damascus*:
the Stranger's idea that his first wife might re-marry and give his
children a stepfather is made to haunt him, in Parts One and Two,
with a frequency which tells us as much about Strindberg's obsession as about the Stranger's. This obsessional quality is characteristic of the whole of *A Dream Play*: each scene is a grim
demonstration of the grimness of all experience, made grimmer still
by the Advocate's words that the worst thing of all is 'Repetition.
Repeating the pattern'. 'Life consists of doing things again.'[129]

The stunning technical virtuosity of *A Dream Play* should not blind us to Strindberg's lack of emotional control over his material. *Waiting for Godot* is a play where the author's control is complete; but *A Dream Play* has two things in common with it. One is that the people in it learn nothing. Experience impinges on some of them to the extent of making them aware of their misery, but not to the extent of teaching them how to alleviate it. The only one who learns anything is Indra's Daughter, but she does not belong to the world we see: she is the child of the god Indra, and she comes to Earth not to save men but to report back to Indra on their reputation as a race steeped in misery. Indra clearly knows this already, and says that the journey will be a trial for his daughter. This turns out to be true only in the sense that she has a miserable time; in the end her departure is as abrupt as her arrival, and the only thing she seems to have learned is summed up in her repeated cry, 'Alas for mankind!' She is nothing more than a wretched observer of wretchedness, with no power to heal or help. Moreover, she is the daughter, not of the god who made the world (we are told that Brahma did that), but of another god who bears no responsibility for it. That makes Indra's Daughter a helpless observer representing another helpless observer. Strindberg has created a world which is not only wretched but also beyond redemption: its inhabitants suffer constantly and its creator is absent. And if the Daughter learns a lesson, however banal, we note that she learns it very early on, and that nothing that happens after that deepens her experience. Indeed, Strindberg could have added several more scenes of human unhappiness without changing anything about the play except increasing its length.

Now Strindberg may have had insufficient emotional control over his material, but his technical control was complete: among other things he knew when to stop. This may sound a simple matter; but it turns our attention to a crucial feature of Strindberg's late plays. It is one thing to know when to stop if you are writing *Comrades* or *The Father* (or *A Doll's House*, or *Macbeth*, or *Agamemnon*). With such plays the nature of the event partly dictates both pace and length: the story has a dynamic of its own which will control its unfolding and which the playwright has to keep in step with. In this sense, dramatic control is relative: the narrative and its characters also have their own demands. With *A Dream Play* we sense that the play does not exert this kind of pressure on the playwright. When we say that Strindberg 'knew when to stop', we mean that he knew that one more scene might have begun to lose him the audience's attention, rather than realised that the events and characters at his disposal had run their natural course.

The reader may reply that Strindberg did not have, or want, the events and characters at his disposal that Ibsen or Shakespeare had: but this is precisely the point about plays like *A Dream Play*. Strindberg has chosen an (in theory) infinitely expandable structure, and our experience of the play includes a sense that it is expandable: that we are in the presence of a mind which arbitrates over the narrative, rather than one which works partly in response to the narrative's natural demands. We are reminded of Kafka's *The Trial*, of Proust's *A la Recherche du Temps Perdu*, both of which are structurally held together by their beginning and end, but yet give us a sense of being infinitely expandable in between. This is the other similarity between *Waiting for Godot* and *A Dream Play*. We know perfectly well that it would have been superfluous for Beckett to write a third act; and yet it is an essential part of the play's impact and of its meaning that we should sense a possibility of endless repetition, of eternal recurrence, at the end.

In Ionesco's *The Lesson* we have a sense of recurrence because it is quite blatantly stated: the Pupil is the Professor's fortieth victim that day and the play ends with the offstage arrival of the forty-first. If *The Lesson* ends in order to be repeated, Ionesco's *Rhinoceros*, by contrast, ends as something unrepeatable: the entire world of the play (and there is no indication of any other) has turned into another kind of world, just as Georg Kaiser's *Gas* trilogy describes the complete disintegration of one world and the entirely unconvincing rise of another. Such plays have, in their different ways, a Wagnerian sense of annihilation and apocalypse. Both kinds of ending, the recurrent and the apocalyptic, undermine the nature of narrative — if narrative is something that tells a unique event in context. The events of *Macbeth*, for example, are not infinitely repeatable: but it is not entirely beyond belief that events like them might happen again. The ending leaves behind a world steeped in the concerns and problems of the events we have just witnessed. The characters, some of whom are still alive, have provided the uniqueness of those events; the time, place and background, in other words the context, imply the possibility of their repetition. Thus the classical narrative tells us of unique events springing from a context which is knowable and lasting: like a unique tree springing up from the enduring soil.

Making the dramatic narrative infinitely repeatable or apocalyptical-
ly final has the same effect as giving characters generic names: the
Stranger and the Lady, the Billionaire and the Engineer, the Professor and the Pupil. The unique character, like the unique event,
becomes universal, approaching the condition of the mythical.
Closed drama lacks unique characters because they would invite the
kind of questioning which the play's essential attitude is designed to
prevent. It also, not surprisingly, has to do with the imaginative
temperament of the playwright. Strindberg held that

> one person's life depicted fully is more truthful and more
> enlightening than a whole family's. How can one know what is
> occurring in the brains of others, how can one know the
> involved motives of another's deed, how can one know what
> this one or that one said in a confidential moment? . . . One
> knows only one life, one's own.[130]

Strindberg, we sense, is both impatient and puzzled: he reminds us
of Kafka's uneasiness at having to cope with more than one character
in a narrative. R.J. Kaufmann has said about Strindberg that 'the
more purely felt his plays, the more they approach the monologue as
a limit.'[131] When Yeats says that

> we move others not because we have understood or thought
> about those others, but because all life has the same root,[132]

he is describing a quality of what we might call the monological
imagination, circling around, and projecting, the inner self. Peter
Brook has admitted that

> The job of shifting oneself totally from one character to another
> — a principle on which all of Shakespeare and all of Chekhov is
> built — is a superhuman task at any time. It takes unique
> talents and perhaps ones that do not even correspond with our
> age.[133]

Coming from a director of the widest range in subjects and styles,
this could stand as a diagnosis of a monological culture.
 Ionesco goes so far as to

> disapprove of stressing individual differences when one is creat-
> ing a 'character'. What interests me above all is the deep-rooted
> identity of people, precisely because *my need* is to establish
> contact with all men everywhere (my italics).[134]

This is drama as therapy; and it also sounds as if it had been inspired by Jung's theories of the collective unconscious and the archetypes. But in drama, as in life, those deep-rooted identities strike us much more strongly through character differences. We realise that there is something of a Hamlet in us, something of a Gregers, or an Alceste; and the realisation leads us to question the characters and the plays, as well as ourselves. What Ionesco says amounts to a declaration that we are all fundamentally alike — a cliché which is beyond argument either because it is irrefutably true or because it is not worth arguing with. One of the most perceptive diagnoses of such writing was made by Walter Sokel, who noted that

> Wedekind applied the identical idiom of stilted phrases and caustic epigrams to all his characters from newspaper publisher to ragpicker ... By his peculiar idiom he created a *closed world* similar to the autonomous space of the Cubists or the *closed universe* of Kafka and Trakl.[135]

The relevance of these words (the italics are mine) to the argument of this book need not be emphasised. They remind us that the depersonalisation of language, which is so noticeable in Expressionist drama and Ionesco, is an aspect of closed drama: you cannot question characters who use language as if they were not quite, or something more than, persons, and as if the words were not of their own choosing. Take the following exchange from Beckett's *Endgame*:

> CLOV: Do you believe in the life to come?
> HAMM: Mine was always that.[136]

If we did not know the speakers and the play, we might think that these lines came from *Godot*: they have that quality of a cerebral joke, grim, impersonal and painful, which would fit Vladimir and Estragon perfectly. What this means is that in Beckett's plays, and in all closed drama, the range of dialogue, in the sense of speech representing or suggesting individual character, is so restricted that we tend to identify the voices in the plays with the voice of the dramatist. Character becomes a mouthpiece, beyond our questioning. We do not engage with the life in the play, but with the author's ideas. The playwright as lecturer.

We have said at the beginning of this book that characters in closed drama are not made by their world, any more than the world is made by them. One aspect of this is their essential innocence.

Kafka's and Proust's narrators had, as Radomsky in *The Idiot* said of Prince Myshkin, an 'inherent inexperience'. The characters of closed drama share this quality. Even Beckett's highly (and oddly) literate characters have a quality of 'innocence', on which no experience really impinges, and which also prompts them to ask fundamental but unanswerable questions. Like Ionesco's Bérenger, or those garrulous old men and haunted toddlers in Maeterlinck, they are the wise fools of modern literature. In open drama such roles are filled by jesters, madmen, children or the uneducated: professional naives or real innocents. In closed drama such characters are central. The effect on us is that we, too, are made to ask only those unanswerable questions which they are facing. Is life really a random and purposeless meeting of blind people? Does it really consist in waiting for the unknown? One reason why we cannot question such characters is that they themselves cannot effectively question their own lives.

In closed drama all characters are usually on the same level of intelligence (or naiveté), so that we cannot quite measure people within the same play against each other. When we compare Shakespeare's Ulysses, say, with Achilles and Ajax, or Ibsen's Hedda with Tesman and Brack, we understand each of them better: they express values, they have moral and imaginative energies, whose differences help to shape the play. It also gives us a sense of how they were moulded by the play's world, and it by them. The unique abides our question; the general is free.

The characters in Harold Pinter's plays spend a lot of their time sizing each other up. These are no mere innocents. Pinter's name is often bracketed with Beckett, and so he has often been regarded as a different playwright from what he really is. Far from being a writer in the tradition of the absurd, Pinter is a psychological realist. He has often been compared to Kafka; but Harold Hobson was much closer to the mark when, in his first review of *The Birthday Party* in *The Sunday Times*, he compared him to Henry James. This is not as eccentric as it sounds. What the two have in common is that, unlike Kafka, they both write about a known and knowable world: a world in which things are *caused*. Like James's novels, Pinter's plays are always confrontations in a specific sense that Beckett's, or even Ionesco's, never are. James's circumlocutory narrative style can, especially in the late novels, be a barrier between us and what he wants to say: but what he wants to say is, finally, never in doubt.

This style is both a stratagem and an evasion; and Pinter has seized on the human proneness to such stratagems and evasions as the stuff of his plays. But with him, what is really being spoken of is never far beneath what is being said. His characters deliver themselves in a curious mixture of brutal directness and oblique formality.

After seeing a play by Pinter we often catch ourselves speaking with the apparently inconsequential circumlocutions of his characters, and then conclude that the world we live in is really rather like a Pinter play. But this is not entirely true. The real world may conduct itself according to certain oblique rules, and the English world especially so; but a degree of directness is part of language and of its relation to behaviour. In Pinter's world this directness is systematically dislocated: what people say usually means something else as well. Even the apparently straightforward opening exchange in *No Man's Land* is laden with unspoken meaning.

> HIRST: As it is?
> SPOONER: As it is, yes please, absolutely as it is.[137]

Hirst is brief and to the point; Spooner verbose and ingratiating: twelve words map out the relationship between the man of power and the supplicant. The opening of *Old Times* is almost naturalistically matter-of-fact: we catch a married couple in mid-conversation, talking about someone they are expecting: clearly a woman, and clearly someone the wife knows but the husband does not. Then comes the following exchange:

> KATE: She was my only friend.
> DEELEY: Your best and only.
> KATE: My one and only.
> *Pause.*
> If you have only one of something you can't say it's the best of anything.
> DEELEY: Because you have nothing to compare it with?
> KATE: Mmnn.[138]

This sums up the relationship, and it is done through an oblique use of language. I do not mean dialogue: it is a matter, specifically, of how people use or misuse words. For Deeley, language is not a precision instrument: even when Kate corrects his tautology he misses the point. Throughout the play his character is subtly defined by his use of language, and his attitude to how other people use it. He is affronted when others use what he considers recondite words such as 'lest' and 'gaze'; he himself is given to odd expressions, such as 'I touched her profoundly all over': 'You smiled fit to bust', or 'something luscious if not voluptuous'. When cornered, Deeley reacts with the garrulous sarcasm of the insecure.

> I use the word globe because the word world possesses emotional political sociological and psychological pretensions and resonances which I prefer as a matter of choice to do without, or shall I say to steer clear of or if you like to reject.[139]

The point of the famous exchange of thirties songs between him and Anna (it is Deeley who starts it) is that he can most confidently express himself in familiar words written by other people.

Deeley's uneasiness with language is a clue to his uneasiness with life: they both spring from a sense of insecurity and an urge to dominate. In *Betrayal*, which tells the story of the collapse of an adulterous love-affair, scene by scene, in reverse order, the dialogue of the first scene (the end of the affair) is bleak, spare: the clichés of disenchantment. That of the last scene (the beginning of the affair) is distraught, passionate: the lyricism of infatuation. On the face of it, language matches the action. But here, too, it is the final scene that determines the nature of the play as a whole: we take in the magnitude of the loss only when we have witnessed the excitement of the promise. And so the language of the play describes a trajectory which is precisely the opposite of that described by its story.

Pinter's plays can at first be puzzling because their language operates at a distance from its meaning as expressed in the plot. When we say, as we sometimes do, that we do not understand his plays we mean that we cannot bridge the apparent gap between what his characters say and what they might be driving at. Therefore we tend to suspect that, to take up our old terminology, the plays are *about* something rather than tell a story. But in fact language in Pinter's plays is an unfailing guide to what is happening. It defines people's nature, their motives, and their social background. The clash between Deeley and the two women may be expressed in the way they use words; but the real nature of this conflict is sexual and social. Pinter employs language in the way Ibsen employs symbols. Words and phrases in his plays are not only means of communication: they are also a system of specific signs. When Gregers Werle in *The Wild Duck* says that he would like to be a clever dog he means something else, and so does Lenny in *The Homecoming* when he asks Teddy whether he can 'detect a certain logical incoherence in the central affirmations of Christian Theism'[140]. The difference is that we need much of the rest of the play to understand what Gregers is after, whereas the alert ear can clearly hear, in Lenny's words, the cunning brutality of the predator.

We might call Pinter's plays closed in the sense that all this can amount to a statement about the world. His characters are constantly on the alert, ready to fend off menaces lurking behind commonplace words, and hidden threats in apparently innocuous situations. This might seem to be Pinter's picture of the world: we know that the world we live in is not entirely like that. This is not the same as saying that Pinter gives us an inaccurate account of the world — which is what we would mean if we were talking in these terms about the plays of, say, Beaumont and Fletcher, or Peter Shaffer. An inaccurate play is an open play which we find does not have the consistency of the world it claims to depict. In the case of Beaumont and Fletcher, and Shaffer, we might say that they sacrifice probability and psychological realism in the interests of theatricality and lyrical eloquence; whereas Pinter's seemingly oblique dialogue roots his characters, with unerring precision, in social and psychological reality. Pinter's characters may initially seem elusive to us, but they do not appear elusive to each other. And since they understand each other, their actions, too, are held together by the logic of personal behaviour. Pinter had a brief early flirtation with the world as a place ruled by mysterious forces in *The Room* and *The Dumb Waiter*; but even in these plays we soon notice how mundanely logical his characters are: how quick they are, for instance, to spot inconsistencies in others. Even *The Dumb Waiter* could be described, without too much exaggeration, as a real situation manipulated by someone with a sadistically bizarre sense of humour.

Pinter's work might appear to belong to closed drama, too, because of its pervasive sense of ritual. A ritual is a ceremonial action: it signifies something other than what is being done. When McCann, in *The Birthday Party*, slowly tears a page of a newspaper into strips, he is performing a ritual of menace. The exchange of songs in *Old Times* is a ritual of erotic boasting. But the most characteristic ritual in Pinter is not so much the action as the big speech. The big speeches of classical drama, including the monologue, served to define and sum up personalities and situations. They were concentrated dramatic statements, delivered at crucial moments, rather like arias in opera. Modern drama has gradually come to dispense with the big speech, (just as modern opera relies much less on the aria): its text has aspired, more and more, to the texture of conversation. Not that the speech disappeared altogether: many of Shaw's characters make them all the time; Strindberg's *The Father* reaches its climax with a speech by the Captain; and even Borkman's lyrical outburst at the end of *John Gabriel Borkman* has the impact of a concentrated speech.

In closed drama the big speech reappears as parody. Perhaps the most famous is Lucky's 'thinking' in *Waiting for Godot*: a speech which, under its demented verbiage, conceals one of the most important ideas in the play — the idea of divine indifference. I say 'conceals' because, unless we know the play well, the speech is impossible to grasp in performance, bearing witness to Beckett's

> dream of an art unresentful of its insuperable indigence and too proud for the farce of giving and receiving.[141]

(This sentence is the apotheosis of monological art.) Plays like *Not I* and *Play* are all one speech (or parallel speeches). The long final speech by Bérenger in Ionesco's *The Killer* is, in its ineffectiveness and sense of futility, almost an anti-speech: its point is that it is not worth making it. (The verbosity of the writing contributes to this, to an extent that Ionesco cannot have intended.)

Pinter has revived the big speech for a specific purpose. The climax of *The Caretaker* is Aston's speech. The play is about solitudes; and this speech, about Ashton's electric shock treatment, is a statement of his complete loneliness. It tells us that he is both beyond help and beyond intimidation. Deeley's speech, near the end of *Old Times*, about the Wayfarers Tavern and the Edgware Road philosophers, is his last throw to assert his mastery, sexual and intellectual, over the two women. Spooner's closing speech in *No Man's Land* is the final attempt of a supplicant to gain a foothold in hostile territory. Lenny, in *The Homecoming*, is one of Pinter's characters (like Mick in *The Caretaker*, Goldberg in *The Birthday Party*, Foster in *No Man's Land*) who are given to long, apparently rambling speeches full of underworld braggadocio, and a recondite, parvenu vocabulary which do not quite come naturally from them. These speeches convey, without openly expressing it, a sense of menace which is intentional on the speaker's part, and of hollow boastfulness which is not.

In closed drama the same function is performed by the dance. I am indebted for this idea, and for some of what I have to say about it, to Frank Kermode's *The Romantic Image*, whose fourth chapter,

'The Dancer', is a meditation on the dancer and the dance as poetic icons in modern literature. Yeats's poetry is one of Kermode's central concerns in this book, and he calls the Dancer

> one of Yeats's great reconciling images, containing life in death, death in life, movement and stillness, action and contemplation, body and soul.[142]

Taken in the late Romantic context which Kermode is looking at, this image of the dancer has among its qualities impersonality, formal and rhythmical perfection, and a sense of passion tinged with sadism. Oscar Wilde's Salome is a representative dancer of this late Romantic spirit. Of course she is a dramatic character, whereas Kermode is more interested in the use of such figures in poetry. We may note, too, that the plot of Wilde's play actually turns on Salome's dancing: it is not only a formal expression of impersonal and sadistic eroticism, but also an example of an art she is clearly good at, and an action she performs for a price. It is both a symbol and a dramatic narrative device, expressive as well as functional, like the dances at the end of Shakespeare's *As You Like It*, and in Act IV of *A Winter's Tale*. In Brecht's *Mother Courage*, Eilif, the elder son, performs a war dance, sabre in hand, to celebrate his latest exploit ('Hungry job cutting down peasants'[143]). This is perfectly in character with Eilif's innocent and thick-witted brutality. (Six scenes later, when he is shot for carrying out the same sort of exploit in peace time, his dance takes on, in retrospect, a horribly ironical significance.) Again, this is a very different kind of dance from that movement of impersonal perfection which Kermode so perceptively analyses. It expresses a specific type of child-like murderousness, set in the concrete context of a particular war. It is both innocent expression and sardonic political comment: Eilif does not understand what it means, but it helps us to understand the play. In Brecht's *Baal*, which is still steeped in the tradition of Expressionism, the dance occurs at a moment of apprehension. This is a dance with a difference. Baal has been on the run since his young mistress Johanna drowned herself and he lost his lodgings. Now he is drinking in a dismal bar, where a beggar tells the story of a man who walked deeper and deeper into the forest to see how independent he was, and ended up crying bitterly on the ground, clutching at the wild, hard roots. Baal glimpses himself in this spare, bleak parable, and he is troubled. The conversation around him is moralising and resigned; he is touched with guilt and a sense of futility, and he sings.

BAAL: (*brutally*)
   Float down the river with rats in your hair. Everything's
   lovely, the sky's still there. (*He gets up, glass in hand*)
   The sky is black! Did that scare you? (*Drums on the
   table*) You have to stand the roundabout. It's wonderful.
   (*He sways*) I want to be an elephant in a circus and pee
   when things go wrong . . . (*He begins to dance and sing*)
   Dance with the wind, poor corpse! Sleep with a cloud,
   you degenerate God![144]

Baal dances because, for the first time in the play, he is beyond
words: he is thrown off-balance by what he probably recognises as
remorse. The dance plays no functional part in the play: Baal's dance
is not as psychologically apt as Eilif's. But the young Brecht is reaching
for something that will express both what Baal feels at that moment,
and what he himself feels about Baal and about life. In its savagery
and pain, Baal's dance sums up Brecht's picture of the world.

In the same way, the hero of Ernst Toller's *Hinkemann*, a soldier
who has returned sexually crippled from the Great War, performs a
wild and violent dance in front of a little bronze Priapus he has just
bought and put on the mantelpiece, with a lighted candle next to it.
The dance and its setting are as clumsy and as crushingly emotional
as the whole play: Hinkemann, having lost his manhood and his
self-respect, has now been betrayed by his wife, and he is expressing
an unspeakable desperation. Toller is in no doubt that there is
something self-lacerating about his hero: his wife Greta might have
become unfaithful to him out of simple sexual hunger, but she has
tried hard to hold on to him, and it was partly his crushing self-pity
that wore her down. It would not be quite true to say that Hinkemann is expressing something that is entirely beyond words, for
Toller is all too able to make his characters express everything he
wants to; but there is something in the dance that sums up things
not openly said. Performed in front of what is meant to remind us of
an altar, it is a horrendous comment, at once grossly obvious and
moving, on a pointless sacrifice. In the same way John Arden, who
seems to have learnt all that was worth learning from Expressionist
drama, just as he learnt all the important lessons that Brecht had to
teach, made the central moment of *Serjeant Musgrave's Dance* a
dance of frustrated anger and conviction.

Another of Toller's plays, *Masses and Men*, includes a kind of
dance of death in one of its dream scenes, set in a prison yard. A

man, condemned to death and with a rope around his neck, asks as a last favour to be allowed to dance:

> Dance is the kernel
> Of all things:
> Life, born of a dance,
> Urges to dance —
> Dance of desire,
> Dance of the years
> And dance of death.[145]

He and the other condemned then dance with the sentries to the sounds of a concertina played by a character called the Nameless. He is the sinister antagonist of Toller's revolutionary heroine, and throughout the play he embodies the kind of doctrinaire ruthlessness which, for Toller, undermined the true revolution from within. This dance of death, then, is more than a ritual farewell to life: it is an expression of a larger anger and horror. Toller is telling us that the tune played by this merciless demagogue is the death-song of the revolution. And it is deeply characteristic of Toller, who had a great deal to say but limited dramatic talent for saying it, that he had to employ a dream-scene to create this picture of apocalyptic politics. Leonid Andreyev, whose *The Life of Man* (1906) both draws on Symbolism and foreshadows Expressionism with its attempt at moral profundity and its reliance on the impassioned cliché, expresses both the prosperity and the downfall of his anonymous hero in a dance. This device is entirely appropriate to a play where the scenery, and the grouping of the huge cast, are both more important than the deliberately banal dialogue. (We may note in passing that Andreyev indicates the Man's cocksure prosperity by a lengthy description of his house in the stage directions. These contain the following solemn reservation: 'Yet the pictures are but few in number, and confined to the side walls.')

For Yeats the dance expressed the divine as well as the menacing; and he found its most appealing expression in the Japanese Nōh plays. He was introduced to them by Ezra Pound, who had been editing the papers of the Japanese scholar Ernest Fenollosa; and one of Fenollosa's remarks that must have greatly appealed to Yeats was that whereas in Greek drama

> the chorus danced and the god was represented by an actor . . .
> in Japan the god danced alone.[146]

Accordingly, there is an apartness, a sense of a distant, almost indifferent divinity, in the dances of some of Yeats's plays. He, as well as some of the Expressionist playwrights, reminds us that the dance was also one of Nietzsche's favourite figures: in his mature writings it expresses excitement, superiority, apartness and intellectual passion. And the interest in the impersonal expressiveness of the dance at the turn of the century went hand in hand with an interest in the spiritual expressiveness of marionettes and masks. The writings of Gordon Craig and Arthur Symons are both required reading to a full understanding of Yeats's plays.

Perhaps the most characteristic Yeatsian dance is the dance of the Guardian of the Well in *At the Hawk's Well*, the first of the Cuchulain plays. Cuchulain comes to the well because its water, which bubbles up from the ground only at rare intervals, is said to give eternal life to whoever drinks of it. An Old Man has already waited fifty years for it to flow. When the Guardian of the Well gives a cry like a hawk, Cuchulain is surprised because he has heard it before.

> As I came hither
> A great grey hawk swept down out of the sky,
> And though I have good hawks, the best in the world
> I had fancied, I have not seen its like. It flew
> As though it would have torn me with its beak,
> Or blinded me, smiting with that great wing.
> I had to draw my sword to drive it off,
> And after that it flew from rock to rock.
> I pelted it with stones, a good half-hour,
> And just before I had turned the big rock there
> And seen this place, it seemed to vanish away.[147]

There is something deeply ambiguous about this hawk: it both threatens Cuchulain and lures him on. The Old Man thinks the Guardian is possessed by

> The Woman of the Sidhe herself,
> The mountain witch, the unappeasable shadow.[148]

The play's climax comes when the Guardian rises and, bearing a shape suggesting a hawk, begins to dance. It is an eerie moment. The Old Man falls asleep and Cuchulain, following the dancing figure, leaves the stage in a daze. When the Old Man wakes he finds that the water had flowed and dried up again while he slept. Cuchulain, on coming back, finds not only that he missed the rising of the water but that the hawk woman has roused his enemies, the fierce mountain women, and he goes off to a life of fighting.

On the face of it the Guardian's dance is a dramatic device: its purpose is to protect the life-giving water by casting a spell on both men. Yet the Guardian herself both dances and does not dance: her body is not her own now, because she is possessed by the same spirit who lured Cuchulain to the place in the shape of a hawk. It is this sinister ambiguity which makes me reluctant to accept Richard Ellmann's interpretation that the hawk 'symbolises logic and abstract thought'[149]. The point of the hawk is that it evades such precise interpretation. Yeats is describing a world in which the same mysterious force both tempts us to find out the secrets of life and frustrates our attempts when we try. Cuchulain's defiance is as vain as the Old Man's dogged persistence; and the fact that the former is ignorant of the real power of the Sidhe and the latter all too familiar with it makes no difference to either of them. The well is like the gate in the priest's parable in Kafka's *The Trial*: it stands for the most profound human values (knowledge, eternal life), which draw us to themselves but remain unattainable. Cuchulain's decision to fight rather than wait for the water to rise again amounts to a choice of action in preference to eternity; yet, like Nietzsche's Zarathustra and Proust's Narrator, he experiences his revelation in a state of trance.

The play ends with a song of five terse stanzas: a lament for the weakness of fallible humanity. It is a lyrical meditation on the bitterness of all action and the futility of all but a homely existence, thus recommending a way of life which neither of the two human characters follow. The play is grave, beautiful and nihilistic; and the Guardian's dance is its most complete expression. For here the dancer is not really the one who dances; and the spell cast by the dance cancels out that same supernatural aid which brought Cuchulain to the well. This dance expresses the authority of something powerful, supernatural and hostile; something that annuls all action; something that is beyond questioning. The Guardian never speaks. Pure movement stands for what is beyond words and beyond human will.

In *The King of the Great Clock Tower*, written eighteen years later, a Stroller comes to court because he is in love with the Queen whom he has never seen. The King, after a year of marriage, still does not know the Queen's name; she, in turn, does not speak to him. The Stroller is disappointed in the Queen when he sees her, but is determined to go on singing her praise; and he announces that the Queen will dance for him and then he will sing to her. The King has him beheaded for insolence; but the Queen dances, taking the severed head on her shoulder, and the head, with the voice of one of the Attendants, sings to her. This is a drama of personal tensions which never come close enough to each other to become relation-ships. Yeats's stage directions call for an inner curtain with a stencilled pattern of dancers on it, and for the Queen to have 'a beautiful impassive mask'[150]. Clearly, the dance is the culmination of this savage and lyrical play. The Queen, like the Guardian, never speaks. She embodies a feeling which can hardly be called love: it is impersonal, remote and sadistic — but then the Stroller's love for her had nothing personal about it either. Both of them are un-appeasable shadows. The dance is Yeats's picture of love in the world: the dead being kissed by the indifferent living.

Finally, when Lucky dances in *Waiting for Godot*, the dance which he performs without enthusiasm, or indeed a show of any other feeling, means nothing. Vladimir and Estragon surmise that it might be called 'The Scapegoat's Agony' or 'The Hard Stool', as if they were trying to grasp the subject of an abstract painting by giving it a title. According to Pozzo the dance is called 'The Net', and signifies that Lucky is entangled in one. These widely differing interpretations suggest that none of them is correct; and the pre-ceding dialogue has already indicated that Lucky's accomplishments as a dancer are meagre. The weary little pantomime takes its place in the play, Beckett's picture of the world, as a wordless expression of his aesthetic which he himself has summed up, in an often-quoted sentence:

> The expression that there is nothing to express, nothing with which to express, nothing from which to express, no power to express, no desire to express, together with the obligation to express.[151]

CHARACTER, MORALITY, ACTION

The first draft of *At the Hawk's Well* ends with the words;

> Accursed the life of man — between passion and emptiness
> what he longs for never comes. All his days are a preparation
> for what never comes.[152]

The word 'accursed' would be entirely out of place in the play as we know it, with its measured and detached lyricism; but otherwise this cancelled passage contains the same sense of passionate aridity. When I speak of aridity I do not comment on the poetic achievement of the play: I mean that Yeats sees the world as an arid place. But the distinction is not a simple one. The play is a moral comment on an amoral world. The play's world is a moral no man's land, but Yeats's description of it as such is a moral act.

The relationship of closed drama to morality is made more complex by the fact that all drama is to a great extent impersonal. When Yeats wrote of 'Character isolated by a deed'[153], he empha-sised the apartness of the dramatist and his creation from each other: an apartness that is usually greater than in the novel. In older drama the connection between moral intention and moral content is more intimate. The comedies of Jonson and Molière are moral acts: they concern themselves with a world which has a moral basis. Many of their characters are immoral and are savagely exposed as such. Wedekind stated that when he wrote his Lulu plays he

> wanted to exclude all ideas which are logically untenable, such
> as love, loyalty, gratitude[154]

— yet all three have made their way into the play, albeit more honoured in the breach than in the observance.

The world of *King Lear* is one where the immoral threatens to engulf the moral. The play contains moral lessons about the nature of trust and credulity, generosity and loyalty. Shakespeare may not have written the play expressly to convey such lessons, but they can be validly concluded from what happens in it. The result is not a guide to conduct ('be as nice to your illegitimate children as to your lawful heir'), but a weighing up and affirmation of values such as fairness and justice. Shakespeare makes sure that we do not regard these values as abstractions: they have to do with the actual destruction or survival of people. Indeed, they are values rather than merely ideas precisely because they are established or, as with

Edmund's values, discredited in the pressure of events and at the cost of personal honour, happiness or life. The storm scene may 'feel' like something out of Beckett, but only if we isolate it from the events that brought it about. Put the scene in context, and Lear is no longer a victim of the universe which is how, at first, he sees himself. His claim, that he is 'more sinn'd against than sinning', may not be justifiable, but the matter becomes open to argument. There is no morality without context. We approach plays as moral beings because we live in a world where conduct and values are judged by moral standards.

I repeat these commonplaces to emphasise the inherent difficulty of encountering and evaluating the amoral, which I take to be the ethical equivalent of weightlessness. Camus's *The Outsider*, which is a portrait of an amoral man, is a profoundly moral work; but Gide's *The Vatican Cellars*, which is a deliberate attempt to write an amoral book about an amoral man, is a failure because ultimately Gide cannot do without morality. When his hero Lafcadio saves people from fires from no motive at all, that is, gratuitously, for amoral reasons, the world remains relatively indifferent; but when he equally amorally kills someone, the world catches up with him and he is doomed. Gide is equally fascinated by all amoral acts, but the world, in which his story has perforce to unfold, is not.

It is this difficulty of encountering the amoral which lies at the heart of our initial difficulty with closed drama. We assume that we are having a moral experience, but also sense that the people in the play are not. This is rather like the way we react to the closed play as a story: we can see that things are happening, and yet we feel that we do not understand what is going on. This is because we live in, and are conditioned by, a dynamic world where things happen, and happen with causes and consequences; so that we are naturally baffled by a play in which things happen with neither. A spectator who accepts a closed play on its own terms is therefore someone who already sees the world as a place which lacks the known dynamics of life — or is at least willing to suspend his belief in them for the duration of the performance.

When we say that the characters of a closed play do not seem to have a moral experience, we do not mean that there is nothing good or bad about them, but that they exist in an amoral situation. Vladimir and Estragon, for example, are clearly friends rather than enemies; though in the context of the play this friendship has a limited value. It is based on need, rather than loyalty or affection: it could not be compared with the attachment of Kent to Lear. But then Kent is part of a world where disinterested personal loyalty, or the lack of it, distinguishes people from each other, the very idea being conditioned by a causal way of thinking. (Compare the unselfish loyalty of Kent with the time-serving loyalty of Oswald.) And all such ideas about loyalty are part of the coherence of things, which is what we conceive of as the moral world.

It is precisely this coherence of things in drama that Brecht was impatient with. He complained in *The Messingkauf Dialogues* that in what he called Aristotelian plays

> the audience's deception with regard to the way in which the incidents shown on the stage come about and take place in real life is helped by the fact that the story's presentation forms an indivisible whole. Its details cannot be compared one by one with their corresponding parts in real life. Nothing must be taken 'out of its context' in order, say, to set it in the context of reality.

Note Brecht's intellectual sleight-of-hand: he makes us assume automatically that an act of deception is taking place. This allows him to present himself as a liberator. 'The answer,' he goes on

> lies in the alienating style of acting. In this the story line is a broken one; the single whole is made up of independent parts which can and must be compared with the corresponding part-incidents in real life. This way of acting draws all its force from comparisons with reality; in other words, it is continually drawing attention to the causality of the incidents reproduced.[155]

This sounds obscure because it is the logic neither of life nor of a play: Brecht's perversity as a commentator can be seen as a case of a logical mind trying to operate according to arbitrary rules. It has often been said that his best plays invalidate some of his theories: the case of Eilif in *Mother Courage*, which we have just discussed, is a case in point. The Eilif who gains praise for his brutality is the same man who later gets shot for committing a similar act of brutality at the wrong time. These are not 'part-incidents'. There is continuity here. Brecht's lesson for us is that killing innocent people is always wrong: it is only war which can make it a virtue. War, and what Brecht tells us about it, form the context, the indivisible whole, which allows us to judge Eilif; and what we think of him is part of what we think about the whole play. Eilif may have been deceived, but we are not: Brecht himself has seen to that.

We can see what happens when he practises his theories by looking at *The Good Person of Setzuan*. Its theme is first stated by one of the Gods: 'no one can be good for long if goodness is not in demand.'[156] This is amplified later, in the Song of Defencelessness, sung by Shen Te:

> The good can't defend themselves and
> Even the gods are defenceless.
>
> You can only help one of your luckless brothers
> By trampling down a dozen others.[157]

What Brecht is implying is that the good in people is weak and the evil in them is strong. This is not the same thing as saying that good people are weak and evil people strong (an idea which is at the bottom of Edward Bond's plays); yet the play ends up demonstrating just that. It is entirely Brecht's fault. This is because he is doing to a character what, in *The Messingkauf Dialogues*, he advocates doing to plays: he is taking a person's qualities (good and self-sacrificing, evil and ruthless) out of their context, presenting them as two separate characters, and then comparing them with corresponding qualities in 'real life'. We could call this process a dispersal of character. It is a self-defeating process.

It is not only that in 'real life' the purely good and the purely bad cannot be distinguished like this. It is also that we cannot make the claims and criticisms of real life when we are dealing with half a person. Neither Shen Te, nor her *alter ego* Shui Ta, are in a proper sense responsible for what they do; and when, at the end, responsibility is shifted on to the kind of world we live in, we must ask whether this world was not after all created by people who are both Shen Te and Shui Ta. But the fact is that Brecht is interested, not so much in such people, as in their Shen Te-ness and Shui Ta-ness as independent and identifiable forces. For him, the Shui Ta in us all is responsible for all the evils of the world; and to the extent that the play presents this as an irrefutable, unquestionable truth, it is a closed play. Brecht ducks the moral and artistic responsibility which the author of *Major Barbara*, for example, confronted head on: that of putting before us someone who is a Shen Te and a Shui Ta at the same time. For such a character is open to our questions. We can ask how Undershaft, being a civilised man and a kindly father, can make his living out of selling lethal weapons. Through such a character the play, and the world, too, are open to our questions: it is natural to go on to ask whether a nation's defence needs people who can overcome or ignore their own native kindliness; or indeed whether nations need defence. But we cannot question Brecht's Shui Ta because he is simply the Exploiter: a type, a function, a political version of one of Ben Jonson's humours.

It is no good saying that Shui Ta is a dramatisation of an aspect of Shen Te's personality: we are asked to believe that to other characters in the play 'he' actually appears as Shui Ta, and if Shen Te herself suddenly started behaving like 'him' it would, in the terms of this play, have no effect. Conversely, if a real Shui Ta had been the hero of the play, then his transformation into a Shen Te would have simply made him look feeble. Brecht is asking questions typical of open drama: why is society the way it is? What is the nature of generosity, exploitation, selfishness? Is unselfish goodness actually relevant to the way people live? But he then fends off any real answers by putting at the centre of his play a dramatic device which is simply not open to questions. In the same way Toller, in *Transfiguration*, presents characters in some scenes 'with the features of' his hero Friedrich, which only weakens our sense of him as a person and an accountable moral being. (Nor is it clear how this can be staged without confusion.) The character becomes detached from his own personal existence. Toller is *stating* Friedrich's experience, instead of showing him having it.

Character is vital to open drama. The truth of this was summed up by Freud when he said that it was natural for man to want to personify anything he wanted to understand. Applying this to Brecht, we might say that in *The Good Person of Setzuan* he dramatised, or personified, aspects of a character rather than a whole complex character, because what he wanted to understand was tendencies rather than people. In other words he wrote parables rather than stories. The paradox of the parable is that it is a moral form of expression which tends often to subject character to its purpose: an open form working with the methods of closed art. Brecht's *Man Equals Man* is a good example of this, because it is actually a parable about the subjection and dispensability of human character. Brecht is interested in how and why ordinary people can be transformed into killing machines; but the result is a play which shows you what happens without showing you how.

The huge comic potential of the play should not blind us to the fact that, as far as Brecht is concerned, something very serious is at stake. The subject is the obliteration of the identity of a human being. The trouble is that, in Galy Gay, Brecht has given us a human being who shows little resistance to having his identity obliterated. He, too, has an 'inherent inexperience'. It is not that, as the three soldiers think, he cannot say no: for just as they say this, he has very dexterously said no to the solicitations of Widow Begbick. It is rather that there is something lackadaisical about him, even to the point of dimness. If, at the end of scene three, once he had helped the soldiers out of trouble, he did not, rather improbably, stay behind, thinking he might be needed again, there would be no play. And if he were not so preposterously gullible, he could not be persuaded to get involved in the allegedly lucrative business of the selling of the elephant. The difference is between creating a character with suitable motivations and creating one who is suitable to one's own. Brecht wants to warn us about how easy it is to get caught up in evil, but he makes his case through a character with whom few of us would identify ourselves, and who therefore does not serve as a warning to us. Compare Galy Gay with Jaroslav Hasek's Schweik, and you will see how Brecht avoided the challenge he had set himself. The play is weakened by having, not a character to demonstrate a conflict, but a cipher to make a point.

Galy Gay's improbability is underlined by the contrasting figure of Sergeant Fairchild, known as Bloody Five. If Galy Gay does not really care much about what people call him, Bloody Five cares about nothing else. He confesses that his manhood makes him weak in Widow Begbick's presence, and when she challenges him to pluck it out he goes off and castrates himself with a pistol shot because, with his reputation as Bloody Five, he cannot afford to be known to be weak. There is a certain amount of grim and implausible fun in all this; but what it reminds one of, unexpectedly, is Jean Genet's *The Balcony*. Here Roger, the leader of the failed revolution, comes to Madame Irma's brothel, or House of Illusions, to impersonate the Chief of Police; and he castrates himself to express the impotence both of the revolution and of state power. The comparison with Brecht may sound fanciful, but the two playwrights have a surprising amount in common. Both are fascinated by the condition of men who have power; both are interested in theatricality as an art of deception; and both are drawn to the idea of character and appearance. *Man Equals Man* could be used as a subtitle for *The Balcony*, for Genet's thesis is that power resides in mere impersonation;

indeed, that power is not real, and the thirst for it is not wholly satisfied, until a sense of impersonation gives it the pleasure of physical splendour and the satisfaction of pride. Genet is interested in the nature of human identity and, like Brecht, he bends his entire intellectual energy and emotional fervour on constructing a dramatic argument which shows how fallacious that identity is. The characters of *The Balcony* not only do not resist: they seem to yearn to lose what is barely discernible as their character in the insubstantiality of appearance.

Genet extends what might have been a psychological *grand guignol*, along the lines of *The Maids*, into a dramatic metaphor of politics and power: he applies the technique of a static image to a subject which is by definition dynamic and causal. This is why the play loses power and conviction after the first four scenes in the brothel: the rest is an animated argument about the power of appearance and the appearance of power, which has limited value as politics, and almost no conviction as drama. The Bishop is in reality a man who works for the gas board, but it would be pointless to ask how he can afford to come regularly to what is clearly an expensive establishment. He is obviously not meant to have a life, only a significance. As for living, Genet might be saying, our metaphors will do it for us. If in *Man Equals Man* character aspires to the condition of a didactic example, in *The Balcony* it aspires to the condition of a poetic image. In this sense both are closed plays, for both playwrights severely limit the scope of our questioning. In both plays, but especially in *The Balcony*, the central image which carries the meaning is presented rather than explored. To return to Martin Esslin's remark, it is true that such plays are more interested in situation than in event. But plays, as we have seen, are by definition events; and the closed play's lack of interest in character weakens that sense of dynamism, that sense of an event, which is the essential quality of all drama.

One of the reasons why Surrealist drama produced so little that is worth reading (let alone staging) is that Surrealist writers had no interest in events. The Surrealist film succeeded because, being almost devoid of 'human interest', that is to say, recognisable stories, it could exploit the imaginative dynamism of visual images. Human beings are but one of the elements of these images. The human and social connotations in films like *L'Age d'Or*, *Le Chien Andalou*, or *The Shell and the Clergyman* is almost nil: they do not create events in the sense of things which happen and then cause other things to happen. We see some recognisable social settings, but without a sense of society. We are in a dislocated world which the camera welds into visual unity. Now a play is much more handicapped than a film if it has a total lack of interest in events; and Surrealist playwrights display an adolescent hostility to the tedious tendency of events to form themselves into plots. The Surrealist playwright wants to shock by disrupting this process, and he is thwarted by the fact that he is working in an art form of which events are the essence. A play like Tristan Tzara's *The Gas Heart*, which has for characters parts of the human body such as Eye, Mouth, Neck and Eyebrow, but who never say anything that has to do with their identities as anatomical functions, seems to have been written for no other purpose than to show dislocation in action.

Dislocation is also at the heart of Surrealist painting. But it expresses itself in a recondite visual language, which means that we can learn how to 'read' the pictures of Miró, Dali, Ernst or Magritte. We can ask what they 'mean': windows and field guns, limp watches and ants have a significance, and they give these pictures a language, however private. The Surrealist play lacks such language: it exists in the act of dislocation. If a play is a story which tells itself by taking place, the Surrealist play might be called the true anti-play, for it is an 'event' the 'story' of which is that nothing is taking place. Tzara's play is not held together by images, and there is no dialogue in any normally comprehensible sense. Here is a typical exchange:

MOUTH: I have made a great deal of money.
NOSE: Thank you not bad.[158]

Sometimes what sounds like a recognisable note is struck:

EYE: Clytemnestra the wind is blowing ... Have you felt the horrors of war?[159]

Set in the frivolity of such deliberate dislocations, this is clearly meant as an affront to the conventional morality of the time (the play was written in 1920). Indeed, logic is identified as Tzara's Public Enemy Number One in the following brief meditation:

EYEBROW: 'Where', 'how much', 'why', are monuments. As, for example, Justice. What beautifully regular functioning, practically a nervous tic or a religion.[160]

This is pure intellectual hectoring. The idea of any critical engagement with such a play is too absurd to need going into, and nothing was further from Tzara's mind than to ask for such a response. The man who created the phrase 'the dictatorship of the spirit' knew better than to provide us with an opening. Ionesco, the principal heir of the Surrealists, takes the view that 'plots are uninteresting', and therefore, he has decided,

> it is my dream to rediscover the rhythms of drama in their purest state, and to reproduce them in the form of pure scenic movement. I should like to be able to create an abstract, a non-representational theatre.[161]

In other words, Ionesco's ambition was to write a completely closed play; and in so far as he succeeded as a dramatist, his success can be measured by the failure of that ambition.

Ionesco's phrase 'pure scenic movement' recalls Gordon Craig, and painters like Malevich and Lissitsky, with their attempts to create a sense of pure movement unrelated to the context of objects. And indeed, the most 'closed' play known to me is by a painter: Kandinsky's *The Yellow Sound*, which he subtitled 'A Stage Composition'[162]. This is probably the nearest anyone has ever got to Ionesco's dream of an 'abstract' theatre: dramatic rhythm in its purest state. It has events: the shapes we see on the stage move, change shape and colour, to the accompaniment of music. The Prelude, with its 'indistinct chorus from the orchestra' and its impression of a 'dark-blue dawn', recalls the opening of *The Rhinegold*, while the apocalyptic visual effects of the final scene remind one of the ending of *Götterdämmerung*. There are even figures, clad in various colours, who utter sounds and occasionally fragments of sentences. These things *happen*; but they are not dramatic events, because there are no people to provide a context in which we can make sense of them. Drama is relations in action; and neither relations nor dramatic action has any meaning without character.

Nor has character any meaning except as expressed in action and relations. The Student in Strindberg's *The Ghost Sonata* is not a character we can question: he is Strindberg's means of leading us into his moral parable. We would find it difficult to think of him as someone who, in some hypothetical past, might have behaved differently. In any case, Strindberg drops a heavy hint that the whole play is happening somewhere other than in the real world: for if the Student's description of how he had saved a child from a collapsing house is correct, he ought really to be dead. This would explain the play's otherwise puzzling title, and its atmosphere of elaborate insubstantiality.

The story is a kind of unfolding: it is the revelation of what happened to its characters in the past. But though these people are all prisoners of their past deeds, their actual past is unspecific. Behind its technical virtuosity and its elaborate, sometimes faintly comical symbolism, the play is like the aftermath of a conventional melodrama of stock characters. What matters is not their actual past and what they did, but the way they are bound and fettered by the consequences. Strindberg is more interested in their guilt than in its cause; more in the play as a picture than in the story that lies behind it or in any story that could follow from it. Appropriately, the final stage direction reads:

> The room disappears. Böcklin's painting of the 'Island of the Dead' appears in the background. Soft music, calm and gently melancholy, is heard from the island outside.[163]

The moral import of *The Ghost Sonata* is not unlike that of *A Dream Play*: 'Alas for mankind!' Artaud, who composed a bizarre production plan for it, noted shrewdly that death is the only deliverance the play provides, and that this Buddhist thought is one of its faults. He added perceptively that the ending

> may also clarify the play for those in the audience who would be frightened by the purely unconscious.[164]

What Artaud means is that the play's content is futile suffering, and the ending glorifies it by softening it. And indeed, it is one of the weaknesses of Strindberg's plays that in them suffering in itself acquires a moral significance. In *To Damascus* everyone suffers because most of the characters are either alter egos of the Stranger or are linked to him by love or marriage. All this suffering is then sanctified by the Stranger's religious and mythological self-identifications: he sees himself at various times as Christ, Prometheus, Orpheus — and of course, as the title implies, St Paul, the misguided persecutor who becomes one of the chosen, and is persecuted in turn. He also sees himself as Cain, with his alter egos as his victims: one of them, significantly, has a scar on his forehead. This heavy-handed symbolism tells us that those who suffer and those who cause suffering are essentially the same — rather as Artaud declared it in *The Cenci*. This gives the whole trilogy a moral circularity which is entirely consistent with the fact that its liberator

liberates no one. *To Damascus* is monological art at its most
obsessional. Its pervasive sense of guilt and suffering is made unreal
by the insignificant nature of the past events that caused them: the
trilogy is based on a sense of moral questioning which is never
fulfilled. The revelation St Paul received on the way to Damascus
spurred him to action; for the Stranger there is neither an actual
revelation nor any action, but only a growing sense that human
existence is unendurable, and that the only solution is to escape into
a life of resignation and sorrowful but self-righteous contemplation.
It is nothing more than redemption by resignation. I cannot think of
another work of moral literature which ends up by so completely
contradicting its own title.

The point about Strindberg likening the Stranger to Christ is that
he seizes on only one aspect of him. 'He suffers for all mankind,'[165]
the Lady says, which might be taken to mean that the Stranger's
sufferings represent those of all humanity. This is a large claim, for
it would mean that this unstable neurotic, tormented by a monstrously exaggerated sense of guilt, stands for us all. The words
might also mean that the Stranger's sufferings will in some way help
others: but this is clearly untrue. He helps no one in the play; and
he teaches us, the spectators, nothing about our lives, since his own
is represented not through experience but through reflection. The
Stranger is Strindberg's picture of man, and, like the state of anxiety
which defines his character, he is beyond questioning. And the world
of *To Damascus* is a closed world because, to the extent that it is a
projection of the Stranger's mind, it is a world ruled entirely by
anxiety.

Strindberg sees the Stranger as Christ simply because he suffers:
the redeemer as victim. This is as one-sided as Wagner's presentation of Parsifal: for suffering in itself no more makes you a
redeemer than innocence. Even Toller's Hinkemann does not really
earn his comparison to Christ: he has indeed suffered, but merely as
a helpless instrument and victim of higher powers, and not as a
conscious agent of redemption. Christ knew He was the Redeemer
all along; the suffering Christ-figures of Strindberg and others are
only made to appear so when they are in trouble. But morality in
drama, as in real life, is character in action. A play like Toller's *Transfiguration* has greater moral authenticity than *To Damascus*, not
because its subject is public while Strindberg's is private, but because
its hero, the saintly and tormented Friedrich, himself experiences the horrors of war, and this contributes to his transfiguration

from anxious patriot to unselfish revolutionary leader. Yet even Toller is obsessed by the idea of the suffering hero as Christ: in Scene IX, significantly entitled 'Death and Resurrection', we see a Prisoner (again 'with Friedrich's features') lying at the bottom of a staircase, 'his head flung back, his arms flung out as though he were crucified'[166]. We have no idea why the Prisoner/Friedrich has been brought here: in the previous scene he was arrested by a character called the Night Visitor, as abruptly and without explanation as Joseph K. in *The Trial*. Nor do we know why he killed himself, except that when the Warder taunts him that he broke the Church's commandment, he replies:

PRISONER: What do you know about it, brother?
It is so far beyond all good and evil,
Repentance, heavenly recompense.
I heard a voice; it said: —
All, all deluded;
He was not nailed upon the Cross by men,
He crucified himself.[167]

Thus, for Toller, Christ's crucifixion loses its essential moral content and becomes a Nietzschean metaphor of self-sacrifice; and Friedrich, whose name may not be a coincidence, duly turns into a benevolent Socialist Superman. In Scene XII we see him (that is, we yet again see 'a man with Friedrich's features') climbing a precipitous rock with his friend: a scene whose narcissistic and artificial sense of danger unmistakably recalls *Zarathustra*. The friend warns 'Friedrich' that up there no one will hear him, but 'Friedrich' replies:

The mighty walls of rock rejoice to hear
The sound of shouting voices
And echo them in joyful repetition.[168]

There is a breathless, solipsistic excitement about all this, which Nietzsche would have recognised, but which is totally contradicted in the next, and final, scene. Here Friedrich, again like Zarathustra, addresses people at noon in the market place; but, quite unlike Zarathustra, he reminds them of their common humanity and rouses them to revolution. They respond with fervour; and so, the personal morality of action goes, for Toller, hand in hand with the impersonal and entirely private amorality of the visionary.

The idea of redemption and self-redemption haunts all Expressionist drama. Take Claudel's early play, *Tête d'Or* (1889), which is like some monstrous passion play written by Nietzsche, and which, like Villiers's *Axël*, has both Expressionist and Symbolist qualities. Its hero, Cébès, complains that his companions who watch with him cannot keep awake by his side. They mutter that he is a bad king and curse him; but the accusation is never substantiated. Claudel is clearly on Cébès's side; and when Cébès dies in the rugged mountains of the Caucasus, calling out to God and wondering when he will appear again, we realise that, once more, the image of the Redeemer (combined with that of Prometheus) is being used to convey a sense of heroic but amoral suffering.

The Billionaire's Son, in Kaiser's *Gas I*, too, presents himself as a saviour of humanity in the inhumanity of the industrial world: when the workers fail to respond to his vision, he feels 'Ultimately alone, like all who tried to become one with all men!'[169] But this Christ-like attitude is as unconvincing as the Stranger's in *To Damascus*; and the sense of failure it conveys is made unreal by the fact that we never see any real men, only impersonal crowds.

Kaiser's morality here, like the morality of Villiers's *Axël* and Claudel's *Tête d'Or*, resembles the morality of science fiction. A cosmic confrontation takes place: the writers face ultimate values in the context of an improbable event, preferably on a vast scale. The effect is often like a sermon: a moral imagination is at work, but it is weakened by the very size and improbability of what is happening. Classical science fiction, like Mary Shelley's *Frankenstein* or Stevenson's *Dr Jekyll and Mr Hyde*, takes us artfully into the improbable by first rooting its stories in a recognisable, even narrow world. They appeal irresistibly to our moral sense as well as our imagination, because we can question each step the narrative takes. We are, paradoxically, in an open world. By contrast, the Billionaire's Son in Kaiser is the hero of a cosmic event. We know that the plant makes gas, but the way in which the product is said to fuel the industry of the entire world remains obscure and is indeed beside the point. Kaiser conveys a sense of conflict on a vast scale, to which such details are immaterial. His concerns are profoundly moral, but the way he goes about them finally eludes moral inquiry.

In *Gas II*, where the Billionaire's Son becomes the Billionaire-Worker, we find him battling with the Engineer in furious debate for the soul of the workers. The workers are there only as a faceless crowd; their function is to be swayed in alternate directions, and they end up, predictably, agreeing to their own destruction. Unlike Toller, who is a late-born Romantic, Kaiser takes an aristocratic view of the human crowd; but for both of them political drama is a drama of leaders. The same is true, for example, of Walter Hasenclever's *Antigone*; and when, at the end of that play, the crowd takes over, it is as an impersonal force rather than a collection of individuals. In such dramas of redemption it is always the soul of the leaders that is lost or saved.

If morality in drama is character in action, we come to the heart of a play by asking: what is the purpose of its action? What does it achieve?

The action of a play is the organisation of its events. Surrealist drama, for example, is closed drama because it has neither character nor action: it is pure event which is as contradictory and as difficult to grasp as the 'purely human' of Wagner's theories, or the purely visual pursued by the Cubist painters and their followers. What we know as Expressionist plays have the moral inspiration of open drama, but they are closed plays to the extent that their characters lack accountability: they are part of a passionately felt, personally inspired, but impersonally presented vision. Plays like Kaiser's *Gas* make their moral point by presenting an action that fails. The Billionaire and his Son are both on a hopeless quest: this failure is what the play is about. Strindberg's *To Damascus* is both a quest and a flight: the Stranger is both fleeing from his past and searching for his salvation: he tells the Confessor that he seeks 'death without dying'. Hence the pervasively static quality of this vast and verbose trilogy. The Daughter in *A Dream Play* and the Student in *The Ghost Sonata* are also on quests that fail: the sense of unalterable human misery suffuses both plays so much that there is virtually no sense of progression — even in *The Ghost Sonata* where we actually make discoveries about people. Like the trilogy, both plays are *statements* of human misery: pictures of the world. The static sense of the *Damascus* trilogy is strengthened by the fact that the moral argument of each part turns on a sense of recognition which is sudden, irrational and inexplicable: a transfiguration without cause. Such recognitions are at the heart of mystical poetry, but they make for a very special kind of theatre. A moral transfiguration without cause is, in the theatre at least, a closed event.

Such a closed event is the victory of the Demogorgon in Act Three of Shelley's *Prometheus Unbound*: an event which transfigures the play and, on Shelley's reading of the legend, the world. Yet in dramatic terms it is not at all clear what has happened: there is no explanation in the text for the sudden fall of Jupiter. M.H. Abrams argues that Demogorgon is

> postulated . . . as the course of events which is in itself purpose-less and amoral, but carries out the ineluctable consequences of man's decisions or acts;

and that his victory represents Shelley's conviction, that

> man is ultimately the agent of his own fall, the tyrant over himself, his own avenger and his own potential redeemer.[170]

This could be summed up by saying that man is his own fate: a conclusion which we reached after our reading of Artaud. But what Professor Abrams's cogently presented case ignores is that the story of *Prometheus Unbound* is a moral argument, not an amoral vision; and that the achievement of a moral end by the amoral means of an inexplicable event is both dramatically and morally feeble.

Another kind of closed event occurs when we are asked to accept a moral event for the wrong reason. When, in Kaiser's *The Burghers of Calais*, the town is finally saved, the emotional action of the play makes us feel that it is the result of Eustache de Saint-Pierre's self-sacrifice: by a great, lyrical paradox, his suicide marks the birth of the new man who will give his life for the community. But in the actual action of the play Calais is saved because the King of England, who is besieging the town, had a son during the night and 'for the sake of this new life'[171], he has decided to relent. In other words, Kaiser presents us with a sense of transfiguration which is false. The town's survival is a merciful coincidence; the death of Eustache actually earned the citizens nothing; and when Jean de Vienne declares that Eustache is the King of England's conqueror, he is putting a moral interpretation on the play which is not borne out by its action. In Toller's *Transfiguration* we witness the horrors of war with Friedrich in the early scenes; but Friedrich's own moment of recognition comes only after the war, when he is visited in his studio by the war's crippled victims; and it is only after the 'Death and Resurrection' scene, another three scenes later, that he is reborn as a revolutionary. The hero of those scenes, as we have seen, was not Friedrich himself but someone 'with his features'. By this device Toller wanted to universalise what happened to Friedrich; but what he actually achieves is a sense of transfiguration which is unconvinc-ing because it is detached from the person who is supposed to experience it, and remote from the experience which caused it.

A quest that both fails and does not fail might seem to be no quest at all; yet such is the subject of Maeterlinck's *The Blue Bird*, whose first performance in London in 1909 prompted Yeats to compare its author to 'a little boy who has jumped up behind a taxi cab and can't get off'[172]. The play is a quest, because the children search for the bird and find it; yet it is not really a quest, because the bird turns out to have been in their house all along. Maeterlinck complicates matters by a speech from the Cat, who claims that all animals and elements possess a soul: man does not know this, but the finding of the Blue Bird will reveal it to him. (It is entirely unclear how this would happen.) But the children know nothing about the soul of things; they are looking for the bird only because the Fairy needs it for her little girl who is ill; and when the Oak challenges Tyltyl that he is after the secret of things, the little boy denies it vigorously. In the end the bird flies away anyway; man finds out nothing about the soul of animals and elements; and we find out nothing about what advantage he would have gained if he had. Maeterlinck's play, with its crushingly obvious symbolism, is the denial of all action. We have simply been told that the solution to all things is in ourselves.

Krapp's Last Tape has been called a Proustian play, but almost the opposite is the case. Marcel, in Proust's novel, has no idea, throughout the events he relates, that he is in search of anything. By contrast, the entire action of *Krapp's Last Tape* is about Krapp's re-experiencing his past and then rejecting it. He knows that the scene in the punt is where his life went wrong: this is precisely why he keeps replaying his account of it. But just as the younger Krapp wanted none of the past, the old man before us rejects it too.

> Be again, be again. (*Pause*) All that old misery. (*Pause*) Once wasn't enough for you. (*Pause*) Lie down across her.[173]

The last words take us back again to the scene in the punt, which Krapp now replays, staring motionlessly before him.

The play ends on a triple sense of loss: for the young Krapp had lost both the chance of a different life and the desire to have it back again; and the old Krapp has lost all desire for the past altogether, except that it is present, unwanted but unforgettable; an obsession, not an achievement. It is not so much that he has regained lost time: rather, it is something that he wants to lose but cannot. Krapp lives in a permanent state of quest in which his past is his present; and when he finds what he thinks he wants he rejects it. Action resents its fulfilment.

Another thing about Krapp is that his quest has no moral purpose. Nor has that of Mouth, the disembodied 'heroine' of *Not I*. Like the three characters of *Play*, Mouth exists in an act of endless recall. Indeed, it can fairly be asked of these characters whether they have any purpose at all. When, in *Play*, the Man asks, 'Am I as much as ... being seen?'[174], he is expressing both the bewilderment of someone who has been trying to conceal part of himself from other people, and the uncertainty we might all feel in the face of all or any experience. He is also expressing that sense of ultimate desertion in the world which was sounded in *Waiting for Godot*:

ESTRAGON: Do you think God sees me?
VLADIMIR: You must close your eyes.
Estragon closes his eyes, staggers worse.[175]

Beckett dramatises this sensation in *Not I*. Mouth's existence has no apparent purpose, and her identity, too, is hedged with doubt. When the play's American director, Alan Schneider, pursued Beckett with inquiries as to 'the birth, life experience and physical circumstances' of Mouth, Beckett put an end to the questioning with a terse note: 'I no more know where she is or why than she does.' As far as he was concerned there was only the text and stage image. 'The rest,' Beckett said, 'is Ibsen.'[176] He may be said to have dramatised one of Nietzsche's most vertiginous ideas, which we discussed in Chapter IV, when Nietzsche questioned, in the phrase 'I think,' the identity of 'I', and the substance of 'think'. For Mouth has a terror of the self she describes — if indeed that self is hers. Her cries of 'who? ... no! ... she!' are screams of rejection from a mind struggling to turn away from its sense of personal experience — which is what having an identity means. If, as we said at the beginning of this book, character means the possibility of an alternative past, Beckett has here created someone whose existence consists in trying not to be a character. It is both a recognisable experience, and a denial of experience. Closed drama could hardly go further and still have human content.

But if Mouth has no purpose, the play has: it is that the Auditor should hear what Mouth says. The Auditor is 'intent on Mouth'[177]; and his arm-movements, which always follow Mouth's cry of 'who? ... no! ... she!', are 'gestures of helpless compassion'[178]. I take him to be a figure of divinity, whose silent presence is unknown to

Mouth, and whose gesture of compassion implies a powerless sense of responsibility. The characters of *Play*, too, are 'victims', in Beckett's own words, in the presence of 'a unique inquisitor'[179], which takes the form of the light that focuses on them. Their compulsive recall is a response to an endless, impersonal summons. But Mouth, like the people in Strindberg's *A Dream Play* and in Andreyev's *Life of Man*, is in the presence of a being who may or may not be responsible but who is certainly helpless, and whose compassion, inevitably, diminishes with time. Isolated from herself, Mouth is also isolated from the moral power that watches her — though not over her. She is 'as much as being seen', but no more. This is the ultimate disconnection. On this reading life is devoid of any significance; and our reaction can only be an unqualified yes or no to that bleak proposition.

Again, if the moral content of drama is defined by character in action, can a closed play have a moral content? Does it embody a moral experience, and if so, of what kind? Moral experience is a process of enrichment. Morality is bound up with experience and experience with actions: we are enriched only when we experience events. And we cannot be enriched without some understanding of what is happening to us. Life and literature are the same in this respect. On this account, no one in *Waiting for Godot* can have a moral experience, for they do not fully understand what is happening to them. Vladimir compares his and Estragon's condition to that of the two thieves on Calvary; but this famous remark has no real basis because they have not committed any crime. Like other characters in closed drama, they suffer without cause. Estragon says that all his life he has compared himself to Christ, an idea which Vladimir finds preposterous and which we, too, find hard to square with Estragon's treatment of Lucky. Is either of them aware of this contradiction? We do not know.

But if the characters of the play do not have a moral experience, we, the audience, do. In other words, *Waiting for Godot* has a moral content in which its characters take no part: something which could not be said about an open play. The moral content resides not in the action but in the writing: the play is suffused with Beckett's immense sympathy for his characters, and the humour with which he sees their situation. Of course, in the last analysis, we cannot separate the writing from the action, for the writing is that in which the action exists. But the characters themselves do not have the humour and the compassion which the writing has. They are certainly short on compassion. When Pozzo cries 'Pity!', Vladimir says 'Poor Pozzo!'[180], but he and Estragon do nothing: instead, they embark, first on a discussion about who Pozzo really is, then on the expediency of helping him, and then on the nature and conditions of generous actions in general. Yet the core of the play's moral imagination lies in a sense of sympathy, which gains ours. It is quite an achievement to make us feel *with* Pozzo, let alone to make us feel *for* him: the latter follows from the former. This is a moral achievement. Meanwhile what the play, its action, tells us, is the impossibility of enrichment, of moral growth, of causing things to happen. It is an amoral message. It is in this profound sense that *Waiting for Godot* shows us one thing and tells us another.

And it is by showing us one thing and telling us another that the play eludes the logic of questioning. An Ibsen play is a series of events all of which might have had alternatives, and all of them together make up a moral web of facts and events. The moral action of such a play takes place within a framework of physical and psychological action: the two are intimately related. It is the absence of moral action within that framework that is the great paradox of *Waiting for Godot*, and the essence of its nature. When we say that nothing happens in it, what we mean is that its physical action contains a core of moral stillness.

In Ionesco's *Rhinoceros* there is both physical and moral action. The former consists in the transformation of the community into a herd of rhinoceroses; the latter in Bérenger's reaction to it. Ionesco himself described the inspiration for the play: it was an account, by the Swiss writer Denis de Rougemont, of a Nazi rally he witnessed in Nuremberg in 1938. We are told that

> something rose from the depth of his being and resisted the storm ... it was not his mind that resisted, not arguments formulated in his brain, but his whole being, his whole personality, that bridled.[181]

In other words, Rougemont was about to witness a perlocutionary act, and reacted to it in one of two possible ways: instead of mindlessly accepting it like everyone else around him, he mindlessly rejected it. This implies no disrespect for Rougemont, for such an occasion could hardly have been suitable for dispassionate thinking. Indeed, it was one of the purposes of Nazi rallies that people present at them should not think dispassionately.

But basing a play on such a reaction is something else again.

Bérenger in *Rhinoceros* reacts, not to a sudden appearance of a herd of wild animals, but to a process of animalisation over a period of time. Ionesco further clouds the issue by the way he presents this process. It is not only that it is crushingly simpleminded to represent the rise of Nazism in this way; it is also that the play is deeply ambivalent on how people react to it. Do they become rhinoceroses because they want to be, or because they have to be? Is it something that could be resisted? We are never told. The first identifiable person to become one is M. Boeuf, and he gives every sign of being an unwilling victim. Dudard, who says he does not approve of rhinoceroses, thinks that

> one has to keep an open mind – that's essential to scientific mentality. Everything is logical. To understand is to justify.[182]

This is a crucial moment in the play. Dudard's last sentence is quite out of character: he is made suddenly to renounce his faith in the objective validity of logical thinking. It is not just that this turns him from a character into a spokesman: it is also that, through him, Ionesco is now making the point that logical thought leads to moral capitulation. Within minutes, Dudard will join the rhinoceroses. Already, at the beginning of the play, we had a certain amount of harmless fun at the expense of logic, personified in a dotty professional logician; now it is becoming clear that logical thinking is becoming as much of an enemy as the rhinoceroses. Ionesco has written a play to express that bridling of the personality which Denis de Rougemont felt at the Nazi rally in Nuremberg: it is his own perlocutionary act. And when Bérenger announces that he refuses to think, he, too, submits to its spirit.

Ionesco once said: 'Nature against mind — there you have the whole of Nazism.'[183] He is perfectly right as far as that goes, though of course it is far from defining the whole of Nazism. Indeed, by presenting it as nothing more than mindless and brutish energy, Ionesco comes near to saying that it is not an evil force, and to implying that dealing with it is not really a moral matter. It is therefore quite appropriate that he should confront it with an attitude of simple, unquestioning innocence: an attitude which is embodied in Bérenger, and which is both the essence and the weakness of *Rhinoceros*. It is this innocence, this unquestioning astonishment in the face of monstrous events, which makes Bérenger think, towards the end of the play, that there may be something beautiful about rhinoceroses after all, and that they are perhaps superior beings. And this turns out to be more than the inevitable, passing self-doubt of a cornered man: we read in Ionesco's own stage directions that the animals' voices 'have become melodious'[184]; that stylised rhinoceros heads gradually cover the rear wall, and that

> in spite of their monstrous appearance [they] seem to become more and more beautiful.[185]

If this is meant to be irony at our expense, it misfires catastrophically. Here the moral abdication of the dramatist is complete: he becomes an acquiescent part of the apocalypse of which he has so far been the appalled spectator. The enemy becomes beautiful because he is victorious. This is Ionesco's picture of the world; and it tells us that we, too, are part of it. It is a perlocutionary play: we agree with it, or else our personality bridles at it, like Denis de Rougemont's at Nuremberg.

Rhinoceros illustrates the difficulties of the closed play in dealing with the complex moral and psychological pressures of a political subject. *The Lesson* and *The Killer* have similar preoccupations; and even *The Lesson*, the most powerful of these three plays, is weakened by its implication that the victim acquiesces in her destruction and even lends herself to it. And who exactly is this Professor? In Ionesco's world this is a senseless question. His plays are invasions from an unidentifiable source. We do not know where the first rhinoceros comes from, nor how exactly people are turned into rhinoceroses. We do not know who the Gentleman, the main character in *The New Tenant*, might be, or where he might have lived before, to have so much furniture; nor is it part of our experience of the play to ask. No one watching *The Chairs* would think of inquiring where this ancient couple could have stored so many chairs, or why. The Killer who terrorises the city, and who finally arrives in person at the end of the play that bears his name, is a puny, one-eyed, expressionless creature, with his toes peeping out of his torn shoes. 'Or possibly,' Ionesco's stage directions surmise, 'there is no *Killer* at all. Bérenger could be talking to himself, alone in the half-light.'[186] Could Ionesco be suggesting that the Killer really only exists in Bérenger's mind? Hardly: for that would not explain all the corpses that are being found all over the city. What such stage directions betray is a sense of ambiguity about evil which is so profound that it weakens Ionesco's own sense of its monstrosity. It looks as if he could only oppose evil by not understanding it;

and as if Dudard's statement, in *Rhinoceros*, that to understand is to justify, was a symptom of a deep moral uncertainty in Ionesco's inspiration.

These plays of invasion, from a source beyond understanding, are the reverse of plays of quest without an end: in both, the event we see bears no causal relation, to either its origin or to its end. Such events are either terrible or incomprehensible or both: we protest vehemently or we submit, overwhelmed. Yeats pointed to an important truth, both about his own plays and about the way we respond to closed drama, when he said that in tragedy 'all the chimeras . . . haunt the edge of trance'[187].

A sense of impersonal will drives such plays, and both executioners and victims are its tools. Hence the paradox that, within these moral parables, there is no moral will at work. Like the Whipper in Kafka's *The Trial*, the victims are simply there to suffer, and the executioners to kill. The world of these plays is certainly not one in which nothing happens: indeed, monstrous and incredible things happen, sometimes at a monstrous and incredible rate. The stasis of these plays is a moral stasis.

All this might suggest an explanation for a sombre paradox of our time: the hostility of closed societies towards closed art. This is an enormous subject, which needs a study to itself (not by the present author). Closed societies regard closed art with a mixture of fear tinged with admiration. These are not unlike the feelings Plato had for the arts in general; but his ideas for a closed society never actually took political shape. The problem is a strictly modern one. The two major totalitarian regimes of the twentieth century have both been essentially conservative, in some respects even reactionary, organisations, but they subjected their populations to unceasing propaganda demanding action and promising progress. The nature of the action they demanded was always defined as moral; at the same time its outcome was presented as being also inevitable, which meant that man had to strive for something that was to happen in any case. This is not unlike the procedure of closed art. *The Ring*, *Tristan and Isolde*, *A la Recherche du Temps Perdu* or *The Trial* all combine a sense of movement and moral purpose (which is their open aspect) with a sense of the static, the circular, the inevitable. They contain characters who are both prisoners and activists.

The aesthetic dilemma of such works is very like the aesthetic-political dilemma of Socialist Realism. The problem can be traced back to 1905, when Lenin asserted:

> We want to establish . . . a free press, free not simply from the police, but also from capital, from careerism, and what is more, from bourgeois-anarchist individualism.[188]

Lenin is talking specifically about the press, but his argument is so fundamentally about free personal expression that we may fairly relate it to personal expression in literature and art. Lenin's problem was the same which exercised all radical political leaders: given that freedom is good in principle, and indeed, that it is what most radical movements claim either to create or to defend, how much of it can be allowed to exist without endangering the Movement, and the State towards which the Movement strives? Lenin has no doubt about the matter: absolute freedom of expression is not to be tolerated. The phrase 'absolute freedom' is, in any case,

> a bourgeois or an anarchist phrase (since, as a world outlook, anarchism is bourgeois philosophy turned inside out). One cannot live in society and be free from society.[189]

Note the sleight of hand with which Lenin is able to devalue and dismiss both 'bourgeois' and 'anarchist', by using both words as terms of abuse and then identifying them, albeit rather speciously, with each other. He can then dismiss them both by concluding that the total freedom of expression, which they are supposed to stand for, is by definition harmful.

Lenin's argument gives us a glimpse of a closed society being born, under the influence of an immensely able totalitarian mind, and acquiring characteristics that are very like those of closed art. We now know how unimportant, in the event, real freedom was to be to Lenin; but here he presents himself, at least for the purposes of the argument he is conducting, as being torn between the claims of freedom, with its inevitable dependence on personal will, everyday causation and human relations, and the claims of Party rule, which must impose its own definitions on the fabric of life, and which is ultimately beyond questioning. This inner conflict of Lenin's, if it really was one, did not last long. And in the same way, Socialist Realist art, too, is torn between the claims of simple realism, the need to represent life as we know it, with its elaborate texture of moral dilemmas, personal responsibilities and alternative possibilities of action, and the claims of the Party, which imposes on all this the Will of an impersonal political imperative.

This is why works of Socialist Realism resemble works of closed art, such as *The Ring* or the *Recherche*, in a specific and paradoxical sense. Wagner and Proust, as we have seen, represented life as a moral spectacle, in a world in which things are *caused*; and, at the same time, as an amoral vision. Socialist Realist art wants to satisfy the artistic needs of ordinary moral narrative, but at the same time it wishes, or is compelled, to pay homage to a monolithically stable supra-moral system which is beyond questioning. As Andrey Sinyavsky puts it:

> Socialist Realism starts from an ideal image to which it adapts the living reality.[190]

Or, according to the terse wording of the Soviet Writers' Union, Socialist Realism is

> the representation of reality not as it is but as it ought to be.[191]

The most important product of Socialist Realism is the Positive Hero. His role is to fight for, and to represent, the qualities of the supra-moral system which the Party constantly declares to exist, and yet for which a constant struggle must still be carried on. Hence one of the most predominant characteristics of Socialist Realism: its tendency to set its works in times of revolution or war, or, if the setting is peaceful, to give the story a sense of struggle — for the highest productivity, or the best tractor. This explains the importance of the positive hero: he is a congenital fighter, and yet he also possesses all the stable qualities of moral excellence such as wisdom, will-power, generosity, ideological clarity and optimism. He must know where he is going, be certain that he will get there, and display nobility on the way. The novelist Leonid Leonov called his positive hero

> a peak of humanity from whose height the future can be seen.[192]

Perhaps the earliest appearance of the positive hero is in Gorky's play *Philistines* (1901), in which one of the characters, talking about the condition of Russia, declares:

> You have to be as straight and unbending as a sword to make your way through.[193]

This is not unlike listening to Nietzsche on the subject of Superman;

and it is at this point that Nil, the gentle, fervently optimistic and utterly dedicated young engine driver, enters, as if to respond to a call. Like Nietzsche, Socialist Realism has created a dream hero, majestic, kindly, lyrical, nobly brutal and unspecific, who commands even less conviction in fiction than in philosophy because he is both so much more and so much less than human, and because he embodies revolutionary struggle as eternal action, decreed by a Party imperative which is beyond questioning.

The totalitarian spirit may be repressive, but it worships the idea of action and has no patience with the ideas which advocate or imply none. The totalitarian spirit does not question: it asserts. It also claims the right and the ability to carry out the ultimate imposition on the structure of life: the creation of a new kind of man. Stalin described writers as engineers of the spirit — a phrase whose deeply sinister meaning is not often understood. Brecht understood it perfectly and prophetically. He told an interviewer in 1926 that he was working on a comedy called *Man Equals Man*, 'about a man being taken to pieces and rebuilt as someone else for a particular purpose'.

QUESTION: And who does the rebuilding?
  ANSWER: Three engineers of the feelings.
     Q: Is the experiment a success?
     A: Yes, and they are all of them much relieved.
     Q: Does it produce the perfect human being?
     A: Not specially.[194]

Stalin's engineer of the soul was an important part of the closed social system: he was charged with putting together the new man, that is, with creating the positive hero. Nietzsche's idea of the transvaluation of all values receives here its most appalling formulation.

The artistic vehicle of this transvaluation is *kitsch*. Milan Kundera defines *kitsch* as an aesthetic ideal which is based on 'a categorical agreement with being', and which simply denies the existence of anything it dislikes[195]. (Thus *kitsch* is a picture of the world.) When this is done in the name of a single political movement, 'we find ourselves in the realm of *totalitarian kitsch*'[196]. This is a perfect description of Socialist Realism: an inauthentic art-form in which a superficial realism is undermined by a pervasive sense of extra-artistic manipulation. Like certain representational paintings, which are 'legible' but which we cannot understand because we cannot grasp what is being represented, a Socialist Realist novel or play has the appearance of open fiction, but is presented under political and aesthetic constraints which make its openness deceptive. In such works we are always in the presence of things that are meant to be beyond our questioning: the great purpose, the struggle, inevitability, Communism, the Party, the Leader.

In their way, such works can be as predictable as average Westerns or Hollywood success-stories. Their ostensible open-ness is hedged about with severe restrictions. Just as the future is inevitable, the past, too, can only be questioned, indeed presented, within well-defined limits. No Socialist Realist play or novel could describe the dispossession of millions of peasants, or the forcible uprooting of entire nationalities. Similarly, no such novel or play could truthfully depict Leon Trotsky or Marshal Tukhachevsky. If character consists of past actions and alternative actions, then the figures of Socialist Realist fiction seem one-sided and somewhat unreal, precisely because there are no alternative pasts which they could have had. Past and future are both predetermined. The lawmakers of Socialist Realism not only create the life to come: they also *will backwards*. Putting it in yet another way, characters in Socialist Realist fictions become closed characters because they suffer from an incoherent story: they are obliged to give an inadequate narrative account of themselves. They suffer from an enforced amnesia.

What George Steiner calls the great ultimates of tragedy are placed, in these fictions, not in a poetic or mythological distance, but in the very web of the narrative: they both ordain and emasculate that striving which is the essence of the action. And unlike the moral remoteness and religious grandeur of Steiner's ultimates, these are secular imperatives, derived from political or economic arguments: they are placed, as warning beacons of the closed society which created them, into the body of an ostensibly open art work. But they are duplicitous in their effect, because they are presented as though they were natural parts of the 'open' life which, we are asked to believe, is being depicted. Their presence is underhand, inauthentic: like informers disguised as guests at one's table. That which cannot be questioned, denied or argued with is constantly at the back of every action and every actor. It transforms the entire fictional action into something to be unconditionally accepted. This is the way closed society creates its own, unique type of closed art.

Now real closed art is the fruit of a rival revolution. A-logical, impersonal and amoral, it makes a similar and rival appeal to the mind. It also, like closed society itself, calls for unconditional consent. But it holds, too, the possibility of unconditional dissent, and here lies its dangerous quality. From the point of view of closed society closed art is unpredictable and therefore dangerous. Being beyond argument, it cannot safely be used to advocate either argument or action. Brecht, whose understanding of the totalitarian spirit was based on first-hand experience as well as the nature of some of his own politics, once described how he and his colleagues discussed a literary work with workers — or, to be precise, 'with the most progressive cadres of the working class'. 'I shall never forget,' Brecht goes on,

> how one worker looked at me when I answered his request to include something extra in a song about the USSR ('It must go in — what's the point otherwise?') by saying that it would wreck the artistic form: *he put his head on one side and smiled.* At this polite smile a whole section of aesthetic collapsed. The workers were not afraid to teach us, nor were they afraid to learn (my italics).[197]

In this chilling scene we can see the totalitarian aesthetic in action: the artistic imagination is subjected to a will which is both imperative and external to the work. The artist can no longer question his material and, through it, the world: his sense of moral inquiry and engagement is replaced by submission to an extra-artistic force. The 'polite smile' of Brecht's interlocutor implies a peremptory, unspoken order for the creation of perlocutionary art.

In a closed society, whose purposes are specific actions and specific attitudes, open art is amenable to manipulation: for stories can be subverted and re-interpreted, but pictures of the world can only be wholly accepted or rejected. We could explain Mrs Alving's books as symbols of the bourgeois spirit, indulging in a private revolution of the mind but unable to carry out a real transformation of society. We could interpret Clytemnestra's tapestries as symbols of the helpless voraciousness with which the pre-feudal ruling class of Argos destroys itself. It would be far more difficult to show that Vladimir's carrot represented, say, the meagre sustenance of the dispossessed. To repeat our paraphrase of E.M. Forster: Oh dear, yes, a play tells a story; but nothing in the story that is *Waiting for Godot* tells us who might have dispossessed Vladimir, or of what. We are alone with him and his author. Closed society regards this as a dangerous privacy.

*   *   *

The characters of closed drama live in a closed world. This means that their world is not a place they can understand, nor one that we, the audience, can rationally explain. Not once throughout *Waiting for Godot* does either of the two men show any sign of realising the true purpose, or purposelessness, of their situation. They accept their world as we accept it. The difference is best understood by comparing the play with Brecht's *Mother Courage*. For when Courage says that 'Corruption in humans is the same as corruption in God'[198], she is being perfectly sincere as well as accurate. But if she understands this about the world, there is something else she does not: that she herself might be responsible for that corruption. But if she does not understand this, we do: again, Brecht sees to that. This is what dramatic irony means; and it springs from our critical engagement with the play.

That kind of critical engagement is not possible with *Waiting for Godot*: for we cannot make sense of its world any more than its characters can. And we may note, too, how limited is the characters' awareness and understanding of each other. Pozzo and Lucky come and go, twice, without making, or wanting to make, any sense of Vladimir and Estragon and their appointment. They in turn are interested in Lucky's extraordinary appearance, and Vladimir is at first shocked at Pozzo's treatment of him; but they show virtually no interest in their changed appearance in Act Two, or in what might have caused it, except to ask when it happened. People in closed plays are closed worlds to each other.

This is part of a greater moral isolation. Hamm and Clov in *Endgame* give this isolation one of its most extreme statements:

> HAMM: We're not beginning to ... to ... mean something?
> CLOV: Mean something! You, and I, mean something! (*Brief laugh*) Ah that's a good one![199]

These famous words go beyond critical clichés like the impossibility of communication. We are dealing with a world where people's inability to make sense of each other and of themselves reflects a greater inability: that of making sense of the world. Closed drama talks to us about this inability as about a shared experience which is beyond questioning. Wanting to make sense of the world means wanting to know the purpose of our existence in it: it is partly a solipsistic quest, but also an objective moral inquiry. Thus Vladimir,

having held forth verbosely about generosity while the blind Pozzo
lies helplessly on the ground, solemnly concludes:

> ... But that is not the question. What are we
> doing here, *that* is the question. And we are
> blessed in this, that we happen to know the
> answer. Yes, in this immense confusion one thing
> alone is clear. We are waiting for Godot to come —
> ESTRAGON: Ah!
>   POZZO: Help!
> VLADIMIR: Or for night to fall. (*Pause*) We have kept our
> appointment, and that's an end to that. We are not
> saints, but we have kept our appointment. How
> many people can boast as much?
> ESTRAGON: Billions.[200]

Vladimir is cheering himself up with a little moralising eloquence,
but Estragon knows better. What he says does not amount to
making sense of the world, but to accepting that he cannot. It also
sums up the moral value of their situation — which is none.
Vladimir is proud of their endurance; but endurance is only moral if
there is an alternative. Aeschylus' Prometheus has an alternative,
which is to submit to Zeus: his refusal to do so establishes his moral
status within the play. Sophocles' Philoctetes has an alternative,
but only when Odysseus arrives on the island and offers to negotiate
with him. Until that happens, Philoctetes has no alternative: his
situation is horrible, and what has been done to him is monstrous,
but he can do nothing except *be*.

One of the reasons why a play like *Waiting for Godot* speaks to us
with such immediacy is that, in this sense, too, it is a work of its
time. It is a unique characteristic of this century that it has been
able, quite systematically, to devise ways of inflicting unspeakable
suffering on vast numbers of people and, at the same time, reduce
them to mere things that have no choice in the matter. The Polish
priest who offered to die in the place of another prisoner at Au-
schwitz was privileged in this respect: he was allowed a personal
choice. The others had not even that. For them no moral courage
was of any use: there was nothing to which it could be applied. The
human faculties that are said to distinguish men from animals have
no function in such situations. Pascal's 'thinking reed' has had the
scope and the reason for thinking taken away from it: man is indeed
but a reed. Human suffering is even more monstrous because it is

deprived of any moral value: its cause is beyond protest, and no protest could hope to have any effect. The relations of ordinary human life have no practical validity here; the ideas of time, and of the passage of time, are meaningless. The past has no bearing on the future. The factuality, the logic, and the morality of life are power-less. There is no willed human action or movement; the characters of such an event can only be certain of moving towards extinction. This is the most closed world of all. The ending of Kafka's *The Trial* expresses this with a terrible perfection.

But suffering itself is not moral: it is simply demeaning. As the Little Monk says in Brecht's *Life of Galileo*:

> hunger is no trial of strength, it's merely not having eaten: effort is no virtue, it's just bending and carrying.[201]

We must not confuse our sense of outrage, itself a product of self-identification, fear, and moral anger, with the actual situation of the victims. We see their suffering in context; they have not even a context to think in any more. The point about Vladimir and Estragon is that, like 'billions', they kept their appointment, the nature of which they do not understand. By doing so, they have done nothing except exist. What Estragon confirms for us is that this in itself has no moral value. For the two men can only keep their appointment; not to do so has no meaning in the context of the play. They have neither the luxury nor the challenge of an alternative.

The only possible alternative, that of suicide, is suggested by Estragon quite early on. The passage has no sense of despair about it: the two men are curious and excited about the fact that hanging is supposed to give you an erection, and that even ejaculation may follow. But they drop the idea of suicide on the grounds that the bough of the tree might not be strong enough, and might hang one of them but not both. Estragon's explication of this suggests, not so much that he cannot bear to be parted from Vladimir, but that he cannot bear the thought of Vladimir surviving him. At the end of the play this little ceremony, like all the others, is repeated: the tone is now more weary, and the idea comes to nothing, this time because the two men have no rope.

Shortly before this, they do consider abandoning the appoint-ment, but decide not to because, Vladimir claims, Godot might punish them. Estragon does not disagree. But we cannot help observing that Godot's powers of punishment have no reality in the play, since he himself is never real. The expectation of punishment by someone you do not know and may never have seen, and whose very existence is in some doubt, is very like a neurosis: it reminds us of that deep-seated feeling of guilt, with no factual or personal cause, which Freud so persuasively anatomised. On this reading, the play would be a dramatisation of anxiety: a picture of the world in which anxiety is the principle of existence. It might be saying to us that we live in an abandoned world and invent for ourselves a figure of authority with powers of reward and punishment. It is typical of closed art that such a reading of the play would exclude all other readings: if this is what Godot is, he cannot be God, for example, or death.

What such a reading confirms, too, is the play's picture of abandoned humanity, without the fetters or the consolations of either morality or logic. We are in the presence of a world out of context. Experiencing such a play is always somewhat like experiencing both arbitrary imprisonment and unexpected liberation. We sense that no personal will is at work in these characters, but that a single, impersonal, 'unquestion-able' will, rather than the multiple causes and complications of life, drives forward its events. We sense that, though the play is clearly an artefact of human imagination, both its beginning and its end are beyond our computing. This is why the experience of a closed play is, ultimately, always the experience of being alone.

London, November 1978 — May 1985

IN MEMORIAM
P.A.
1903—1944

Notes

1. *The Treasure of the Humble*, tr. Alfred Sutro, London, 1907, pp. 106−8.
2. In *Casebook on 'Waiting for Godot'*, ed. Ruby Cohn, New York, 1967, p. 65.
3. By R.J. Kaufmann, in 'Strindberg: The Absence of Irony', in *Strindberg: A Collection of Critical Essays*, ed. Otto Reinert, New Jersey, 1971, p. 62.
4. Strindberg: *The Plays*, tr. Michael Meyer, London, 1975 (2 vols). II p. 119.
5. *ibid.*, p. 140.
6. Bertolt Brecht: *Collected Plays*, ed. John Willett and Ralph Manheim, London, 1970 −; Vol. 5 i, (1980), p. 128.
7. In *Explorations*, Harmondsworth, 1964, p. 17.
8. *ed. cit.*, p. 129.
9. In *Dramatis Personae*, London, 1925, p. 115.
10. In *Essays*, London, 1924, p. 414.
11. In *Wheels and Butterflies*, London, 1934, p. 101.
12. *Towards a Poor Theatre*, ed. Eugenio Barba, London, 1969, pp. 22−3.
13. *The Savage Mind*, London, 1972, p. 26.
14. In *The Birth of Tragedy*, ed. cit., p. 135.
15. Esslin, *op. cit.*, p. 393.
16. *Aspects of the Novel*, p. 87.
17. *Waiting for Godot (WG)*, London, 1959, pp. 87−9.
18. In *Dramatis Personae*, p. 310.
19. *WG*, p. 80.
20. In *The Sense of an Ending*, Oxford, 1967, p. 39.
21. In 'Any Way You Like, Alan: Working with Beckett', *Theatre Quarterly*, Vol. 5, No. 19, 1975, p. 34.
22. Ibsen: *Plays* (I-IV), tr. Michael Meyer, London, 1980, I pp. 152−4.
23. In *The Symbolist Movement*, London, 1908 (2nd ed.), p.1.
24. *Macbeth*, I. 6, 3−10.
25. Knights, *op. cit.*, p. 33.
26. See *The Letters of W.B. Yeats*, ed. Allan Wade, London, 1954, p. 469.
27. In *Wheels and Butterflies*, p. 135.
28. *The Intruder*, tr. Hall Caine, London, 1892, pp. 216−7.
29. Quoted in *Artaud and After* by Ronald Hayman, Oxford, 1977, p. 49.
30. *Plays*, Vol. 2 p. 632.
31. *Endgame*, London, 1964, pp. 31, 39.
32. *Samuel Beckett: A Biography*, by Deirdre Bair, London, 1978, p. 490.
33. Georg Kaiser: *Five Plays*, tr. B.J. Kenworthy, R. Last, J.M. Ritchie, London, 1971, p. 143.
34. *ibid.*, pp. 139−41.
35. *ibid.*, p. 184.
36. Georg Kaiser: *Plays Volume Two*, tr. B.J. Kenworthy, H.F. Garten, Elizabeth Sprigge, London, 1981, p. 134.
37. *Studies in Seven Arts*, London, 1906, p. 349.
38. *ibid.*, pp. 359−60.
39. Quoted in *The Theatre of Edward Gordon Craig*, by Denis Bablet, tr. Daphne Woodward, London, 1981, pp. 87−8.
40. See Michael Meyer: *Henrik Ibsen*, Vol.3 p. 176. When Duke Georg II of

Saxe-Meiningen was preparing for his production of *Ghosts*; he asked Ibsen for suggestions about staging. Here is part of Ibsen's reply:

The interior decoration of Norwegian country houses today shows no distinctly pronounced national character. The living rooms of the oldest family houses of this class are usually papered with dark-coloured wallpaper. Below this, the walls are finished in *simple*, polished wood. The ceiling as well as the doors and window frames are finished in this manner. The stoves are large, *ponderous*, and usually *cast iron*. The furnishings are often in the style of the First French Empire, but throughout the colours are darker. .

The italics are Ibsen's own. Quoted in *The Theatre Duke* by Ann Marie Koller, Stanford, 1984, pp. 93–4.

41. Quoted in Bablet, *op. cit.*, p. 148.
42. Konstantin Stanislavsky: *An Actor Prepares*, tr. Elizabeth Reynolds Hapgood, Harmondsworth, 1967, pp. 48–9.
43. *ibid.*, 27–8.
44. Konstantin Stanislavsky: *My Life in Art*, tr. J.J. Robbins, Harmondsworth, 1967, p. 371.
45. Quoted in Bablet, *op. cit.*, p. 142.
46. Michael Meyer: *Strindberg: A Biography*, Ch. 29, p. 477.
47. 'A Note on Marionettes', by 'Adolf Furst', in *The Mask*, Vol. II pp. 4–6.
48. In *Plays, Acting, and Music*, London, 1903, p. 193.
49. In *The Mask*, V.2, October, 1912.
50. In *The Mask*, I. 1, March, 1908.
51. Bablet, *op. cit.*, p. 119.
52. Quoted *ibid.*, p. 140.
53. In 'The Theatre of the Soul', *The Mask*, IV. 3, January 1912.
54. *The Gay Science*, *ed. cit.*, p. 324.
55. *Letters*, p. 610.
56. See Yeats's Introduction to *Certain Noble Plays of Japan*, by Ernest Fenollosa, ed. Ezra Pound, Dundrum, 1916.
57. Quoted in Meyer: *Strindberg*, p. 202.
58. *ibid.*, p. 203.
59. *ibid.*, p. 85.
60. *ibid.*, p. 139.
61. *ibid.*, p. 127.
62. *ibid.*, p. 158.
63. Appia: *The Work of Living Art*, tr. H.D. Albright, Florida, 1960, p. 74.
64. *ibid.*, p. 18.
65. Appia: *Music and the Art of Theatre*, tr. R.W. Corrigan, Mary Douglas Dirks, Miami, 1962, p. 52.
66. *ibid.*, p. 198.
67. *ibid.*, p. 221.
68. Quoted in *Adolphe Appia: actor-space-light*, exhibition catalogue by Pro Helvetia – Arts Council of Switzerland, designed by Denis and Marie-Louise Bablet, London, 1982, p. 38.
69. *Music and the Art of the Theatre*, pp. 198–9.
70. *ibid.*, p. 181.
71. *The Work of Living Art*, p. 53.
72. *ibid.*, p. 65.

73. *Music and the Art of the Theatre*, p. 70.

74. *ibid.*, p. 5.

75. In *Modern French Plays: An Anthology from Jarry to Ionesco*, ed. & tr. Michael Benedikt and George E. Wellwarth, London, 1965, p. 66.

76. See Konstantin Rudnitsky: *Meyerhold the Director*, tr. George Petrov, Ann Arbor, 1981, p. 269.

77. *ibid.*, p. 273.

78. Quoted in *Meyerhold on Theatre*, tr. & ed. Edward Braun, London, 1969, p. 164.

79. Quoted in *The Playwright as Thinker: A Study of Drama in Modern Times* by Eric Bentley, New York, 1946, p. 232.

80. In his Preface to *Four Plays for Dancers*, London, 1921, p. vi.

81. Quoted in Allardyce Nicoll: *The World of Harlequin: A Critical Study of the Commedia dell' Arte*, Cambridge, 1963, p. 41.

82. See Michael Patterson: *The Revolution in German Theatre 1900–1933*, London, 1981, p. 148.

83. W.B. Yeats: *Collected Plays*, London, 1952, p. 214.

84. In *Four Plays for Dancers*, p. 136.

85. In *The Symbolist Movement*, p. 4.

86. *Axël*, tr. M. Gaddis Rose, Dublin, 1970, p. 104.

87. *ibid.*, p. 110.

88. *ibid.*, p. 129.

89. *ibid.*, p. 175.

90. Antonin Artaud: *Collected Works*, tr. Victor Corti, London, 1968, Vol. 4 pp.80–93.

91. *ibid.*, Vol. 3 p. 162.

92. *ibid.*, Vol. 4 p. 89.

93. *ibid.*, p. 10.

94. *ibid.*, p. 13.

95. *ibid.*, p. 16.

96. *ibid.*, pp. 14–5.

97. *ibid.*, p. 17.

98. *ibid.*, p. 19.

99. *The Journals of Anais Nin*, London, 1973, Vol. I pp. 200–1.

100. Artaud, *Collected Works*, Vol. 2 p. 151.

101. *ibid.*, Vol. 4 p. 20.

102. *ibid.*

103. *ibid.*, pp. 38–50.

104. More than a decade earlier, in June 1920, Kandinsky submitted his *Program for the Institute of Artistic Culture* to the First Pan-Russian Conference of Teachers in Moscow. He paid particular attention to the study of movement which, he said, presented an escape to 'many spectators, tired of the excessive psychology of the theatre'. He recommended the study of ancient cultures and their rituals in so far as they could be identified from monuments, etc. In these rituals, he said, 'Certain gestures, distinguished by their extreme schematicism, possess a superhuman power of expression.' Kandinsky wanted to study the sensory and psychological effects of such movement and gestures; he even wanted the results of such research to be 'tabulated, indexed, and entered in directories'. His approach is a fascinating combination of subjectivism and a passion for a system rigidly encoded in tables and indexes.

The program was rejected in favour of another, compiled by the Working Group of Objective Analysis, which put less emphasis on the subconscious and the fortuitous, and more on industrial and applied art. Within a couple of years, the whole Institute lost its artistic and academic autonomy anyway. See Kandinsky, *Complete Writings on Art*, Vol 1 pp. 455—72.

I have not come across any evidence that Artaud knew this Program, or even that he knew Kandinsky's play *The Yellow Sound*.

105. See Hayman, *op. cit.*, p. 117.
106. Grotowski, *op. cit.*, p. 121.
107. *Collected Works*, Vol. 4 pp. 175, 177.
108. *Shelley's Poems*, Everyman Edn., London, 1953, pp. 222—3.
109. *Collected Works*, Vol. 4 p. 215.
110. *ibid.*, p. 144.
111. *ibid.*, p. 153.
112. *The World as Will and Idea*, I, 457.
113. *Plays, ed. cit.*, I p. 134.
114. *ibid.*, III pp. 48, 51.
115. Bentley, *op. cit.*, p. 140.
116. *The Plays, ed. cit.*, I p. 82.
117. *ibid.*, p. 68.
118. *ibid.*, pp. 36—7.
119. Quoted in Evert Sprinchorn: 'Strindberg and the Greater Naturalism', *Tulane Drama Review*, Vol. 13, No. 2, Winter 1968, pp. 127—8.
120. *The Plays, ed. cit.*, I p. 68.
121. In *The Death of Tragedy*, London, 1961, pp. 128—9.
122. *The Plays, ed. cit.*, p. 86.
123. ibid., p. 109.
124. *Axël, ed. cit.*, p. 170.
125. Meyer: *Strindberg*, p. 114.
126. Kermode: *The Sense of an Ending*, esp. pp. 35—89.
127. WG p. 18.
128. *The Plays*, II, p. 586.
129. *ibid.*, pp. 606—7.
130. Quoted in C.E.W.L. Dahlstrom: *Strindberg's Dramatic Expressionism*, Michigan, 1930, p. 99.
131. In Reinert, *ed. cit.*, p. 68.
132. In *Plays and Controversies*, London, 1923, p. 161.
133. In *The Empty Space*, Harmondsworth, 1972, p. 38.
134. Quoted in Richard N. Coe: *Ionesco*, London, 1961, p. 77.
135. In *The Writer in Extremis: Expressionism in Twentieth-Century German Literature*, Stanford, California, 1959, p. 61.
136. *Endgame*, p. 35.
137. *No Man's Land*, London, 1975, p. 15.
138. *Old Times*, London, 1971, p. 9.
139. *ibid.*, pp. 40—1.
140. *The Homecoming*, London, 1966, p. 51.
141. In Beckett: *Proust and Three Dialogues*, London, 1965, p. 112.
142. *Romantic Image*, London, 1971, p. 61.
143. *In Collected Plays*, Vol. V, ii p. 15.
144. *ibid.*, Vol. I, pp. 45—6.

145. In Ernst Toller: *Seven Plays*, tr. Edward Crankshaw and others, London, 1935, p. 134.

146. In *Noh and Accomplishment*, by Ernest Fenollosa and Ezra Pound, London, 1916, p. 108.

147. *Collected Plays*, p. 214.

148. *ibid.*

149. In *Yeats: The Man and the Masks*, London, 1949, p. 219.

150. *Collected Plays*, p. 633.

151. In *Proust and Three Dialogues*, p. 103.

152. Quoted in Ellmann, *op. cit.*, p. 219.

153. In 'The Circus Animals' Desertion', *Collected Poems*, London, 1950.

154. Quoted in *The Playwright as Thinker*, p. 44.

155. *The Messingkauf Dialogues*, tr. John Willett, London, 1965, p. 104.

156. In Bertolt Brecht: *Parables for the Theatre*, tr. Eric Bentley, Harmondsworth, 1966, p. 37.

157. *ibid.*, pp. 61–2.

158. In Benedikt and Wellwarth, *ed. cit.*, p. 139.

159. *ibid.*, p. 140.

160. *ibid.*, p. 136.

160. *ibid.*, p. 136.

161. Quoted in Coe, *op. cit.*, p. 19.

162. 'The Yellow Sound' is reprinted in *The Blaue Reiter Almanac*, ed. Klaus Lankheit, London, 1975, pp. 207–25.

163. *The Plays, ed. cit.*, Vol I p. 467. Strindberg's letter to his translator is quoted on p. 420.

164. In *Collected Works*, Vol. II p. 99.

165. *The Plays*, Vol. II p. 46.

166. *Seven Plays*, p. 90.

167. *ibid.*, p. 92.

168. *ibid.*, p. 99.

169. *Five Plays*, p. 240.

170. In *Natural Supernaturalism: Tradition and Revolution in Romantic Literature*, Oxford, 1971, p. 302.

171. *Five Plays*, p. 131.

172. See *Letters*, p. 542.

173. *Krapp's Last Tape*, London, 1959, p. 18.

174. *Play*, London, 1964, p. 22.

175. *WG*, pp. 76–7.

176. Quoted in Schneider, *art. cit.*, pp. 33–4.

177. *Not I*, London, 1973, p. 6.

178. *ibid.*, p. 16.

179. *Play*, p. 23.

180. *WG*, p. 77.

181. In *Notes and Counter Notes*, tr. Donald Watson, London, 1964, p. 205.
Rougemont's instinctive repudiation of what he saw and heard is paralleled by the reactions of the audience at the first great Dada evening in Zurich, on July 14, 1916, organised by Tristan Tzara and his friends. Hugo Ball, dressed in cardboard cylinders, was carried to the platform to recite his first 'abstract phonetic poem'. It began:
    gadji beri bimba glandridi laula lonni cadori

gadjama gramma berida bimbala glandri glassassa laulitalomini
gadji beri bin blassa glassala laula lonni cadorsu sassala bim . . .

and so on. Hans Richter, who was also present, records:

This was too much. Recovering from their initial bafflement at this totally new sound, the audience finally exploded.

This is the only alternative reaction to a perlocutionary act.

For a full account, see *Dada: Art & Anti-art* by Hans Richter, tr. David Britt, London, 1965, esp. pp. 11–80.

182. Eugene Ionesco: *Plays*, Vol. 4, tr. Derek Prouse, London, 1960, p. 83.
183. Quoted in Coe, *op. cit.*, p. 98.
184. *Plays*, Vol. IV p. 104.
185. *ibid.*, p. 94.
186. *Plays*, Vol. III, tr. Donald Watson, p. 98.
187. In his Preface to *Plays for an Irish Theatre*, London, 1911, p. viii.
188. In 'Party Organisation and Party Literature', *On Literature and Art*, London, 1967, p. 25.
189. *ibid.*, p. 26.
190. In *Beyond Socialist Realism* by 'Abram Tertz' (Sinyavsky), New York, 1960, p. 76.
191. Quoted in Jurgen Ruhle: *Literature and Revolution*, tr. Jean Steinberg, London, 1969, p. 138.
192. Quoted in Sinyavsky, *op. cit.*, p. 48.
193. *Philistines*, by Maxim Gorky, tr. Dusty Hughes, Act Four, p. 108. I am quoting from Mr Hughes's unpublished script.
194. See *Brecht on Theatre*, tr. John Willett, London, 1974, p. 16.
195. In *The Unbearable Lightness of Being*, p. 248.
196. *ibid.*, p. 251.
197. *Brecht on Theatre*, pp. 110–11.
198. *Collected Plays*, V. ii, p. 40.
199. *Endgame*, p. 27.
200. WG, p. 80.
201. *Collected Plays*, V. i, p. 66.

INDEX